Life and Death Matters

Life and Death Matters

Human Rights and the Environment at the End of the Millennium

edited by
Barbara Rose Johnston

ALTAMIRA
PRESS
A Division of Sage Publications, Inc.
Walnut Creek ■ *London* ■ *New Delhi*

For information contact:

AltaMira Press
A Division of Sage Publications, Inc.
1630 North Main Street, Suite 367
Walnut Creek, CA 94596
explore@altamira.sagepub.com
www.altamirapress.com

SAGE Publications Ltd.
6 Bonhill Street
London EC2A 4PU
United Kingdom

SAGE Publications India Pvt. Ltd.
M-32 Market
Greater Kailash 1
New Delhi 110 048

Library of Congress Cataloging-in-Publication Data

Life and death matters: human rights at the end of the millennium / edited by Barbara Rose Johnston.
          p. cm.
          Includes index.
          ISBN 0-7619-9184-0 (cloth: acid-free paper). —ISBN 0-7619-9185-9 (pbk.: acid-free paper)
          1. Economic development—Environmental Aspects—Developing countries
2. Environmental Policy—Developing Countries. 3. Human rights—Developing countries. I. Johnston, Barbara Rose.
HC59.72.E5L4   1996
333.7—dc21   96-51290
                                                        CIP

98 99 00 01 02 03 04 05 06 07 08 09   7 6 5 4 3 2

The Gold Miners Statue photograph on page 101 is used with permission of the photographer, Linda Rabben.
The CODDEFFAGOLF activist photograph on page 175 is used by permission of the photographer, Susan Stonich.
The map on page 214 originally appeared in *Basta! Land and the Zapatista Rebellion in Chiapas*. Collier, George and Elizabeth Lowery-Quaratiello. Food First Books, Oakland, CA. © 1994. Page 1.

Cover Photo by Lorraine V. Aragon
Interior Design and Production by Labrecque Publishing Services
Cover Design by Denise M. Santoro

CONTENTS

Acknowledgments

The original impetus for this book came from a November 1994 conference session on "Human Rights and the Environment" at the American Anthropological Association meetings in Atlanta, Georgia. To all who originally participated in that session, and to AAA President Jim Peacock, who asked me to organize that session, I owe my thanks. I am especially grateful to those session participants who worked, reworked, updated, and reworked once again their papers for this volume. Thank you, Lorraine Aragon, Paula Garb, and Al Gedicks, for seeing this through from beginning to end. Thank you, Holly Barker, for responding so enthusiastically to my previous book, and writing the companion piece on the Marshall Islands for this book. Thank you, Les Sponsel, for your amazing ability to write and submit a chapter two weeks after receiving the book proposal. Thank you, Lindsey Swope and Margaret Swain, and Yang Fuquan and Jack Ives, for graciously allowing me to merge your two papers into one chapter. Thank you, David Stea, Silvia Elguea, and Camilo Perez Bustillo, for working on various drafts and revisions, and for communicating changes back to me under the arduous and chaotic conditions that typify daily life in post-NAFTA Mexico. And, thank you, Bill Derman, Bob Hitchcock, Shan McSpadden, Brooke Thomas and Oriol Pi-Sunyer, Jim Phillips, Val Wheeler and Peter Esainko, and Ben Wisner, for allowing me to twist your arm and for agreeing to write up your work for this book, despite your harried schedules. Thank you, Tony Oliver-Smith, Duncan Earle, and Bill Loker; your ideas, worries, and conceptual meanderings helped me more than you may know.

Some of the contributing authors received institutional support for their research and writing as well as assistance from colleagues. Individual acknowledgments are listed in chapter endnotes. Except for a travel grant to attend an August 1996 International Union of Anthropological and Ethnological Sciences/International Geography Union conference from the Center for Political Ecology, my involvement with this project was not supported by any institutional source.

Taking this material and turning it into a book involved two years of proposal writing, negotiating with publishers, communicating with contributors, attending conferences, editing, procrastinating, and busting out of horribly cranky moods, especially those related to writer's block and technodysfunctionalism. Thanks to the economic, psychological, and physical support of my family, I survived the burnout of my old computer, learned the ways of a newfangled machine, and regained my sanity after my new hard drive self-destructed, taking an almost completed version of the book with it. Ted Edwards, my husband, kept the kids out of my hair, paid the bills, prodded me back to work, and always loved me. Thanks, Ted, for the last-minute, late-night editing, and helping me meet the endless deadlines. Daniel Johnston helped figure out what was going on with that damn machine. Denise Santoro, my editor at AltaMira Press, exhibited patience and empathy when these crises pushed submission deadlines further into the future. Ben and Chris Edwards helped in numerous ways, especially by turning the television down, ignoring my grumpy moods, rubbing my shoulders, and telling me that they loved me. Shadow kept me company. Dr. Terry Johnston, my mom, worried, gave me money when I needed it, and brought over a bottle of wine whenever it was required. My friends did the same. Thanks, Ingrid.

Finally, editing these chapters meant continually confronting and embracing the reality of many lives around the world so different from my own. These life and death matters are hugely intense—at times, overwhelming. Babies proved to be the best antidote. Now and then I desperately needed to hug, tickle, and play with a baby. Babies continually remind me that life goes on, that even in the worst situations people live, love, and laugh, and that this is an essential part of human survival. So, I thank my brothers and sisters for the use of their babies. Give them a hug and a kiss from me.

Life and Death Matters
at the End of the Millennium

Barbara Rose Johnston[1]

Preface

In my mind's eye I see human history as a journey over the mountains of time. We have reached the summit of a pinnacle—a high, rocky crag. Humanity has traveled to this point by confronting challenges, experiencing setbacks, transforming the world we traveled through, and continually reinventing ourselves along the way. So here we sit and catch our breath, looking back on the familiar distance we have traveled, scanning the horizons ahead, looking for paths through the unknown that is our future.

Having achieved this summit, we now realize that our perch is quite perilous. A wrong move in any direction might cause us to fall. Sitting on this pinnacle, we find ourselves temporarily frozen, feeling around the rock for handholds, but unable to grasp and move, unable to make a commitment for fear that it will lead us in the wrong direction.

As we sit here, near the end of the millennium, we confront a world of escalating population; growing inequities; increasingly polluted air, water, and soil; and ever dwindling resources—a world in which environmental quality and social justice are, for many, but a dream. It is a world sharply defined by fear. We fear violent conflict in our homes, on the streets, between strangers, even between friends. We fear our growing numbers, and what they might mean for our present and future ability to enjoy the luxuries and necessities of life. We fear the horrible health consequences of our modern life—of cancers, of infectious diseases, of genetic mutations. We fear the seemingly irrational actions and beliefs of the many who turn to cultural traditions (such as fundamentalist religions or ethnic-based nationalism) for meaning and stability.

We are right to be fearful. The human environmental crises of our time threaten the lives and future, not only of some of us, but increasingly of us all. Political and economic institutions (state, multinational, multilateral) are struggling to find those handholds to back off, climb down, get back to firm, flat, stable ground. Social institutions (civic organizations, local communities, and religious and cultural groups) are struggling with similar needs. Which direction will take us to solid ground—retracing our steps, or forging new paths? Will fear paralyze effective action?

Introduction

Life and Death Matters presents a collection of stories, events, and experiences that attempt to provide you, the reader, with some sense of what life is like for the people who must daily confront the environmental crises of our time. The title and the selection of topics addressed in this volume both reflect an understanding that the life-and-death struggles of people in the distant corners of this planet are struggles that matter: to those involved, to those intimately and distantly responsible, and to the many who will, unless lasting solutions are found, experience similar difficulties sooner or later. Three things significantly influenced the way I defined and shaped this project: the November 1994 *Atlantic Monthly* publication of "The Coming Anarchy" by Robert Kaplan, a conversation with a colleague, and the death of a friend. I begin with the last.

A good friend of mine died this past summer. While writing a letter to his wife, I found myself transported back to the time, setting, and conversations shared with my friend. I met Phil and Mimi Caesar at the beginning of my professional life, as an archaeologist working in the Virgin Islands. They were a retired couple living on St. John who donated their time to many community activities—the Lion's Club, the library, the Historical Society, and the government Office of Archaeological Services. I worked for the territorial government, locating, mapping, and designing preliminary resource management plans for all the prehistoric sites in the islands. The Caesars were my volunteer crew, and I was one of their archaeology daughters. The summer I worked on St. John I lived in an apartment below their house, and we spent our days scouring the island and offshore keys, locating sites . . . looking for archaeological treasures. A good part of each day was spent traveling to remote bays, usually on board their sailboat, which allowed us ample time to talk. Island culture, race relations, politics, local events, and global crises were all open for discussion, and, given the huge differences in our views, all were debated in heated fashion. When I think of Phil, I think of the many long, loud arguments we had. Although we never succeeded in changing each other's opinion, over the years we did learn, eventually, to listen. And, in listening, we acknowledged reality from the other's point of view.

Phil Caesar spent his professional career as a scientist. He was a chemist who worked during World War II on a collaborative government/industry research project aimed at cracking the petroleum molecule and developing more highly refined fuels, efforts that they hoped would help the Allies win the war. They were successful. A catalytic converter was built that allowed more refined fuels to be developed, and in the process created a whole host of new chemical compounds. Tens, and eventually tens of thousands, of new compounds found their way into almost every item of our material culture, and into the air, the water, the soil, into the food we eat, into our selves. From his perspective, he had helped save the world. From my perspective, his efforts may eventually destroy our world. Both our perspectives are real.

A colleague of mine works for a large, multilateral organization that funds numerous development projects. Her job is to review the social and environmental integrity of proposals, projects, and assessments, and her decisions affect the lives of millions of people. During one of our conversations in cyberspace I asked her what social scientists can provide, in terms of research and analysis, that will truly have an effect on policy makers in the donor community. How can our work have more direct policy implications?

She responded (I am paraphrasing her comments here) that much of what she sees in reports prepared by consultants, as well as the published "development" literature, are case studies in which the research energy is directed toward documenting the role of development projects and policies in creating situational disasters, yet in which minimal critical attention is given to recommendations. A great deal of time, energy, and funding is spent analyzing the origins and anatomy of various case-specific crises, yet an equal measure of rigor is seldom applied to the issues of response. Investigations that critically examine the praxis aspects of recommendations—documenting the conditions and contexts in which recommendations actually work on the ground in targeted communities (and pointing out where they do not)—are relatively scarce. The situation is complicated by changes in the donor community. More and more development project funding is flowing from nongovernmental organizations (NGOs), and less from governments and multilateral entities. NGOs typically have limited budgets for analysis, and as a result rely on other sources (often the existing literature) for information. This means that policy and funding priorities may be defined with little understanding of community-based realities, proposals may project a naive sense of feasibility, and programs may be initiated with little chance of succeeding. There is a huge need for accessible data that demonstrates how people respond to human environmental crises.

The third factor shaping this book is a reaction to the November 1994 *Atlantic Monthly* article written by Robert Kaplan entitled "The Coming Anarchy: How Scarcity, Crime, Tribalism, and Disease Are Rapidly Destroying the Social Fabric of Our Planet." Using examples from West Africa, Asia, and the Middle East, Kaplan argues that population growth, environmental degradation, and subsequent competition for increasingly scarce resources are interrelated factors that contribute to increased aggression and violent conflict in many places around the globe. With photographs, interviews, and descriptions, Kaplan paints a picture of life in some of the more desperate regions of the world: environmental hot spots, where people act solely through self-interest; where power lies in cultural, ethnic, and religious group membership; and where the state and other governmental institutions are weak (or nonexistent), while cultural-based institutions are strengthening (or dominate). Regions no longer are sharply defined by political borders, but rather reflect ethnic affiliation and the fluid movement of populations. Given current population rates and continually escalating levels of resource extraction and consumption, Kaplan suggests that the criminal anarchy characterizing life in these crisis areas may represent the shape of things to come in a "few decades hence" for the entire planet. "The coming upheaval," Kaplan predicts, "in which foreign embassies are shut down, states collapse, and contact with the outside world takes place through dangerous, disease-ridden coastal trading posts, will loom large in the century we are entering."[2]

Kaplan's article was reportedly one of the most reproduced essays of the year. His vision and conclusions were matter for much academic and public policy debate. Will the events of the next 50 years be characterized by environmental scarcity leading to cultural and racial clashes, to a remaking of the geopolitical map reflecting "geographic destiny and the transformation of war"? Are cultural allegiances simply a matter of immediate family and "guerrilla comrades"? Is humanity doomed to employ cultural strategies for self-serving ends?

In reaction to the comments offered by my unnamed colleague, I distributed a call for contributions (intended for this volume) that asked environmental social scientists to take a critical look at how people in communities, organizations, and governmental institutions respond to the human environmental crises that structure their lives. The resulting case studies of human environmental crisis are presented in this book. The contributors document a broad range of responses (including individual, community, state, and international responses) that include denial, migration, and the formation of social and political movements, as well as efforts to renegotiate power and consequence from within existing systems, efforts to transform systems, and efforts to build new hierarchies of power.

In some cases, Robert Kaplan's vision was validated: people *do* use cultural notions and mechanisms in an attempt to respond to human environmental crises, and at times these responses are reactionary, repressive, abusive, and violent. One can draw identifiable connections between ineffective response and the rise of violent conflict. However, other cases suggest that while chaos and anarchy may be inevitable byproducts of human environmental crisis, neither is necessarily the endpoint. There is much more to the story.

As the chapters in this book illustrate, life-threatening situations tear at the fabric of culture and society. Some people are caught in an escalating cycle of degradation and human rights abuse: they die, they flee, they passively accept their lot. Others fight to survive in more violent ways, embracing and engaging in confrontational politics and actions. Sometimes the common experience and urgent need to respond blurs previous lines of cleavage: new leaders emerge, innovative networks and coalitions are formed, community identity is reshaped. Organization, activism, and the changes that these sociopolitical movements promote all threaten the status quo. Conflict, and the chaos and anarchy that conflict engenders, is inevitable—hence Kaplan's vision. However, the process of shaping solutions requires confronting and engaging problems—for substantive change emerges from what appears, at a temporal glance, to be anarchy.

The human environmental crises plaguing our planet are difficult to define, to understand, and to resolve—because they are, by their very nature, the manifestation of historical processes and events with consequences that are both synergistic and cumulative. If we are to recognize and support the new strands of order emerging from the chaos and anarchy of our times, we must refocus our questions. Kaplan asks an important question: Is the violent anarchy that plagues Africa today the shape of things to come for the entire planet tomorrow? In this book we rephrase the question to ask, How are people responding to these crises? What works in what settings? What doesn't work? What are the social and environmental consequences of inadequate response to human environmental crisis? What structural mechanisms are employed, or needed, to resolve crises successfully?

For my late friend Phil Caesar and me, resolving our differences of opinion required learning how to listen, learning how to see from the other's vantage point, learning how to recognize the validity in each other's understanding of reality. At times we ended our verbal duels with a polite agreement to disagree. Over the years we learned to seek the common threads, those we both could agree on, and in doing so, we bridged the distance between us.

If we, as a species, are to survive and even thrive, we must approach human environmental crisis in the same way: by listening, by learning how to see reality from the multiplicity of vantage points that structure each and every crisis, and by devising strategies and creating opportunities that let us bridge the distance between those who struggle to survive in the midst of environmental crisis and those who helped create the chaos that has fundamentally transformed life.

Human Environmental Crisis

Environmental degradation is by no means a new challenge to human survival. The rise and fall of many past societies were tied to the ability to modify the immediate environment and subsequent inability to prevent escalating environmental degradation.[3] In the past, when peoples were faced with deteriorating environmental conditions, their success in adapting was dependent on sufficient time to develop biological responses or, more typically, on behavioral responses that recognize changing environmental conditions, identify causality, search out or devise new strategies, and incorporate new strategies in ways that allow the society to survive and thrive.[4] Often the strategy of choice for such threatened peoples was simply to go somewhere else. Our situation at the end of the millennium differs from past crises in a number of ways.

First, the problems we are experiencing are rarely confined to a local context. Changes in upper atmospheric composition are global, and these changes present a host of problems tied to fluctuating weather patterns and increased ultraviolet radiation. Other environmental crises are local, yet their origins and consequences are tied to global trends. For example, water quality problems vary throughout the world and involve contamination from human waste, agricultural chemicals, industrial solvents, and mining byproducts. These local crises contribute to a global trend of water scarcity, where an estimated one in five persons on this planet lacks access to clean water. And some environmental crises defy our conception of time. The nuclear hot spots of the world, places where nuclear weapons were developed, tested, and their waste stored, will continue to contaminate life processes for thousands of years. Our ability to contain, reduce, or even remove their threat is seriously inhibited by the changing nature of our sociopolitical systems. Who, for example, is responsible for managing the radioactive legacy of defunct regimes?

Second, the environmental constraints faced by our ancestors were in large part defined by the nature of their surroundings—by the biophysical parameters of nature (water availability, soil fertility, altitude, temperature). Today's problems represent the biodegenerative products of humanity. These products—polluted air, water, soil, food;

depleted forests and fisheries—are cumulative and synergistic. Problems compound each other. Our ability to respond both as individuals and as a human society is significantly inhibited by the synergistic nature of these problems.

For example, a colleague of mine just returned from Chiapas, Mexico, having spent a good part of the summer in the Lacandon rain forest attending an international solidarity conference. She was quite ill with giardia, E. coli, amoebic dysentery, hepatitis, and malaria. In Chiapas, safe drinking water was difficult to find; even the bottled water was contaminated. Lack of safe drinking water is tied to the underdevelopment of the region where two-thirds of the nation's hydropower is generated but the majority of the residents lack electricity or potable water. Malaria is on the rise because of intensified deforestation—historically associated with the expansion of cattle ranches and in-migration of Mayans and other peasants, and recently tied to the settlement and land-use patterns of the Mexican military and Zapatista revolutionaries. (Malaria is carried by mosquitoes whose natural habitat is in the upper levels of the rain forest; deforestation broadens their habitat.) Increases in malaria infection rates are also related to the influx of people going to and through the region (peasants, revolutionaries, Mexican military, journalists, national and international Zapatista supporters). At the individual level, my friend's ability to fight off opportunistic infection was inhibited by the cumulative assault on her immune system as one exposure followed another, and her recovery was compromised by the synergistic effect of the multiple assaults. At a broader level, the cumulative and synergistic effects of resource inequity—the continued denial of critical resource rights for Mayans and other peasants in the region, the patterns of land use over time, and the lack of physical infrastructure development—have contributed to the human environmental crisis that exists in Chiapas.

The cumulative and synergistic nature of environmental crises have other meanings as well, including the bioaccumulative or mutagenic consequences of environmental degradation. "Bioaccumulative" suggests the process of passing toxic substances through the food web at ever increasing levels. Many pesticides, for example, when ingested find a home in the fatty cells of the consumer, and when this organism is consumed by others, the toxins work their way outward in the food web. "Mutagenic" refers to substances that cause mutation at the cellular level, and thus can be passed through to the next generation. Radioactive elements are an example of mutagenic substances that adversely affect the cellular structure of this and future generations. Thus, we face not only biophysical change, but also continual degenerative change.

Third, the experience of environmental crisis is highly differentiated. As suggested in the above example of crisis in Chiapas, some populations are more vulnerable than others, and this vulnerability is at times structurally reinforced by government action. In spite of international and national structures establishing inalienable rights for all people, powerless groups are often denied rights to land, resources, and health and environmental protection—in the name of economic growth and national security.[5] This selective victimization is a product of cultural notions (for example, racism, ethnocentrism, sexism) as well as political economic relationships and histories (of colonialism, imperialism, ethnocide, and genocide). Cultural values and ideals inform and structure the goals and agenda of local and national governments, of national and multinational corporations, as well as of local elites. Powerless groups and their rights to land, resources, health and environmental protection, and thus their future are "expendable" in the name of national security, national energy, and national debt. While victimization is not a new facet of the human experience, the nature and extent of environmental threats, coupled with the interconnectedness of human communities, means that it is increasingly difficult for victimization to occur in isolated, solitary contexts.

And, finally, in the past, human adaptation to changing environmental circumstances required time, space, and the means to implement change (optimally, viable sociopolitical structures). Today, time is an increasingly scarce commodity, especially given the rapid pace of degenerative change. Migration of peoples is less and less a viable option; there are few frontiers, few unmapped spaces to disappear into. Our nation/state structures respond in clumsy and ineffective ways, because the origins and experience of human environmental crisis transcend geopolitical boundaries.

The Culture and Structure of Power

Life and death matters at the end of the millennium are matters pertaining to the global dimensions of environmental crisis; the biodegenerative, cumulative, and synergistic nature of crisis; the social context of inequity; and the inadequacy of existing strategies and structures to respond effectively. The past few generations have seen a rapid expansion of technology and industries, intensified use of environmental resources, exponential population growth, and unprecedented destruction of our global habitat. Accompanying these changes in human action are changes in the culture and structure of power: fewer and fewer people control more and more of the world's resources, and most people are far removed from the consequences of their actions.

As an ideal, a government's structures serve the needs of its citizens. Nonetheless, decisions are made daily that adversely affect the health and well-being of some of its citizens and institutions, while enhancing the standing and situation of others. Inequity is institutionalized in ways that allow immoral actions to appear socially palatable and legally defensible. Physical, cultural, and conceptual mechanisms maintain illusions of both legitimacy and distance from the consequences of decision.

Physical Mechanisms

Perhaps the most common and obvious mechanism used to distance decision makers from the consequence of their decisions is siting hazardous activities and storing hazardous wastes in "peripheral" regions (the "not in my backyard," or NIMBY, approach to decision making). Peripheral regions can be a matter of actual geographic distance, as well as "cultural" distance (that is, areas populated by less powerful groups).[6]

The decision to use the Nevada test site as the United States' nuclear weapons "proving grounds" illustrates the geographic and cultural facets of distancing mechanisms. A review of U.S. government documents pertaining to the selection of the Nevada test site indicates that the prime continental U.S. site, in terms of minimizing public exposure to fallout, was located on the East Coast, south of Cape Hatteras, North Carolina. This site was rejected. The rationale for this decision, as articulated in the federal records, was that the federal government did not own the land, and did not want to go through the process of acquiring it. Choices were then redefined to lands the federal government already owned or controlled, with less consideration given to possible health effects than to geographic proximity to Los Alamos Laboratory in New Mexico. The Nevada test site was ultimately chosen—with the explicit knowledge that prevailing westerly winds would blow fallout over most of the country.[7]

Both physical and cultural distancing mechanisms were at work in this example of decision making. The Cape Hatteras site was located uncomfortably close to the seat of political power (Washington, D.C., and the eastern seaboard) in both physical and cultural terms, while the Nevada test site was comfortably distant ("out of sight, out of mind"). Most of those living in the western area were Native Americans, people who spoke other languages, or people whose relatives were not in political office or even whose relatives of relatives of relatives were not in political office. Neither the Cape Hatteras or the Nevada test site was owned by the federal government. The Nevada test site, however, because it was located on Native American reservation land, was federally controlled land. The Department of Defense obtained control on a "temporary" withdrawal basis from Western Shoshone and Southern Paiute use in 1951, without the tribes' approval, and without compensation.

Cultural Mechanisms

In addition to physical mechanisms, cultural mechanisms also play a crucial role in legitimizing immoral actions. Efforts to exert political and economic control over other human groups involve the use of socially constructed images and terms in both language and behavior, terms that reinforce hierarchy and legitimize action.[8] As anthropologist Robert Hitchcock demonstrates, much can be learned about social relations by examining the simple matter of a name. The indigenous former foraging peoples occupying the African Kalahari desert are referred to by the Setswana-speakers in Botswana as Basarwa. Some social scientists call these people the "San"—a name that replaced the derogatory term of "Bushmen" (whose "primitive" lives and simple-minded notions were popularized, and ridiculed, in the movie "The Gods Must Be Crazy"). The people themselves, particularly those in Namibia, now again use the term "Bushmen." A number of Basarwa have expressed the wish to be called N/oakwe, or simply "first people." The Botswanan government, a bit antiseptically, refers to these people and other rural poor as Remote Area Dwellers, or RADs. And the popular term in Botswana used to refer to Remote Area Dwellers is *Tengyanateng*, meaning "the farthest people" or "the deep within the deep." And finally, Hitchcock notes, some of the more politically aware Basarwa call themselves simply "the dispossessed."[9] This shaping and use of cultural terms implies and reinforces relationships between groups.

Examining the rationale for economic development illustrates the central role of cultural notions in making the immoral moral. The social context of development is often one of co-optation of traditionally held lands and resources, with little or no recognition of resident peoples' rights, and little or no compensation for their subsequent environmental health problems. People living in targeted areas are described as living in extreme poverty. Their subsistence or barter-based economies are ignored or belittled, their cultures deemed primitive. They are called lazy, backward, ignorant, illiterate, stupid. Their situation of inequity is "their own fault." Surrounding lands are seen as unoccupied, empty, or "wilderness" areas that can be claimed and used by the state. Legally, state co-optation of peripheral peoples' territory and resources is supported by western notions of property rights: the contention that resources held in common—common property—do not in fact constitute "actual" property rights. [10]

Creating and maintaining inequity requires control over systems that produce and reproduce these cultural notions. Recent armed conflict in Afghanistan starkly illustrates how control over information is central to systems of power. When the Taleban took over the Afghanistan capital of Kabul in late September 1996, armed militias went from house to house, seizing televisions, videocassette recorders, satellite dishes, magazines, tape recorders, cassettes, and even musical toys that introduce "un-Islamic" sounds. In a world where thought and behavior are increasingly shaped through the media, control of those media and systems of knowledge is essential to legitimizing action and maintaining power. [11]

Conceptual Mechanisms

While cultural notions structure the way agendas are built, programs designed, and decisions made, it is conceptual mechanisms that provide an aura of objectivity, and thus legitimacy. Scientific methods are used to study reality, and economic frameworks are erected to make rational decisions. For much of the world, the notion of environmental crisis is defined, assessed, and articulated by a western-dominated science. Biologist Mary Clark has argued that western science is a product of a cultural mind-set that views the world as a set of categorizable, governable objects—resources that are human property that can be managed. Hence, we have the idea that whales and volcanos can be governed. This world view also includes a Darwinian vision of nature that emphasizes the central roles of violent, competitive, and self-serving behavior within and between species, rather than a vision of nature as a series of interrelated systems based on cooperative and collaborative relations. As Clark puts it, "modern western science . . . is being offered to cultures globally as a problem-solving device, dragging along with it its particular set of assumptions and its selected, and biased, vision." [12]

The development process again provides a useful example. The first phase of development process typically begins with resource inventories. Biological, geological, and other natural resource surveys are conducted, providing planners with resource maps of a given region. Projects are designed and funded using cost/benefit models that assess social, economic, and environmental costs relative to predicted benefits; these models rely on the accuracy of baseline studies to identify the full extent of the resource as well as the full range of potential costs to extract and develop that resource. Public participation is a component in some development planning processes, usually in the early stages of project implementation, occasionally during the cost/benefit analysis phase, though rarely at the initial planning phase. The role of public participation is generally limited to identifying potential problems and designing strategies that will minimize adverse impacts associated with the project. There are few or no opportunities for resident peoples to assess (or, more importantly, to decide) whether the development of resources in itself is an appropriate path to take.

For much of the world, science is controlled by nonnative experts, or experts trained in western institutions. The biases and cultural assumptions of a western world view significantly influence the ideological and institutional construction of ecology, environmental crisis, and resource management. This is the case with fishery resource management efforts in the U.S. Virgin Islands. In interviews, at public hearings, and in recorded minutes from fishery council meetings, biologists repeatedly framed the problem of declining fish stocks as a consequence of over-fishing and the self-serving, competitive behavior of fishers, rather than a problem of habitat degeneration due to overdevelopment and pollution in the coastal zone. The focus on fishing rather than habitat integrity is partly tied to political realities. Biologists recognize that pollution and habitat integrity are important, but their regulatory power is limited to the fishing industry. They lack authority to control activities that adversely impact on fishery habitat—namely, coastal development and related pollution. Fishery resource managers have concentrated on limiting fishery access (establishing seasons, marine reserves, and in some cases closing down the fishery altogether) and restricting the size and use of various gear (regulating the size and shape of fish traps and seines). Regulation and technological intervention have promoted competition and individualism, with a few fishers investing considerable resources in boats, radar, and storage facilities. Biologists argue that limiting access allows efficient management and economic "growth" while striving to achieve sustained yields. Fishers, especially the small-scale and part-time fishers, complain that commercial enterprises capture a greater share of the resources and sell their catch at lower prices—effectively squeezing them out of the marketplace. Resource scarcity continues, the number of full-time fishers continues to decline, and the incidence of conflict between fishers still rises. Along the way, collaborative and cooperative strategies have been replaced, and fishers have been transformed via the resource management process from experts who control the rules of access and use, to the ignorant and uniformed who themselves need to be controlled.[13]

"Developing" or "managing" the resources of previously peripheral regions requires a reformulation of resource relations, transferring the loci of power over resource value, access, use, and control from resident peoples to external power structures.[14] Conceptual mechanisms are used to redefine the meaning and value of resources, from those valued as critical to a traditional way of life, to those valued as economic commodities supporting progressive growth in the national and global economies. Nature is commodified and labor redirected from household subsistence and regional markets to the national and global economic arenas. Accompanying this centralization of authority and capital is an increase in distance between those who decide and those who experience the consequence. Thus, decisions are made that reinforce the status quo by providing short-term benefits, while ignoring or failing to consider the long-term and hard-to-quantify consequences of action.[15] Communities experience a loss of meaning, power, and integrity over their own natural settings, a loss that contributes to a declining ability of the communities to respond to crises.

Responding to Human Environmental Crises

Environmental problems, such as polluted air, water, and soil, become human environmental crises when biophysical conditions significantly threaten human health, society, or way of life. What is suggested here and illustrated in the following chapters is that human environmental crises emerge as a result of the culture and structure of power as well as the biophysical implications of political economic action. Physical, cultural, and conceptual distancing mechanisms are structural features of decision-making systems. These mechanisms, together with the inherent contradictions and conflicts of interest that accompany their use, contribute toward dysfunctional governance—where the abuse of fundamental human rights is deemed socially palatable and becomes legally justified.

Human rights and environmental crisis are inextricably linked. The emergence of crisis and efforts to respond to it involve conflicts between individuals, communities, peoples, and/or the state over rights to define, use, and control resources. For the state, the "nation" is the salient population for whom decisions are made. For resident communities living in the path of change, the community is the salient group.

Anthropologist Eric Wolf has argued that "the arrangements of a society become most visible when they are challenged by crisis."[16] Those who suffer the most are typically those with the least power in society—either the power to insulate themselves from the threat or, later, the power to rebuild their lives.[17] Not only does the experience of crisis expose the power relations of society, but it also tests the viability of political systems. The common experience and urgent need to respond blurs previous lines of cleavage—the cultural notions and historical relationships that divide groups in society are temporarily pushed aside as people struggle to survive a common threat. Life-threatening situations prompt people to act, organize, and transform the conditions of their life. New leaders emerge, new networks and coalitions are formed, community identity is reshaped. Responding to human environmental crisis creates opportunities to rearrange the hierarchies of power in society.

Across the world, communities and groups are linked in a struggle for protection of civil and human rights, equally. They are struggling for access to information, for the right of the worker and the community to know the risks and dangers involved in industrial activity, for the right to request and receive environmental and community health safeguards, for the right to monitor conditions, for the right to question the reasons for and benefits from development, and even for the right to say "no." Their struggle involves documenting the human context of environmental crisis, using this information in ways to establish culpability, and forcing changes in the status quo to prevent future abuses. They seek strong systems of law and regulation as well as user representation in policy formation. In short, these environmental quality and social justice movements seek a restructuring of the cultural values and assumptions on which decision-making systems are built.

Life and Death Matters closely examines this tension between problem and response, raising such questions as: Who has the authority to define resource use—the "state" in its actions or granting of permits to outside economic interests, or the affected communities? Who are the affected peoples? Who participates in shaping the development agenda? Who has the authority to evaluate, modify, assess, or reassess the implications of development activity? Who holds social and environmental culpability when development brings adverse affects—and who is responsible for remediation? How do we respond to human environmental crises that are the legacy of prior governments? What is the basis for determining socially just measures of compensation?

These are difficult questions, and, as illustrated in the following cases, the answers are by no means clear. Resolving human environmental crises requires fundamental transformations in local, national, and international decision-making systems that, first, allow people living with the problem to gain greater control in defining the nature of the crisis, devising equitable responses, and prohibiting recurrence; and, second, allow institutions and organizations that played a significant role in creating the problem to acknowledge their culpability and (through their efforts to respond) to carry a greater share of the burden for resolving the consequence. The struggle to achieve these transformations in decision-making systems requires confronting, challenging, and changing the status quo. Backlash is inevitable. Thus, we come to what may be the crucial question as we approach the end of the millennium: Can we build environmentally sound and socially just solutions to our problems in ways that minimize or prevent the incidence of violent conflict?

Notes

1. Thanks to Valerie Wheeler, Peter Esainko, Denise Santoro, and Ted Edwards for their editorial comments on portions of this chapter. Jim O'Connor provided helpful criticisms of an earlier paper. Bill Loker helped stimulate my thinking on the relationships between unresolved human environmental crisis and the rise of violent conflict; my thanks to him for sending me the Kaplan article.

2. Robert Kaplan's essay "The Coming Anarchy" was printed in *The Atlantic Monthly* 273 (1994) 44–76, quote from p. 49. After the publication of the *Atlantic Monthly* article, Kaplan revisited the regions described in his article. The ensuing book, while based on the original article, acknowledged that his earlier representation of cultural belief systems as a negative force contributing to the rise of violent conflict may have been somewhat simplistic. See Robert D. Kaplan, *The Ends of the Earth: A Journey at the Dawn of the 20th Century* (New York: Random House, 1996). Kaplan's thoughts were strongly influenced by the work of Thomas Homer-Dixon (*c.f.* "Environmental Scarcities and Violent Conflict: Evidence from Cases" *International Security* 19 (1994) 5–40). A growing body of literature frames environmental crisis in the language of national security, *c.f.* the extensive annotated bibliography contained in P. J. Simmons, ed., *Environment and Security Debates: An Introduction: Woodrow Wilson Environmental Change and Security Project Report*, Issue 1 (spring 1995), and Issue 2 (spring 1996). Also contained in these volumes are reprints of "environmental security" speeches given in 1995 and 1996 by various members of President Clinton's administration.

3. *C.f.* Clive Ponting, *A Green History of the World* (New York: Penguin Books, 1991).

4. *C.f.* Emilio Moran, *Human Adaptability* (Boulder, Colo.: Westview Press, 1982). Some of the ideas discussed in this section on Human Environmental Crisis and in the following section on the Culture and Structure of Power have appeared in Barbara Rose Johnston, "Human Rights and the Environment," *Human Ecology* (June 1995); and Barbara Rose Johnston, *Who Pays the Price? The Sociocultural Context of Environmental Crisis* (Washington, D.C.: Island Press, 1994).

5. See the United Nations Declaration of Human Rights, and the United Nations Commission on Human Rights Draft Declaration on Human Rights and the Environment, in the appendices to this volume.

6. See, for example, Bunyan Bryant, ed., *Environmental Justice: Issues, Policies and Solutions* (Washington, D.C.: Island Press, 1995); Robert Bullard, *Unequal Protection: Environmental Justice and Communities of Color* (San Francisco: Sierra Club Books, 1994).

7. This information is drawn from IPPNW International Commission to Investigate the Health and Environmental Effects of Nuclear Weapons Production and the Institute for Energy and Environmental Research, *Radioactive Heaven and Earth* (New York: Apex Press, 1991), 50–56. The

authors' sources include recently declassified U.S. Atomic Commission planning documents pertaining to the site selection process. See Gordon Dean (Chairman, U.S. Atomic Energy Commission), "Location of Proving Grounds for Atomic Weapons—selection of a continental atomic test site," report by the Director of Military Application, U.S. AEC Document 141/7, Dec. 13.

8. These thoughts are strongly influenced by the works of George Appell, especially his paper "The Social Construction of Dependent Peoples: The Rungus of Northern Borneo" presented at the Borneo Research Council Symposium: The Transformation of the Societies of Borneo Produced by the Expansion of the World System (Dec. 3, 1992).

9. Robert Hitchcock, "Settlements and Survival: What Future for the Remote Area Dwellers of Botswana?" (unpublished paper presented at the National Institute of Research [NIR] Seminar, University of Botswana in Gaborone, Botswana, Oct. 13, 1995).

10. *C.f.* Erling Berge, "Democracy and Human Rights: Conditions for Sustainable Resource Utilization," and other case studies in Johnston 1994, *op. cit.,* note 4.

11. For examples of the media as a force in shaping cultural beliefs, affecting social behavior, and reinforcing the status quo, see various issues of the journal *AdBuster*. For an analysis of the methods and means used to reshape public perception of industry and government's role in creating and responding to environmental crisis, see Tom Athanasiou, "The Age of Greenwashing," *Capitalism, Nature, Socialism* 7:1 (March 1996) 1–36, and his lengthier treatment in *Divided Planet: The Ecology of Rich and Poor* (New York: Little Brown, 1996). Neil Middleton, Phil O'Keefe, and Sam Moyo argue in *Tears of the Crocodile: From Rio to Reality in the Developing World* (Boulder, Colo.: Westview, 1994), 210–211, that capital controls education and health to suit its own ideologies, and that "no matter what 'knowledge' NGOs may feel that they possess about the right ways in which to proceed, no matter what 'expertise' they are able to provide, the administration, use, and finally the appropriation of that knowledge and expertise must be by the people for the South. . . ." I have argued elsewhere that control over the culture and structure of power in scientific information systems is a key variable in determining the shape and face of resource management systems (where people are trained, who structures the curriculum, how problems are defined and studied, where funding comes from, and how scientific knowledge is interpreted and used in the policy arenas). Barbara Rose Johnston, "Environmental Alienation and Resource Management: Virgin Islands Experiences" (194–205) in Johnston 1994, *op. cit.*, note 4.

12. Mary Clark, Keynote Address to the third annual congress of the International Common Property Studies Association, Washington, D.C., Oct. 1993.

13. See Barbara Rose Johnston, "Environmental Alienation and Resource Management: Virgin Islands Experiences," *Capitalism, Nature, Socialism* 3(4), issue 12 (1992) 99–108. For a description of the collaborative and cooperative traditions in Virgin Islands fishing communities, see Stephen Koester, "Socioeconomic and Cultural Role of Fishing and Shell-fish in the Virgin Islands Biosphere Reserve," Subtask 2.5 (St. Thomas: Island Resources Foundation).

14. See Barbara Rose Johnston, discussion of resource relations in "The Political Ecology of Development: The Impact of Tourism in St. Thomas, U.S. Virgin Islands," Ph.D. Diss., Dept. of Anthropology, University of Massachusetts–Amherst, 1987.

15. This point is particularly well demonstrated in The Ecologist, *Whose Common Future? Reclaiming the Commons* (Philadelphia: New Society Publishers, 1993).

16. E. Wolf, "Facing Power: Old Insights, New Questions," *American Anthropologist* 92, pp. 586–596, p. 593. Thoughts here were influenced by discussions with Anthony Oliver-Smith and developed in the context of natural disaster in a paper by Barbara Rose Johnston and Judy Schulte, "Natural Power and Power Politics," presented to the Society for Applied Anthropology, Memphis, Tenn., March 1992.

17. See Ben Wisner and his examination of the political, economic, social, and cultural factors that influence vulnerability to "natural disasters" in "Disaster Vulnerability: Scale, Power and Daily Life," *Geojournal* 30:2 (1993) 127–140.

PART ONE

Economic Development
Global Forces/Local Responses

In the first chapter of the book, we examined how "developing" or "managing" the resources of previously peripheral regions requires a reformulation of resource relations, transferring the loci of power over resource value, access, use, and control from resident peoples to external power structures. Conceptual mechanisms are used to redefine the meaning and value of resources, from those valued as critical to a traditional way of life to those valued as economic commodities supporting progressive growth in the national and global economy. Cultural mechanisms are used to legitimize this process, presenting traditional beliefs, actions, and endeavors as "primitive" or "backward," and imposed projects and activities as "progress." Nature is categorized and commodified and labor is redirected from household subsistence and regional markets to the arenas of national and global economics.

Development may be imposed, but it is rarely a passive process. In Lorraine Aragon's chapter on local responses to global forces in Outer Island Indonesia, we see how the seductive promise of development (progress, material wealth, enhanced quality of life) raises expectations, obscures perceptions, and structures reactions to development. People are able to ignore or deny the negative consequences of development and go on to act as collaborators, even initiators. Once development programs are initiated (such as transmigration, timber harvest, mining, and tourism) and problems begin to emerge, lack of information contributes to the problems villagers face in devising solutions. Access (or, more typically, *lack* of access) to information concerning a proposed project, the problems of development elsewhere, and the strategies used by other communities to assert their voice in the decision-making process can significantly influence local experience and local response to development.

Aragon's chapter also illustrates the varied ways *distance* factors into the information flows and power structures of a nation. Indonesia is the fourth largest nation in the world, consisting of some 1,400 islands stretching across more than 4,000 miles of ocean. The geographic structure of the nation inhibits information flow and facilitates Javanese control over the huge territory and its diverse population: people are separated by water, mountainous terrain, language, religion, and poverty. These factors affect access to education and other communication tools (including the opportunity to learn other languages). When problems emerge, local people blame those responsible locally (such as resettled peoples, or timber and mining companies) rather than assigning culpability to national government policies.

Distance between national policy makers and the communities experiencing development can sometimes work in favor of villagers. Given the repressive political context

(Indonesia has a well-documented record of human rights abuses), fear of violent reprisal encourages passive resistance rather than proactive responses to development-related threats. Given the great distance between power centers and the rural periphery, opportunities to delay, obstruct, and subvert development projects occur with some regularity. Distance and the lack of accountability mechanisms means that local behavior and action are not closely monitored. Thus, swidden farmers can set forest fires on lands being logged in an effort to reclaim traditional lands.

Other local response strategies include co-opting the national language and goals of development to use in interest-specific ways (thus, allowing village leaders the means to communicate and negotiate with local government or industry representatives). And, in those rare cases where information flows and communication tools are accessible, another strategy is to work in collaboration with other communities in negotiating the development experience.

The chapter by Lindsey Swope, Margaret Swain, Fuquan Yang, and Jack Ives on Lijiang County, Yunnan Province, China, similarly examines local response to larger development forces, focusing on the tension between individuals, communities, peoples, and the state over rights to define, use, and control resources. For the state, the "nation" is the salient population for whom decisions are made. For resident communities in the path of change, the community is the salient group. Swope and colleagues argue that the pattern of control over common resources—who decides what happens, where, how, who benefits, to what end—is a key indicator in determining the viability and integrity of rural conditions. In exploring the different dimensions of resource use in Lijiang, China (tourism and timber), the authors also demonstrate the difficulties of depicting the development experience in definitive terms, either positive or negative.

Rural conditions for minority peoples in Yunnan Province have been influenced by China's strong central government and history of ethnic-based underdevelopment, a history that presented both opportunities and constraints to managing and maintaining local control over common resources. Irregular and contradictory regulatory structures presented opportunities for self-interest exploitation—opportunities that, in the long run, contributed to the degradation of biological resources. The distance between those who decided (national policy) and local communities, coupled with the lack of accountability mechanisms, provided local peoples with opportunities to circumvent restrictive regulations (in the case of forestry, to run a timber-smuggling network). Economic opportunities, especially those tied with ecotourism and cultural tourism, had far-reaching effects on social organization, economic activity, cultural expression, and the construction of ethnicity. For both resident minorities and the nation, tourism emphasized cultural differences even as it enhanced the standing of cultural minorities.

As mentioned in the preface to Swope and colleagues, solving the human environmental crises of the urbanized core requires confronting the contexts and conditions of life in rural regions. In mapping out the development history of Lijiang, China, the authors give us some sense of how a regional economy has been transformed from what was, for the most part, a regional-oriented market with villagers engaged in household production, to an economy highly dependent on national and international economic forces. This chapter ends with a brief mention of the devastating earthquake in Lijiang, China, in February 1996. Will the region, with its newly acquired dependency on tourism and timber, be able to meet the demands of rebuilding without further degrading forest resources or compromising the cultural attractions that drew tourists to Lijiang in the first place? Have Lijiang and other previously peripheral regions traded regional self-sufficiency for short-term gain—losing community flexibility and resilience in the process?

CHAPTER 1

Distant Processes
The Global Economy and Outer Island Development in Indonesia[1]

Lorraine V. Aragon

The View of a Highland Sulawesi Farmer

During my 1986–1989 fieldwork in highland Central Sulawesi, I held the following conversation in a mixture of Indonesian and Uma languages with one of my closest acquaintances, Tina Mase'. We were relaxing on the veranda of her family's field house, a one-room bamboo and bark structure set about five feet above the ground on wooden stilts. We sat gazing out over the swidden rice fields and vast mountain silhouettes that stretched before and below us in a late afternoon at the start of the harvest season. Chewing on her betelnut and tobacco leaf quid, Tina Mase' turned to me and broke our calm silence by asking, "Ronald Reagan, he is president of the United States, right?" I was struck by her political knowledge and reflected quickly how few of my college students in the United States would be able to provide the name of Indonesia's president.

Tina Mase' is an elementary school-educated grandmother in her forties with seven of her ten children still living. Besides household work and child care, Tina Mase' farms rain-fed crops of rice, corn, and vegetables on steep mountain slopes. Her husband, Tama Mase', also farms, builds houses, and hunts game animals. They both tend coffee trees and harvest the beans, which he carries to the coast to trade for cash or supplies.

After a brief interlude Tina Mase' continued her political questioning. "And Father Suharto, he is president of . . . out there?" She paused midsentence, looked me straight in the eyes, and then nodded slowly in the direction of one of those faraway mountain ranges in the distance. This interchange startled me not because I was surprised by a rural Indonesian's knowledge about the United States. Millions of Indonesians, after all, watch Bill Cosby on television in urban areas, listen to cassette tapes of American pop musicians, and regularly view Hollywood action films. Rather, her words moved me because I realized just how distant western Central Sulawesi highlanders feel, not only from the government capital in Jakarta but also from the province of Central Sulawesi and the political nation as a whole. As a state, Indonesia is one of the most rapidly developing nations in the world, but the path of development set by the nation's leaders

Lorraine V. Aragon is a cultural anthropologist who has worked in Central Sulawesi, Indonesia since 1984. She teaches anthropology at East Carolina University in Greenville, North Carolina, A-214 Brewster Hall, Greenville, NC 27858. She can also be reached via email (anaragon@ecuvm.cis.ecu.edu).

has been created without the participation, or sometimes even the knowledge, of the hundreds of ethnic minority groups in the hinterlands. The established ways of life of millions of people in the so-called outer islands hinges on their elusion of, or at least partial control over, expanding development projects linked to global market forces. This essay includes descriptions of early responses to development projects such as logging, transmigration, and tourism in western Central Sulawesi and some parallel events already moving forward in other parts of the Indonesian archipelago. Only a greater understanding of the connections between global economic forces and such changes on the periphery can lead to the legislative and diplomatic measures needed to promote local autonomy as well as the protection of human and environmental rights in Indonesia.

The Periphery Meets the Center

Millions of North Americans begin their mornings with a "cup of java" and regularly purchase clothes, running shoes, tropical wood furniture, or toys manufactured in Java or Bali, the most populous islands of Indonesia. It is less widely known, however, that the country that includes these islands is the fourth most populous nation in the world and has a per capita economic growth rate that is over three times the world average. International economists who have studied Indonesia during the "New Order" political regime beginning in 1965 laud the rapid growth of a middle class and cite Indonesia as "among the world's outstanding examples of poverty reduction."[2] Nevertheless, what remains relatively unexamined is the political and economic relationship between the state and its multiethnic hinterlands, peoples and lands that are being radically affected by economic projects controlled from the center. The Indonesian national development program is founded on, and literally fueled by, regional inequities that often entail the rapid debasement of ancestral lands occupied by ethnic minorities who reside on the less populated "outer islands" of the archipelago.

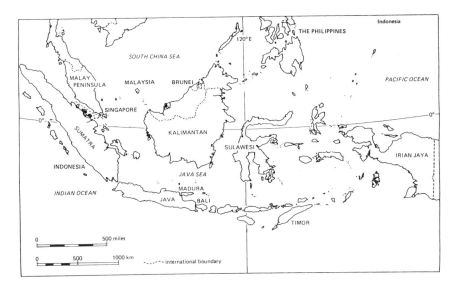

A Da'a Kaili family who were moved from their ancestral highland village to a local transmigration village in Central Sulawesi. Photograph by Lorraine V. Aragon.

For many decades, the peoples of western Central Sulawesi, one of those outer island ethnic minority regions, have participated indirectly in the global economy by growing and selling coffee for export. Now, however, they are confronting new economic development programs, including transmigration, timber harvesting, and tourism, which more severely threaten their ecological and cultural environments. Many indigenous Central Sulawesi people are startled by these transformations and they are cautious in their replies to the initiatives of a powerful military-based government. Below I describe some of their initial responses along with reactions to earlier development programs encountered by other Indonesian minority regions. These latter ethnic groups' efforts to negotiate, evade, or counter government-imposed development proposals provide models for anticipating future outcomes in less developed regions such as Central Sulawesi. Ultimately, actions on the part of American consumers and legislative representatives may be necessary to affect the western businesses whose operations encourage environmental and human rights violations in Indonesia. Such multilateral approaches to human rights and careful modifications of Indonesian development policies would attenuate periodic outbreaks of disruptive regional violence and thus facilitate the cause of Indonesian national stability as well as international investment.

International Business and Human Rights Problems in Indonesia

President Clinton's 1994 visit to Jakarta for the APEC (Atlantic-Pacific Economic Cooperation) meetings highlighted Indonesia's increasing importance to American foreign trade. It also drew national attention to Indonesia's most troubling human rights problems. As in his earlier 1994 diplomatic encounter with China, President Clinton was concerned about human rights violations in Asia—but did not wish to jeopardize the United States' potential trade opportunities in this rapidly expanding region. Indonesia's gross national product grew at an average of 6 percent annually from 1970 to

1992, and the United States and Japan were Indonesia's two biggest trading partners for both imports and exports.[3] Therefore, although the United States public may have little notion of Indonesia's importance to the future of American-Asian trade, our leaders, understandably, are highly motivated to further American business interests in the region.

The Clinton administration's insistence that western nations' commercial engagement will have a more positive effect on Indonesia's human rights progress than commercial disengagement is compatible with the widespread claim among Asian governments that economic development will naturally lead to greater democracy and political freedoms—despite the fact that nearby Singapore provides a glaring counterexample.[4] My view is that increased commercial engagement may or may not affect human rights improvements in Indonesia, depending on the strategic nature of our commercial interactions and the particular human rights issues of political concern to our government and business leaders. In general, however, the United States government weighs economic and security concerns over humanitarian ones, and the stakes for the former are high with respect to Indonesia's rapid development and strategic Pacific location.

Secretary of State Warren Christopher raised the following five human rights issues during the 1994 APEC meetings: the government's cancellation of several Indonesian newspapers' licenses, the arrest of labor leaders in workers' disputes, a decree restricting the existence of nongovernmental organizations, a "cleansing" operation in Jakarta that cleared opposition figures before the APEC summit meeting, and human rights abuses in East Timor.[5] Given the United States' own ambivalent record on environmental conservation and the fair treatment of ethnic minorities, these two issues were less a point of focus for human rights discussions at APEC than were increased freedoms for the press, labor unions, and nongovernmental organizations—issues where United States representatives can stand on higher ground.[6] Overall, the Clinton administration's human rights agenda at the APEC meetings was very limited in scope with respect to Indonesia's myriad of lesser known environmental and ethnic minority questions.

Indonesia is no exception to the general rule that a state's economic development most adversely affects the environment and human rights of its marginal populations, particularly its ethnic minority groups. The historical basis for Indonesia's asymmetrical development, however, is geographic as well as demographic. Untapped natural resources are most abundant in what are commonly called the "outer islands," meaning the islands of the archipelago outside of the most densely populated islands of Java, Bali, and Madura. Given that about 60 percent of the nation's population is clustered on those three "inner islands," which comprise only 7 percent of the country's land mass, the remaining 6,000 inhabited islands appear in the eyes of the government to be relatively unoccupied and unproductive. Thus, the outer islands—home to most of Indonesia's over 300 ethnic minority groups—have been viewed by the postwar Indonesian governments as primary locales for "human development" (*pembangunan masyarakat*) as well as resource development for the purposes of mining, forestry, tourism, oil extraction, and plantation agriculture.[7]

The Indonesian program for economic development (*pembangunan*), which is implemented by civil service and military personnel in their dual role as security and development forces, has two matching facets: first, the creation of large Indonesian businesses that pull foreign cash into the national economy and, second, the management or guidance (*pembinaan*) of more "modern" citizens who will cooperatively participate in the growing economy. These twin goals, supported by a powerful military, create the potential for large-scale environmental and cultural debasement in Indonesia.

Economic development projects, often funded by foreign aid monies or multinational companies, have made territorial consolidation in the outer islands a priority of critical "national interest" to the regime of President Suharto. Possibilities for profitable development, especially in the fields of mineral and offshore oil extraction, have led to the relatively recent incorporation of regions such as Irian Jaya (the western half of New Guinea subsumed in 1969) and East Timor (seized by military occupation in 1975), despite the resistance of indigenous inhabitants. Reports by organizations such as Human Rights Watch and Amnesty International have publicized these most dramatic environmental and human rights crises in Indonesia, yet the widespread problems associated with development efforts in other outer island areas have received little international attention largely because few outsiders have observed them.[8]

Unlike in the United States, where diverse colonial settlements voluntarily joined together to form an independent union, the political boundaries lassoing Indonesia's diverse peoples are a legacy from centuries of Dutch colonialism. Some of the ethnic groups held under Indonesian military rule have ancient historical and cultural ties to one another, but many do not. This situation creates a potential tension between the interests of minorities in the hinterlands and those of the central government on Java, which sets national development policies. Local responses to incipient human environmental rights problems in western Central Sulawesi illustrate the varied perceptions about development programs held by local villagers, entrepreneurs, Indonesian government officials, and social scientists. The Central Sulawesi cases described can be matched with parallel examples from other Indonesian regions where ethnic minorities have sought to negotiate for their community rights or to evade development initiatives designed without their input. Ultimately, western consumers, businesses, and governments play a large role in providing incentives for ecological and cultural degradation in Indonesia, yet the contexts for western policy formulation leave the foreigners involved largely unaware of their effects on Indonesian minorities. It is important, therefore, when our government formulates foreign policy, technology transfer agreements, and human rights positions, that it include state versus minority ethnic relations in the equation. As several Asian governments have correctly pointed out, western governments have no right to exercise neocolonial demands in the human rights arena. Such issues benefit more from multilateral discussion and the participation of nongovernmental organizations (NGOs). Western citizens and their governments, however, do have the right to raise human rights issues and withhold their business from companies profiting from unethical development ventures.

Tourism, Transmigration, and Roads Forward in Central Sulawesi

From 1986 to 1989 I conducted anthropological research on social and religious change in Central Sulawesi, one of the less developed outer island provinces. The one western visitor I received during those three and a half years of fieldwork commented that Palu, the provincial capital, was one of the least attractive cities that he had ever visited during his 30 years of travel in Indonesia. In a certain respect his judgment mirrored mine: that tourism was one facet of economic development that would not likely gravitate to Central Sulawesi, a province with few impressive "traditional" buildings and even fewer paved roads, flush toilets, or other amenities favored by foreign visitors. When I returned to the area in 1993, however, I understood that we were mistaken. We had grossly underestimated the vision of both Indonesian and western entrepreneurs.

In 1992 a European man married to an Indonesian woman purchased land from a coastal fishing village and built a scuba diving resort beside a coral reef. That reef formerly was considered a village right-of-way but locals accepted the passage of resident foreigners who occasionally stopped by for a few hours to swim, snorkel, and watch colorful tropical fish. The new resort, by contrast, privatized the previously open beach. Bungalow accommodations, priced comparably to Palu's urban hotel rooms, catered to European backpacking tourists. Once the facility was listed in a major guidebook along with provincial bus routes, a stream of tourists arrived who were interested to sunbathe, scuba dive, and then go trekking in the mountains to see local flora and fauna and to visit groups of highland villagers.

I asked the European businessman how the coastal inhabitants, members of the Bugis and Kaili ethnic groups, felt about moving their houses to accommodate the resort. He smiled proudly and answered, "No problem, they all work for me." The new owners first asked the locals to evacuate a portion of their village to create space for the bungalows. Then they hired cooperative villagers as cooks, maids, and custodians. By 1993 the resort also was sponsoring guided trekking tours, including one to a distant highland area where I knew the indigenous peoples' prior experience of westerners had been confined to an occasional Protestant missionary. I was told by a nurse that the influx of tourist dollars into the highland economy was severely inflating prices for transportation services and local commodities, including clinic medicines.

In 1993 the European entrepreneur and his wife were receiving unprecedented support for their tourism ventures from provincial military officials. Although the resort's charges for scuba diving were considered a bargain by the European diving patrons I interviewed, the daily fees—calculated at the resort in U.S. dollars—were far above the average monthly income of a local Indonesian family. In the long run, the owners and government officials issuing permits stood to gain a very high profit from these tourism activities while the villagers, even if some acquired a new access route to cash, stood to lose their land rights, their privacy, and their independent coastal subsistence patterns.

In my four-year absence from Central Sulawesi, increased tourism and new development programs had become prominent topics of local discussion. I learned from highland villagers and local government officials that new transmigration sites, to which Javanese and Balinese would be moved from overpopulated regions on their home islands, were targeted for the forested interior. The Dutch colonial idea of "transmigration" was designed to control overpopulation, mainly on Java, by moving peasants from the densely populated inner islands of Indonesia to the sparsely populated outer islands. This policy has been pursued with vigor by postwar independent Indonesian governments despite many reported difficulties for both the migrants and indigenous groups.

The low-population areas of western Central Sulawesi selected by the government for new transmigration sites are locales known to the indigenous people for their potential health risks. In one of these targeted areas, Banggaiba, the population suffered from an unusually high incidence of malaria, insufficient access to clean water, and no health care clinics. Another area adjacent to Lake Lindu was known for its problems with schistosomiasis, a liver disorder transmitted by water-borne parasites. Local people in these regions said they hoped that better health care and water purification facilities would arrive with the transmigration programs. Research indicates, however, that inter-island transmigration often results in poorer health and higher mortality for the migrants, as well as altered ecological habitats conducive to disease transmission for both migrants and indigenous residents.[9]

Between 1989 and 1993 electric lines had progressed 80 kilometers up into the Kulawi district highlands and the vehicle road had been extended by bulldozer 20 kilometers deeper into the forest. I was told that some government officials had made a deal with the villagers of the area: if the locals would vote 100 percent for the government party (GOLKAR) in the 1993 election, the government would arrange for a vehicle road to enter their region. If indeed such a promise was made, the bargain apparently was kept on both sides.

The new roadbed, however, was not paved and its creation quickly resulted in landslides along the steep mountain paths. Following heavy rains the deforested trail became a morass of sticky mud useless for foot travel, the customary mode of transportation in the region. Within days of the bulldozer's arrival locals already were complaining about the so-called road and were busy cutting new walking trails through the forest. If government officials wanted a road enough to bully elections in order to achieve it, they likely were less interested in the transport of highland crop surpluses, which are not substantial, than in the undeveloped resources of the highland forests, probably timber or minerals. For the moment, such questions did not concern the villagers. They had hoped for improved transportation facilities but were thus far tolerating and coping with the developmentcreated landslides much as they would any other natural disaster.

The Charms of Development

The situations observed in Central Sulawesi during the early 1990s illustrate some processes by which Indonesian ethnic minorities can be "selectively victimized" and left with a degraded environment.[10] They also reveal how Indonesian villagers often are passive observers in these processes. Many residents of rural areas initially are attracted to the proposals that government officials and other outsiders present to them. Under pressure to "make progress" from international economists and foreign investors, the New Order Indonesian government has made a conscious effort to promote economic development as an abstract value to the citizenry. The cooperation of minority communities is secured with promises of advancement and new opportunities to obtain cash and imported goods. Central Sulawesi highlanders, who have long lived without electricity or vehicle roads and exchanged subsistence crop surpluses primarily with relatives, now find themselves labeled as impoverished and "backward" (terbelakang) by development project leaders who tour the region.

Pervasive Indonesian media campaigns and community education programs equate economic development with moral righteousness as well as economic prosperity. These so-called "guidance" (*pembinaan*) programs seek to draw Indonesia's ethnic minorities into a national culture about which they had little knowledge (or with which they had felt little affiliation) until recently. Members of smaller ethnic minorities also see that citizens of the nation's "more advanced" (*lebih maju*) ethnic groups own a range of possessions that they themselves cannot afford. Thus Central Sulawesi villagers often are anxious to participate in development programs and they cannot foresee the environmental and related human rights problems that may accompany the projects entering their region.

In various areas of Central Sulawesi, I heard people say that they wish they could attract wealthy foreign tourists to their village, that they would love to have a vehicle road to help them transport their produce to coastal markets, that they are interested in forestry or building projects that would give them more access to cash, and that they await infrastructure improvements promised by government transmigration programs.

These pleas for "progress" are troubling, given the extensive environmental and human rights problems that such programs have generated in other regions of the country.[11] Nevertheless, foreign observers are in no position to dismiss Indonesian villagers' desires to improve their families' and communities' fragile socioeconomic status within the nation. Nor should we dismiss the Indonesian government's desire to improve its national economic status in the world. Rather, members of Indonesia's smaller ethnic groups need more information, participation, and options with regard to the development schemes that will undoubtedly transform their particular regions in diverse ways during the forthcoming decades.

Local responses in Central Sulawesi confirm that, despite past government assertions to the contrary, Indonesian villagers are open to both internally and externally generated change.[12] What villagers are *not* open to is unwarranted additional risk to their subsistence, or severe social disruption. Thus resistance to development programs often rises dramatically as actual costs and benefits become increasingly understood by the individuals affected. At present, local villagers gain knowledge about their future far too slowly to participate in its formulation, because the Indonesian government permits the circulation of only positive or neutral data about past development program achievements.[13]

Blaming Tourists, Migrants, and Swidden Farmers

Indonesian villagers have limited information to guide them in assigning responsibility, once development programs are initiated and their consequent difficulties become manifest. In the case of tourism, Central Sulawesi residents assume that tourists who flaunt local cultural rules are powerful independent agents: people with magnificent inherited wealth who need not work for food or their family's needs. Tourists also hold extraordinary political power to obtain passports and visas that are unattainable for the average Indonesian citizen. Highland villagers generally know little about tourists' and tribal art collectors' motivations. They also are unaware of their own government's promotion of Indonesian tourism with advertisements that promise views of exotic tribes, "lost worlds," and splendid natural surroundings along with western food and comfortable accommodations.[14] Villagers only envision what they themselves have to gain from development such as cash needed for school fees, taxes, medicines, and imported commodities. Rarely do villagers imagine what they have to lose—such as ancestral land rights, fish and game habitats, cultural autonomy, and even their present form of subsistence.

In the case of transmigration projects, Central Sulawesi highlanders generally blame problems on the other ethnic groups who have been relocated to their region, rather than assigning culpability to the government policies that require and structure trans-migration. The situation in Central Sulawesi is not currently as dire as that in regions such as Irian Jaya, where government plans for transmigrating hundreds of thousands of Javanese will leave Irian people as a minority population in their home province. Nevertheless, the expansion of interisland transmigration sites in Central Sulawesi is carving away the ancestral domains of indigenous inhabitants with efforts to establish wet-rice agriculture in steep and infertile areas that often are better suited to their prior swidden farming uses.

Besides the island transmigration projects, "local transmigration" (*resetelmen pen-duduk*) programs are being implemented to move "isolated ethnic minorities" (*suku terasing*) into model villages near the coast where the government can supervise them more closely (see photograph). In the transmigration settlements away from their ancestral lands, the migrants usually are found to be more amenable to Muslim or Christian conversion, transformations to monotheism that the government considers conducive to national development. As in other regions of Indonesia, many of the houses and villages set up by the Central Sulawesi transmigration program are neglected or soon abandoned because, as Michael Dove puts it, the people who move from their ancestral domains are asked "to change too much, too fast, in exchange for too little."[15]

Indonesia's policy on "isolated ethnic minorities" condemns as antithetical to devel-opment goals and national security three cultural features that characterize several indigenous Central Sulawesi groups. The first is these peoples' supposed lack of "relig-ion" (*agama*), meaning that they have not yet converted to one of the nationally recog-nized world religions, which include Islam, Protestantism, Catholicism, Hinduism, and Buddhism. World religion is considered a necessary step in the modernization of "back-ward" groups and a protection from communism, still considered a looming political threat by the Indonesian government. Moreover, the government closely regulates all official religious organizations, which in turn can be useful to spread government mes-sages to local congregations. A second objectionable characteristic of these isolated ethnic minorities is their subsistence strategy of shifting cultivation, meaning the regular movement of rice and other rain-fed crop fields throughout an otherwise intact forested environment. A third problem, in the eyes of the government, is the movement of farm houses with shifting fields, a potential problem for government control and tax collec-tion.

The Indonesian government perceives shifting cultivation as a potential threat to national security and as unproductive in terms of crop harvests. Shifting or "swidden" farmers often move their residences along with their field plots, making government supervision and military mobilization difficult. Moreover, swidden or dry-rice fields produce smaller harvests annually than fixed location wet-rice fields, although swidden cultivation allows for the regrowth of forests and the periodic use of land where irrigated agriculture is not feasible.

Officially, swidden farming is proclaimed to be detrimental to the environment, although the government often replaces swiddened forests with transmigration projects or timber concessions that do far more ecological damage. The government also over-looks the significant contributions of forest peoples to the national economy, including their harvest of wild forest products such as rattan and resins.[16] In Central Sulawesi, most highlanders participate in the global economy indirectly through the sale of forest-grown cash crops such as coffee, cacao, vanilla, and cloves.

In essence, just as most Americans are unaware of the human rights violations leading to the inexpensive Indonesian products they consume, most Indonesians do not comprehend the global market forces and central government strategies behind the appearance of development projects such as tourism and transmigration. Simultane-ously, Indonesian government officials criticize the subsistence strategies of indigenous farmers as an environmental rationale to escalate development projects, such as lucrative timber concessions and transmigration. These programs, however, really are aimed at solving other national problems, including uneven population distribution, military security, and economic advancement. Until the larger forces propelling change in the outer islands are better known to local villagers, they will not be able to negotiate effectively for greater local participation.

National Versus Local Rights

According to the 1945 Indonesian constitution the government has rights to all "natural forest" and assigns concessions averaging 100,000 hectares in size for approximately 20 years to timber companies.[17] In one western Central Sulawesi highland region where logging concessions have been operating for years, the forest has been widely clear-cut despite official Indonesian regulations that require "selective felling." Anna Tsing describes a civil servant report from an interior South Kalimantan region that advised the Forestry Department to waive official rules for selective cutting in the area because otherwise the logging companies were likely to ignore those regulations in order to obtain a sufficient profit.[18] In this way, environmental ordinances are repudiated to prevent any loss of face that would accrue if they were ignored by business magnates far more powerful than local inspectors or village residents.

November 1994 international news briefs indicated that forest fires raging in Kalimantan and Sumatra were set by ethnic minority peoples protesting the logging of their lands. This drastic means by which swidden farmers try to reestablish claims to ancestral land cleared by timber companies has been reported for over a decade.[19] Interior villagers learn too late that loggers will remove not only "valuable trees" but also locally useful species that timber companies define as "troublesome plants" growing in "unoccupied" territories. One of the greatest problems faced by swidden farmers whose ancestral territories are desired by developers is that their long fallow cycles ensure that they will be absent from most of their customary homelands at any given time. This situation provides developers with many opportunities to seize legally unoc-cupied land.

In western Central Sulawesi there is often a passive acceptance of new development projects based on local peoples' certainty of their inability to reject government proposals. Aggressive actions by foreign human rights activists or mobilized resistance by local ethnic minorities are potentially dangerous, given the severity with which the Indonesian government can respond to protest of its policies. Like other marginal ethnic minorities, Central Sulawesi highlanders recognize the intimidation of state power and have a long, and in certain respects successful, history of choosing detached or passive resistance strategies.

Historical evidence concerning past migrations indicates that many ethnic minorities in Indonesia adopted their interior locales and difficult subsistence strategies precisely to avoid overbearing state control, including interference from Dutch colonialists as well as prior coastal rulers. Yet no longer are there many areas of primary forest to which swidden farmers can flee. Therefore, when government-approved enterprises build roads to their villages and request "hospitality" for army troops and nonlocal workers, what realistic options do ethnic minority communities have? Future negotiations about resource management in areas such as Central Sulawesi may benefit from knowledge about events already played out among other Indonesian groups facing earlier development proposals.

Negotiations in North
Sumatra, Bali, and South Sulawesi

Some Indonesian ethnic groups outside Central Sulawesi have a stronger track record of negotiating directly with the government for consideration of their community rights. For example, villagers in southern Bali and villagers in the Gayo region of North Sumatra have invoked locally favorable interpretations of government doctrines and used their version of national rhetoric to achieve their community's interests in the execution of development projects.[20] As Carol Warren argues concerning a Balinese water dispute case, skillful use of the national rhetoric with army leaders was not in itself sufficient for successful resistance to the government. Nevertheless, when combined with the organizational power of village institutions and popular control over local leaders who mediated with the state, the villagers' will prevailed.

In the Balinese case, a village excluded from the benefits of a clean water project refused to contribute labor and matching funds unless their needy area would receive its own water tank. The villagers collectively used nationalist-style oratory, passive resistance, and implicit threats of sabotage to gain their way with the military troops sent in as supervisors on the water project. In the Gayo region of North Sumatra, by contrast, John Bowen describes how local villagers avoided donating labor and matching funds to the yearly "Presidential Order [concerning the] Village" program (*Inpres Desa*) simply by using the subsidy funds as they saw fit and then falsifying records provided to the government. Thus negotiation for local interests through organized village politicking, and the avoidance of change through deception, have been successful on occasion in various parts of the archipelago.

Geographically closer to the Central Sulawesi situation is the case of tourism development in the Toraja region of South Sulawesi. There tourism problems have involved not only land degradation but also theft of cultural properties. Anthropologists have served as informal advocates of Toraja rights in Indonesia and have worked in the United States to stop the trade and display of stolen ancestor statues that fuel tourism-related thefts and ecological destruction.

Pursuant to the immense financial success of Bali as a tourism center and the increasing interest of foreigners in scouting out other exotic Indonesian locations still "unspoiled" by tourism, the Toraja region of South Sulawesi became the outer island tourist mecca of the 1970s. Although the concept of "tourist" was still unknown in Toraja in the late 1960s, by the early 1980s approximately 40,000 foreign tourists per year were arriving via newly built roads and airports to view Toraja houses, spectacular mortuary ceremonies, and life-size grave statues.[21]

The environmental disturbances caused were not only in the natural world, such as problems with tourist refuse, but also in the cultural environment. In Indonesia there are few forests or "natural" resources that have not been subject to some forms of human manipulation through the past millennia. Thus there is usually no radical disjunction between the "natural" and cultural environment. Rather, tourism's disruption of local settlements and human grave sites in the forests occurs parallel to its degradation of waterways and trees in the forests.

In the process of tourism promotion, inhabitants of selected villages in the Toraja region had their houses, their villages, and even their mortuary statues designated by the government as official "tourist objects," which by definition could be controlled by government regulations and made available to foreigners' intrusions.[22] The most heinous result of Toraja tourism is the thievery of consecrated ancestor statues, called *tau tau*, from the limestone cliff balconies where they formerly watched over their living descendants. By the late 1980s almost all major Toraja burial sites had been looted. Local thieves working in collusion with western "primitive art" dealers had exported hundreds of complete statues—and even disembodied heads—to galleries and museums located throughout Europe and the United States.[23]

Crystal, Volkman, and Adams publicized the tau tau theft crisis and documented its origins and process, including ineffective responses by South Sulawesi and Indonesian government authorities. With the collaboration of affected Toraja families, the graveyard origins of particular ancestral images in the hands of western collectors were identified and efforts were made to repatriate ancestral images and prevent further publicity or exhibition of these invariably stolen religious artifacts. In the United States a plan to exhibit Toraja tau tau and carved grave doors in the 1990–1991 Festival of Indonesia exhibit "Beyond the Java Sea" was terminated through timely petitions to the Smithsonian Institution by anthropologists who conduct research in Sulawesi. A message regarding collection and display ethics was sent to exhibit planners, the National Museum of Natural History, and individual art collectors who hoped that the Toraja statues in their possession would gain further value through the Smithsonian exhibition.[24]

By contrast, the case of Toraja tourism also illustrates that development can benefit groups who successfully parlay foreign interest in their minority cultures. Kathleen Adams describes how tourism and anthropological interest in Toraja bolstered the group's regional prestige and gave them sudden ethnic recognition and economic clout at the national level.[25] Foreign interest in Toraja funerals and anthropological reports helped persuade Indonesian government officials that Toraja mortuary feasts were not simply a waste of money and buffalo meat but that they served an important subsistence function for poorer Toraja families who otherwise had little access to meat protein.

Although unrestrained tourism in new locations such as Sulawesi may evoke cultural conflicts and resentment among local populations, cautious tourism development that allows residents a significant part in planning and economic gains may provide indigenous communities with increased employment options and national visibility. Such cooperative tourism in the outer islands may also allow regional minorities to maintain greater control over cherished ancestral lands that otherwise would be targeted for more ecologically destructive logging, mining, or transmigration projects. The aim is not to stall national development in Indonesia, but rather to couple international economic initiatives with efforts to augment local participation while safeguarding environmental and human rights.

Government Officials, Foreign Investors, and the Future

The Indonesian government is faced with a difficult balancing act to meet the often conflicting demands of foreign investors and its own socially heterogeneous, multiethnic populations. At one meeting of foreign investors held on July 8, 1994, in Paris, an Indonesian representative was asked to comment about the impact on indigenous peoples of a proposed $5.2 billion 1995 regional development program. The official reportedly answered that "although the Indonesian government does not want to leave its populations in the Stone Age, good only for anthropologists, if they [the local people] want it so, we respect them." This statement communicates the official government view that ethnic groups outside of national development programs are neglected as well as unproductive.

Given Indonesia's unprecedented economic growth and rising middle class, it is unlikely that objections to development from either outside or inside the nation will turn this tide of change. Nevertheless, resistance and insurgency in the islands—expressed most violently in East Timor and Irian Jaya, but also among indigenous farmers, urban workers, and students in Kalimantan, Sulawesi, Sumatra, Bali, and even Java—indicates that the Indonesian government stands to improve its negotiations with minorities who seek greater local autonomy and their share of development decisions and profits.

Although the Indonesian military, through the application of force, has been capable of suppressing past outbreaks of resistance, a greater openness to local input could help Indonesia elude future political turmoil and the resulting depletion of resources and crises of confidence that such chaos entails. Riots, such as those occurring near a Freeport-McMoran Copper and Gold mine in Irian Jaya in March 1996 or those resulting in the death of students protesting an increase of public transportation fares in South Sulawesi in April 1996, create international opprobrium as well as national embarrassment. Even the Javanese, who make up the majority of Indonesians, view governmental exercises of force as a sign of weakness rather than political strength. Governments are considered less viable when they resort to violent tactics because such measures imply a fallen authority to rule.[26]

Beyond investors' demands and the Indonesian government's efforts to increase the nation's economic productivity and political security through development lies the purchasing pressure of foreign consumers and businesses that unquestioningly seek inexpensive labor and raw materials. Aside from the tiny "Made in Indonesia" tags attached to our imports, the nature of the global economy allows us to buy inexpensive commodities seemingly detached from their origin processes, thereby disguising the potentially disturbing circumstances of their production. The unprincipled pursuit of precious metals, low-cost toys, running shoes, clothes, and teak furniture manufactured abroad has helped to create many of the environmental and human rights crises now facing Indonesia. In this respect, commercial engagement with the United States does not contribute to improvements in human rights overseas, but rather the opposite occurs: commercial engagement without adequate research and ethical considerations undermines any leverage that the United States might gain in the diplomatic discussion of human rights issues.

At the 1994 APEC meetings the Clinton administration witnessed or signed 15 agreements for projects worth over $40 billion to U.S. companies involved in telecommunications, energy, transportation, and the environment. One of these projects was a $104 million agreement between Motorola and Indonesia's Ministry of Forestry. Motorola agreed to provide a "state-of-the-art, integrated, radio communication system" designed to "improve forestry management" by minimizing "rain forest destruction and illegal exploitation." At first glance this appears as a laudable program designed to protect Indonesia's vast tropical rain forest, which is the second largest in the world. This technology, however, could readily be used to track and eliminate members of ethnic minorities who attempt to cultivate their ancestral lands in the face of development programs aimed to usurp their occupation.

Incautious commercial engagement with governments regularly accused of human rights violations is a dangerous game in technology transfer, a lesson learned previously when U.S. weapons were sold unthinkingly to Iran and Iraq. Despite the admitted business risks, such technology transfer agreements should be coupled by our government with corollaries that address the protection of local human rights and environmental resources. Although it may be unreasonable and unfair to demand U.S. standards of production from developing nations, some regionally appropriate guidelines concerning environmental degradation, labor conditions, and indigenous peoples' participation should be formulated and ensured for overseas operations. Foreign commercial opportunities should not be accepted or rejected out of hand, but rather assessed for their various impacts, both home and abroad, and activated with human rights safeguards on their implementation.

At the end of October 1994, the Indonesian government signed an agreement with the United Nations High Commission for Human Rights whereby they agreed to cooperate with the UN to develop a national action plan to improve human rights. This positive step came in the wake of a series of news magazine shutdowns, persecutions of East Timor dissidents, and other indications of regression in the human rights arena. The Indonesian government's publicly stated aim to improve its human rights record is to be applauded and supported. This humanitarian aim also should be matched with a form of international commercial engagement that no longer ignores the distant processes through which wealthy foreigners obtain inexpensive clothes, handmade furniture, exotic vacations, and gourmet coffee.

As a final note, a March 1996 *New York Times* article on human rights violations at an Indonesian Nike sport shoe factory catalyzed a "Justice: Do It Nike!" call-in campaign to protest that company's reportedly unethical sweatshop practices abroad. A series of *New York Times* opinion columns on the same topic followed in June 1996.[27] When U.S. citizens become familiar with the extreme human rights and environmental safety violations tacitly supported by U.S.-based companies manufacturing overseas, businesses can be lobbied, and laws can be proposed, to prohibit the import of products created under ignoble conditions. Even a few such actions could resonate overseas to affect the Indonesian government's development policies. Economic development that respects the environments and human rights concerns of indigenous populations drawn into the global economy will help to undercut violence between the Indonesian state and its minority communities, thereby enhancing the political equilibrium of the nation as well as future international investments.

Notes

1. I am grateful to the Fulbright-Hays program and the National Science Foundation for fieldwork support between 1986 and 1989. For research support in 1993 I am indebted to the Association for Asian Studies and the Luce Foundation. A Richard Carley Hunt Fellowship from the Wenner-Gren Foundation for Anthropological Research provided funds for writing in 1994. I would like to thank the Indonesian Institute for Sciences (LIPI) and Tadulako University in Palu for research permits and, finally, to acknowledge Stuart Kirsch for excellent comments on an earlier draft.

2. See Edwin S. Mills, *Growth and Equity in the Indonesian Economy,* Background Paper No. 1 (Washington, D.C.: United States-Indonesia Society, 1990), xi.

3. *Ibid.*, 1–11.

4. Besides the well-known Singapore example, the deleterious effects on human environmental rights that have occurred with economic development in the Philippines, Thailand, and China were examined at a research panel organized by Sidney Jones of Human Rights Watch/Asia for the annual meetings of the Association for Asian Studies. The panel, titled "Human Rights and the Underside of 'Progress' in the Urban Peripheries of Asia," was presented on March 26, 1994, in Boston. For a succinct account of how "constructive engagement" in Burma (Myanmar) during the 1990s has primarily served the interests of the repressive military junta, see Michael Hirsh with Ron Moreau, "Making It in Mandalay, Burma: Where Trade Meets Human Rights—Again," *Newsweek,* June 19, 1995, 46. For a lucid Southeast Asian perspective on human rights issues that argues against economic sanctions in most cases, see Jusuf Wanandi, "Confrontation on Human Rights," *Indonesian Quarterly* 21:3 (1993) 245–249.

5. Voice of America, "U-S/Indonesia/Human Rights," Voice of America radio broadcast, Nov. 16, 1994. Correspondent Report No. 2-169364, by Ron Pemstein, dateline Jakarta.

6. The one exception to this pattern was the topic of East Timor where the Indonesian government's aggressive military actions in the region engendered vociferous protests at the U.S. Embassy at the time of the trade meetings. These protests, well-reported by the international media, compelled the United States to make some concerned comments about the Indonesian government's forced control over this former Portuguese colony whose leaders have sought secession from Indonesia.

7. See William H. Frederick and Robert L. Worden, eds., *Indonesia: A Country Study* (Washington, D.C.: Federal Research Division, Library of Congress, 1993), and Lorraine V. Aragon, "Multiculturalism: Some Lessons from Indonesia," *Cultural Survival Quarterly* 18:2/3 (1994) 72–76. A

summary critique of Indonesian development programs can be found in Marcus Colchester, "Unity and Diversity: Indonesia's Policy Towards Tribal Peoples," *The Ecologist* 16:2/3 (1986) 89–98.

8. See, for example, Amnesty International, *Power and Impunity: Human Rights under the New Order* (New York: Amnesty International USA, 1994). By contrast, see J. Kadjat Hartojo, "Indonesia's Political Modernization and Economic Development," *Indonesian Quarterly* 18:3 (1990) 253–261 for a compelling explanation of why the Indonesian army became so involved with economic development and why the political process must admit greater public participation.

9. See Bakir Bakir Abisudjak and Rusydi Kotanegara, "Transmigration and Vector-Borne Diseases in Indonesia," in *Demography and Vector-Borne Diseases*, Michael W. Service, ed. (Boca Raton, Fla.: CRC Press, 1989), 207–223; P. M. Laksono, "Perception of Volcanic Hazards: Villagers Versus Government Officials in Central Java," in *The Real and Imagined Role of Culture in Development: Case Studies from Indonesia*, Michael R. Dove, ed. (Honolulu: University of Hawaii Press, 1988), 191–198; Mariel Otten "'Transmigrasi': From Poverty To Bare Subsistence," *The Ecologist* 16:2/3 (1986) 71–76; M. Sudomo, "Ecology of Schistosomiasis in Indonesia with Certain Aspects of Control," *Southeast Asian Journal of Tropical Medicine and Public Health* 15:4 (1984) 471–474; Kartini Binol, "Transmigration and Health in Connection with Tropical Diseases in Indonesia," *Southeast Asian Journal of Tropical Medicine and Public Health* 14:1 (1983) 58–63.

10. See Barbara R. Johnston, "Human Rights and the Environment," *Practicing Anthropology* 16:1 (1994) 9, and Barbara R. Johnston, ed., *Who Pays the Price? The Sociocultural Context of Environmental Crisis* (Washington, D.C.: Island Press, 1994).

11. Appell notes that "every act of development or modernization necessarily involves an act of destruction." See George N. Appell, "Costing Social Change," in *The Real and Imagined Role of Culture in Development: Case Studies from Indonesia*, Michael R. Dove, ed. (Honolulu: University of Hawaii Press, 1988), 272. See also Marcus Colchester, "The Struggle for Land: Tribal Peoples in the Face of the Transmigration Programme," *The Ecologist* 16:2/3 (1986) 99–110, and related articles in the same issue.

12. See Michael R. Dove, "Introduction: Traditional Culture and Development in Contemporary Indonesia," *ibid.*, 23–24, 31.

13. *Ibid.*, 27–28.

14. See the Garuda National Airlines advertisements discussed in Paul Taylor and Lorraine Aragon, *Beyond the Java Sea: Art of Indonesia's Outer Islands* (Washington, D.C., and New York: National Museum of Natural History and Abrams Press, 1991), 52, and also in Shelley Errington, "Unraveling Narratives," in *Fragile Traditions: Indonesian Art in Jeopardy*, Paul M. Taylor, ed. (Honolulu: University of Hawaii Press, 1994), 139–164.

15. Dove, *op. cit.*, note 11, p. 19.

16. See Carl L. Hoffman, "The 'Wild Punan' of Borneo: A Matter of Economics," *ibid.*, 89–118. A good overview of the "isolated ethnic minorities" issue that considers Indonesian government policies from an Indonesian anthropological perspective can be found in Koentjaraningrat, "Penda-huluan" ("Introduction"), *Masyarakat Terasing di Indonesia* (*Isolated People in Indonesia*), Koentjaraningrat, 3d ed. (Jakarta: PT Gramedia Pustaka Utama, 1993), 1–18.

17. See Malcolm Gillis, "Indonesia: Public Policies, Resource Management, and the Tropical Forest," in *Public Policies and the Misuse of Forest Resources*, Robert Repetto and Malcolm Gillis, eds. (Cambridge: Cambridge University Press, 1988), 43–113, and Kathryn G. Marshall, "The Economy," in *Indonesia: A Country Study*, William H. Frederick and Robert L. Worden, eds. (Washington, D.C.: Federal Research Division, Library of Congress), 137–205.

18. Anna Lowenhaupt Tsing, *In the Realm of the Diamond Queen: Marginality in an Out-of-the-Way Place* (Princeton: Princeton University Press, 1993), 167.

19. Dove, *op. cit.*, note 11, p. 15.

20. For the Sumatra case, see John R. Bowen, "On the Political Construction of Tradition: Gotong-royong in Indonesia," *Journal of Asian Studies* 4:5 (1986) 545–61. For the Balinese case, see Carol Warren, "Rhetoric and Resistance: Popular Political Culture in Bali," *Anthropological Forum* 6:2

(1990) 191–205, and *Adat and Dinas: Balinese Communities in the Indonesian State* (Oxford: Oxford University Press, 1993), 224–230.

21. Eric Crystal, "Rape of the Ancestors: Discovery, Display, and Destruction of the Ancestral Statuary of Tana Toraja," in *Fragile Traditions: Indonesian Art in Jeopardy*, Paul M. Taylor, ed. (Honolulu: University of Hawaii Press, 1994), 29–41.

22. See Kathleen M. Adams, "Cultural Commoditization in Tana Toraja, Indonesia," *Cultural Survival Quarterly* 14:1 (1990) 31–34, and Toby A. Volkman, "Visions and Revisions: Toraja Culture and the Tourist Gaze," *American Ethnologist* 17:1 (1990) 91–110.

23. Crystal, *op. cit.*, note 21, pp. 34–39.

24. Taylor and Aragon, *op. cit.*, note 14, pp. 51–54.

25. Kathleen M. Adams, "Carving a New Identity: Ethnic and Artistic Change in Tana Toraja, Indonesia," Ph.D. dissertation, University of Washington, 1988.

26. See James T. Siegel, *Solo in the New Order: Language and Hierarchy in an Indonesian City* (Princeton: Princeton University Press, 1986), 37, and Benedict R. O'G. Anderson, "The Idea of Power in Java," in *Culture and Politics in Indonesia*, Claire Holt, B. R. O'G. Anderson, and J. T. Siegel, eds. (Ithaca, N.Y.: Cornell University Press, 1972), 1–69.

27. Edward A. Gargan, "An Indonesian Asset Is Also a Liability," *New York Times*, March 16, 1996; two columns by Bob Herbert, "Nike's Pyramid Scheme," *New York Times*, June 14, 1996, p. A17, and "Nike's Bad Neighborhood," *New York Times*, June 14, 1996, p. A15 were followed by a response from Nike CEO Philip H. Knight, "Nike Pays Good Wages to Foreign Workers," *New York Times*, June 21, 1996, p. A18.

CHAPTER 2

Uncommon Property Rights in Southwest China

Trees and Tourists

Lindsey Swope, Margaret Byrne Swain,
Fuquan Yang, and Jack D. Ives

Editor's Note: By the year 2000, over half the world's population will be struggling to survive life in the city. One in three of these urban residents will breathe unhealthy air. An estimated one billion will be homeless, living in squatter settlements, garbage dumps, in shacks and boxes on streets. Many of these people will find clean water a rare resource (in 1995, some 220 million urban residents lacked access to clean drinking water). Their struggle to find housing, jobs, and food will be complicated by ill health—unsafe drinking water, according to the World Health Organization, causes some 90 percent of all disease including diarrhea, dysentery, typhoid, and cholera.[1]

China, with one-fifth of the world's population, provides numerous examples of problems of life in the megacity, as well as efforts to respond to these situational disasters. In 1996 some 300 million people lived in China's 633 cities, 11 million living in and around Beijing alone. A new sewage plant built in 1990 handles some 25 percent of Beijing's daily sewage load; the remaining effluent drains directly into the Tonghui and Lianghui rivers. Air pollution in Chinese cities has increased the death rate by cancer by 6.2 percent and lung cancer by a staggering 18.5 percent since 1988. If life is so horrible in the city, why do people continue to move there? In a word, opportunity. Economic opportunities have been traditionally limited in rural areas, and since the 1991 easing of legal restrictions on the right to choose one's own town or city, many Chinese have opted for city life.

The Chinese government responses to the problems of megacity growth include efforts to improve the public health, housing, and environmental conditions of residents living in urban areas (by building public works, erecting housing projects, and enforcing pollution regulations). In the long run, resolving the human and environmental crises of megacity life will require proactive as well as reactive strategies—most importantly, halting and even reversing the flow of people from the country to the city.

Lindsey Swope holds a graduate degree in geography from the University of California–Davis. Margaret Byrne Swain is a research anthropologist at the University of California–Davis. Fuquan Yang is a member of the Yunnan Academy of Sciences, Kunming, Yunnan Province, People's Republic of China. Jack D. Ives is a geographer and Professor of Environmental Studies at the University of California–Davis. Comments can be sent via email to Margaret Byrne Swain (mbswain@ucdavis.edu) or Jack Ives (jdives@ucdavis.edu).

Thus, China has initiated a program of economic incentives to encourage settlement in small to medium-sized "sustainable" cities being built in rural areas (by the year 2000 there will be 800 cities, and by 2010 some 1,200 cities). Whether these strategies succeed depends on numerous factors, not the least of which is developing economic opportunities in traditionally isolated and marginal regions, many of which are populated by ethnic minorities.

This chapter examines the tensions between state policies and local responses, focusing on the struggles of rural people to shape economic opportunities while maintaining or regaining some degree of control over critical resources. In Lijiang County, Southwest China, rural struggles include access and control over timber resources, problems from deforestation, increased tourism, and deterioration of traditional culture. Slowing down migration to urban centers requires confronting the contexts and conditions of life in rural regions.

Lijiang County

In northwestern Yunnan Province Lijiang County sits astride the 27-degree north latitude, on the edge of the Tibetan Plateau. Until the modern airport was opened in August 1995, it required two long days by road from Kunming, the provincial capital, to reach Lijiang City. The western and northern boundary of the county is the Jinsha Jiang (Yangtse River). The crowning feature of the Lijiang landscape is its sacred mountain, Yulong Xue Shan (Jade Dragon Snow Mountains, 5,595 meters), in conjunction with the Tiger-Leap Gorge, which has cut a chasm almost 4,000 meters deep between the Yulong summits and the neighboring Haba Xue Shan (5,400 meters). This enormous landscape relief of nearly 4,000 meters in a horizontal distance of 3 to 4 kilometers has produced a great range of vegetation, from rich agricultural terraces with oranges and bananas, through a series of altitudinal forest belts, to bare rock and talus slopes, and the southernmost glaciers and permanent snowfields in Eurasia. Wildlife includes snow leopard, red panda, bears, wolves, and endemic pheasants, although several of these species are seriously endangered.[2]

CHINA: ADMINISTRATIVE DIVISIONS
Showing the location of Yunnan Province and Lijiang County

Naxi pictograph depicting the legend of Love-Suicide Meadow. Photograph by Jack Ives.

Some seven nationalities inhabit the area, with Naxi (numbering 300,000) as a clear majority.[3] Until recently, extreme poverty was widespread, with most people involved in subsistence farming and earning an estimated per capita annual income as low as U.S. $40 per year. The physical environment brings many obstacles to economic development. The mountainous terrain is characterized by poor-quality land that is difficult to farm, and the short growing season at higher elevations further limits agricultural production. Many villages are not linked by roads, making access to markets difficult and restricting transportation, further limiting the potential for development. There are, however, abundant natural resources, including timber, medicinal herbs, and considerable hydroelectric power potential. Recent policies established by central and provincial governments have encouraged the development of tourism as the primary economic activity in the region, as a means both to improve standards of living and to protect a fragile environment.

Policies to encourage a tourist economy were designed while severe environmental disturbances occurred between 1985 and 1989, when the entire region of northwestern Yunnan was progressively "opened" to the world market. At the same time that economic regulations were eased, forest policy was confused and unpoliced. The Yi, and neighboring Tibetan and Naxi villagers, began a process of excessive logging. During this short "boom" period, individual per capita income from illegal logging in the Yi village of Hei Shui exceeded 1,700 yuan (US$1.00 = about 8 yuan). Additional Tibetan and Yi people moved into the area; many were able to acquire large trucks for transporting illegally cut logs. The improved (though still unsurfaced) road south to Lijiang City was choked with lumber trucks day and night. Logging occurred in forests throughout the region, including within the Yulong Xue Shan Nature Preserve. Deforestation was claimed to have contributed to soil erosion, to increased runoff of water and sediments, and to flooding in the lower reaches of the drainage. As Lijiang County borders on the upper reaches of the Yangtse River, the health and extent of the forest cover not only impacts villages in the immediate area, but also may have serious implications for the heavily populated Sichuan basin located downstream.

By 1990 the central government began to react strongly to the devastation caused by both illegal and legal logging, and began strengthening the forest laws and, in places, vigorously enforcing them. Degradation slowed, though the extreme poverty of the rural population results in continued use of forested areas to practice traditional agriculture, collect fuel wood and other forest products, and—through timber harvest—acquire scarce capital.

In the following sections we will examine two questions: How are villagers responding to the problems of deforestation? And, is tourism the answer? Data for these sections are derived from a joint University of California–Davis and Yunnan Academy of Social Science research project examining the relationships between poverty, development, and environment in poor mountain ethnic communities.[4]

Forest Ownership and Management Policy

"There has been much deforestation in the past decade. Now we must go much further to collect firewood and pine needles (for compost) . . ."

"The hillsides are eroding, and some streams are now dry. The problem is that there is no one to manage the forests; no one is in charge . . ."

"If the managing ability of local cadres were improved, they could take more responsibility . . ."

"We need village laws like in old times, and different levels of government should work together to forcefully control illegal logging. The Forestry Bureau has tried, but is unsuccessful. Besides, they do not know what the local situation is, and would give the same punishment if someone is rich and cutting trees to make money or poor and cutting because they need to build a house . . ."[5]

According to official policy, the forests of Lijiang are managed by the village communities. In interviews villagers expressed the desire to conserve their forests, but said they cannot control the deforestation because they do not feel empowered to do so, even though the forests belong to them in the form of village collectives. The villagers express interest in the conservation of the forests, yet they do not feel they have control over their environment. The reduction in quantity and quality of the forests is already felt by the local people through the reduced availability of firewood, building materials, compost, and, in some cases, access to legitimate income. Deforestation continues.

The pressure for development stems from both national and local sources. Lijiang County is relatively remote from the main production centers of China, is populated by ethnic minority groups, and is viewed by the national government as lagging behind the rest of the nation. Official Chinese policy urges minorities to "catch up" to the majority Han population, encouraging them to improve their economic standing.[6] Most of China's remaining natural resources are located in the rural, marginal regions of the country, and areas such as Lijiang are the focus of the national government's resource-use plans. Development enterprises that exploit natural resources are encouraged by the government both for its own interests as well as a means of helping minority populations (though, in actuality, resource development often works to the detriment of the local population, as the resulting environmental degradation usually far outweighs economic improvements). Recent economic restructuring, such as the Household Responsibility System[7] and the introduction of a market economy, also encourages the local populace to take advantage of local development opportunities to increase their income. The forests present a readily available means to this end.

The problem of extreme overexploitation of the forest resource has its roots in the history of Chinese forest ownership and management policy, which has been characterized by a pattern of continually changing directives from the national government since the beginning of this century. This has caused a high level of distrust on the part of the peasantry, and the uncertainty of tenure discourages any investment in the forests, resulting instead in a tendency to liquidate holdings. The domination of coercive policies over incentives, which serve to alienate the people from the resource, can be seen throughout this century.[8]

Pre-Liberation policy allowed for the ownership of private forest plots, but during the Land Reform of 1949–1953 many of these forests were redistributed. Many landholders felled their trees in anticipation of land reform, wishing to keep the assets for their families, and those peasants who received forest land as a part of the reform viewed the wood as a "windfall" to be harvested immediately. The failure of land reform to protect the forest led to the introduction of forest cooperatives in 1953. Foresters recognized that cooperatives would only be successful for forestry if they were well organized, but the local cadres tended to be overzealous in their support of socialism and the fulfillment of their missions, so that collectives were formed more under coercion than voluntarily and many of the peasantry were alienated. The collectives were to allow for continued private ownership of small groups of trees, and furthermore were to provide compensation for any trees expropriated; still, many trees were wrongfully expropriated and the collectives were often unwilling to provide compensation, because from the Marxist point of view the value of trees is considered to be a "fruit of nature" rather than a result of labor.

From 1956 to 1957 the collectives underwent a consolidation phase, during which an attempt was made to remedy many of the previous wrongs. Trees that were wrongfully collectivized were returned to their owners, and compensation was paid to others for their confiscated property. However, this consolidation phase was short-lived, and by late 1957 a new set of policies was introduced that came to be known as the Great Leap Forward, placing a strong emphasis on socialist ideals. Collectives were reorganized into large-scale communes, which were supposed to provide better management opportunities for forestry, as the larger organizations could handle delays on their investments and weather periods of financial hardship without needing to liquidate their assets. This essentially resulted in yet another change of ownership, from the smaller agricultural cooperatives to the larger communes. Smaller household holdings were also confiscated at this time.

Thus the first decade of communist rule was marked by a series of fluctuating policies that essentially contradicted each other and resulted in forests changing ownership several times, between individuals, small cooperatives, and larger communes. Forest policy after the Great Leap Forward experienced a higher degree of continuity overall, in that ownership remained collective and adjustments were merely a matter of scale. In the early 1960s there was a move to decentralize the communes and return forest management back to the smaller production units, as it seemed they could better manage and protect the forest. By the 1970s it was recognized that forest management by the smaller production teams was less efficient and there was a move to place them again under the management of the larger production brigades.[9]

Another significant shift occurred at the end of the 1970s and early 1980s with the introduction of the Household Responsibility System, which returned the unit of production to the household, loosening control over people and land in the hopes of encouraging greater productivity. This was accompanied by the opening up of rural markets, including timber markets, in the hopes that the market system would provide more incentives for management. In some cases this did involve the return of forest plots to individual households, and there was overall a general increase in the rate of tree-felling on both collective and private plots. These events support the notion that forest preservation has less to do with ownership regime incentives than other factors, such as trust in tenure or other strong incentive programs.

Currently, the village forests in Lijiang County are held as common property—they are owned by the village as a whole in the form of village collectives. Forests are not a completely public, "open-access" resource, as the idea of "property" implies the exclusion of nonowners.[10] The resource is shared among a group of users who have equal rights of access to the goods and services provided by the resource.[11] To accommodate access by multiple users, a viable common property management system also requires a set of institutional arrangements for managing the resource. This governing facility should incorporate both administrative as well as managerial duties, by recognizing the rights of the users to determine the set of rules governing the resource, along with the rights to make decisions regarding the resource and its management. In Lijiang, the Forest Bureau determines how much of the forest may be logged and is responsible for protecting the forest and prosecuting offenders. However, the forest area is large and the Forest Bureau staff is small. Thus, villagers, whose rights to use forest resources are determined by outsiders, find themselves in the unique situation of being alienated from the decision-making system while at the same time being responsible for enforcing that system (as there is no effective enforcement by the managers, they are expected to protect the forests of their own accord). The introduction of a market economy has increased the demand beyond sustainable limits, and the result in this open-access situation is extreme overexploitation of the resource. Villagers feel they do not have the power to improve the situation, despite being official owners of the resource, because the Forest Bureau has usurped their management rights and responsibilities.

Village Response

In the fall of 1993 a team of researchers from the University of California–Davis and the Yunnan Academy of Social Sciences surveyed four villages in Lijiang County to examine the villagers' attitudes and perceptions of their forest resources. In two of them (Yu Hu and Jiazi, both Naxi villages), deforestation is acknowledged and the harm to the environment is recognized, but there is no effort to mitigate it. People in these villages expressed feeling powerless to effect positive change. In the village of Hei Shui (a Yi village) the introduction of tourism has led to a response by the government, through the offices of the Tourism Bureau and the Forestry Bureau, of stricter oversight. The forest is patrolled on a more regular basis to check for illegal loggers, and those caught are thrown into jail (in other villages, guilty parties are only reprimanded). In Wen Hai (Naxi), village leaders responded to the impending crisis by taking the initiative and rallying the villagers to conserve their resource. These latter two villages will form the basis of discussion.

Wen Hai

Two villages compose Wen Hai, Upper and Lower Wen Hai, and it is populated by people of the Naxi minority group. It is accessible only by footpath, about a three-hour walk from the nearest road, at an elevation of 3,110 meters. Forest policy in the upper and lower villages has followed slightly different routes in the past decade. In 1982 the government introduced a self-kept forest system, whereby every household in a village was allotted a private piece of forest land, in the same way that agricultural land was parceled out. In the Wen Hai villages, an area of collective forest was maintained in the center of the self-kept forest. This area could be used for firewood collection only, so that cutting was supposed to be limited to trees, such as oak, that were crooked and unusable for construction. The collective forest was surrounded by the self-kept forest with the aim of protecting it, an aim that proved ineffective as people still cut timber in the collective forest. According to a retired village official, the people of the upper village recognized this problem after two or three years and returned all forest to collective management. In contrast the lower village maintained this policy despite the problems, and it was discontinued only in 1995. Thus there has been a continuous history of logging in the lower village forest for over a decade, and the difference between the two village forests is visible in the landscape. Logging in the area has continued to the point that the township (Bai Sha) recently decided to terminate the quota for the Wen Hai collective forest, stating that all suitable trees have already been cut.

The villages also have access to a "public mountain forest," in other words an area not associated with any particular administrative village, located over the ridge from the village. This area was also established in 1982 and is used by people from several neighboring villages, purportedly for the collection of pine needles and firewood. Because of the lack of direct control, it has consequently also been the site of much illegal logging. At this point most of the suitable trees have been cut so that the forest of the neighboring La Shi township has now become the site of increased timber poaching. This township is unable to patrol or regulate the forest and so is unable to prevent this type of illegal activity. Illegal logging in this area is thus not limited to Wen Hai village, making it more difficult to control. For instance, trees are also cut illegally in the Long Pan forests but are then transported through Wen Hai to Lijiang, setting a negative example for the people of Wen Hai and encouraging them also to participate in the logging trade.

One research respondent, a former village official, pointed out that because of the harsh climate, income from agriculture in this area takes a long time to realize—at least one year—whereas it only takes two days to earn money from logging. Larger logs are worth 20 to 30 yuan, and it is possible to average 70 to 80 yuan a day. They are dried in the home before being transported by mule or horse to be sold, either in Lijiang or elsewhere. The black market in this area is very broad; there are many channels and many arrangements for transactions. Logs are sold between villages, and people also come to Wen Hai from the lowlands to buy timber that they will then resell in Lijiang. Many local people also make boards that can be sold at a higher price than logs; the logs are at least stripped of their bark on site for easier transport and increased value.

It was estimated by the respondent that 20 percent of the villagers from Lower Wen Hai are involved in illegal logging activity. They are certainly aware of the laws, but are easily tempted by loggers coming through the village. Apparently, it is mostly young people doing the cutting, who typically use the money to buy cigarettes and alcohol. The close nature of the community makes it difficult to control illegal activity. There were many comments that when people are caught, nothing is done because more often than not those involved are socially acquainted, and therefore it is too awkward to enact any real punishment. As one villager noted, "village life is too confined to make enemies." The government believes that people cannot control themselves, but does not have the staff to do much local enforcement. There is also a strong network of informants, so that those involved in transporting logs are warned if officials are present and they will wait to move their logs to prevent getting caught.

In Upper Wen Hai, on the other hand, there is very little illegal logging within their village forest. This was attributed by several villagers to the commitment of the village leaders, who try to set an example of forest preservation. They remind the villagers that the forest does in fact belong to them, and regardless of the management regime it is they who live with the effects of excessive logging. People also mentioned problems with soil erosion as a result of deforestation. The village is situated on the shores of a seasonal lake, and it was reported that the lake is now much larger than in previous times because every year more sediment fills in the bottom of the lake, so that it becomes broader. These points are disputed by outside observers, who claim that historical evidence proves the lake cannot be any larger than it was in the 1920s. Whether true or not, it seems to be an effective story for the promotion of forest conservation.

The location of Wen Hai on a trade route to Lijiang presents some difficulties in controlling illegal logging, though the people of Wen Hai also benefit from this situation. While they refrain from cutting trees in their own forest, they are involved with transporting timber from other village forests. Thus they have managed to profit from the burgeoning timber market without adversely affecting their own immediate environment.

Nevertheless, all those questioned in Wen Hai believed that the forest cover has decreased in the past ten years. It was almost unanimous that the main causes were commercial and illegal logging. A majority of 53 percent of those interviewed expressed dissatisfaction with the current management, while 33 percent abstained, stating they were unsure of their opinions. Only two households (13 percent) were satisfied with the current management. People said they hoped the government would punish those who participated in illegal logging, and that different levels of government (village and county) should work together to control the logging.

The low incidence of illegal logging in the Upper Wen Hai village forests is attributed to the positive examples set by village leaders. This suggests that local control can work, given leaders who can effectively motivate the villagers into adopting a cooperative strategy in dealing with local resources.

Hei Shui

The village of Hei Shui is comprised of three settlements, with a total population of 246 people, all of whom belong to the Yi minority. They are located on the road to the north of Lijiang town at an average elevation of 2,880 meters, and within the Yulong Xue Shan Nature Preserve. From 1986 through 1988 this area experienced a period of very heavy logging. People from outside the village were hired to assist in the logging, and timber was sold to the county timber company, private businesspeople, or a township factory that was set up for timber processing. A logging quota, or allowance, determined by the Forestry Bureau, was introduced in 1989 and was divided among the families according to the amount of labor available in each household. The quota was enforced by the county, who sent an inspector to confiscate any timber over the allotment, but was then revoked in 1991 because of overharvesting. Currently, villagers are allowed to cut trees for self-use only, and solely with permission from the village council. There is strict punishment for illegal logging in this village—several villagers were jailed for two years for cutting within the Nature Preserve.

The establishment of the Nature Preserve is a fairly recent phenomenon, and its purpose and relationship with the villages have evolved since its conception. It was originally conceived in 1979, although the on-site management office was not fully functioning until 1984. It was designed to protect certain wildlife species and habitats, such as the Yunnan monkey and the high-mountain duck. From 1984 to 1988 the policy on the local use of forest resources was fairly free, and there was much logging both on the part of the villagers as well as by commercial enterprises. In 1988 the park was approved as a National Tourist Area and came under the joint administration of the Lijiang Tourist and Forestry bureaus, and all large-scale public logging was prohibited. The forest is now patrolled regularly by the staff of the Nature Preserve, who check for illegal logging and potential fires.

The park is divided into a core and an outer experimental area, with the villages located in the outer area. The inner area is supposed to be free from any human impact; the villages' collective forests are delineated in the outer area for their own self-use, with any commercial uses expressly prohibited. Thus all forests in this area come under the management of the Nature Preserve, with the villagers given limited access to very specific areas.

The presence of the villagers within the Nature Preserve is somewhat controversial, with differences in opinion between the Tourist and Forestry bureaus. The head of the Forestry Bureau would not give any specific details, but did say that he believed there should not be people within the Preserve, as the purpose of the Preserve is to protect the area from human impact. The Tourist Bureau, on the other hand, views the villagers as a tourist attraction and encourages their presence. The villagers, meanwhile, have had mixed experiences with the presence of tourists in their villages (as elaborated further in this chapter in the section on tourism development).

When queried about changes in the forest cover over the past decade, more people in this village believed that the forest cover had increased than in the other villages surveyed. There may have been some confusion over the time period, as the period of heaviest logging was in the late 1980s, which was less than ten years ago. Some 50 percent of those questioned (from a total sample of 23 respondents) believed the forest cover had increased, and of those, 82 percent attributed this to government regulations, so perhaps what they really mean is that the increased government control has reduced the amount of logging.

All but two of the respondents expressed satisfaction with the management of the forest. It is a controversial subject in this village, however, and the headman was present during several of the interviews, so these responses should not be accepted without question. Several people said that life is more difficult now that logging is illegal, as this was an important source of income. There were even one or two cases of families leaving the village because of the loss of income, although they had in fact only immigrated to the village within the past generation, so their ties to the locale were not strong. Another respondent remarked that the government cuts too much, and should allow the villagers a greater quota allotment. (There are also national forest farms in the region where heavy logging is taking place, and trucks carrying logs from these forests are often seen on the road through the village.) The older people of the village, by contrast, were glad that the logging had stopped, as they could recognize the damage that was occurring.

Increased regulation of forest resources by government agencies has been effective in curbing the illegal logging in this village. In terms of the common property management issue, they have effectively limited access to the forest resource. In so doing they also serve to separate the people from their environment; thus there is no incentive for the people to protect the resource, and the situation is only stable with continued government supervision. In this village, several people were punished severely as examples so that others might obey. The presence of tourism is the stimulating factor in the government's interest in protecting the environment, and so the focus of preservation is not primarily to the benefit of the local people.

Love-Suicide Meadow: Is Tourism the Answer?

Between 1985 and 1989 it was still possible to walk through Lijiang's Yulong Xue Shan Nature Preserve and enjoy peace and serenity in solitude. By 1993 word had spread along tourism channels of prospects for a beautiful and tragically romantic trip—and the trek to Love-Suicide Meadow, a subalpine meadow at about 3,500 meters elevation on the east slope of the Yulong Xue Shan, became increasingly popular.

Lijiang is the site of the mythical Kingdom of the Naxi. This "kingdom" bears several names, including "the forgotten kingdom," "the love-suicide center of the world," and "the kingdom of powerful and brave women." According to folklore, the Naxi forebears (an ancient culture called the "Dongba," also the name for Naxi high priests, or male shamans) developed a literary script in pictograph form (the *lubberluraqt*) which preceded creation of the Chinese script. Thanks to the efforts of the Dongba priests who protected the literature as well as traditional forms of painting, music, dance, and religion, many hundred of the early Naxi pictographs have survived and have become the object of serious and extensive research. Today there are five Dongbas working at the Dongba Research Institute translating the pictographs (the youngest Dongba is 65 years old, and a few other Dongbas are known to live in Naxi villages), including one that gives the legend of Love-Suicide Meadow[12] (see photograph):

The Queen of the Kingdom of Love-Suicide called on the girl Kaimeijjiumiji (believed to have been the first suicide), to join her in paradise:

Kaimeijjiumiji!

there is so much suffering in this human world, you see it all around you;

farmers begin to worry about what they shall eat for supper when they have barely finished their breakfast, they work hard in the fields all day only to return home in the evening tired and hungry;

herdsmen do not have meat to eat, even though they herd many yaks and sheep;

girls have no beautiful clothes for themselves, even though they weave from morn till dark for harsh task masters;

and lovers cannot share that splendid ecstasy of life even though they know

their heart's desire

Kaimeijjiumiji!

by seeing the world your eyes are suffused with so much suffering;

you must come to my kingdom to see the lovely flowers in the meadows;

your feet are injured from walking in the human world; you must come to me where you can walk barefoot in the cool grass;

come to live in this world of gentle breeze and refreshing clouds;

come here and fill your hair with garlands of flowers;

where the birds will sing with you in chorus;

here you will be able to weave beautiful clothes from the clouds of the morning;

here you can eat the white pine sugar of the meadow;

here you can drink the rich milk that flows from the mountain spring;

come to us and live in harmony with nature, with birds and animals and enjoy a life of youth everlasting, of rapture that never falters.

Under the Ming and Yuan dynasties (prior to 1723) the ethnic minorities of present-day southwest China were ruled according to a code named *suisushizheng* (rule minority people according to a policy of no interference with their traditional customs). After 1723, the Qing Emperor Yongzheng introduced a new policy for ethnic minorities called *giatuguiliu* (conversion to the official system of the central government). This new policy caused serious cultural conflict between Confucianized political institutions and the diverse traditions of many ethnic minorities in the southwest. The traditional Naxi marriage and family system was based on matrilineal and patrilineal modes, with marriage being a free choice of love partners; teenage love relations were open and predominant. As part of the imposition of Han-style customs, all indigenous traditions and institutions came to be looked down on as primitive and barbarian. The Han-style marriage contract arranged during infancy was enforced; cremation of the dead was forbidden; there was even an attempt to eliminate the wearing of the Naxi woman's costume. In particular, under Han Confucian morality, childbirth before marriage was considered shameful and virginity was emphasized.

Despite heavy political suppression and Confucian ideological influence, remnants of the Naxi way of life survived. Free love before marriage continued to exist, together with the Han-enforced marriage arrangements by parents. In this way, a highly romanticized sexual relationship developed informally. Nevertheless, the two, frequently mutually exclusive approaches to marriage often came into conflict. The love-suicide pact became the dramatic response of young lovers unwilling to face forced separation for a loveless marriage with prearranged and unknown partners.

In some instances, these events were group contracts with participation of several couples. In anticipation of this ultimate act, the lovers would spend several days visiting beautiful natural locations; high mountain meadows with a backdrop of spectacular snow peaks became favored places. By the 18th century, the Love-Suicide Meadow above the White River section of the Yulong Xue Shan became the most revered place. From this meadow (*Yunshanping* = meadow in the spruce forest) can be seen one of the most magnificent landscapes in southwest China, including the highest summit (*Sanzidou* = Fan Peak) of the Naxi sacred mountain. While Yunshanping is the most famous meadow for ritual suicide, many other sites were also used: the *hualeibu* cliff, for instance, above the village of Yu Hu from which place views of the Tiger-Leap Gorge can be obtained. And near Yunshanping, the valleys of the White and Black rivers are frequently mentioned in the Dongba religious scripts.

The suicides, dressed in their finest clothes, as if for a wedding, sang sad and beautiful love songs (*Yeqbee*) accompanied on traditional instruments. They built simple rustic shelters decorated with garlands of flowers, feasted, and indulged in physical love. When the food was eaten they would hang themselves on rope suspended from tree limbs, or else jump over the cliffs to their deaths.

The lovers believed that after death they would be transported over the mountain top to a paradise (a kind of *Shambala*, or Shangri-la) where they would live forever in perpetual youth and in good health. They would dwell deep in the mountains in harmony with nature. Stags would assist in plowing the fields; they would be awoken in the mornings by colorful pheasants; during the days they would ride on red tigers or sing together with wild animals. At night, bright stars and the moon would cast sufficient light so that lamps would not be necessary. Clothes and pine sugar would be available in abundance. Above all, they would be totally removed from the bitterness and sorrows of the world. In turn, they would call upon young lovers in the common world to escape from their suffering and so join them.

In the 1930s groups of up to ten couples committed this tragic ritual. Love suicides occurred until as recently as the 1950s. In that decade artifacts of the rituals were still being discovered in the meadow, including instruments that were used by the suicides. The local Naxi revere the meadow even today; no one should whistle in the meadow for fear that the spirits of the young lovers will seduce them and they themselves will commit suicide in a form of ecstasy; it would be impossible to escape.

Love-Suicide Meadow Today

The Love-Suicide Meadow remained a much revered site of myth and mystery, quiet, sad, and dramatically romantic. Save for the suicides themselves, only occasional herders brought their animals, or farmers from distant villages came to collect herbs for which the meadow was also famous. The first certain human impacts began about 60 to 70 years ago when the Yi people from Ninglang County to the east immigrated to the vicinity. They established small subsistence villages in the forests below the meadow and began to practice their traditional slash-and-burn agriculture (swidden). The first disturbance of the forest was not particularly significant and did not reach the actual meadow.[13] While the "opening" of northwestern Yunnan between 1985 and 1989 meant settlers pouring into the area and excessive logging in the nature preserve, the meadow itself remained scarcely touched.

With the 1990 tightening of forest laws, access to the forests of the Nature Preserve became tightly controlled. Tourism development, at first spontaneous and opportunistic, by 1994 came to be the dominant economic activity in the region.

The headquarters to the Nature Preserve is situated immediately below the Love-Suicide Meadow (a walk of about two hours). It sits on the main road from Lijiang City north to Daju, the northern "gateway" to the Tiger-Leap Gorge. A modern hotel and restaurant opened in October 1993. Tourists, mainly domestic, but with an increasing trickle of foreigners, began to visit the hotel, driving the unsurfaced road from Lijiang City by taxi or minibus. Some of them would walk to the meadow and picnic. The nearest of the three Hei Shui natural villages is only a 20-minute walk from the hotel and base of the trail to the meadow. Yi entrepreneurs, with government assistance, began to acquire horses and to offer them for hire to the tourists. The standard pattern was for Yi women, appareled in their spectacular traditional costumes, to lead the tourists, who were seated on gaily decorated horses. The exotically costumed guide was obviously as much an attraction as the horse ride itself.

Business began to flourish. More and more Yi families were able to acquire horses. A point was soon reached, however, whereby the Yi women were in fierce competition with each other for clients; shouting matches, scuffling, and underbidding began to occur.

The Yulong Xue Shan Nature Preserve staff estimate that 4,000 people visited the meadow in 1990; 5,200 in 1991; 7,500 in 1992; and more than 10,000 in 1993. By 1994 the Yi villagers had acquired 56 horses and were building temporary shacks along the road adjacent to the hotel, the better to conduct their trade. By October 1994 a modern chairlift had been constructed and began operation, complete with parking lot, restaurants, and a program to widen and surface the road from Lijiang City. Despite the relatively expensive chairlift fees, this novel mechanization severely undercut the Yi entrepreneurs. During the next 12 months a series of compromises between the Yi villagers and Tourist Bureau of Lijiang Prefecture were attempted. These included an effort by the Yi to hire out horses to cover the 1 kilometer distance over the gentle sloping ground through the forest from the top of the chairlift to the meadow; horse rides for hire within the meadow; and horse races in the meadow. The Yi villagers themselves replaced individual family competition with a strict schedule of equal allocation of clients and fixed prices. This reduced the importance of female costumes in the competition, and most of the horse attendants became indifferently dressed males.

The compromises, however, caused serious damage to the meadow itself, in addition to the spread of tourist litter, and the short trail from the chairlift to the meadow became a quagmire. This type of environmental damage added to the existing damage of tourist litter, which had been a problem on the original main trail from the beginning. Tourists liberally cast litter, especially plastic bags and bottles, across the forest floor. Domestic animals ingested the plastic and choked to death on it. Eventually, the Tourist Bureau and the Nature Preserve staff instigated more secure restrictions on the use of horses—riding in the meadow was prohibited, and a heavy wooden boardwalk with handrails was constructed between the top of the chair life and the meadow.

By October 1995, the Yi villagers had 104 horses, most idle, and no subsistence food crops. The short-lived tourist boom had led many of them to neglect their traditional subsistence farming. During the boom period, Yi horse owners had been able to earn up to 1,600 yuan per month for each horse; a good day could bring 100 yuan. But the idle horses of 1995 had become a burden on their owners, who could hardly afford to feed them. Horses are not traditional to Yi subsistence agriculture, and consequently their acquisition has become a serious liability.

Tourist visits to the meadow continue to increase. By October 1995, only one year after opening, the lift, financed jointly by a Hong Kong business company and the Prefecture Tourist Bureau, had been amortized. During the 1995 Spring Festival several thousand tourists visited the meadow each day.

Economic participation in tourism for Yi villagers is now concentrated on activities in the meadow itself, where several booths have been set up. They are operated by Yi women who hire out Yi and Naxi costumes to tourists so that they can dress up to be photographed. Even these costumes are a mix of the authentic original and gaudy modifications, presumably the more likely to attract clients. Trinkets are also sold. At the base of the chairlift small tourist lodges for overnight stays are being added.

In addition, two Yi dance teams perform for tourists daily in the meadow. One team, consisting of nine girls and one boy, is from the village of Wen Hui, one of the poorest of mountain villages. This team had won the county championship for excellent performance in ethnic dancing. Now they dance in a meadow far from home, paid 5 yuan per day. The other team is a group of seven girls from Ninglang County managed by an old Yi woman. The Yi dance teams are also invited to perform for tourist groups at the hotel and the lodges. The prospects of this element of the tourist trade to degenerate into prostitution is greatly feared.

Other jobs available for Yi men involve the management of tourists to minimize environmental damage to the meadow and aid in litter collection in the meadow and along access routes. Wages of about 300 yuan per month are paid by the Tourist Bureau for these activities.

Naxi villagers, whose ancestors created the legends and traditions of Love-Suicide Meadow, participate in the tourist development in quite a different manner. Farmers from Jiazi village, located 15 kilometers east of the meadow, bring their surplus products (fruit, chickens, and pigs, for example) for sale to the hotel, to tourists directly, and to associated traders. Some Naxi women from the Lijiang Old Town come to the meadow by bus to sell traditional *liangfen* (black bean curd) to the tourists.

Discussion and Conclusion

There is obviously confusion in Lijiang over the management of the forests, as they are termed "village collective forests"—yet the villagers do not feel they have any management rights, and state that their rights of use are heavily regulated by the government through the offices of the Forest Bureau. Ideally, government regulations should serve to support the local authority of communal institutions and to assist in enforcing local regulations. In practice, government resource management policies vest control of the commons in government agencies rather than in the communities directly affected.[14] The Forest Bureau has, for all practical purposes, usurped the control of the local peoples, thus making the forests, in effect, state property. The danger of this arrangement, in removing responsibility from the community to the state offices, yet without adequate state enforcement, is that it encourages poaching and results in a situation whereby the state is obliged to protect the resource from the local people.[15]

In Lijiang, the Forest Bureau is not effective in enforcing the laws and protecting the forest (with the exception of Hei Shui where tourism related to the Nature Preserve and Love-Suicide Meadow provides an incentive to do so); villagers are excluded from decision-making systems that invest them with resource management responsibility. No one is in control and illegal logging proliferates. Those management decisions that are enforced are typically those that serve the "public interest"—interests defined by officials far removed from the actual minority nationality village (whose cultural needs may be overlooked or deemed insignificant).[16] The situation in Lijiang seems to support the contention that development in areas occupied by minority nationality groups often comes at the expense of the environment,[17] despite the stated local government's aspirations.

With the current shortage of timber in China as a whole, there may be no easy solution to the forest resource management problems of Lijiang. The market for forest products will probably remain strong for some time to come, encouraging the overuse of forest resources. Although common property systems, properly employed, seem to offer hope for reaching a successful resolution of the deforestation problem, the troubled history of imposed forest management may also create difficulties in achieving this. There has been no certainty of tenure for China's forests since the beginning of this century. This inconsistency actively discourages any investments in the forests and does not encourage any desire to protect them, especially since the local people suspect that forest access regulations may well change again in the future. This attitude, in turn, contributes strongly to the general feeling of alienation between local peoples and their own environment, setting the scene for increasingly severe problems.

As shown above, local villagers have responded in a range of ways to the problems of deforestation, with tourism playing a central role. Capitalizing on the unique aspects of Naxi tradition, history, and legend in a spectacular natural setting, tourism has had a marked effect on the region. The economic potential of tourism is underlined by the rapid amortization of the costs of installing the chairlift, and by the large and increasing number of visitors. Tourist visits in 1995 to Lijiang City and County exceeded over 700,000 overnight stays (mainly domestic, but more than 20,000 foreign tourists). Also in 1995, five new modern hotels were under construction. Lijiang County, together with its neighboring counties, was attempting major infrastructure improvements, especially a high-quality road network. Lijiang Old Town was nominated as a World Cultural Heritage Site, and there are prospects for World Heritage nomination for the Yulong Xue Shan–Tiger-Leap Gorge–Haba Xue Shan region.

Placed in broader regional perspective, sustainable development and maintenance of the entire Yulong Xue Shan Nature Preserve, and the enhancement of living standards and cultural security in a large number of mountain villages, including Naxi, Yi, and Tibetan peoples, are at risk. Increasing environmental degradation attributable to tourism development makes problematic any assertion that tourism is truly the answer to economic issues in Lijiang. A significant underlying issue is: who controls the access to environmental, scenic, and cultural resources, and who pays the price for their degradation?

The situation is further complicated by the stresses and demands of disaster recovery: on February 3, 1996, Lijiang County was hit with a 7.0 Richter scale earthquake. The epicenter of the earthquake was beneath the Tiger-Leap Gorge, about 25 kilometers from Lijiang City. Damage was enormous: 24 towns and townships and 152 administrative villages were affected. In Lijiang City alone there were 293 deaths, 3,706 seriously injured, 11,727 other injuries; some 180,000 people were rendered homeless. There was extensive damage in the entire region to the public utilities and communications systems. Large sections of the Old Town collapsed, and considerable expanses of the beautiful five-colored stone streets were destroyed. Provincial authorities estimate that U.S. $700 million will be required to offset losses.

Mass tourism, rapid development, and submergence in external financing had proceeded far enough by 1995 to raise the specter of increased wealth for the few, exploitation of the rural poor, and loss of cultural heritage. Given the pressures on the local authorities from village level to county level, the dilemma had become severe. There is no doubt of the sincerity of the local authorities in their concern for both rural people and the spectacular environment. Certainly, the rapidity of change (1985–1995) renders evolution of sound development policies doubly difficult, even if the way ahead was clear. Nevertheless, the enforced pause, brought about by the disastrous earthquake, even despite the enormity of human and material losses, may facilitate the interjection of a more balanced and equitable approach to development. The prospects for rebuilding the Old Town—so that its cultural and historic integrity is protected and, hence, it gains eventual designation as a World Heritage site—are considerable. Similarly, autonomous village development and establishment of a Biosphere Reserve (as a first step toward World Cultural Heritage designation) for the Yulong Xue Shan–Tiger-Leap Gorge–Haba Xue Shan landscape could conceivably provide a sustainable showcase for Southeast Asia. To lose this opportunity could result in this magnificent mountain region, with its many minority peoples, becoming another Kathmandu.

Notes

1. Information for this editor's note was drawn from sources reported in World Resources Institute, World Resources 1994–1995, "Population and the Environment" (pp. 27–42) and "China" (pp. 61–82); and from the Earth Times News Service (theearthtimes@igc.apc.org). See William C. Burns, "The Habitat II Conference and the Future of the World's Cities," Earth Times News Service, June 6, 1996; Bruce A. Silverberg, "Best Practices: China," Earth Times News Service, June 6, 1996; Ashali Varma, "How Beijing Handles Sewage Problems" and "New Cities Being Planned in China," Earth Times News Service, June 6, 1996. Earth Times News Service articles reported on material presented at the Second United Nations Conference on Human Settlements (Habitat II), Istanbul, Turkey, June 3–14, 1996. Country reports, summary conference reports, and "Best Practices" case material can be found on a number of United Nations and NGO sites on the Internet, including the Earth Negotiations Bulletin (for access information write: enb@igc.apc.org).

2. Jack D. Ives and He Yaohua, "Environmental and Cultural Change in the Yulong Xue Shan, Lijiang District, NW Yunnan, China," in *Montane Mainland Southeast Asia in Transition*, proceedings of a symposium, Chiang Mai University, Thailand, Nov. 12–16, 1995, B. Rerkasem, ed. (Chiang Mai University, 1996), 1–18.

3. Han, Yi, and Tibetan are the other nationality populations in the study area.

4. Funding for this study was provided by the Ford Foundation and the United Nations University as part of a larger study on poverty and gender relations in Lijiang County. Dr. Jack Ives (Dept. of Environmental Studies, University of California–Davis) and He Yaohua (Yunnan Academy of Social Sciences) were the principal investigators on the project.

5. These comments were voiced by various informants during our village surveys in Lijiang County.

6. Colin Mackerras, *China's Minorities: Integration and Modernization in the Twentieth Century* (New York: Oxford University Press, 1994).

7. The Household Responsibility System returned agricultural production responsibility from village collective organizations to individual households. For a detailed discussion, see Elizabeth Croll, "Some Implications of the Rural Economic Reforms for the Chinese Peasant Household," in *The Re-emergence of the Chinese Peasantry*, Ashwani Saith, ed. (London: Croom Helm, 1987).

8. The historical information included here is largely based on L. Ross, *Forestry Policy in China* (Ann Arbor, Mich.: University Microfilms International, 1982); for further discussion and information on current forestry policies in China, see also L. Ross, *Environmental Policy in China* (Bloomington: Indiana University Press, 1988); and S. D. Richardson, *Forests and Forestry in China* (Washington, D.C.: Island Press, 1990). For region-wide assessments see L.S. Hamilton, *Forest and Watershed Development and Conservation in Asia and the Pacific* (Boulder, Colo.: Westview Press, 1983); and Jack D. Ives and Bruno Messerli, *The Himalayan Dilemma: Reconciling Development and Conservation* (New York: Routledge, 1989).

9. Nicholas Menzies and Nancy Peluso, "Rights of Access to Upland Forest Resources in Southwest China," *Journal of World Forest Resource Management* 6 (1991) 15; and Changjin Sun, "Community Forestry in Southern China," *Journal of Forestry* 90:6 (1992) 38.

10. A. P. Grima and Fikret Birkes, "Natural Resources: Access, Rights-to-Use and Management," in *Common Property Resources: Ecology and Community-Based Sustainable Development*, Fikret Birkes, ed. (London: Belhaven Press, 1989), 36.

11. See C. Ford Runge, "Common Property and Collective Action in Economic Development," in *Making the Commons Work*, D.W. Bromley, ed. (San Francisco: ICS Press, 1992), 17–39; and Elinor Ostrom, *Governing the Commons: The Evolution of Institutions for Collective Action* (Cambridge: Cambridge University Press, 1990).

12. Fuquan Yang, *Mysterious Suicide for Love Among Naxi People (Shenquidexunqing)* (Hong Kong: Joint Publishing Company, 1993) (Taipei: Hanyang Publishing House, republished 1995).

13. In 1985 tree-ring counts indicated trees exceeding 900 years of age; comparison with 1930s photographs taken by Dr. Joseph Rock showed little noticeable change in the meadow.

14. Ronald Oakerson, "Analyzing the Commons," in *Making the Commons Work*, D. W. Bromley, ed. (San Francisco: ICS Press, 1992), 48.

15. Piers Blaikie and Harold Brookfield, "The Degradation of Common Property Resources," in *Land Degradation and Society* (New York: Methuen, 1987), 192. The history of forest policy in Nepal offers a good example of the problem with government control of forests; see D. A. Gilmour and R. J. Fisher, *Villagers, Forests and Foresters: The Philosophy, Process and Practice of Communal Forestry in Nepal* (Kathmandu, Nepal: Sahayogi Press, 1991).

16. Menzies and Peluso, *op. cit.*, note 7, 18.

17. Mackerras, *op. cit.*, note 4.

PART TWO

Biodiversity
Preserving What, for Whom?

By some accounts, the world is on the edge of an episode of major species extinction. Habitat loss as lands are converted to other uses; the rapid spread of introduced plants and animals; overharvesting of fish, plants and animals; pollution; global climatic change—all contribute to the loss of natural ecosystems and the species within. Habitat loss, by most accounts, is considered the biggest threat to biodiversity. A reduction in biodiversity has numerous implications, not the least of which is the declining ability of ecosystems to carry out vital functions such as maintenance of soil fertility, water retention, and the cycling of nutrients. These changes have not gone unnoticed. Biologists, planners, nongovernmental organizations (NGOs), and governments increasingly consider threats to biodiversity as a problem that tops the resource management agenda. In the past two decades a number of conservation management strategies have been developed, including international conventions and agreements that restrict commerce in endangered species; enactment of national endangered species protection legislation; the declaration and gazettement of national parks, game reserves, and other kinds of conservation areas that shelter specific species and populations; and the development of programs aimed at protecting habitat integrity. Whether these programs have been or can be successful is debatable, with the key questions being: preserving *what*, for *whom*, at *what cost?*

The following two chapters closely examine the social justice dimensions of activities designed to conserve biodiversity, especially wildlife, in Africa. Bill Derman critically explores a case of integrated conservation and development in the Zambezi Valley of Zimbabwe, where the failure to acknowledge local knowledge and institutions or to involve local peoples in the planning and implementation process significantly inhibited project implementation, and certainly contributed toward the failure of project goals. As is typical in many projects designed and funded by nonlocal (and often foreign) entities, ambitious and unrealistic goals, coupled with contradictory means, undermined project success. The Zambezi Valley, like many African regions, is home to endangered species and cultures, and attracts numerous "development aid" projects, many of which operate in isolation and conflict with each other and, because of the level of funding and promised outcome, encourage immigration. Derman argues that these development projects physically and psychologically undermine the ability of local peoples to generate the resources and expertise necessary to improve their own livelihoods and standards of living. Projects fail for a multitude of reasons, not the least of which is that the loci of power in defining problems and shaping response, and the means to implement response, no longer reside in local hands.

In Robert Hitchcock's chapter we consider the human rights and environmental quality implications of international wildlife management programs in a number of communities in Southern Africa. Hitchcock describes incidents and situations where people are forcibly evicted from traditional lands to set up wildlife reserves, restricted from hunting and gathering in the reserves, arrested, beaten, and sometimes even killed for daring to hunt meat defined by the state as a protected species. He also details incidents where people have been killed because they were gathering wood, searching for water, or merely visiting friends. The incidents described by Hitchcock emerge from the clash of well-meaning efforts aimed at preserving biological diversity the struggles of resident peoples to preserve some measure of cultural diversity. Response has included attacks on game scouts and tourists by local people, as well as politically motivated spearings of rhinoceros and other large mammals. Hitchcock argues that efforts to preserve biodiversity generally served to exacerbate problems of poverty and resource stress among local communities in Africa. He acknowledges that antipoaching operations have, in some cases, slowed down the rate of destruction of some endangered species. But he raises the question whether the mistreatment and killing of people is the most effective way to promote conservation.

Both authors argue that effective conservation and development activities in Africa can only come about when coercion gives way to cooperation. Both note that the failure by governments and international NGOs to incorporate local people (including women, children, the elderly, and indigenous minorities) into decision-making has led some African communities to plan and implement their own projects and devise their own sets of rules by which conservation and development will be conducted.

At a more fundamental level, these chapters engage the ideological debate over ways to define environmental crisis and to shape appropriate responses. Are threats to biodiversity simply a matter of declining species numbers and habitat loss? Or are these problems the inevitable outcome of human crises (such as the spread of export agribusiness and the displacement of peoples, with the subsequent intensification of subsistence activities in marginal lands)? Will human environmental crises be resolved by implementing socially-just solutions that protect basic human rights and improve the human condition? Or are environmentally sustainable solutions only achievable with the restriction—or complete abolishment—of human rights?

CHAPTER 3

Nature, Development, and Culture in the Zambezi Valley[1]

Bill Derman

With the assistance of Mr. Mike Makina (Mushumbi Pools) and Mr. Lazarus Zhuwao (Basiyao, Zimbabwe)

Preface

Royal ancestral spirits (known in the Zambezi Valley as *mhondoros*) have guided the conduct and conscience of Zambezi Valley communities. These representatives of the past speak through their contemporary mediums. They serve a critical role in both past and present events by facilitating discussion on controversial issues. In addition, they examine how and in what ways current practice is or is not consistent with past understandings and current community practice. The *mhondoros* are arguably no longer as respected as in the past, although when difficulties arise (drought, murder, famine, and so on) they are consulted. Nonetheless, their comments on contemporary environmental and developmental issues represent many older residents' sentiments about current development projects in the Zambezi Valley. Yet, as the text below demonstrates, *mhondoros* perspectives were not sought in either the planning or implementation stage of the Mid-Zambezi Rural Development Project. Their doubts emphasize why local participation and democratic processes have an environmental significance that has, all too often, been ignored.

The text comes from an interview with the *mhondoro* Karembera on April 23, 1991:[2]

I wasn't told about it [the Mid-Zambezi Project]. What happened was the District Councilor[3] came with his friend to peg [pegging refers to demarcating an area] an area which included my tsopero [a tsopero is a sacred place in which it is forbidden to cultivate or live; it is best called a shrine]. I waited to see if they would inform me but they did not. On the fourth day I travelled around my territory. When I reached the place where I conduct tsopero, I found a peg. I asked a local leader what is this and he said it's a peg for a residential plot. I asked him, who did this? He said it was the Councilor. I told him to call the Councilor but the Councilor said he would not come that way. The Councilor said he would come at his own time when he heard that I am angry. They [the project] had pegged an area to be for an animal's path.

Bill Derman is an anthropologist and Director of the African Studies Center at Michigan State University, 100 Center for International Programs, Michigan State University, East Lansing, MI 48824-1035. He can also be reached via email (bderman@ibm.cl.msu.edu).

We then asked if the *mhondoro* was told that your people (meaning those living within the boundaries of the *mhondoro*) could no longer cultivate on the river banks and what were his thoughts about that decision:

> That is not a good idea because here in Mbire [one of the local terms that refer to the valley] the sun is very hot. When the river is in flood it spills into the valleys. When the water dries it is when my people will grow their crops and the crops we sell there. Do you know snuffing tobacco? Here we don't grow it on this land [upland] but along the river banks and now this crop is beginning to disappear [snuff tobacco is an essential part of the sacred paraphernalia as well as being a cash crop]. If you want to know how bad are their plans, they will tell you that we will put you in prison if you cultivate there.[4]

The issues are clear: a large development project in the name of protecting a fragile ecology has sought to bar valley residents from cultivating along the rivers, the source of both water and good land. In addition, a project meant to benefit citizens did not inform their leaders nor consult with them about how to proceed. How did this happen, and what are the implications? How does a government come to override the views and aspirations of its own citizens in the name of both environment and development? This is part of the story of the Mid-Zambezi Rural Development Project located in the Zambezi Valley in northern Zimbabwe. It is not an unusual story, yet it demonstrates the multiple and often unforeseen consequences of disempowering local communities. This is not an effort to romanticize what was but to point to how ignoring local knowledge and institutions can intensify environmental degradation and social conflict.

Introduction: The Zambezi Valley and Zimbabwe

The Zambezi Valley, which traverses the northern border of Zimbabwe, serves as one of the most important wildlife reservoirs in Central and Southern Africa. The valley provides extraordinary opportunities for tourism, including Victoria Falls and Lake Kariba. It also contains several national parks and safari areas. These are visited by thousands of people each year who are excited by the sight of lions, elephants, buffalo, zebra, elands, and many others. The valley has also been the site for some of Africa's

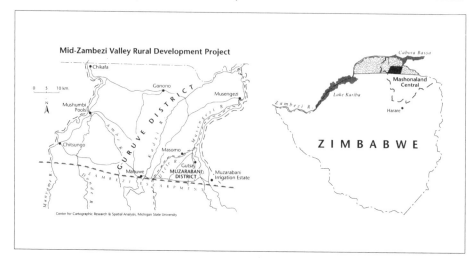

Woman working in a riverine garden, an activity deemed illegal by the Mid-Zambezi Valley Rural Development Project. Photograph by Bill Derman.

bitterest conflicts between poachers and National Park rangers in the difficult and ultimately unsuccessful campaign to protect the last remaining black rhinos. At the same time, the valley is characterized by the poverty of many of its human residents.

Contrary to popular images, the valley is not exemplary of wilderness in Zimbabwe; instead, it represents a very large ecosystem experiment. In 1959 a large dam and lake were created, known as Kariba. The human-created lake flooded the prime agricultural lands of a people known as the Tonga, altering irrevocably the valley's ecology. Downstream of Kariba to the east, many communities were removed to create a habitat for animals, while, further east, major projects to create environments more favorable for human settlement are under way. These changes do not take place without debate. One major unresolved issue centers on the best economic use of the semiarid lands of the Zambezi Valley. On one side are those who argue that wildlife programs are both more economic and sustainable in the longer term. On the other side are those who contend that with appropriate land-use planning and water management, intensive agricultural systems are viable. Both are human-designed programs to utilize the environment in quite distinct ways. Another long-term ecological and human experiment has been the effort to control and eradicate the tsetse fly, the vector for both human and bovine trypanosomiasis (sleeping sickness). This effort has been ongoing since 1917 but without full understanding of what the consequences would be if the effort were to be successful. The measures used to eradicate the fly have included the mass destruction of wild animals, the movement of human populations, aerial spraying, ground spraying, and the like. This long-term continuous effort remains a site of contestation between development planners and valley residents, since the presence of tsetse reduces to some measure the possibilities of keeping livestock. In short, the Zambezi Valley continues to be a site of multiple social, cultural, and ecological experiments whose outcomes remain unknown.[5]

It is clear that for wildlife and environmental programs to succeed, they will also have to incorporate the multiple developmental needs of valley residents. Two different strategies have emerged. The first, which has attracted much international attention, is the Communal Areas Management Program for Indigenous Resources (popularly known as CAMPFIRE). Less attention has been given to the second, the Mid-Zambezi Valley Rural Development Project (MZVRDP), which began in 1987 and which technically ends in December 1996. This second project, while lacking the intense international scrutiny and criticism that CAMPFIRE received, is apparently the model of choice for future land-use planning and programs in the valley. The principles underlying both the CAMPFIRE program and the Mid-Zambezi Project reflect how divergent approaches can be utilized in the same ecological and geographic area. In the case of the Mid-Zambezi Project, they demonstrate why investment in top-down, blueprint types of projects can lead to both disillusionment with a government and greater ecological degradation than if the project had been planned and implemented in a more democratic fashion. It has led to the vast deforestation of what had been a dryland forest area with gallery forest along seasonal rivers. The government has attempted to bar people from cultivating along the riverine areas where people have been cultivating for centuries. In fact, the practice of riverine cultivation has made living possible in this drought-prone environment. In sum, democracy and participation are more than slogans in examining development projects in fragile environments when the longer-term sustainability of an environment is envisioned.

Zimbabwe's independence, gained through a guerrilla war and sustained until recently by a socialist ideology, has led many scholars, including anthropologists, to conduct research in this strikingly beautiful but glaringly inequitable nation.[6] The inequities derive primarily from colonialist alienation of one-half of the best land from African residents and the differential infrastructure put into place in the former European areas (now called Large Scale Commercial Farmers) and the Tribal Trust Lands (now called Communal Areas).[7] This structural inequality persists. Increasingly small numbers of black Zimbabweans are becoming large-scale commercial farmers.[8] Land, and the nature of the war for independence, remains a critical focal point for contemporary research, along with the contemporary situation in the communal areas. Unfortunately, the commercial areas have not been adequately researched.[9] The current land categories in Zimbabwe are classified as follows:

1. Large-scale commercial farm land = 40 percent total area (157,000 sq km and 1,713,000 people, of which 4,400 are owners and the remainder are farmworkers
2. Small-scale commercial farm land = 4 percent total area (14,200 sq km)
3. Communal lands = 42 percent total area (163,500 sq km and 4,662,000 people living on small-scale commercial and communal lands)
4. National parks and safari areas = 14 percent total area (56,200 sq km)

The commercial farms are located in the regions of highest rainfall and good soils. The European colonialists seized the best lands for themselves, a historical legacy that has been difficult to overcome. Moreover, there remains a dual property regime in which the commercial areas are privately owned and are fully commoditized, whereas the communal areas are owned by the national government and managed by a combination of newly created local structures emphasizing the elected Rural District Councils. The "traditional authorities" of chiefs and headmen, while legally barred from allocating land, are, in practice, quite influential. This system created by the new government in 1982 is currently being reversed. "Traditional authorities" are once again being emphasized and valley residents believe, and *sabhukus* are acting as though they can, once again, allocate land.

The communal lands were created along racial lines to hold the indigenous African populations. Issues of sustainability, adequacy, viability, or economies of scale were not considered.[10] The large-scale farm areas were created to be vast in order to deny Africans the best lands. The small-scale commercial areas served the rising elite of black Zimbabwean farmers. These, on the whole, have been nonviable as farming enterprises. The national parks and safari areas, while outside the scope of this paper, are important in understanding the role of tourism and wildlife utilization. Indeed, there has been a long perceived historical conflict between livestock and wildlife. Much energy and many resources have been allocated to ridding the Zambezi Valley of the tsetse fly in order to make Zimbabwe safe for cattle.

The Tsetse Fly and Land Use Planning

Nature is not necessarily benign. The Zambezi River valley supports a large population of tsetse flies, which carry both human and bovine trypanosomiasis (sleeping sickness). Since the discovery that sleeping sickness was carried by the tsetse fly there have been continuous efforts to eliminate or at least diminish the presence of the fly. Since the discovery of the vector, efforts have been directed to eliminate wild animals that might carry the disease and to destroy tsetse habitats. Thus there were yearly kills of large amounts of game in order to reduce bovine and human trypanosomiasis. These indiscriminate killings came to an end as other tactics were employed to eradicate the tsetse fly in the 1950s. However, it was not until the 1980s that a linkage was made between tsetse control and land-use planning. In practice, this meant opening up new sections of the valley for increased human and livestock habitation.

> It was only in the 1980s that the land use issues relating to reclamation of tsetse-infested areas came to the fore in Zimbabwe. The newly developed methods for tsetse control provided real scope for moving from defence to attack against the tsetse . . . furthermore Government objectives towards the development of the marginal hinterland of Zimbabwe changed radically since 1980.[11]

The European Economic Community (EEC), following a consultancy study in 1983, funded the establishment of a Regional Tsetse and Trypanosomiasis Control Programme (RTTCP) to investigate the best methods to control and eliminate the fly belt in Zimbabwe, Zambia, Malawi, and Mozambique. The government's aim was to expand the frontiers of prosperous communal farming. Tsetse control was to support these rural development programs, which relieve the population pressure in other parts of the country. Additionally and perhaps most importantly, alternative land-use options were not seriously entertained by the GOZ and the EEC in these critical years. The EEC aerially sprayed the length of the Zambezi Valley, stopping only in 1988 because of the development of alternative cost-competitive techniques.[12] In light of the range of potential long- and short-term consequences of tsetse eradication, or at least its dramatic reduction, new studies were commissioned to examine land-use in the valley. The basis of such policies—which remained unstated—was that the division of land between communal and large-scale commercial lands would remain unchanged. In addition, land for land-poor communal farmers had to be found in "marginal" areas like the Zambezi Valley. The European Economic Community consultancy proposed a series of projects that, at least in hindsight, had contradictory objectives of both large-scale projects and emphasis on environmental conservation. Among the projects they proposed was the Mid-Zambezi Valley Rural Development Project.

The Mid-Zambezi Valley Rural Development Project

The MZVRDP was the first major post-independence development project in the Zambezi Valley. It was initiated in 1987 with funding from the African Development Bank, and it was staffed entirely by Zimbabweans. The project was supposed to run for five years but, because it was not completed in that time frame, it was granted first a three-year extension with additional funding and now an additional one-year extension. It is expected to terminate in December 1996.

The MZVRDP responded to a political priority of the state to resettle populations from other, more crowded rural areas to either commercial farm land or to frontier areas. The political rationale for the project was to be able to claim that 7,600 households (of which 3,000 were to be new settlers) were being resettled, thus demonstrating the government's ongoing commitment to resolving historic land grievances.[13] It was designed to fit within the larger land-use planning strategy recommended by the EEC to the government of Zimbabwe and the government's developmental objectives. The African Development Bank through its Africa Development Fund provided the external funding.

Its objectives were to greatly increase agricultural production, to increase commercial agriculture production, to protect the fragile environment, and to provide a resettlement zone for 3,000 farming families from other communal areas in Zimbabwe. Specifically, the MZVRDP was to provide boreholes, schools, clinics, roads, and improved agriculture for all residents—both new and old. Planning documents stated that the valley was so underdeveloped and so many critical aspects of infrastructure were missing that *any* intervention would be better than none.[14]

The project was originally recommended by an FAO (Food and Agriculture Organization) team conducting a land-use study of the entire valley in response to the question What would the valley look like if the tsetse fly were indeed eliminated?[15] It is located in Central Mashonaland Province (one of Zimbabwe's eight provinces) in Guruve and Muzarabani Districts between the Manyame River to the east and the Musengezi River to the west. It lies below the escarpment that marks the end of the high plateau and extends north all the way to the Mozambique border. The project's area is approximately 2,500 square kilometers.

Resettlement projects within the government of Zimbabwe ordinarily fall within the purview of the Department of Rural and Urban Development (Derude), which is located in the Ministry of Local Government and Rural and Urban Development

(MLGRUD).[16] This department was given primary responsibility for the MZVRDP's implementation. Most members of Derude were trained by the Department of Rural and Urban Planning at the University of Zimbabwe, and there were strong continuities with colonial planning.

The Department of Agricultural Extension and Technical Services (Agritex) drew up the project plans in collaboration with Derude following the guidelines for an Accelerated Model A Resettlement Scheme.[17] This entailed an allocation of five-hectare arable plots to eligible household heads, setting aside lands for grazing, and consolidating villages. The project has involved resettling and reorganizing the local population into consolidated villages grouped around boreholes. Arable plots were found for 7,600 households through aerial photograph identification. Planners thought that there were only 3,600 resident families living in the project area, but this turned out to be a gross underestimate. As a result of this miscalculation, the government's objective of providing land for new settlers could not be achieved.

The project's planning process exemplifies how government and the project related to the proposed beneficiaries. Government planners believed that they had a successful model for rural development programs and thus felt that it was unnecessary to consult with valley residents.[18] This model and its accompanying procedures were strikingly similar to that used by the Rhodesian colonial state and were so viewed by many valley residents. The model was virtually identical to that proposed in the Native Land Husbandry Act of 1951, which was detested by black Rhodesians. The act attempted to compartmentalize the land into areas for concentrated villages, fields, and grazing areas. It was ultimately withdrawn because of widespread opposition and the incapacity of the Rhodesian government to implement it.

Employing colonial terminology, the MZVRDP named the new villages, calling peoples' homesteads "residentials" and fields "arables." In addition, grazing areas were delimited. These are state-imposed terminologies. The identification of arable, residential, and grazing areas was carried out by Agricultural Research and Technical Services (Agritex) in the Ministry of Agriculture.[19] The principles were simple: vegetative complexes were used to identify arable areas, grazing areas were set aside along the rivers, and residentials were located where boreholes were sunk. Although the practice of riverine cultivation was central to human adaptation and agriculture in the valley, the project set out to rupture this agro-ecological adaptation by prohibiting riverine or stream-bank cultivation, by moving the designated arables away from rivers, and by allocating riverine land for grazing areas.

This contemporary planning pattern has its roots in the colonial period. During the 1930s colonial officials believed that there was an immediate soil conservation crisis, which they regarded as a result of destructive African agricultural practices.[20] They blamed overpopulation and poor farming methods in the reserves for creating degraded soils, deforestation, and low agricultural productivity. Overstocking of cattle was added to the causes of rapid soil deterioration, and thus compulsory destocking became part of agricultural policy toward African producers. Scientists and Rhodesian agricultural specialists thought that there was a growing ecological crisis of erosion because of African cultivation practices. Their views became part of the scientific and knowledge system of those attempting to understand and alter African agricultural systems. There has been little analysis and study, for example, of the ecological outcomes of a tobacco-led agricultural export economy.[21]

As the practice of stream-bank cultivation was regarded as one of the major factors promoting erosion, laws were enacted during the colonial period to prohibit it. The all-white Parliament of Rhodesia passed the Water Act of 1927 (amended in 1976) to control use of Zimbabwe's wetlands. The act stated:

> No person shall conduct any operations which interfere with the bed, banks or course of a public stream or any swamps or marshes forming the source of a public stream or found along its course without permission.

This concern with water use and erosion was reinforced by the Stream Bank Protection Regulation, which formed part of the 1942 Natural Resources Act (amended in 1975). This law prohibits cultivation within 100 feet (now 30 meters, but often interpreted as *100* meters) of the normal flow of a stream or wetland.

The policies on stream banks and wetlands grew out of studies conducted in the high plateau. Nevertheless they were applied nationwide regardless of ecological variation and river slope. While the regulation has been enforced in other portions of Zimbabwe's communal lands, it was not enforced, until recently, in the Zambezi Valley. To make matters more difficult in the valley, normal flow was defined by Agritex planners as the flood stage of the rivers, which meant that large areas of alluvial soils were, in principle, to remain unutilized for cultivation.

Colonial policies reflected the view that African knowledge and practices were inimicable to progress. The MZVRDP planners, in essence, accepted these views, especially as they pertained to riverine cultivation. As a consequence, local voices and knowledge were not incorporated into the design or implementation of the project, although they have had a decided impact on its operation. Indeed, from the valley residents' perspective the most objectionable part of the project has been the effort to ban riverine cultivation.

Riverine Cultivation in the Zambezi Valley

Before considering resident responses to this plan, a brief description of riverine cultivation is presented as it is currently practiced in the Zambezi Valley. Stream-bank cultivation in this area is not a single practice. It encompasses both rainy and dry season cultivation, and involves the cultivation of current river beds and former river beds, as well as the use of stream banks. Rainy season areas of cultivation are referred to as fields, while the dry season areas are termed either fields or gardens. They are gardens when they are small in size or contain vegetables rather than maize or snuff tobacco. Rainy season crops include maize, with smaller areas of sorghum, squash/pumpkins, and, increasingly, cotton. In the dry season, farmers cultivate maize, sweet potatoes, and a range of vegetables for sale and household use. Depending on the depth of ground water, most gardens are now hand irrigated during the long dry season from hand-dug wells. It has become increasingly difficult for women to sustain these gardens as they have been moved away from the rivers and as the increasing numbers of livestock drink from the shallow wells, thereby filling them in.

Because of the large number of migrants into the valley, riverine land for rainy season cultivation is hard to obtain. Riverine cultivation allows people to have harvests if the rains are poor, as often occurs in the valley. When the rains are heavy and damage or destroy a crop, then the moist soil of these gardens permits a reliable dry-season harvest.

When the MZVRDP was initiated, residents were told that their lands would be demarcated and they would get schools, boreholes, clinics, tractors, and even electricity. They were *not* told that the project would decide where they were to live and farm. Indeed, the project got under way when peggers entered two areas in the valley and began demarcating arables. The peggers were employees of the project whose job was to peg (stake) the areas demarcated as arables and residentials by the Agritex planners. When residents inquired what they were doing, they were told not to ask questions or else they would be arrested. That night all the pegs were pulled out of the ground by local residents (who remained anonymous) and placed at District Council offices. The District Councils and Administrators along with project staff then had to explain the project to valley residents.[22]

The most contested part of the MZVRDP was moving residents away from the rivers and converting these most highly valued riverine lands to grazing areas. Valley residents describe this process as "throwing away land." In general, it is the long-term residents, often from the most influential families, who own or have user rights to large tracts of riverine land. More recent migrants have obtained access only to riverine gardens, and thus have had much less of a stake in this issue. The major cash crop in the valley is cotton, which for the most part is cultivated in the uplands, away from the alluvial riverine soils. While many migrants were able to keep their existing lands, which were located away from the rivers, those with lands along the rivers were relocated. In addition, wealthier migrants who owned cattle are not as opposed to the project's setting aside of grazing areas. Even though residents do not speak with one voice, project and Agritex personnel, who overwhelmingly come from outside the valley, tend to listen to the wealthier, cotton-growing, cattle-owning families.

In 1990, a new ward councilor was elected for one of the project wards, or political districts. As part of his platform, he argued that the MZVRDP needed to be changed. At an early meeting following his election, he made known his views on what he thought the relationship should be between the government and its citizens, and between the project staff and valley residents:

> All government civil servants should be listening to you. The Mid-Zambezi Project has dis-torted our lives and brought problems in the valley because of not listening to the dwellers of this area who know best about what they want. Some of you have been threatened by the VIDCO Chairmen [the heads of Village Development Committees, which in turn are made up of several villages] and Councilors that failure to cooperate with the project will result in your losing your land. Most of you have become afraid to say anything at meetings.

He continued:

> The project did not spend time listening to anybody. People were frightened and got nervous until the whole project was viewed as a bad idea. Resettlement has allocated sacred land, taken good soil for cattle grazing which people don't have.[23]

He spoke clearly and forthrightly about the importance of local knowledge and participation to the success of development efforts, including the project.

His activities and speeches did not go unnoticed. In a letter to the District Administrator reporting on the activities of this Council, the Resettlement Officer observed that this Councilor:

> ... involves Spirit Mediums and Kraal Heads [sabhukus] in development issues. I feel he does this to get their support. These people tend to give him the wrong advice which he fails to object to. As far as I have observed traditional leaders oppose changes and this could be the reason why the councillor goes to meetings with negative attitudes. These leaders have their role in society and if properly used can help in mobilization other than as advisors. The Councillor made this mistake from the very start and I cannot find a way out.
>
> I feel that the Councillor needs to be told as to who to consult on developmental issues.

The Resettlement Officer expressed the prevailing view that local authorities and local practices were not relevant to development. The Ward Councillor was engaged in a process of mobilization utilizing recognized and long-established voices in the area. He attempted to incorporate spirit mediums and sabhukus into the discussion of local development rather than accepting the resettlement officer's notion that they were not relevant to government decision-making. It is not without irony that sabhukus and chiefs have been given increased authority over all issues. Indeed, it is strongly rumored that the Village Development Committees will be ended. Thus, a Ward Councilor who actually tried to represent his constituents and engage in an appropriate process of consultation found his hand slapped. In the final irony, the agency responsible for resettlement, Derude, has been ended. The first and only project manager for the project has taken early retirement.

While valley residents do not speak with one voice on most issues, there is strong consensus that riverine cultivation is essential to the valley economy and to household well-being. Almost all those who can obtain access to riverine gardens and fields do so, be they project employees, ward councilors, Village Development Committee chairmen, or virtually everyone else.[24] Once again, it is not without some irony that those charged with moving people away from rivers, Ward Councilors, VIDCO Chairs, and the like, all have riverine fields and gardens.

On several occasions, farmers and researchers have debated the rationale that streambank cultivation causes erosion, in meetings with Derude officials, resettlement officers, Natural Resources Board officers, and Agritex planners. In general, officials, planners, and technicians uniformly asserted that riverine cultivation causes erosion. They argued that unless valley residents ceased this practice, the rivers would widen, would choke with sand, and ultimately would stop flowing. When questioned as to how the erosion process worked in the relatively flat valley, the answers they gave were appropriate to steeply sloped river beds and not to those that characterized most of the valley.

Valley residents were far more nuanced in their explanations of why riverine cultivation did not usually cause erosion. They pointed to how their crops and cultivation practices held the soil in place. They described their practices of shifting their fields and the rationale that underlay these moves. They identified and recognized erosion as a natural process that could be affected by human action. In a conversation with a former Ward Councilor whom I first interviewed in 1990, he asked me if I believed that stream-bank cultivation was causing erosion and causing the rivers to stop flowing. I reversed the question and asked him if he and his family found themselves unable to cultivate their riverine fields and gardens due to soil erosion. He laughed and said no. Since he was an elder, I asked him what change had there been in the land that he has continuously cultivated for 16 years. He replied, "None," continuing, "They are just as fertile now as when I first returned to the village after the war." Although the processes of erosion are at least partially understood, they are not necessarily acted on by younger farmers, many of whom were expanding cotton cultivation in riverine fields despite the cautions on pesticide bottles not to use these chemicals near water or fish.

The MZVRDP's commitment to a blueprint planning approach has made real dialogue very difficult between residents, technicians, planners, and other development personnel. The structure of the resettlement program and its shortage of resources (including trained people) has made it difficult for project personnel to learn and incorporate the results of research that would be relevant to the success and failure of the project. The outcome to date in the Zambezi Valley has been a pattern of serious resistance by valley residents to different aspects of the MZVRDP, but especially to the notion of ceasing riverine cultivation. The project also attempted to bar residents from having livestock. The maximum number was to be two oxen per household. The project was to provide 50 tractors to make up for lack of animal traction. This guideline has been totally ignored and the project has given up any effort to limit livestock in the project area.

Ongoing Contestation

A fascinating dimension of this whole process of project implementation has been the outspoken opposition to the project by some residents, combined with much foot-dragging and resistance to project implementation. This is a major reason why the project fell so far behind its schedule of implementation. A workshop was held in September 1993 organized by the District Councilor in order to resolve problems in two wards along the Manyame River. The workshop was attended by local leaders and Government Department Heads, including the Mid-Zambezi Project, Tsetse Control and Eradication, and the Department of Co-operatives as well as many residents (older men). After the requisite introductions the representative of the Mid-Zambezi Project spoke. He stated:

> Most people think that the MZP is for we the employees, but the project is yours. You got arables, boreholes, roads, clinics and schools. All these facilities are for the community, not for us the employees. When we ask people to come and help us on the construction of the school, few people come to do the work. This has become a major problem for school construction especially in this ward. We had to buy bricks [instead of their being made by residents] for Mushumbi School [Mushumbi is a small town, site of a major bus stop, a small market, several stores, and a few government offices]. Here at Nyambudzi [a central village] we are paying those who are digging the toilet pits. These works should be done by you, the parents. The school is yours! The children who will attend this schools are yours. You, the local leaders, should encourage people to participate in these construction projects. In Kanongo [a village situated across the Manyame river from Nyambudzi] people are refusing to mold bricks. This project has its time period. When the period is over we are going to leave some of these schools incomplete and you will be to blame.

Following a brief discussion the representative from Tsetse Eradication and Control spoke:

> After the aerial spraying which was carried out in 1987 we then introduced [tsetse fly] traps. Before 1984 there were no cattle here in the valley [this is a gross oversimplification] especially in Guruve District. We are killing the tsetse because of your domesticated animals, especially cattle. These traps are not mine or for tsetse control, but for the community. Whenever we put these traps it's our responsibility—both of us—to take care of these traps. These traps are now being stolen in areas such as Chikafa, Gonono and Chidodo. The cloth on each trap is worth $30.00 (Zimbabwean).[25] There was one month when 300 cloths between Chikafa and Gonono which means $9,000 were stolen. So let us work together and make sure that our traps are not being stolen.

These speeches make clear that local populations are resisting central components of the government's strategy for this area. Local populations have not taken ownership of a project, which, they are told, was meant to benefit them. It is more than likely that the speakers are not familiar with the project's history and really do believe what they say. In the first instance, people are resisting building schools. This is not a straightforward issue since education is highly valued, and school attendance is relatively high. However, many residents don't know which school to work on since they are or were in the process of moving. Second, those who do mold bricks then refuse to mold more if others haven't carried out their share. In the second instance of stolen tsetse fly-cloth traps, there has been increasing conflict between cattle owners and cultivators. In addition, there is much cross-border movement between Mozambique and Zimbabwe, and it is possible that Mozambicans are more responsible for the thefts.

There are many residents who have supported elements of the project. More recent migrants to the valley who did not have clear rights to land or who had relatively small areas were delighted to receive more secure tenure and larger areas. Most residents supported the construction of roads and boreholes. They have also supported increased numbers of stores and markets. The project has created centers of temporary employment for the construction of roads, boreholes, schools, and the clearing of one acre for new fields. This has intensified economic activity in the valley. Moreover, there has been a dramatic increase in the numbers of cement or brick dwellings and livestock. This reflects the residents' use of savings for their homes and agricultural production. This intensified economic activity has also meant that the valley continues to draw migrants into the valley. These migrants and kin of residents settle on unpegged or nonallocated land, thus undermining all efforts at land use planning. To add to the confusion, one ward in the project area remained undemarcated and unpegged until 1995. In this ward, the local *mhondoro* opposed pegging, as did many of the family heads.

The *mhondoro* named Chidyamauyu has been responsible for the territory of a major spirit (known as Nehanda) whose medium died during the war for an independent Zimbabwe. In 1993 and 1994 the project made a concerted attempt to have Chidyamauyu accept the project in Nehanda's territory (his was outside the project). This was his account of the project's efforts:

> I am the only one who looks after Ambuya Nehanda [the other royal ancestral spirit]. If you want me to tell you the wrong things which are done by Government to the *mhondoros* Chiefs I can tell you. But if you are after the pegging [he is referring to the demarcation of land by the Mid-Zambezi Project, which I will explain shortly] and you are just hiding, that is what I

don't want. Chief Matsiwo came here hiding by saying that he had been sent by his children. And yet it was him and Maziofa [the Project Manager for the Mid-Zambezi Project]. You should not take me that way. I fought for this country for eight years. When I went to Mozambique I had been with this Medium Nehanda. I represented all the *mhondoros* of Dande [the Shona term for this part of the valley]. If you come with an idea of destroying this area by pegging, that is what I don't want to hear. Even if it is Mugabe [the President of Zimbabwe] telling me [to accept the pegging] then I will tell him to stop it. If we are talking of pegging it is a very disturbing issue. The Government has just used its powers without asking. . . . When they started their war [against the Rhodesians] they asked us, the *mhondoros* and the *mambos* [the chiefs]. The chiefs gave them their children to go to war until today some of their children didn't return home. . . . The Government has forgotten us, the *mhondoros* and the chiefs, the owners of the land.[26]

In the end, the project proceeded. Its supporters were able to carry it forward only after the election of a new, younger Ward Councilor who was told in no uncertain terms that the area would not get a new clinic or schools without the project. Nonetheless, he did genuinely support the project. He said in his campaign that it would bring development to his ward. After eight years the value and worth of the project should have been demonstrated, but it had not been. The pegging is in process as of July 1996. It should be completed by October. People have yet to begin to move to take up their new arables and residentials, although in this ward they have been given greater input into land use planning. Let us briefly examine the broader ecological changes in the valley and how new plans continue to rely on blueprint models.

Since the mid-1980s, the eastern Zambezi Valley has been transformed from a verdant zone to a deforested, dust-filled region, with thousands of new farms. The contemporary patterns of migration into the valley (not only the east) are historically rooted in an effort by the Rhodesian government to reorganize what were then termed the Reserves and to find new areas for displaced farmers. In addition, the use of frontiers for human settlement results from the growing scarcity of good farm land and pasture in the communal lands of Zimbabwe. It is indicative of the land-scarcity in other portions of Zimbabwe that so many migrants choose the drought-prone Zambezi Valley in which to settle. The current government, with the assistance of the European Economic Community, Food and Agriculture Organization, Overseas Development Administration, and the African Development Bank, has continued to press for the intensification of population and production in the Eastern Valley.

This is being done through a new generation of projects only slightly different than the Mid-Zambezi Valley Rural Development Project. While there is not space to detail them, one deserves mention: the Dande Irrigation Project. This proposed project will irrigate much of the land where people have just been resettled. The project assumes that families in the area will rely totally on irrigated crop production and give up their upland and riverine fields. If they don't do this, then they will be removed from the project. This is clearly a top-down, blueprint approach to development.

All development interventions and projects in the valley claim that the standards of living will be raised and that the environment will be protected. This has been the case since colonial times. At the same time, farmers' knowledge is discounted, community social structures are regarded as irrelevant, and planners ignore them. Meanwhile, as described earlier, the division of lands into arables, residentials, and grazing areas takes no account of microecological variations. Past and present projects, with the exception of CAMPFIRE, do not begin with the assumption that valley residents are knowledgeable agents who are making a living in a tough environment. Indeed, their experiences are deprecated. Moreover, I have heard it argued by social scientists, planners, and project implementers that valley residents are used to moving because of the needs of their system of shifting cultivation. While considerable movement took place in both precolonial times and even during colonial years, this kind of voluntary movement involved searching for new fields and villages, as well as fissioning of kin groups. It had a decidedly different character than that which took place following establishment of the Native Land Husbandry Act of 1951, which proposed to determine the size of people's fields, how many animals they could own, and where they could be employed. During the war, the Rhodesians forced valley residents into keeps (which were equivalent to strategic hamlets created by the United States in Vietnam). Past mobility was similarly different from the coercive resettlement continued within the MZVRDP and now, in our estimation, the new irrigation proposals. On the more pragmatic side, a large-scale irrigation project involves heavy management costs and operations, which may be beyond the capacity of the different project management entities that are to be established. Most importantly, these projects will prevent communities from creating the organization and structures necessary to manage their natural resources on a sustainable basis.

However, there is no turning back to earlier land use systems. Because of the heavy in-migration into the valley, there is a dramatic shift from a more diverse natural resource management system to primary reliance upon cotton and maize. These population and agricultural changes are profoundly altering both the valley's ecology and relationships between people and nature. To date, centralized planning has not worked. Efforts to control in-migration have been ineffective, and alternative solutions need to be generated. New efforts are required to see if local populations regard current patterns of in-migration into the valley as a major problem and what solutions can be found to reduce it in those areas where local communities find it objectionable or unmanageable. It is ironic that government officials who had attempted to solve these kinds of problems find themselves virtually powerless to stop these processes. Thus, while in the past they disempowered local communities, now they need to reempower them to find solutions.

Conclusions

The Mid-Zambezi Valley Rural Development Project illustrates how a complex mix of developmental, environmental, and political objectives have led to overriding local knowledge and local practices. The experiences of project residents are, unfortunately, not unique in the annals of large-scale development projects. The Mid-Zambezi experience fits with other efforts to plan lives for people deemed "underdeveloped" or "undeveloped" in ways and manners that would not be done for wealthier or more powerful individuals. This type of development has had multiple consequences, for both the people and the environment. While it is perhaps too early in the process to draw final conclusions, one can point to how the project has missed accomplishing its central goals. Partly, this was due to the ambitious, if not unrealistic, nature of those goals and the contradictory means employed to achieve them. The nature of the planning process and the incorporation (or rather the lack thereof) of environmental concerns demonstrates once again the importance of finding and following appropriate democratic means and structures in the design and implementation of large-scale development projects.[27] This process is now far more complicated than before, owing to the dual pressures of development projects and continued in-migration. Let us examine these in turn: government-sponsored (if externally funded) development projects send a message that local peoples cannot generate the resources and expertise necessary to improve their own livelihoods and standards of living. In short, external intervention combined with government takes responsibility for valley residents' development. The assumption is that different agencies of government and development assistance agencies can "know" how to develop a region. This message is precisely wrong. The true message is not that external assistance and governments aren't necessary, but that the responsibility lies ultimately with local populations, village communities, and their organizations to generate, within their capacities, the means to determine their futures. Governments and development assistance organizations can facilitate a process, though to date they have intervened far too deeply so that, as argued earlier, communities, villages, and local organizations have acquiesced and shifted the ultimate responsibility for change to others.[28]

Second, the Zambezi Valley as a whole, and the eastern valley in particular, is now threatened by blueprint and inappropriate approaches to its environment. The central government and donors by their continued emphasis on large projects imply by their actions that the Zambezi Valley should continue to be the site of major development interventions. These actions, combined with land scarcity and sustained drought in southern Zimbabwe, mean that migrants are drawn to the valley to find adequate land, pasture, and employment in the valley. These processes are leading to increased populations of humans, cattle, goats, and other animals. The major cash crop remains cotton, which requires extensive land areas and essentially mines the soil while utilizing large quantities of pesticides. Deforestation has proceeded at a frightening pace. This all can work while cultivable land remains available and when rainfall is adequate. The system, however, remains highly vulnerable. Potential solutions are complex, involving greater community controls to now regulate, if possible, overgrazing conflicts between livestock and agriculture, deforestation, and experimentation to use more drought-resistant crops. Failure to address these issues will lead to the continued encroachment on the National Parks and Wild Life estate, which in turn is viewed globally and nationally as one of Zimbabwe's treasures. It will also lead to a deteriorating living standard for valley residents and increased dependence by these residents on government during drought years.

Notes

1. The research on the Mid-Zambezi Rural Development Project could not have been possible without the support of a Senior Research Fulbright Fellowship, a Wenner-Gren Foundation grant, a Social Sciences Research Council grant from their African Agriculture Project, Michigan State University, and the Centre for Applied Social Sciences of the University of Zimbabwe.

2. The interview was conducted on April 23, 1991, by Lazarus Zhuwao.

3. Zimbabwe is divided into provinces, districts, and wards. The Councilor is an elected official from the ward.

4. According to the project all land is divided between arables (fields), residentials (homesteads), and grazing areas. The project pegged these areas without discussion or approval by local populations. The project threatened to arrest those who cultivated outside the arable areas.

5. For a consideration of these issues see John Barrett, "Economic Issues in Trypanosomiasis Control: Case Studies from Southern Africa by John Barrett," Ph.D. diss., University of Reading, 1994, p. 31; Bill Derman, "The Unsettling of the Zambezi Valley: An Examination of the Mid-Zambezi Rural Development Project," Centre for Applied Social Sciences Working Paper, Sept. 1990; S. Metcalfe, "The Zimbabwe Communal Areas Management Programme for Indigenous Resources (CAMPFIRE)," *Natural Connections: Perspectives in Community Based Conservation*, David Western and R. Michael Wright, eds. (Washington, D.C.: Island Press, 1994), and "Livestock, Wildlife and the Forage Commons. Prospects for Rangelands Reform in a Semi-Arid Communal Area of Zimbabwe" (CASS Occasional Paper–NRM: University of Zimbabwe, 1995); Marshall Murphree "Communities as Resource Management Institutions," International Institute for Environment and Development Gatekeeper Series, No. 36. (London: IIED, 1993); "Traditional and State Authority/Power in Zimbabwe" (CASS Occasional Paper Series–NRM: University of Zimbabwe, 1995), and "Optimal Principles and Pragmatic Strategies: Creating an Enabling Politico-Legal Environment for Community Based National Resource Management (CBNRM)" (Harare, Zimbabwe: Centre for Applied Social Sciences, 1995); Marshall Murphree and David H. M. Cumming, "Savanna Land Use: Policy and Practice in Zimbabwe," in *The World's Savannas: Economic Driving Forces, Ecological Constraints and Policy Options for Sustainable Land Use* (London: Parthenon Press, 1993), 39–177; and John Peterson "Campfire: A Zimbabwean Approach to Sustainable Development and Community Empowerment Through Wildlife Utilization" (Harare, Zimbabwe: Centre for Applied Social Sciences, University of Zimbabwe, 1991).

6. The best-known work is that of David Lan who explored the interaction of the ideology of the peasants of Dande (the local term for the eastern portion of the Zambezi Valley) with that of the guerrillas who lived among them during the war of liberation; see *Guns and Rain: Guerrillas and Spirit Mediums in Zimbabwe* (Berkeley: University of California Press, 1985). Prior to the war one can signal the following anthropological studies of the Shona and Tonga: Elizabeth Colson, *Social Organization of the Gwembe Tonga* (Manchester: Manchester University Press, 1960), A. K. H. Weinrich, *The Tonga People on the Southern Shore of Kae Kariba* (Gweru, Zimbabwe: Mambo Press, 1977), Marshall Murphree, *Christianity and the Shona* (London: Athlone Press, 1969), and Thayer Scudder, *The Ecology of the Gwembe Tonga* (Manchester: Manchester University Press, 1962). More recent are the works of Michael Bourdillon, *The Shona Peoples: An Ethnography of the Contemporary Shona, with Special Reference to Their Religion* (Revised Edition) (Gweru, Zimbabwe: Mambo Press, 1982) and "Guns and Rain: Taking Structural Analysis Too Far?," *Africa* 57:2 (1987) 263–274; Angela Cheater, *Idioms of Accumulation: Rural Development and Class Formation among Freeholders in Zimbabwe* (Gweru, Zimbabwe: Mambo Press, 1984); and Pamela Reynolds *Dance Civet Cat: Child Labour in the Zambezi Valley* (London: Zed Books, 1991). The best-known anthropological studies are those of Thayer Scudder and Elizabeth Colson, *The Social Consequences of Resettlement* (Manchester: Manchester University Press, 1971), focusing on the Tonga displaced by Kariba Dam conducted on the Zambian side. Their research is summarized in Elizabeth Colson, *The Social Consequences of Resettlement* (Manchester: Manchester University Press, 1971), and Thayer Scudder and Elizabeth Colson, "Long-Term Research in Gwembe Valley, Zambia," forthcoming in Robert V. Kemper, ed., *Long Term Field Research in Social Anthropology* (in press).

7. For example, all of the commercial farm areas were electrified, while communal areas were not. The roads in most LSCFs were paved while in the CAs they were not, and so forth.

8. There have been numerous efforts to address this question, including an ambitious resettlement program, the 1992 Land Acquisitions Act, which permits the national government to confiscate up to one-half of commercial farm land and give it to others without specifying how it should be

done, and most recently a National Commission on Land Tenure, which is to address the questions of multiple tenurial systems within the nation. See Mandivamba Rukuni and Carl Eicher, eds., *Zimbabwe's Agricultural Revolution* (Harare: University of Zimbabwe Press, 1994).

9. Blair Rutherford from McGill University is the only anthropologist that I know examining a large-scale commercial farm. See Blair Rutherford, "Traditions of Domesticity in 'Modern' Zimbabwean Politics: Race, Gender, and Class in the Government of Commercial Farm Workers in Hurungwe District," Ph.D. diss., McGill University, 1996. There is the earlier valuable study by Rene Loewenson, *Modern Plantation Agriculture: Corporate Wealth and Labour Squalor* (London and Atlantic Highlands, N.J.: Zed Books, 1992).

10. Government of Zimbabwe, *Report of the Commission of Inquiry into Appropriate Agricultural Land Tenure Systems,* under the Chairmanship of Prof. Mandivamba Rukuni, Vol. 2: Technical Reports (Harare, Zimbabwe: The Government Printer, 1994), 107.

11. Barrett, 1994, *op. cit.,* note 5, p. 31.

12. *Ibid.*

13. There is a large and important literature that reviews the land question in Zimbabwe. There are relatively good statistics to demonstrate that, overall, the government did not meet its own specified commitments to acquire land from commercial farmers to give to communal area farmers. The government has said that this is due to the lack of funds for the purchase of such land. This question has become moot since 1992 when Parliament passed the Land Acquisition Bill whose intent is to acquire 6.9 million hectares from the large-scale commercial sector to add to the resettlement and state farm sectors. The government's initial efforts to acquire land has been met with a great deal of opposition and skepticism because of the lack of clear guidelines and data base for the GOZ to systematically acquire and productively redistribute land. For a much more detailed treatment of these issues see Sam Moyo, *The Land Question in Zimbabwe* (Harare, Zimbabwe: SAPES Books, 1995); Michael Bratton, "Land Redistribution," in Rukuni and Eicher, 1994, *op. cit.,* note 10; and Michael Roth, "Critique of Zimbabwe's 1992 Land Act," in Rukuni and Eicher, *op. cit.,* note 10.

14. The two primary project documents are the Food and Agriculture Organization of the United Nations, *Zimbabwe: Mid-Zambezi Valley Rural Development Project Preparation Report* (Main Text and Annexes), No. 119/85 AF-ZIM 10, Oct. 1985, and the African Development Fund, *Appraisal Report: Mid-Zambezi Valley Rural Development Project, Zimbabwe,* Agriculture and Rural Development Dept., July 1986. It has often been argued by personnel of the Dept. of Rural and Urban Development that much of the fault lies in the documents that had not been properly prepared. The implication is that they were rushed through without a real project preparation document, which left DERUDE the unenviable task of implementing a project without sufficient design.

15. The FAO study sought to develop an overall plan for the valley, anticipating the successful eradication of the tsetse fly by the EEC aerial and ground spraying program. It was anticipated that much of the valley would be opened for livestock and thus there would be a great need for such planning. The consultants did not appreciate the historical legacy of land use planning in Zimbabwe that would lead to projects like the MZVRDP.

16. There are a few examples of the management placed in the hands of the para-statal Agriculture and Rural Development Authority (ARDA). Indeed, DERUDE has just been phased out, replaced by the District Development Fund at District Level and by ARDA at the national level.

17. There are four different types of resettlement schemes. In general they are voluntary, and Zimbabwean citizens apply to become eligible. Accelerated Type A means that the government provided no support (either logistical or monetary) for citizens having to move their residences or fields.

18. Jocelyn Alexander, "State, Peasantry, and Resettlement in Zimbabwe," *Review of African Political Economy* 21:61 (1994) 325–344; Bill Derman, "Changing Land-Use in the Eastern Zimbabwe Valley: Socio-Economic Considerations," A Report Prepared for WWF-Zimbabwe and the Centre for Applied Social Sciences, University of Zimbabwe, 1995; Michael Drinkwater, *The State and Agrarian Change in Zimbabwe's Communal Areas* (London: Macmillan, 1991); and A. H. J. Helmsing, N. D.

Mutizwa-Mangiza, D. R. Gaspar, C. M. Brand, and K. H. Wekwete, *Limits to Decentralization in Zimbabwe: Essays on the Decentralization of Government and Planning in the 1980s* (Harare: Dept. of Urban and Rural Planning, University of Zimbabwe, 1991).

19. Even the terminology negates distinctions made by the different peoples living in the valley.

20. The origin and practice of conservation and centralization has been the subject of an important historical debate between Ian Phimister and William Beinart, "Soil Erosion, Conservationism, and Ideas About Development in Southern Africa," *Journal of Southern African Studies* 11:2 (1984) 52–83. Phimister leans toward viewing the emphasis on conservation as one more way by which the colonialists attempted to control and dispossess Africans. Beinart suggested that conservation was indeed important in its own right and couldn't just be reduced to economic interest, although economic interests were important.

21. Government planners relied on the results of the controversial scientific findings of agricultural research during the 1930s and 1940s, which blamed only African cultivators for land degradation without examining the consequences of land alienation, and the policies of permanent cultivation using hybrid maize promoted by the Dept. of Agriculture itself.

22. The history of this process, not yet complete, forms part of the larger study of the MZVRDP. For partial accounts see Derman 1990, *op. cit.*, note 5; and Bill Derman, "Recreating Common Property Management: Goverment Projects and Land Use Policy in the Mid-Zambezi Valley, Zimbabwe." CASS Occasional Paper, NRM 1993 (University of Zimbabwe).

23. This particular Ward Councilor was sent a severe reprimand by Derude and the District Administrator for his district. The action was initiated by the Resettlement Officer (RO) for his ward, who wrote in a long letter of charges: "While all civil servants are willing to advise and work with the Councillor, he does the opposite. On several occasion he has publicly told people that no civil servant comes from Dande and as a result they are doing nothing good for the valley people. By saying this the Councillor gives people the impression that Government employees are doing more harm than good in whatever they do. I feel this tribalistic attitude should be cast away." (From the letter of the RO to the District Administrator of Guruve District, April 19, 1990.)

24. There are areas in the project where riverine cultivation is not possible because there are not sufficient water resources during the dry season or where the soils are too sandy. These areas tend to be away from the base of the escarpment and the major rivers. A relatively low percentage of the population is located in these areas.

25. As of July 1996 US$1.00 equals approximately $10.00 Zimbabwean.

26. These quotes are from an interview conducted by Lazarus Zhuwao and Marja Spierenburg. Zhuwao has worked with me since 1990. Marja Spierenburg is a Dutch anthropologist who has written an excellent paper on the role of Chidyamauyu: Marja Spierenburg, "The Role of the Mhondoro Cult in the Struggle for Control Over Land in Dande (Northern Zimbabwe): Social Commentaries and the Influence of Adherents," Centre for Applied Social Sciences Occasional Paper–NRM Series (Harare, 1995).

27. This issue is explored in greater detail in Bill Derman and James Murombedzi, "Democracy, Development, and Human Rights in Zimbabwe: A Contradictory Terrain," *African Rural and Urban Studies* I:2 (1994) 119–144.

28. A second major emphasis of contemporary development practice and research has been the Communal Areas Management Program for Indigenous Resources, better known by its acronym CAMPFIRE. This program has become justly renowned for its efforts to redress and redirect the flow of wildlife resources from national government and tourist interests to local communities that live with wildlife. For an account of the contrasts between CAMPFIRE and other valley projects, see Derman 1995, *op. cit.*, note 18.

CHAPTER 4

African Wildlife
Conservation and Conflict

Robert K. Hitchcock

Introduction

Over the past decade a dramatic upsurge has taken place in activities designed to conserve biodiversity, especially wildlife, in Africa.[1] The problem has been that conservation efforts have sometimes had negative effects on local people, including violations of basic human rights.[2] (See table.) As a result, many Africans have called for a new approach to wildlife preservation, management, and development, one that does not cause them harm but that instead leads to improvements in their standards of living.[3]

Biodiversity is on the decline in some parts of Africa as some species have been driven to extinction or reduced in number and as habitats have been altered by a combination of human and environmental factors.[4] A major worry of biologists in Africa is that the ability of ecosystems to carry out vital functions such as maintenance of soil fertility, water retention, and the cycling of nutrients will be reduced by the loss of biodiversity.

In response to the concerns about environmental degradation, African governments, along with nongovernment organizations (NGOs) and international aid agencies, have devised various policies and programs to counteract the problems. The biodiversity preservation strategies employed in Africa range from the enactment of endangered species protection legislation, the control of trade in wildlife products, and the enforcement of conservation laws (species conservation) to the declaration and gazettement of national parks, game reserves, and other kinds of conservation areas (spatial conservation).

Attempts have also been made to implement projects aimed at balancing conservation and development. The basic assumption behind these kinds of projects, which are known as integrated conservation and development projects (ICDPs), is that people will be more likely to conserve resources if they are able to gain direct benefits from them.[5] This paper examines the social and environmental impacts of wildlife preservation and management activities in Africa, with special emphasis on human rights and environmental justice.

Robert K. Hitchcock is an Associate Professor of Anthropology and the Coordinator of African Studies at the University of Nebraska, Lincoln, NB 68588-0368. He can also be reached via email (rkh@unlinfo.unl.edu).

Problems with Biodiversity Conservation Efforts

In the past, a major problem with biodiversity conservation programs in Africa, from the perspective of local people, was that they tended to result in dispossession or to prevent people from engaging in resource procurement activities. As one Ju/'hoansi woman in the Nyae Nyae region of Bushmanland, Namibia, put it, "Government first took away our right to hunt and then tried to remove us from our traditional territories." The efforts to control hunting and collection of wild plants and the setting aside of parks and reserves generally served to exacerbate problems of poverty and resource stress among local communities in Africa.[6]

Conservation Efforts in Africa That Have Had Negative Impacts on the Well-Being of Local Populations

Project	Country	General Comments
Central Kalahari	Botswana	Decision to resettle people out of the Central Kalahari Game Reserve resulted in continued pressure on people to leave, restrictions of food and water, and harassment of local people by game scouts, police, and the military
Korup National Park	Cameroon	Resettlement of villagers was done but was underfunded; assistance and infrastructure promised was not forthcoming; the majority of the benefits from the project went to people living away from the park rather than to residents
Tsavo National Park	Kenya	None of the benefits from use of the park by tourists went to the people removed from there; beatings, shootings of hunters and gatherers
West Caprivi	Namibia	Local Khwe (Bushman) groups in conflict with Mbukushu and Kavango peoples moving into a game reserve with government ministry backing
Virunga Volcanoes National Park	Rwanda	Gorilla protection in the park led to kidnapping of local children, intimidation of nearby residents, and restrictions on access to area
Kruger National Park	South Africa	Local people were moved out of the park and mines were planted to prevent ingress; anti-poaching efforts used to intimidate people
Ngorongoro Conservation Area	Tanzania	Use of region's grazing resources by Maasai restricted; cultivation of crops banned; benefits from tourism went to district councils but were not decentralized to communities
Kibale Forest Reserve	Uganda	30,000 residents were evicted in a six-day operation and had to leave possessions for which they were not compensated; intimidation of people

A village scout group in the Kafue area of Zambia being inspected by an official of the U.S. Agency for International Development (USAID) and a member of a nongovernment organization. Photograph by Robert K. Hitchcock.

Some people in Africa feel threatened by what they perceive to be coercive conservation. Local people were subjected to the imposition of restrictive wildlife laws and periodic search-and-seizure operations from the time of the establishment of colonial institutions in Africa. This was particularly true of foragers or small-scale farmers who hunted and gathered wild plants and animals to supplement their subsistence and incomes.[7]

In the 1970s and 1980s, as the concern over the loss of elephants, rhinoceros, and other large mammal species increased, there were greater efforts by African governments to put pressure on people whom they defined as poachers. Local people were arrested and jailed by police, wildlife department officials, and military personnel. In some cases, suspected poachers were badly mistreated during questioning or while they were in custody.[8] There were also cases in which local people were shot and killed as antipoaching operations were conducted. As Ian Khama, the commander of the Botswana Defense Force, which has an Antipoaching Unit (APU), told *National Geographic* writer Douglas Lee in 1990, "No country can ignore armed men crossing its borders. . . . We took on the poachers aggressively—we actually shot a few of them." Data obtained in the field suggest that at least some of those shot were simply gathering wild plants, obtaining water, or visiting friends.[9]

Exact numbers of people killed by government officials in the pursuit of biodiversity preservation are difficult to come by. Some officials have suggested off the record that there may have been as many as 96 people shot and killed in a single year in one country in southern Africa. The hard-line shoot-to-kill policy has served to anger local people and has resulted, in some cases, in attacks on game scouts and tourists by local people. It has also led to what some feel are politically motivated spearings of rhinoceros and other large mammals, as occurred, for example, in the Ngorongoro Conservation Area in Tanzania and some of the Kenya national parks in the 1970s and 1980s.[10]

The antipoaching operations arguably have served to slow down the rate of destruction of such endangered or threatened species as rhinoceros and elephant.[11] There is a major question, however, as to whether or not the mistreatment and killing of people is really the most effective way to promote conservation. Some local people in Africa have suggested that the actions of government and military agencies are genocidal in intent. Others have said that preservationist actions have been undertaken in order to get them off the land so that it can be used for other purposes, including ranching and recreation. Still others have argued that the arrests and killings of local people have actually had the effect of exacerbating poaching problems.[12]

One Tyua Bushman man from the Nata River region of northeastern Botswana had this to say about wildlife laws:

> Our lives depend mostly on meat, and the laws have kept us from eating. I believe that when God created man, he provided all animals to be the food of the Masarwa. The Bamangwato depend on their cattle to provide their food. The Kalanga depend on their crops. White people live on money, bread, and sugar. These are the traditional foods of these groups of people, so it can be seen that the law is against us, the Masarwa, because it has prevented us from eating. The people who made the law knew that they were depriving us of our food. Even if we raise cattle, we cannot do it as well as the Bamangwato. We cannot raise crops like the Kalanga, and we cannot make money like the white people do. These are the ways of other people. The tradition that God gave us, the Masarwa, is to eat meat. Meat is our life. Small animals to us are not important; we eat kudu, duiker, steenbok, and birds every morning. What we really care about is big animals. These are our food; these are what we care about. Depriving us of meat is depriving us of life and of the tradition that God gave us.

The question that a number of spokespersons of African communities are asking today is whether it is appropriate for government agencies and environmental groups that are supposed to be doing conservation should be so heavily involved in promoting activities that are having such negative effects on their lives. As a Tyua woman from northeastern Botswana put it, "Just because these people say that they are helping preserve the environment does not mean that they should be able to violate our human rights." It is possible, they argue, to promote development and enhance the conservation status of wildlife without engaging in actions that result in the mistreatment and deaths of local people.

Causes and Consequences of Wildlife Decline in Africa

Africans, especially poor ones residing in remote areas, have taken the brunt of preservationist efforts to protect wildlife. Africans note that historically they have had little say in the activities of the various conservation agencies operating on the continent. Eric Edroma, the Director of Uganda National Parks, said at a conference on natural resource management in Africa held in Libreville, Gabon, in October 1993, that "African voices are heard rarely in the halls of the offices of environmental organizations." Other African speakers at that conference argued that the role of the average African peasant in the decline of Africa's game populations has been grossly overstated and that the people who are interested in the well-being of Africa's wildlife should look much more carefully at the root causes.[13]

A significant cause of wildlife decline in various parts of Africa over the past several decades has been military activity. In Angola and northern Namibia in the 1970s and 1980s, game populations were decimated by military personnel in what some consider one of the worst atrocities against wildlife in the 20th century.[14] South Africa, long considered to be a leader in environmental protection, was at the center of what some local people in Angola and Namibia have described as a "wildlife holocaust." Testimony at a series of hearings in South Africa in September–October 1995 suggested that military operatives killed large numbers of rhinoceros for their horns and elephants for their tusks, which were then smuggled out of the region and sold on the black market. The funds that they obtained in exchange were used to carry out covert operations and to enrich individuals, some of them high military officers. An internal inquiry conducted in 1988 cleared South African Defense Force (SADF) officers of any wrongdoing, but subsequent investigations indicated that there had been a whitewash and that SADF officers were directly involved in the poaching and smuggling operations.

Members of Angola's National Union for the Total Independence of Namibia (UNITA), funded by South Africa for over 20 years and by the United States until 1975, was responsible for the slaughter of thousands of elephants in Angola, and rhinoceros were almost totally wiped out. Wildlife continues to be killed in southern Angola and the Western Caprivi region of Namibia by former UNITA fighters in spite of the fact that peace accords have been signed.[15] One way to deal with the problem, according to members of local indigenous peoples' advocacy organizations, is to do a better job of controlling the spread of weapons and promoting strategies that reduce conflict. This is particularly important in West Caprivi, where Namibian government agencies have encouraged people to move in to what is still on the books as the West Caprivi Game Reserve, something that has caused conflicts between resident Khwe (Bushman) groups and the immigrant populations, most of whom are Mbukushu.[16]

Heightened refugee flows arising from civil conflicts in Africa have contributed significantly to the destruction of wildlife in areas where people have taken refuge. This can be seen, for example, in the cases of southern Somalia and northern Kenya in the late 1980s and early 1990s, as well as in Zaire, Tanzania, and Burundi as a result of refugees fleeing the genocide in Rwanda in 1994. One way to get around this problem, according to NGOs working with refugees, is to disarm people. Another way is to promote greater cooperation between the various refugee agencies and wildlife departments. The South African Police have an Endangered Species Protection Unit that has investigated cases of alleged poaching and smuggling by refugees from Mozambique. This unit has called for tighter customs controls and for closer investigations of individuals and businesses moving goods from one country to another.

Community-Based Natural Resource Management Projects

Members of local communities, staffs of nongovernment organizations, and African researchers and development personnel have advocated alternative strategies that will help rather than hurt Africa's people. Some NGOs, with the support of government environmental agencies, are engaged in promoting projects that aim to increase local incomes and raise standards of living while at the same time bringing about biodiversity conservation.

The World Wildlife Fund (WWF–US), The Worldwide Fund for Nature (WWF–International), Conservation International (CI), Wildlife Conservation International (WCI), the African Wildlife Foundation (AWF), and other environmental NGOs are involved in projects that combine conservation and development and that operate at the local level. These community-based resource management (CBNRM) projects are found in a wide variety of habitats in Africa, from tropical forests to savannas and from Afromontane habitats to coastal marine regions. Some of these projects are located on the peripheries of protected areas in what are sometimes referred to as buffer zones, while others are in rural areas under customary systems of land tenure such as those in the communal areas of Botswana, Malawi, Namibia, Zambia, and Zimbabwe. CBNRM projects are also being implemented in specially designated reserve areas that allow for multiple use (for example, hunting, collecting of medicinal plants and firewood, small-scale cultivation of domestic crops, and tourism).[17]

Some of these projects have had unforeseen negative impacts on the well-being of the people occupying the areas where they were implemented. One example is a forestry conservation project established in the late 1980s in the Kibale Forest Reserve and the Kibale Game Corridor in western Uganda.[18] Financed in part by funds from the then European Community (EC), this project led to the eviction of some 30,000 people at the hands of armed parks officers, police, and paramilitary personnel. The residents were forced out so quickly that many of them had to abandon their household possessions. No arrangements were made prior to their eviction to ascertain their assets or to adjudicate their claims; as a consequence, the few compensation payments that eventually were made were minimal.

A major problem with integrated conservation and development projects has been that they have generally underestimated the costs of compensating people for their losses and have not been able to come up with strategies that restore livelihoods or replace income lost as a result of the project implementation. This can be seen, for example, in the case of Korup National Park in Cameroon where some of the villagers inside the park were moved out as part of a program designed by World Wildlife Fund–United Kingdom. While there were plans originally to resettle a total of six villages, only two eventually were established, and much of the assistance and infrastructure that had been promised was not forthcoming. The majority of the benefits from the project have not gone to people residing inside or on the peripheries of the park but instead to people living some distance away.[19]

The implementation of ICDPs in Africa has had mixed results. While they have sometimes led to an expansion of incomes and employment for local people, they have also had costs. These costs range from reduced land and resource availability to impoverishment and expanded rates of wildlife depletion.[20] An example of this situation is the case of the Dzanga-Sangha Dense Forest Special Reserve and the Dzangha-Ndoki National Park in the Central African Republic (CAR), where Baka Pygmy communities were included in a project sponsored in part by the World Wildlife Fund–US and the U.S. Agency for International Development (USAID). Some of the Baka in the forest reserve work as tourist guides, while others sell goods that they obtain from the forest on the commercial market. A local NGO was established, and it receives some of the park gate receipts and plays a role in park management. Unfortunately, logging companies are still allowed to extract timber in the area, and high rates of illegal wildlife offtake continue.[21]

Resettlement in the name of wildlife conservation and tourism promotion has been advocated by a number of African governments and environmental NGOs. This was seen most recently in the case of the Central Kalahari Game Reserve, the third largest game reserve in Africa.[22] In February 1996, Botswana government ministers announced at a community meeting in the central Kalahari that the residents of the reserve would be required to leave the area. Local people reacted strongly to this request, arguing that they should be allowed to stay where they are. They pointed out that the Central Kalahari Game Reserve was established originally as a means of protecting the land-and-resource use rights of local people. They also suggested that the resettlement of people out of the central Kalahari could have a whole series of negative effects on both the people who are moved as well as those people who reside in the areas where resettlement occurs.[23]

In the late 1980s and early 1990s the Botswana government had pursued a policy of "freezing" development in the Central Kalahari Game Reserve. When the borehole at !Xade, the largest community in the reserve, broke down, it took months before it was fixed. Buildings and roads were not maintained in the reserve except for those going to Department of Wildlife and National Parks camps. Even drought relief feeding programs were slower in the central Kalahari than elsewhere in Botswana, a situation that threatened the well-being of people in several parts of the reserve.

Pressures were also brought to bear on people in the central Kalahari through selective enforcement of wildlife laws and what some people perceived to be intimidation. Data collected on households in the central Kalahari and adjacent areas reveal that up to two-thirds of the resident adult males of some communities have been arrested at one time or another by game scouts from the Department of Wildlife and National Parks, police officers, or Botswana Defense Force (BDF) personnel. One of the impacts of high rates of arrest was a considerable withdrawal of sources of much-needed labor from households and communities. This was especially problematic if the person arrested and jailed was a breadwinner or a hunter. Families who had a member arrested often faced both economic and nutritional difficulties. In some cases, people who formerly had been self-sufficient economically had to seek government assistance as destitutes. Local people claim that people in remote areas like the central Kalahari tend to be arrested more frequently and receive higher fines and jail sentences than do people who reside in towns and villages, some of whom actually engage in greater amounts of hunting than do remote area residents.[24]

Even more disturbing than the high rates of arrest were the charges that people have been mistreated by game scouts and other officials. There were a number of incidents where people claimed that they were tortured or received inhumane or degrading punishment when suspected of poaching or when being questioned about others who might be engaged in illegal hunting. According to one report, the most common form of torture included the use of a "rubber ring" placed tightly around the testicles and a plastic bag placed over the face of a person.[25] There were cases where people died of injuries inflicted on them by game scouts, as occurred at !Xade in August 1993, when a 40-year-old man died after being questioned by game scouts. Community leaders in the central Kalahari have argued that authorities have stepped over the line from antipoaching to persecution.

The central Kalahari case provides an excellent example of some of the kinds of responses that Africans are employing to deal with the situations they are facing as a result of wildlife preservation and management efforts. The Bushmen (Basarwa, Khwe) have begun to organize at the grassroots level to protest the ways that they are being treated. They have formed indigenous advocacy organizations, one example being *Kgei-kani Kweni* (First People of the Kalahari), which was established in 1992. The first action of Kgeikani Kweni was to attend a national-level workshop on Sustainable Rural Development held by the Botswana Society in April 1992. There they spoke out on issues ranging from poverty to cultural preservation. They stressed that they wished to be treated with greater respect by officials of the Department of Wildlife and National Parks and other agencies of the Botswana government.

Bushmen spokespersons also attended a series of international meetings, including the Working Group on Indigenous Peoples (WGIP) of the United Nations in Geneva, where they argued forcefully that they should have land and resource rights, the right to practice their own culture and learn their own languages, and the right to have a say in decision-making about development planning. They pointed out that the kinds of treatment that some Bushmen had received were potentially in violation of international human rights law, especially the severe forms of torture employed and what they felt were tantamount to extrajudicial executions. Human rights organizations such as Amnesty International and Survival International took note of these allegations, as did the U.S. Department of State.[26] The defense that some people offered when charged with crimes such as violations of the fauna conservation laws was that they committed these acts "because they were hungry." Poverty and hunger, however, are *not* considered to be extenuating circumstances under Botswana law. As a result, people are jailed or fined for what in essence is an "economic crime."[27]

Bushmen and other indigenous groups in Africa have sought to use the media to positive effect, and they have requested the help of intergovernmental organizations such as the United Nations as well as NGOs, including environmental ones. In their discussions, they have stressed how much damage forced relocation does to local communities. Extensive research by social and natural scientists and by development workers has shown that involuntary community relocation of people with strong ties to the land has nearly always resulted in a reduction in the standards of living of those who were moved.[28] While some of the people moved may temporarily be better off, over the longer term conditions can be expected to worsen, in part because of increased competition for natural resources and employment opportunities.

One of the impacts of the resettlement out of conservation areas has been an increase in interethnic tensions and community conflict. This can be seen around some of the national parks in Africa. There are also cases where ethnic tensions surfaced as a result of the implementation of community-based natural resource management projects. Bakonjo closest to the boundaries of the Rwenzori Mountains National Park—the legendary "Mountains of the Moon"—in western Uganda were underrepresented in the new park management institutions established by the Rwenzori Mountains Conservation and

Development Project (RMCDP). There was also a feeling among the Bakonjo project stakeholders that they had less of a say in decision-making than did the Batoro, another of the ethnic groups in the region.[29] Clearly, it is important to pay careful attention to ensuring that the various ethnic groups in an area are able to participate effectively in conservation and natural resource management activities.

One of the sources of conflict in ICDPs in Africa has been what local people sometimes perceive to be inequities in the distribution of benefits, particularly employment opportunities. Some of the ecotourism projects in Africa, for example, have seen management-level positions occupied by expatriates, while lower-paying and less important jobs go to local people. The experience of tourism in Botswana, for example, has been that tourism companies generally do not hire Bushmen except for such menial positions as camp cleaners or occasionally as trackers for safari hunters.[30] The notion that tourism will provide a windfall of benefits to local people in the central Kalahari, which is being propounded both by the government and by environmental NGOs,[31] is highly unlikely.

One of the strategies employed by Africans in their efforts to deal with environmental and development agencies is to request that they observe international standards such as those pertaining to the resettlement of populations.[32] As John Hardbattle of Kgeikani Kweni has argued in speeches such as one at the UN Human Rights Commission in March, 1996, African governments should be open to negotiation with local people. He and other community leaders in Africa have argued vociferously for planning that is grassroots-oriented rather than top-down. They have also advocated the establishment of more community-based organizations (CBOs), which should be given greater say in policy formulation.

The country where the CBNRM approach has been developed to the greatest extent is the Republic of Zimbabwe in southern Africa. Under the Parks and Wildlife Act of 1975, the Zimbabwe government began to devolve authority over benefits from wildlife to district councils and local communities under the Communal Areas Management Program for Indigenous Resources (CAMPFIRE). CAMPFIRE has been implemented in over half of the districts of the country, and it has been cited as a model of community empowerment and wildlife management.[33] One of the problems with CAMPFIRE is that many of the decisions about resource management come from outside the local communities that are supposed to benefit most from the program. This can be seen, for example, in the case of the Tsholotsho District, which informed communities within its jurisdiction that they would have to leave an area that the district council had designated as a wildlife management area. Some of the Tyua Bushmen who were forced out of the area attempted to move across the border but were arrested, while others, including women collecting bush foods and water, were shot.[34]

The imposition of the ivory ban by the Convention on Trade in Endangered Species of Flora and Fauna (CITES) in 1989 had adverse impacts on the economies of Tyua and Ndebele households engaged in commercial hunting and ivory carving.[35] Ironically, the elephant populations in western Zimbabwe and northern Botswana were on the rise at the time of the ban, so much so that crop damage by elephants became a major problem in the early 1990s. Tyua and other rural Zimbabweans are not allowed to hunt or to shoot animals that raid their fields; they must depend instead on Department of National Parks and Wildlife Management (DNPWLM) game scouts to deal with problem animals. As one Tyua woman put it, "We are not allowed to protect our crops and our children from wild animals, and we are even arrested and shot at for collecting thatching grass and firewood." She was referring to a situation where women had been arrested for collecting resources in an area that had been allocated to a private company by the local district council without the knowledge or consent of local people. The gender effects of wildlife management projects must be considered much more carefully in the future, since women in general tend to bear greater costs and receive fewer benefits than men.[36]

Conclusions

The degree to which conservation and development projects are beneficial is dependent in part on the extent to which local people can take part in project activities. Many of the NGO-sponsored projects that were initiated in Africa have not been as proactive as they might have been in terms of incorporating local people, including women, children, the elderly, and indigenous minorities, into decision-making. It is for this reason that some African communities have sought to plan and implement their own projects and come up with their own sets of rules by which conservation and development will be conducted.

Fledgling grassroots social and environmental movements are springing up in many parts of Africa, seeking to ensure a better balance between conservation and development as well as greater flows of benefits to local people (as opposed to elites and outsiders). Some of these movements have achieved a certain amount of success, as can be seen, for example, in the efforts to prevent the government of Botswana from implementing a water development project that could have had adverse environmental impacts on the Okavango Delta, "the jewel of the Kalahari," and the actions of women's associations in Kenya, Tanzania, Swaziland, and South Africa to promote organic agriculture, soil conservation schemes, and small-scale business activities.[37]

Effective conservation and development activities in Africa can only come about when coercion gives way to cooperation—and when local people are given support, information, and technical assistance. Africans, for their part, are more than willing to cooperate with those organizations that place human rights on an equal footing with species preservation. What they are seeking, they say, is a more participatory process, one in which direct links are made among human rights, the environment, and democratic governance. Successful conservation can only come about, they maintain, if local people are allowed to take part in formulating and implementing policies and programs that incorporate safeguards against abuses and that place strong emphasis on equity and social justice.

Notes

1. Wildlife conservation efforts in Africa have been discussed in the following: Stuart A. Marks, *The Imperial Lion: Human Dimensions of Wildlife Management in Africa* (Boulder, Colo.: Westview Press, 1984); David Anderson and Richard Grove, eds., *Conservation in Africa: People, Policies and Practice* (Cambridge and New York: Cambridge University Press, 1987); Rodger Yeager, ed., *Africa's*

Conservation for Development (Botswana, Kenya, Tanzania, and Zimbabwe) (Hanover, N.H.: African-Caribbean Institute, 1987); Agnes Kiss, ed., *Living with Wildlife: Wildlife Resource Management with Local Participation in Africa* (Washington, D.C.: World Bank, 1990); Jonathan S. Adams and Thomas O. McShane, *The Myth of Wild Africa: Conservation Without Illusion* (New York: Norton, 1992); Raymond Bonner, *At the Hand of Man: Peril and Hope for Africa's Wildlife* (New York: Alfred A. Knopf, 1993); Christoper B. Barrett and Peter Arcese, "Are Integrated Conservation-Development Projects (ICDPs) Sustainable? On the Conservation of Large Mammals in Africa," *World Development* 23:7 (1995) 1073–1084; Clark C. Gibson and Stuart A. Marks, "Transforming Rural Hunters into Conservationists: An Assessment of Community-Based Wildlife Projects in Africa," *World Development* 23:6 (1995) 941–957; Elizabeth Braun, *Portraits in Conservation: Eastern and Southern Africa* (Golden, Colo.: North American Press, 1995).

2. Human rights violations in the context of conservation programs have been dealt with in the following: Nancy L. Peluso, "Coercing Conservation? The Politics of State Resource Control," in Ronnie D. Lipschutz and Ken Conca, eds., *The State and Social Power in Global Environmental Politics* (New York: Columbia University Press, 1993), 46–70; Marcus Colchester, *Salvaging Nature: Indigenous Peoples, Protected Areas, and Biodiversity Conservation*, United Nations Research Institute for Social Development, Discussion Paper 55 (Geneva: UN Research Institute for Social Development, World Rainforest Movement, and Worldwide Fund for Nature, 1994); Robert K. Hitchcock, "Centralization, Resource Depletion, and Coercive Conservation among the Tyua of the Northeastern Kalahari," *Human Ecology* 23:2 (1995) 169–198. General discussions of human rights and environmental justice can be found in Human Rights Watch, *Indivisible Human Rights: The Relationship of Political and Civil Rights to Survival, Subsistence, and Poverty* (New York: Human Rights Watch, 1992); Human Rights Watch and Natural Resources Defense Council, *Defending the Earth: Abuses of Human Rights and the Environment* (Washington, D.C.: Human Rights Watch and Natural Resources Defense Council, 1992); Aaron Sachs, *Eco-Justice: Linking Human Rights and the Environment*, WorldWatch Paper 127 (Washington, D.C.: WorldWatch Institute, 1995); Aaron Sachs, "Upholding Human Rights and Environmental Justice," in Lester Brown *et al.*, eds., *State of the World 1996* (Washington, D.C.: WorldWatch Institute, 1996), 133–151.

3. See Hanne Veber, Jens Dahl, Fiona Wilson, and Espen Waehle, eds., ". . . *Never Drink from the Same Cup,"* Proceedings of the Conference on Indigenous Peoples in Africa, Tune, Denmark, 1993, IWGIA Document No. 74 (Copenhagen: International Working Group for Indigenous Affairs and the Center for Development Research, 1993); Leo van der Vlist, ed., *Voices of the Earth: Indigenous Peoples, New Partners, and the Right to Self-Determination in Practice* (Amsterdam: The Netherlands Center for Indigenous Peoples, 1995).

4. The environmental crisis in Africa has been discussed in the following publications: Rodger Yeager and Norman N. Miller, *Wildlife, Wild Death: Land Use and Survival in Eastern Africa* (Albany: State University of New York Press, 1986); Mort Rosenblum and Doug Williamson, *Squandering Eden: Africa at the Edge* (New York: Harcourt, Brace, Jovanovich, 1987); Lloyd Timberlake, *Africa in Crisis: The Causes, the Cures of Environmental Bankruptcy* (London: Earthscan Publications, 1988); Rodger Yeager, "Democratic Pluralism and Ecological Crisis in Botswana," *Journal of Developing Areas* 23:3 (1989) 385–404; Daniel Stiles, ed., *Social Aspects of Dryland Management* (Nairobi: UN Environment Program and New York: John Wiley and Sons, 1995).

5. For a discussion of some of these efforts, see Associates in Rural Development, *Decentralization and Local Autonomy: Conditions for Achieving Sustainable Resource Management* (Burlington, Vt.: Associates in Rural Development and Washington, D.C.: U.S. Agency for International Development, 1992); Michael Brown and Barbara Wyckoff-Baird, *Designing Integrated Conservation and Development Projects* (Washington, D.C.: Biodiversity Support Program and World Wildlife Fund, 1992); Michael Wells and Katrina Brandon, with Lee Hannah, *Parks and People: Linking Protected Area Management with Local Communities* (Washington, D.C.: World Bank, World Wildlife Fund, and U.S. Agency for International Development, 1992); World Conservation Monitoring Center (WCMC), *Global Biodiversity: Status of the Earth's Living Resources* (Cambridge, England: WCMC,

1992); Biodiversity Support Program, *African Biodiversity: Foundation for the Future, A Framework for Integrating Biodiversity Conservation and Sustainable Development* (Washington, D.C.: World Wildlife Fund, the Nature Conservancy, World Resources Institute, and U.S. Agency for International Development, 1993); World Wildlife Fund, *Community-Based Conservation in Southern Africa: Training Cases* (Washington, D.C.: World Wildlife Fund, 1993); International Institute for Environment and Development, *Whose Eden? An Overview of Community Approaches to Wildlife Management* (London: International Institute for Environment and Development and Overseas Development, 1994); Ruth Norris and Robert K. Hitchcock, *Final Evaluation: Social Science and Economics Program (Formerly Wildlands and Human Needs Program)* (Alexandria, Va.: Automation Research Systems, 1994); Evelyn S. Wilcox, *Lessons from the Field: Marine Integrated Conservation and Development* (Washington, D.C.: World Wildlife Fund, 1994); S. D. Turner, *Common Property Resources and the Rural Poor in Sub-Saharan Africa* (Rome: International Fund for Agricultural Development, Special Programme for Sub-Saharan African Countries Affected by Drought and Desertification, 1995); Barrett and Arcese, *op. cit.*, note 1.

6. Perhaps the best example of the social and economic stress brought about by the creation of a national park is that of Colin Turnbull in his book *The Mountain People* (New York: Simon and Schuster, 1972), which chronicles the cultural dissolution of the Ik, who were removed from Kidepo National Park in northern Uganda.

7. Hunter-gatherers in particular had to give up foraging activities or face arrest and lengthy jail terms; see, for example, Robert Gordon, *The Bushman Myth: The Making of a Namibian Underclass* (Boulder, Colo.: Westview Press, 1992); Daniel Stiles, "Sustainable Development in Tropical Forests by Indigenous Peoples," *Swara* 16:5 (1993) 24–27; as well as the section on Sub-Saharan Africa (pp. 161–178) in Marc S. Miller, ed. with Cultural Survival, *State of the Peoples: A Global Human Rights Report on Societies in Danger* (Boston: Beacon Press, 1993); and Susan Kent, ed., *Cultural Diversity among Twentieth Century African Foragers: An African Perspective* (Cambridge: Cambridge University Press, 1996).

8. See, for example, Alice Mogwe, *Who Was (T)here First? An Assessment of the Human Rights Situation of Basarwa in Selected Communities in the Gantsi District*, Occasional Paper No. 10 (Gaborone, Botswana: Botswana Christian Council, 1992); Casey Kelso, "Hungry Hunter-Gatherers Tortured," and Casey Kelso, "The Inconvenient Nomads Deep Inside the Deep," *Weekly Mail*, July 24–30, 1992, p. 12; Anonymous, "Wildlife Atrocities Exposed: Basarwa Speak Out," *Mokaedi*, Sept. 1992; Anonymous, "Human Rights Abuses Against Basarwa," *Mmegi: The Reporter*, May 29–June 4, 1992; Peluso, *op. cit.*, note 2; Hitchcock (1995), *op. cit.*, note 2.

9. See Douglas B. Lee, p. 49 of "Okavango Delta: Africa's Last Refuge," *National Geographic* 178:6 (Dec. 1990) 38–69. Data on impacts of antipoaching operations include interview data obtained in 1989, 1990, 1991, and 1995 in northern, eastern, and southwestern Botswana; see, for example, Robert K. Hitchcock and Stuart A. Marks, *Traditional and Modern Systems of Land Use and Management and User Rights to Natural Resources in Rural Botswana. Part I: Field Data and Analysis* (Gaborone, Botswana: Natural Resource Management Project, Dept. of Wildlife and National Parks and U.S. Agency for International Development, 1991); and Robert K. Hitchcock, Rosinah Rose B. Masilo, and Poppy Monyatse, *Subsistence Hunting and Resource Rights in Botswana: An Assessment of Special Game Licenses and Their Impacts on Remote Area Dwellers and Wildlife Populations* (Gaborone, Botswana: Natural Resource Management Project and Dept. of Wildlife and National Parks, 1995); for western Zimbabwe, see Robert K. Hitchcock and Fanuel M. Nangati, *Zimbabwe Natural Resources Management Project Community-Based Resource Utilization Component: Interim Assessment* (Harare, Zimbabwe: U.S. Agency for International Development and Dept. of National Parks and Wildlife Management, 1992); Mogwe, *op. cit.*, note 8; Hitchcock *op. cit.*, note 2.

10. Henry Fosbrooke, Daniel Stiles, personal communications. See also Richard Bell, "Monitoring of Illegal Activity and Law Enforcement in African Conservation Areas," in R. H. V. Bell and E. McShane-Caluzi, eds., *Conservation and Wildlife Resources in Africa* (Washington, D.C.: U.S. Peace Corps, 1986), 297–315; L. Talbot and P. Olindo, "Amboseli and Maasai Mara, Kenya," in Kiss, *op.*

cit., note 1, p. 70; K. M. Homewood and W. A. Rodgers, *Maasailand Ecology: Pastoral Development and Wildlife Conservation in Ngorongoro, Tanzania* (Cambridge: Cambridge University Press, 1991); P. Arcese, J. Hando, and K. Campbell, "Historical and Present-Day Anti-Poaching Efforts in Serengeti," in, A. R. E. Sinclair and P. Arcese, eds., *Serengeti II: Research, Conservation, and Management of an Ecosystem* (Chicago: University of Chicago Press, 1995), 506–533. The work in Ngorongoro shows that although the environment has generally been protected, the socioeconomic status of the Maasai is in a serious state of decline; see J. Terrence McCabe, Scott Perkin, and Claire Schofield, "Can Conservation and Development Be Coupled Among Pastoral People? An Examination of the Maasai of the Ngorongoro Conservation Area," *Human Organization* 51:4 (1992) 353–366.

11. For a classic discussion of the utility of anti-poaching efforts, see Dennis Holman, *Massacre of the Elephants* (New York: Holt, Rinehart, and Winston, 1967). Mark and Delia Owens in their book *The Eye of the Elephant: Life and Death in an African Wilderness* (New York: Houghton Mifflin, 1992) discuss various antipoaching actions in the North Luangwa National Park of Zambia along with efforts to promote alternative economic opportunities for local populations. See also N. Leader-Williams and S. D. Albon, "Allocation of Resources for Conservation," *Nature* 336 (1988) 533–535; N. Leader-Williams, S. D. Albon, and P. S. M. Berry, "Illegal Exploitation of Black Rhinoceros and Elephant Populations: Patterns of Decline, Law Enforcement, and Patrol Effort in Luangwa Valley, Zambia," *Journal of Applied Ecology* 27:3 (1990) 1055–1087; Dale Lewis, Gilson B. Kaweche, and Ackim Mwenya, "Wildlife Conservation Outside Protected Areas—Lessons from An Experiment in Zambia," *Conservation Biology* 4 (1990) 171–180; E. Millner-Gulland and N. Leader-Williams, "A Model of Incentives for the Illegal Exploitation of Black Rhinos and Elephants: Poaching Pays in Luangwa Valley, Zambia," *Journal of Applied Ecology* 29:2 (1992) 388–401; Gibson and Marks, *op. cit.*, note 1.

12. This was argued, for example, by Bushman speakers at a conference on indigenous peoples in Africa (see Veber *et al.*, *op. cit.*, note 3) and at two National Institute for Research seminars on Basarwa (Bushmen) held at the University of Botswana in Gaborone, Botswana, in August and October, 1995.

13. See the African Training for Leadership and Advanced Skills (ATLAS) Project, *Natural Resource Management in Africa: Issues in Conservation and Socioeconomic Development* (New York: The African-American Institute, 1993).

14. See S. R. Galster, "Big Game Smugglers: The Trail Leads to South Africa," *The Nation* 256:6 (1993) 195–198; Judith Matloff, "South Africa Decimated Rhinos, Elephants in 1970s for Wars," *Christian Science Monitor,* Jan. 19, 1996, p. 1.

15. See Kyle Owen-Smith, "Caprivi Faces Wildlife Ruin," and "Frontier Dealing Could Wreck Caprivian Hopes," *The Namibian*, March 29, 1996, pp. 1–2, 7–8.

16. For a discussion of the situation in West Caprivi, see Robert K. Hitchcock and Marshall W. Murphree, *Report of the Field Assessment Team, Phase III of the Mid-Term Assessment of the LIFE Project, USAID/Namibia Component* (690-0251.73) (Windhoek, Namibia: U.S. Agency for International Development, 1995).

17. Assessments of some of these projects can be found in Wells and Brandon, *op. cit.*, note 5; Brown and Wyckoff-Baird, *op. cit.*, note 5; World Wildlife Fund, *op. cit.*, note 5; International Institute for Environment and Development (1994), *op. cit.*, note 5; Norris and Hitchcock, *op. cit.*, note 5; and David Western and R. Michael Wright, eds., *Natural Connections: Perspectives in Community Based Conservation* (Washington, D.C.: Island Press, 1994).

18. See Patricia Feeney, *The Impact of a European Community Project on Peasant Families in Uganda*, Briefing Paper No. 6 (London: OXFAM UK/Ireland, 1993).

19. See S. Gartlan, *The Korup Regional Management Plan: Conservation and Development in the Ndian Division of Cameroon* (London: World Wildlife Fund United Kingdom, 1985); R. Moorehead and T. Hammond, "An Assessment of the Rural Development Program of the Korup National Park Project," Report to CARE–United Kingdom (London, 1992); Patrick Sweeting *et al.*, *Evaluation Report: Korup National Park Project, Cameroon* (Geneva: Worldwide Fund for Nature International, 1992).

20. See John A. Hoyt, *Animals in Peril: How "Sustainable Use" is Wiping Out the World's Wildlife* (Garden City, N.Y.: Avery Publishing Group, 1994); Colchester, *op. cit.*, note 2; Norris and Hitchcock, *op. cit.*, note 5; Barrett and Arcese, *op. cit.*, note 1; Gibson and Marks, *op. cit.*, note 1.

21. See Richard W. Carroll, "The Development, Protection, and Management of the Dzangha-Sangha Dense Forest Special Reserve and the Dzangha-Ndoko National Park in Southwestern Central African Republic," Report to the World Wildlife Fund–US (Washington, D.C., 1992); Anna Kretsinger, "Recommendations for Further Integration of BaAka Interests in Project Policy, Dzanga-Sangha Dense Forest Reserve," Report to the World Wildlife Fund–US (Washington, D.C., 1993); G. Doungoube, "The Dzanga-Sangha Dense Forest Reserve," in *Rural Development and Conservation in Africa: A Series of Briefing Papers for Development Organizations* (Geneva and Washington, D.C.: Africa Resources Trust, World Conservation Union, Worldwide Fund for Nature, and World Wildlife Fund–US); Colchester, *op. cit.*, note 2, pp. 32–33.

22. See Suzanne Daley, "Botswana Is Pressing Bushmen to Leave Reserve," *New York Times*, July 14, 1996.

23. See the minutes of the kgotla (public council) meeting at !Xade, Central Kalahari Game Reserve, Feb. 17, 1996, on file at the Ghanzi District Council, Ghanzi, Botswana, and the Ministry of Local Government, Lands, and Housing, Gaborone, Botswana; and the report by Ditshwanelo, *When Will This Moving Stop? Report on a Fact-finding Mission of the Central Kgalagadi Game Reserve, April 10–14, 1996* (Gaborone, Botswana: Ditshwanelo—the Botswana Center for Human Rights, 1996).

24. Interviews of residents of the Central Kalahari Game Reserve and surrounding areas and of officials in the Ghanzi District Council and the Government of Botswana were conducted in 1988–1991 and 1995. See Robert K. Hitchcock, "The Central Kalahari Game Reserve: A Case Study in Remote Area Research and Development," in *Monitoring, Research, and Development in the Remote Areas of Botswana* (Gaborone, Botswana; Ministry of Local Government and Lands, 1988); American Anthropological Association Committee for Human Rights, *Population Relocation and Survival: The Botswana Government's Decision to Relocate the People of the Central Kalahari Game Reserve* (Washington, D.C.: American Anthropological Association, 1996).

25. Mogwe, *op. cit.*, note 8, p. 12.

26. Survival International, "Botswana: Kalahari Peoples Threatened with Expulsion from Game Reserve," *Urgent Action Bulletin*, UAB/BOT/1/APR/1989 (1989); Survival International, Letter to the President of Botswana, April 1996; U.S. Dept. of State, *Country Report on Human Rights Practices for 1993* (Washington, D.C.: Government Printing Office, 1993), 13–14.

27. Mogwe, *op. cit.*, note 8, p. 13.

28. See, for example, Art Hansen and Anthony Oliver-Smith, eds., *Involuntary Migration and Resettlement: The Problems and Responses of Dislocated People* (Boulder, Colo.: Westview Press, 1982); and Thayer Scudder, "Resettlement," in Asit K. Biswas, ed., *Handbook for Water Resources and Environment* (New York: McGraw-Hill, 1986).

29. See Norris and Hitchcock, *op. cit.*, note 5, pp. 35–43. Background information on the Rwenzoris, the groups residing there, can be found in Kenneth Ingham, *The Kingdom of Toro in Uganda* (London: Methuen, 1975); B. K. Taylor, *The Western Lacustrine Bantu: The Konjo* (London: International African Institute, 1962); Guy Yeoman, *Africa's Mountains of the Moon: Journeys to the Snowy Sources of the Nile* (New York: Universe Books, 1989); Guy Yeoman, "Uganda's New Rwenzori National Park," *Swara* 15:2 (1992) 16–22.

30. See Robert K. Hitchcock, "Cultural, Economic, and Environmental Impacts of Tourism among Kalahari Bushmen," in Erve Chambers, ed., *Native Tours: Comparative Perspectives on Tourism and Community* (Albany: State University of New York Press, in press).

31. See, for example, Kalahari Conservation Society, *Management Plan for Central Kalahari and Khutse Game Reserves* (Gaborone, Botswana: Kalahari Conservation Society, 1988) and the speech by President Ketumile Masire on environmental issues in Botswana, Carnegie Endowment for International Peace, Washington, D.C., June 13, 1996.

32. World Bank, "Operational Directive 4.30: Involuntary Resettlement," in *The World Bank Operational Manual* (Washington, D.C.: World Bank, 1990).

33. See, for example, Adams and McShane, *op. cit.*, note 1, pp. 178–183, 242–243; Hitchcock and Nangati, *op. cit.*, note 9; Bonner, *op. cit.*, note 1, pp. 253–278; Gordon Edwin Matzke and Nontokozo Nabane, "Outcomes of a Community Controlled Wildlife Utilization Program in a Zambezi Valley Community," *Human Ecology* 24:1 (1996) 65–85.

34. This information was obtained during interviews in Tsholotsho and Bulalima-Mangwe Districts in western Zimbabwe in July, 1992.

35. Hitchcock, *op. cit.*, note 2, p. 193.

36. See Malcolm L. Hunter, Robert K. Hitchcock, and Barbara Wyckoff-Baird, "Women and Wildlife in Southern Africa," *Conservation Biology* 4:4 (1990) 448–451; and Norris and Hitchcock, *op. cit.*, note 5.

37. See Robert K. Hitchcock, "Zenzele: Swazi Women Say, 'Do It Yourself,'" *Ndiza Natsi* 3:11 (1985) 22–25; Alan Durning, *Action at the Grassroots: Fighting Poverty and Environmental Decline* (Washington, D.C.: Worldwatch Institute, 1989); Thayer Scudder *et al.*, *The IUCN Review of the Southern Okavango Integrated Water Development Project* (Gland, Switzerland: IUCN—The World Conservation Union, 1993).

PART THREE

Mineral Wealth vs. Biotic Health

Gold. Instant wealth. There for the taking. A fistful of treasure with the power to transform the misery of poverty into a luxurious existence. Consuming passion. Feverous dreams.

For hundreds of thousands of years the allure of gold has haunted humankind, sending men and women into forbidden lonely places, living and dying in the worst of conditions, all for the sake of a handful of gold. The presence of gold and other minerals justified the conquering of civilizations, the enslavement of nations of peoples, the devastation of people and land. This is human history, and this is history in the making.

The following two chapters present sharply contrasting experiences in the struggle to halt mining on indigenous peoples' lands. Leslie Sponsel examines the human and environmental impacts of uncontrolled mining in the Brazilian Amazon. Al Gedicks explores the social and political response to proposed zinc-copper mining in northern Wisconsin, United States. The juxtaposition of these two chapters allows us to consider the huge differences in life and death matters for people living in rights-protective states, as well as the limited options for people living in rights-abusive settings.

In the Brazilian Amazon, Sponsel describes a situation where the government is unable or unwilling to keep gold miners from invading indigenous peoples' lands. The peoples affected are caught in the struggle simply to survive the cumulative affects of introduced diseases, degraded and toxic settings, social fragmentation caused by loss of life, and the rise of violent conflict. Despite federal recognition of indigenous land rights, rights-protective mechanisms are lacking, in part owing to the physical distance between the urban power centers and rural "frontier," in part owing to the struggles between state and federal government institutions over respective responsibilities and power domains, and in part owing simply to the lure of gold. Owners, workers, and indigenous peoples are hugely distant from each other, in cultural, socioeconomic, and geographically spatial terms. Controlling powers may wonder, Why bother to deal with occupational health and safety issues, worry over indigenous rights, and show concern about environmental degradation in a distant wilderness, when the people affected are so inconsequential and so much money is at stake?

Given these extreme conditions, how are affected peoples responding? Sponsel describes a variety of responses, including passive acceptance of eco/ethno/genocide, migration, the occasional incidence of violent confrontation, a few instances of collaboration in gold mining efforts, and increasing efforts to organize, educate, and actively seek political change. This latter response relies on the use of informal mechanisms that enhance information flows, allowing isolated groups to share their experiences, organize, document, educate, and disseminate information in national and international forums in ways that pressure policy makers to confront the tangible consequences of their inaction, with the goal of forcing governments to implement rights-protective measures.

Al Gedicks provides sharp contrast to the Amazon experience, describing an effort to stop mining in northern Wisconsin, where legal structures exist and are used by affected peoples to delay mining, and possibly to end immediate prospects *for* mining. This chapter lays out the origins and anatomy of a powerful social movement—one that manages to bring otherwise disparate groups together in a single effort to halt a perceived common threat. In this case, a coalition of Native American, sports fishers, environmentalist, and other community groups formed in reaction to the initial approval of a zinc-copper mining operation in northern Wisconsin. (Previous battles over fishing and resource rights had pitted these groups against each other, fighting in court and in the community, and resulting in incidents of violent conflict.) Dispute about whether the proposed zinc-copper mine will be allowed even to operate has raised such issues as who has authority to decide (state agencies or tribal structures?), and when will economic activity adversely impact tribal resources (such as the health of the watershed, including the viability of fish and rice). In this case the common concern with environmental quality, despite the contested notions of critical resources in that environment, allowed the formation of a political movement that crossed race, class, and cultural lines. This coalition proved to be a crucial factor in transforming the loci of power in decision-making systems.

What is it that allows these people to respond in this way? As documented by Gedicks, affected peoples had access to information before the project was initiated, the opportunity to voice concerns in public hearings and other political arenas, federally recognized tribal rights, and federally recognized biosphere rights (designations of endangered species, as well as of wild and scenic rivers). When decisions were made in spite of public input (the government says yes while its people say no), people were able to challenge decisions through legal means. Legal mechanisms existed to protect the civil and political rights of indigenous peoples and other resident to organize, build collaborative networks, protest encroachments on their lands, and publicly disseminate information that challenged the status quo—activities that were enhanced by access to information and communication tools.

Even with these rights-protective mechanisms in place (allowing affected peoples the opportunity to organize and assert their voice in the decision-making system), the ability to determine the final outcome is questionable. Gedicks' case demonstrates one of the reasons why "success" is fleeting: the struggle over rights to control critical nonrenewable resources will always be contested because the relative power and wealth of government and industry provides the means to ensure that 2 years, 20 years, 40 years later, the issue will resurface.

These chapters ask, What are the conditions and contexts that allow the relatively powerless to succeed in their struggle to seize control, assert their voice, and transform the conditions of their existence? How do we measure success, and in what time frame?

CHAPTER 5

The Master Thief

Gold Mining and Mercury Contamination in the Amazon

Leslie E. Sponsel[1]

Prologue

In 1987 in the town of Boa Vista in northern Brazil, José Altino Machado, a founder and leader of a union of gold miners in the Amazon, swallowed some mercury in front of television cameras to try to dramatically demonstrate to viewers that the chemical was harmless. In a related interview he stated:

> . . . the mercury we employ is inert: it is the same as that in teeth, the same that old people used to cure constipation; it goes in and goes out of the organism. There is no relation with the mercury in Japan (Minamata). . . . It does not contaminate. Even "garimpeiros" [goldminers] who inhale mercury vapours, they are not poisoned. . . . We will measure mercury levels in the waterways. I challenge someone to show me a person, just one person, contaminated by mercury in the Amazon. . . . The point is, as they (ecologists and government) cannot do anything against a citizen pursuing a better way of living, they make up this story of river pollution and shut down all "garimpos." These ecologist "boys" do not realize they are being used as political instruments.[2]

In 1991, an internationally recognized leader for the human rights of the Yanomami, Davi Kopenawa Yanomami, who was awarded the Global 500 Prize of the United Nations Environmental Program and spoke to the UN, stated:

> My Yanomami people now, they see what is happening to our community, and they see what is happening to our relatives in other communities. They are terrified by the miners, and by the [polluted] rivers.

> The miners invaded our reserve and came to our communities feigning friendship; they lied to us, they tricked us Indians, and we were taken in. Then their numbers grew; many more arrived, and they began bringing in machinery that polluted the river. The pollution killed the fish and the shrimp, everything that lived in our rivers.[3]

These are just two of the many contradictory voices in an extremely complex, difficult, and ugly arena of desperate conflict. Other miners and indigenes as well as anthropologists, politicians, officials, missionaries, environmentalists, and advocates of

Leslie E. Sponsel is a professor and Director of the Ecological Anthropology Concentration in the Department of Anthropology at the University of Hawaii, Honolulu, HI 96822. He can also be reached via email at (sponsel@hawaii.edu).

human rights are among the numerous voices. Indeed, it would take several books to place these in context and sort through their claims and counterclaims.[4]

This chapter focuses on one aspect of this conflict—the human and environmental impact of the use of mercury for mining gold by the informal mining sector. The ancient Roman god Mercury was considered to be a master thief, among other things. This fits well the role of mercury, the metal used by most gold miners throughout the Amazon today. Not only does mercury help steal gold, but it also steals the health of human populations and ecosystems, and will continue to do so far into the future.

Gold Rush

For over 6,000 years gold has been one source of wealth, prestige, and power. Greed for gold was a pivotal concern in the discovery, exploration, and colonization of the New World by European kingdoms. Explorers searched for a kingdom of gold, El Dorado. Colonies and states developed principally to exploit gold and other resources. In the process, entire peoples, societies, and environments were degraded and destroyed. This holocaust continues today, and the Amazon is one of its last frontiers.[5]

Brazil has experienced gold rushes since the 17th century, and in the mid-18th century it was actually the world's biggest producer of gold. However, since 1980 the Amazon has been the stage for the largest gold rush ever. During the 1980s gold production in the Brazilian Amazon exceeded US$2 billion per year. Serra Pelada (Stripped Mountain), a huge, deep, open-pit mine worked by up to 100,000 miners, is likely the richest single gold discovery of this century. Since 1980 this mine has produced over half a billion dollars, with an average of a ton per month of gold. The legends of Serra Pelada include the overnight discovery by one team of miners of US$8 million worth of gold, including a single nugget supposedly weighing 120 kg. This mine is a symbol of hope for poor miners throughout the Amazon Basin who would like to become instant millionaires, and it has even stimulated some confidence in Brazil's ability to repay its enormous international debt.[6]

Amazonian gold is not, however, confined to Brazilian borders. By the late 1980s some 30,000 people were prospecting and mining in southern Venezuela. An estimated 4.5 million people are involved directly or indirectly in gold mining in the Amazonian region, working some 2,000 mining sites scattered over 250,000 sq km. Major mining centers include the Gurupí (Maranahao), Serra Pelada (Pará), Cumaru (Pará), Mato Grosso, Tapajós (Pará/Amazonas), River Madeira (Rondonia), and Roraima.[7] Much of this mining activity occurs illegally in the traditional homelands and protected territories of indigenous peoples.

The timing of this modern gold rush reflects not so much any new discoveries as a sharp increase in the price of gold. During the 1970s the price of an ounce of gold rose steadily from US$35 to around US$300. During the 1980s the price ranged from US$300 to US$500, although it briefly soared to US$850 in January 1980. Today the price is still substantially higher than in the 1970s.[8] An increase in production followed the increase in price; thus, between 1980 and 1992 world gold production rose by 78 percent. In Brazil, analysts estimate that about 100 tons per year of gold were produced during the 1980s; however, this is only a rough estimate because the activity is illegal

Giant concrete statue honoring gold miners, erected in the town of Boa Vista in northern Brazil. Photograph by Linda Rabben.

and most of the gold is sold in the black market to avoid taxes.[9] It should be noted that various other factors also influenced the timing of the gold rush. For example, "Coincident with the sharp rise in gold prices was a severe drought that struck northeastern Brazil beginning in 1979. The failure of the Brazilian government to provide drought relief and to develop alternative programs for the unemployed spurred a massive migration to the Amazon Basin in search of new lands and gold."[10]

Both need and greed have driven the invasion of some 300,000 to 1 million miners into the Amazon of Brazil. Many miners are poor, landless, and suffering from hard economic times, including rampant inflation, and they lack other economic opportunities or alternatives for economic and social mobility. Many simply pursue mining as a seasonal alternative when their farming or ranching activities allow. Informal mining has probably had a greater impact on the economy than formal mining, because the profits have generated investments and galvanized local and regional economies in a diversity of ways. An estimated three to four million people are indirectly involved in mining as family members, storekeepers, boat operators, airplane pilots, mechanics, carpenters, traders, cooks, prostitutes, drug dealers, and so on.[11]

The invasion of the Amazon during the last two decades by more than a million gold miners has been an orchestrated, rather than spontaneous, gold rush. Gold mining in the Amazon is part of a largely hidden agenda of nation state governments and military, a combined geopolitical and economic development strategy to conquer, control, integrate, and exploit the Amazon.[12] This is part of a global process that is a continuation of European colonization and industrialization, but with some new components. One common denominator is the exploitation of minerals—the "geological imperative," which Davis and Mathews define as a:

. . . search for mineral and petroleum resources . . . a unique historical phenomenon related to the specific distribution of wealth and power which presently exists in the world. The chief elements in this phenomena are large multinational mineral and energy corporations, and the powerful governments and international lending and development institutions on which they depend. Their *raison d'etre* is profit-maximization and private economic gain."[13]

By the 1970s the geological imperative led the military government of Brazil, mainly through its Department of Mineral Production, to initiate a series of development projects, including a huge aerial survey to detect and map major mineral deposits in the Amazon (Project Radam), and numerous expeditions undertaken by a virtual army of geologists, mining engineers, and other specialists. This campaign was in collaboration with the U.S. Geological Survey and supported by the U.S. Agency for International Development as well as the Brazilian government. Project Radam revealed that the Amazon had one of the most diverse and richest mineral profiles on the planet. Among other sites discovered was the famous mountain of iron, Serra dos Carajas, the mining of which became a US$3 billion joint venture between the state-owned Companhia Vale do Rio Doce and the U.S. Steel Corporation.[14]

Closely connected with the mineral survey and exploration projects was the development of infrastructure that would facilitate mining in the Amazon, namely a network of roads, airstrips, military bases, hydroelectric dams, agricultural colonization schemes, and so on. These activities were part of the Northern Trench Project (Calha Norte), a military master plan started around 1986 and initially kept secret from the public and even the Congress of Brazil. One of the main aims was to "Brazilianize" this zone of the Amazon, a strip 6,500 km long and 150 km wide. This was supposed to help the military control the border security, including combating drug traffic and guerrilla incursions from neighboring countries. One of the highways, the 4,000 km long Northern Perimeter Road, was planned to run near the circumference of Brazil's border with the neighboring countries of Surinam, Guyana, Venezuela, Colombia, and Peru. According to Linda Rabben, an anthropologist specializing in Brazil who is associated with the Rainforest Foundation and Amnesty International, ". . . the Calha Norte program seems ineffective at achieving its stated objectives but all too efficient at facilitating devastation of the environment and destruction of the Indians."[15] (In Venezuela a parallel but short-lived project was termed the Conquest of the South [La Conquista del Sur], but it has recently been revived as the Project for Sustainable Development of the South [Proyecto de Desarrollo Sustentable del Sur].)[16]

These infrastructural developments provided the springboard for the seemingly spontaneous invasion of "illegal" small-scale miners throughout the Amazon of Brazil. The strike at Serra Pelada occurred because people were able to enter and explore the region, thanks to the Transamazon Highway (completed just a few years before the gold strike). The airport in Boa Vista, which had been enlarged by the military for "national security" reasons, served in reality as a transportation hub for airplanes carrying miners, with their equipment and supplies, into Yanomami territory. At the same time as the military was improving transportation infrastructure, FUNAI (the Brazilian National Indian Foundation—the agency in charge of protecting and assisting the indigenous population of Brazil), was administering mineral leases on indigenous lands. In some cases official announcements by the government publicized the existence of gold in the Amazon.[17]

Part of the hidden agenda of the government was surprisingly and candidly exposed when, in March 1975, General Fernando Ramos Pereira, then governor of the northern province of Roraima, stated to the Brazilian press: "I am of the opinion that an area as rich as this—with gold, diamonds, and uranium—cannot afford the luxury of conserving a half a dozen Indian tribes who are holding back the development of Brazil."[18] This statement proved prophetic for many indigenous societies—including the Yanomami.[19]

Mining and Mercury Contamination

The Amazon region contains some of the most ancient geological formations on the planet, the bedrock dating back some 2.8 billion years. During the last billion years, mountains have been uplifted, and then reduced by weathering and erosion to flat plains and highland remnants through several landscape cycles.[20] The Andes are the most recent uplift. Gold is found in two basic types of deposits. Lode deposits are concentrations of gold in solid rock, usually as veins. Placer deposits are found in sand, gravel, and other sediments associated with streams and rivers. They contain particles of gold weathered and eroded from a lode.

Lode deposits are mined by tunneling or sinking a shaft, and this can be a major operation requiring the organization and resources of a regular mining company. In contrast, placer deposits can be worked by simply screening or panning sediments with water along a stream or river. This accounts for only about 17 percent of the gold production.[21] About 83 percent is produced through using heavy equipment for hydraulic techniques. High-pressure hoses wash away the sediment, which is channeled into troughs or sluices. These are riffled to catch the heavy particles of gold. River beds may also be dredged or vacuumed with huge pumps from floating rafts. Prospectors often follow placer deposits upstream to the lode.[22]

Gold mining causes localized deforestation, biodiversity reduction, game depletion and displacement, mercury and other pollution, river and stream bank destruction and siltation, and decline and degradation of fisheries. Enormous amounts of waste result from the mining because huge amounts of material must be worked to extract the gold—one of the scarcest metals on earth. On the average, about nine *tons* of waste are left for every *ounce* of gold extracted. Placer mining is inevitably associated with streams and rivers to have ready access to water for working them, thus this type of mining has a disproportionately large impact on aquatic ecosystems. About two cubic meters of sediments enter water courses per gram of gold extracted by miners. Mining wastes can silt water courses, reduce sunlight penetration and thereby diminish photosynthesis and productivity of aquatic plants, clog the gills of fish, and so on. Also, the water may be undrinkable for tens of kilometers downstream. The other metals associated with gold, plus the chemicals used in the processing, may pollute soils and water bodies for decades or even centuries.[23] Human waste in water courses is yet another pollution problem.

While cattle ranching, pioneering agriculture, logging, roads, and hydroelectric dams are the main causes of deforestation in the Amazon, mining also contributes, in at least two ways. Even though deforestation as a direct result of the mining is very localized, soil and drainage is so degraded that it is difficult for forest regeneration. In addition, mining profits may be invested in economic schemes like cattle ranching, which involve deforestation far from mining sites.[24]

Mercury can be considered the most toxic metal. One of the most pernicious and longest lasting consequences of gold mining is mercury contamination, yet until the last two decades relatively little scientific research had been conducted to document and assess its consequences on human health and ecosystems. Furthermore, little is known about the dynamics of mercury contamination in tropical compared to temperate ecosystems. However, mercury will inevitably follow the basic laws of ecology—namely, that everything is interconnected, is interdependent, and must go somewhere.[25]

Since the 16th century, mercury has been used by miners for extracting silver and gold throughout the Americas. It has been estimated that silver mining in Latin America from 1587 to 1820 released into the atmosphere alone about 180 to 705 tons of mercury annually.[26] Today worldwide, about 400 to 500 tons of mercury are released into the environment every year by small-scale gold miners. Such miners introduce about 90 to 120 tons per year of mercury into the ecosystems of just the Brazilian portion of the Amazon.[27] This is a substantial portion of the global anthropogenic load (releases of mercury from all sources, not just gold mining)—estimated to range around 1,000 to 6,000 tons per year of mercury.[28]

Liquid, elemental, or metallic mercury (Hg) is used to amalgamate (alloy or agglutinate) with smaller gold particles (Au_2Hg, Au_3Hg, and Au_4Hg) so that they will be heavier and more likely trapped in the riffles of sluices. The liquid mercury is poured over crushed rock or sediments. Then the amalgam of mercury and gold is separated from remaining waste by hand. Cloth at the bottom, often a shirt, is also used to collect the amalgam. Some of this mercury is washed away with the water into streams and rivers, some settling in the sediments. The next step is to heat the amalgam in a pan with a blowtorch to vaporize the mercury as a white gas, thereby leaving gold. The mercury vapors go into the local atmosphere and with rainfall return to the surrounding vegetation, soils, and waters, the amount depending on the level of dust particles and humidity. For the production of 1 kg of gold, about 1.32 kg of metallic mercury is used, with 0.72 kg lost to the atmosphere as vapor and 0.60 kg (almost half) lost directly to the stream or river as metallic mercury.[29] Later the gold is again subjected to heating with a blowtorch to remove the remaining mercury in the shops where the miners sell it. Inside these shops and within 100 meters around them, high levels of mercury contamination occur—shop owners may show higher levels of metallic mercury in their hair than even the miners.[30]

The Amazon is essentially an inland sea during the wet season, and aquatic ecosystems are sinks that can accumulate and concentrate mercury and other pollutants. The metallic or inorganic mercury from gold mining is eventually deposited in the soil and sediments of water courses. Indeed, puddles of mercury are common on soils and rock surfaces at the shores of mining areas.[31] Metallic mercury (Hg) becomes organic, or methylated (that is, CH_3Hg+), by microorganisms, in fish guts, and through other biological routes.

While the waters of the Amazon differ in their chemistry, they are rich in metals like iron and manganese, which stimulate methylation of inorganic mercury, as do the high humic acids and overall acidity of black waters in particular. This type of water may be especially liable to high levels of mercury contamination. Curiously, the Tapajós River changed from clear to white water with extensive siltation from mining upstream. This change in water types would in turn profoundly alter the biological and cultural ecology of the area. At the same time, it should be noted that demethylation (when methylmercury is transformed into metallic mercury and methane by microorganisms) also occurs, but apparently at a slower rate than methylation.[32]

Mercury can enter the food chain in various ways: from water through respiration, by absorption of water from the body surface, and by ingestion of food such as through bottom-feeding fish. The mercury is increasingly concentrated at higher levels of the food chain (biomagnification), as when fish eat other fish. The larger or older a fish, the higher the levels of mercury concentration. In turn, other animals and people who consume large amounts of fish in their diet can be contaminated. In the Amazon River, piscivorous animals (fish-eating) include birds like heron and kingfishers as well as caiman (alligator), river turtles, freshwater dolphins, river otters, and even some species of wild cats. Several are already endangered species. Mercury may also cause reproductive failure in animals. Huge fish kills have already been reported in the waters of Pará and Mato Grosso in 1985–86, probably as a result of mercury poisoning. Thus, mercury contamination must be added to the growing number of threats to the rich biodiversity in the Amazon, such as the various causes of deforestation. This region has the highest diversity of freshwater fish in the world, with an estimated 2,500 to 3,000 species.[33] Fish in turn are part of a larger network of ecological relationships that are also being disrupted.

Inorganic mercury can attach to particles of sediments in water courses and be transported by currents over vast distances. Likewise, fish migrations can extend over hundreds or even thousands of kilometers. In such ways, mercury contamination can be spread surprisingly far beyond the original point of pollution.[34]

Mercury contamination can be detected and measured in the ecosystem (air, water, sediments, plants, animals, and especially fish) as well as humans (hair, blood, and urine). Scalp hair is the best indicator in humans. Mercury concentrations in human hair reflect blood concentrations of mercury at the moment of hair formation, and therefore hair strands provide a short time record of mercury contamination.[35] It is important to consider total mercury contamination, both the metallic and methyl forms, since they have different pathways and symptoms. Certain species may be especially good indicators to monitor levels of mercury contamination over time—for example, the floating plant *Salvinia auriculata*; the fish Tucunaré (*Chicla temensis*) and pescada (*Plagioscion squamosissimus*).[36] Mercury appears in sediment cores from lakes, swamps, and other contexts that can be used to reconstruct the historical ecology of a region.[37] The global background level for mercury in surface sediments is 0.4 ppm (parts per million), while World Health Organization[38] safety standards for mercury levels in soil and sediments is 2 ppm, in fish 0.5 ppm, and in human hair 0.6 ppm.

The Tapajós River basin is the oldest (30 years) and most productive gold mining region in the Brazilian Amazon. Research has revealed high and widespread mercury contamination in the upper Tapajós. Fish contained up to 3.82 ppm of mercury, and most fish upstream as well as some downstream exceeded the allowable limit of 0.5 ppm for Brazil.[39] A longitudinal study of hair samples from several fishing villages in the Tapajós area revealed fairly constant and continuous exposure to methylmercury over the last few years. Mundurucú miners had mercury levels up to 31.8 ppm.

However, no cases of the classical Minamata disease from organic mercury poisoning were discovered so far. Another longitudinal study of 12 mining areas revealed higher levels of metallic mercury contamination in gold shop workers than in miners, and higher levels of methylmercury contamination in riverine fishers than in miners.[40]

The Tucuruí reservoir in Pará, Brazil, is 250 km downstream along the Tocantins River from Serra Pelada and other mining sites. Mercury emissions from Serra Pelada have been estimated at 590 tons between 1980 and 86. The Tucuruí reservoir is thoroughly polluted with mercury from the gold mining. Mercury levels in fish exceeded the allowable limit of 0.5ppm, the highest being in predatory fish at 1.3 ppm. Hair samples from fishers in the reservoir area ranged from 0.9 to 240 ppm with a mean value in the main reservoir of 65 ppm. This is certainly high enough to eventually cause health problems, putting many thousands of local people at risk. Furthermore, fish from the reservoir are sold in towns, including in the delta of the Amazon 300 km away.[41]

There has been mining in the Madeira River area for about 15 years. Research reveals that mercury contamination levels in Madeira exceed values for global (0.4 ppm) and background (0.1 ppm) sediments as well as safety (0.5 ppm) by a factor of 25, 100, and 4, respectively. Even fish 180 km downstream from the mining show mercury levels above the safety limit.[42]

These are just a few of the studies, many by independent investigators, that are accumulating to demonstrate widespread and serious levels of mercury pollution in mining areas and downstream in many parts of the Amazon. The delayed symptoms of mercury poisoning should be appearing within a few years, depending on the length of exposure, and these will likewise be progressively documented as research accumulates.

Fish is the most efficient and cheapest form of high-quality protein, and also the only regular source, for millions of poor people in villages, towns, and cities along the rivers of the Amazon. Mercury contamination of some waters and fisheries could jeopardize the income as well as nutrition and health of masses of people in the Amazon. The economic loss for commercial fisheries could be enormous. For instance, since the 1970s the piramutaba catfish (*Brachyplatysoma vaillantii*) has been the single most important species of fish exported from the Amazon. By 1980 the annual harvest value was US$13 million, but it has since declined to US$3 million annually because of depletion. Of course the Amazon is an enormous region, but the fisheries of the Great Lakes of the United States collapsed because of health concerns over mercury contamination and despite an abundance of fish. Contamination could well have numerous other serious negative impacts, because fish are an extremely important part of the cultural ecology of many indigenous and peasant societies in the Amazon.[43]

Gold mining has even contaminated supposedly protected areas, including one of the world's largest wetlands, the Pantanal in Western Mato Grosso. Around 140,000 sq km, it is twice the size of Ireland. It has high biodiversity, with migratory waterfowl and other species. In Pantanal wildlife researchers found 12 ppm of mercury, which is 24 times the level (0.5 ppm) considered safe by the World Health Organization (WHO).[44]

The health hazards of using mercury have been known since ancient times. For example, in the days of ancient Rome prisoners and slaves were forced to mine the rich cinnabar deposits at Almadén in Spain where their life expectancy was only three years.[45] In more recent history the horrible tragedy of people and animals in the small fishing village of Minamata Bay on Kyushu Island in Japan brought the problem of mercury contamination to world attention. Also it revealed that metallic mercury could be methylated by microorganisms and become concentrated in the food chain. There in 1953 people first observed cats developing nervous tremors and then "dancing" that often ended when they jumped into the sea to drown. Eventually similar tremors were observed in other animals—dogs, pigs, birds, and fish. People were next. (Cats showed symptoms earlier than people because they consume more fish for their body weight and are more sensitive to methylmercury.) Subsequent medical and other research identified the cause as methylmercury poisoning from water pollution starting in the 1930s from a factory on the bay. Although mercury is an extremely toxic metal, clinical symptoms of mercury poisoning in humans may not appear for years, more than a decade in Minamata. By the end of 1987, 2,840 individuals had been officially certified as Minamata disease victims, and 999 of them had died. An additional 5,000 with various neurological complaints awaited medical examination and certification. Around 1966 mercury levels in fish were 35 ppm, but with cleanup measures they have since declined to 0.7 ppm, which is still above the 0.3 ppm limit set by the Japan Environmental Agency.[46]

Metallic mercury contamination in the human body can occur in many ways: inhalation into the respiratory system of vapors; absorption through the skin while handling slurries of mercury and gold; ingestion with subsequent absorption in the intestinal tract when dust that is carrying mercury lands on the hands, food, or eating utensils; and so on. There are also several indirect pathways of mercury contamination; however, the principal one is the regular consumption of contaminated foods, the most common being fish contaminated with methylmercury from polluted waters. Obviously gold miners and buyers are likely to suffer direct contamination with metallic mercury, while the masses of poor people in river villages and towns who depend on fish as their only alternative for cheap, high-quality protein suffer indirect contamination with the much more dangerous form methylmercury.

There is a different combination of symptoms of mercury poisoning, depending on whether it is metallic (inorganic, elemental) mercury or methylmercury, and whether it is acute or chronic mercury poisoning. There are also differences depending on age class—fetus, children, or adults—which in turn reflects differences in body size, nutritional needs for growth and development, absorption rates, and physiological vulnerability. Depending on the pathway, inorganic mercury is less of a threat because the prevention of poisoning is simpler and symptoms may be reversible. It is poorly absorbed in the gastrointestinal tract, but readily absorbed through the alveolar membrane in the lungs with inhalation. It accumulates in the kidney, liver, and intestines; chronic toxicity can lead to kidney failure. On the other hand, methylmercury is readily transported by the circulatory system and crosses the blood-brain barrier where it accumulates in brain cells, leading to brain damage and eventually death.

During the latent period in which mercury accumulates in the body, the afflicted person shows no symptoms. Only later do these gradually develop, and early on they may be hard to distinguish from other causes such as malaria. By the time the poisoning is noticeable, irreversible damage has already occurred. However, with gradual intoxication it may only be possible to diagnose mercury poisoning as the cause of death after an autopsy.

Among the many symptoms of chronic poisoning by methylmercury are skin irritations, low fever, headaches, nausea, diarrhea, fatigue, insomnia and irritability, marked decline in sensory acuity (vision, hearing, smell, touch) and eventually blindness, loss of ability to speak properly, memory loss, premature senility, manic depression, kidney problems, crippling and severe tremors, brain damage, and death. Some of these symptoms can result from other causes, ranging from a hangover or minor ailments to malaria. However, in the case of chronic poisoning by mercury, the deterioration gets progressively worse. With less frequent or chronic exposure and lower doses of methylmercury, the symptoms appear more gradually.

Pregnant women may be spared from poisoning because the methylmercury rapidly crosses the placenta to accumulate in the fetus, which reduces the level in the mother. Thus mercury concentrations can be higher in the fetus than in the mother and the latter may even appear normal. Still births, spontaneous abortions, gross birth defects, paralysis, physical impairment, and mental retardation are among the abnormalities that result from mercury poisoning of the fetus.[47] A child weighing 20 kg need only eat regularly 10 to 20 grams of a contaminated carnivorous fish to develop mercury poisoning, given the daily intake limits set by the WHO.[48]

The first longitudinal clinical study of the health hazards of mercury in the Amazon is based on monitoring, for five years (1986–1991), 55 patients with symptoms of mercury poisoning from the Tapajós, Pará/Amazonas, region of Brazil. Of these, 33 had direct occupational exposure to mercury at mines and in gold shops with a mean of 13.1 years (range 2–44). For gold shop workers and miners, respectively, mean blood and urine levels of mercury were 5.1 and 61.0 ppm, and 2.2 and 35.4 ppm. The higher level for shop workers may reflect the fact that they do more burning of mercury than miners, and in an enclosed area with variable ventilation. Furthermore, even urbanites with no direct exposure to the gold industry also showed elevated levels of mercury: a resident living above a gold shop had a blood level of 5.6 ppm. Normal levels of mercury should not exceed 1.5 ppm in the blood and 15.0 ppm in the urine for unexposed patients. Thus, based on the means the subjects in this study showed abnormal mercury levels elevated by a factor of 1.5–3.4 or more in the blood and 2.7–4.0 in the urine. But some individuals had much higher levels. Patients evidenced some combination of the following symptoms: dizziness, headache, palpitations, tremor, numbness, insomnia, dyspnea (difficult breathing), nervousness, poor vision, diminished appetite, forgetfulness, weakness, hair loss, cramps, chest pain, abdominal pain, fatigue, pruritus (itching), impotence, weight loss, and edema (fluid build up in tissue spaces or body cavities).[49]

Such elevated levels and symptoms, present even in persons not directly involved in the gold industry, are obviously a matter for serious concern by government, health personnel, and the public. Furthermore, because extensive medical studies have not been made on people involved in or impacted by gold mining in the Amazon, and because the symptoms of mercury poisoning are readily confused with other diseases (especially malaria, which is common), ailments and death may often be attributed to something other than mercury, though it might well be the real cause.[50]

As if mercury poisoning were not enough, it should be noted that mining has also contributed to the development of other health hazards—drugs, prostitution (even among children), and violence are part of the daily life of boom towns. Syphilis is common and AIDS is likely spreading. Since the miners are a highly mobile population, no doubt they are spreading such diseases over a very wide area, including to indigenous communities.[51]

Responses: Indigenes

The responses of indigenous societies to gold mining vary with their specific circumstances, but in general they fall into two broad categories, depending on whether they have had sustained experience with the national society. Those like the Yanomami who have had very little previous contact are extremely vulnerable and may be devastated. Those like the Mundurucú who have had substantial previous contact are more adaptable and may themselves engage in mining to some degree. However, in either case there are many serious negative consequences. Indeed, tuberculosis and other effects of earlier mining booms may linger for decades.[52]

Yanomami

The Yanomami have been an independent population for around 2,000 years, according to evidence from genetics and linguistics. Obviously they had an adaptive and sustainable society in the tropical forest. Until recent decades, they were one of the more isolated and traditional indigenous societies remaining in the Amazon, and, for that matter, in the world. However, all of that quickly changed in Brazil in the early 1970s when a portion of the Northern Perimeter Highway (Perimetral Norte) penetrated nearly 225 kilometers into the southern portion of the ancestral territory of the indigenous nation of the Yanomami. As predicted, the road construction precipitated the first major crisis for the Yanomami: the spread of epidemic diseases and a population crash in contacted villages. But even worse was the illegal invasion of 40,000 to 100,000 gold miners in the 1980s, which peaked in 1987. The situation in Yanomami territory in Venezuela has been deteriorating rapidly as well.[53]

The Yanomami's lack of sustained contact experience means that they have not had the opportunity to develop immunological resistance against many western diseases, thus these quickly grow to become devastating epidemics. Furthermore, the miners have inadvertently introduced new diseases like tuberculosis and such significantly increased previous diseases as malaria and onchocerciasis (African river blindness). Through prostitution the miners have even introduced disease purposefully to the Yanomami, such as venereal diseases and possibly even AIDS.

In Brazil from 1988–1995 some 2,280 Yanomami died, about a quarter of the population, as a direct result of the invasion of miners, leaving somewhere between 9,000 and 10,000 Yanomami.[54] In Venezuela, government census data indicates 2,955 deaths, a decline from 1982 to 1992 of from 12,082 to 9,127 Yanomami (including Sanema), or 24.5 percent.[55] Illness and death on such a massive scale are severely disrupting the population, economy, society, psychology, and religion of the Yanomami. They are increasingly becoming an endangered people threatened with biological and cultural extinction.[56]

On November 22, 1993, in Venezuela, newspapers reported some 19 Sanema (Yanomami subgroup) dead and 26 others sick from mercury poisoning, although this has yet to be verified by the government, which has never released a report of its investigation to the public. (Some rumors suggest that there are other causes or that the purported disaster never even happened.)

Analysis of hair samples collected in 1990 from Yanomami in gold mining areas in Brazil revealed mercury levels of 1.40–8.14 ppm compared to various standard limits of 5.0–6.0 ppm.[57] Research on Yanomami in Venezuela prior to the gold mining invasion showed hair levels of 0.3–1.4 ppm.[58] Thus, it appears that sectors of the Yanomami may be experiencing some degree of mercury contamination as the result of mining. This should not be any surprise, since over 200 separate mining sites existed from 1986 to 1992 in Yanomami territory in Brazil.[59]

Beyond the indirect violence of disease, the miners have given or traded guns to Yanomami in order to aggravate tensions, conflicts, and violence between villagers and villages. There have also been violent attacks on the Yanomami by miners. The most notorious incident is the 1994 Hashimu massacre in which at least 12 Yanomami were brutally killed: an elderly man, two elderly women, one young woman, three adolescent girls, three boys, and two baby girls. A blind elderly women was kicked to death and one of the babies was knifed. Those not killed immediately by gunfire were hacked to death with bush knives. Then the corpses were mutilated and dismembered. Although the murderers have been identified, they have never been brought to justice.[60] It is surprising that the Yanomami have been relatively restrained in their violence against the miners, but this may not continue.

Because of the deterioration of their economy and society, some Yanomami now go hungry and even beg for food from miners. For the first time Yanomami are experiencing poverty, inequality, theft, alcoholism, and prostitution. The Yanomami simply do not have a world view, a unified political and military organization, or knowledge to effectively confront the sudden mining invasion with its multitude of deleterious manifestations. They sorely need outside help at the national and international levels. A few human rights advocacy organizations like CCPY (Commission for the Creation of the Yanomami Park, now Pro-Yanomami Commission) have been providing some of the needed help, but they are severely constrained by limited personnel and resources as well as government obstacles.

In short, multiple factors that interact in synergy are attacking all levels and aspects of Yanomami life, rendering them literally an endangered people. In 1992 the Brazilian government demarcated the Yanomami territory; however, this legal and physical process has not been followed by the political will to effectively enforce it.[61] Government intervention to expel miners from indigenous reserves and regular surveillance to prevent them from returning are required.[62] The Brazilian and Venezuelan governments have not only failed to protect and advance the human rights of the Yanomami, including the provision of adequate health care, but also they have violated their basic human rights. The government of Brazil, and to a lesser degree that of Venezuela, have allowed, and in some ways even facilitated, the entrance of miners into the territory of the Yanomami nation. This is a clear case of ethnocide, genocide, and ecocide.[63]

At the same time, it should be clear that there is nothing necessarily inevitable in the degradation and destruction of indigenes and ecosystems through contact with "civilization" and "economic development"; instead this is a moral choice of policy makers in government, bank, and corporate offices in Brazil, the United States, and other countries, as well as a result of public apathy.[64]

Mundurucú

In sharp contrast to the Yanomami, the Mundurucú, peoples of the savanna and forest of the upper Tapajós River in Brazil, have long been involved in small-scale extraction of resources for trade, initially tapping natural rubber trees for the latex, and in recent decades occasionally doing gold mining. Tapping and later mining allowed the Mundurucú to obtain some of the western things they came to value including tools and medicines. Until recently they retained their traditional exchange system centered on reciprocity. With the development of rubber tapping in the 19th century the Mundurucú simply added a barter-credit system to their new patron-client relationship with traders and missionaries. However, gold mining and money have been not simply additive, but transformative too. The very nature of social relations as well as their economy has changed profoundly. Even food and time have become monetized.

The mining started developing around 1959 when gold was discovered in and near the Mundurucú reservation. Many Mundurucú moved to the upper Tapajós River and to the Cururú River to small, temporary camps for mining for several weeks or months each year. Thus, mining did not completely replace traditional subsistence and economic activities like hunting and swidden farming. Indeed, the younger men of the community are more likely to engage in mining.

The miners usually pan alone or in pairs scattered along widely separated streams. Stream beds may be dug up, but hydraulic hoses and other machinery are not used. However, mercury is used to amalgamate the gold particles. The Mundurucú miners do not have the typical miners attitude of quickly getting in, striking it rich, and getting out. Moreover, other sources of cash are also exploited, including rubber tapping and wage labor.[65] It seems likely that these factors combine to reduce the environmental impact of Mundurucú mining.

Amarakaeri

Gold mining first came to the Madre de Dios area of southeastern Peru in the 1930s and again since the 1970s. The Amarakaeri have integrated gold mining into their economy while maintaining their sustainable subsistence in their ecosystems and other aspects of their cultural identity. Their small-scale mining of placer deposits of gold focuses on sandy beaches that are exposed in the dry season; they move inland during the wet season. They use a large metal sieve mounted on a sloping wooden board. Water is supplied by hand-carried buckets and in some cases by pumps. Mercury is used as well. The gold production is organized following traditional social criteria that include clan affiliation, close kin, and people with a special exchange relationship. Usually the same men who hunt together also mine together. Unlike other miners in the area, the Amarakaeri have a sustainable subsistence economy, maintain legal right to their ancestral land, use gold mining as a complementary component of their economy, and do not attempt to maximize their profits.[66]

Kayapo

The Kayapo of Brazil are another pointed case. Their Cumaru mine is one of the few instances where an indigenous society has managed to maintain control of the mineral wealth in their territory and benefit from it, although also with serious costs. In 1980 some 10,000 gold miners invaded the Gorotire Kayapo reserve. The Kayapo asked for government intervention and negotiated for a 10 percent royalty on mine production. Initially their earnings were invested in demarcating their lands. They have also developed a video project to archive their ceremonies and other aspects of their culture. However, this success story is tempered by some tragic consequences. For instance, a survey of Kayapo children in 1988 revealed a mean level of mercury in their blood of 4.74 ppm, whereas 2 ppm is an acceptable upper limit. Miners working upstream at Cumaru have 4.97 ppm in their blood.[67]

Ye'kuana

In the Upper Orinoco River region of the Amazon of southern Venezuela, the Ye'kuana have exercised the fundamental human right to self-determination by demarcating with large circles in the forest, to indicate their ancestral territorial boundaries, and then mapping these with a Global Positioning System receiver in a small airplane. They are also documenting their history of settlement, land, and resource use. This is an initiative to document their historic land rights and gain legal title from the government. It is also an attempt to secure their territory before the gold miners invading Yanomami territory move further north into Ye'kuana territory. This is an extremely promising model in applied cultural ecology that could be developed and implemented by other indigenous groups according to their specific situation.[68]

Response: Miners

The response of the miners to controversy surrounding their illegal invasion of indigenous territory, mercury contamination, and other problems has been mixed. They have organized into unions and become a significant force in provincial elections and politics. For some, the miners represent frontier heroes, as evidenced by the giant concrete statue of a gold miner erected in Boa Vista (see photograph). For the most part, however, the miners have tended to ignore, deny, or minimize the human and environmental problems they create, a stance that is reinforced by government action or lack of action. Miners have rarely been held for criminal actions, and there has been little effort to educate them about the human and environmental dimensions of their gold mining in the Amazon. Thus, cultural misunderstanding is a significant factor contributing to violence between indigenes and miners (including in the aforementioned Hashimu massacre).[69]

If the miners were willing to accept lower profits, they could mine without mercury; most recognize this possibility but reject it. If they run out of mercury they will even stop operations until it is procured.[70] Otherwise, relatively simple and inexpensive technological measures could be taken to minimize exposure to mercury and also to environmental pollution. The miners could use a face mask, gloves, and a retort while vaporizing mercury. They could avoid vaporizing mercury in a hut or kitchen and in pans that are also used for cooking. Retorts would reduce mercury lost in the burning of the amalgam to under 5 percent. Gold shops could use proper mercury-condensing exhaust hoods and other simple precautions.[71]

Naturally, it would be easier to try to clean up mining sites where mercury contamination is concentrated than to clean up sediments and water where it is widely dispersed. Several remedial measures have been proposed as possibilities to treat polluted sites: adding selenium or lime, covering a site with absorbent materials, cementing the site with iron scrap, and dredging followed by mercury and residual gold extraction. For instance, one idea is to cover each one-acre site of pollution with seven tons of wool, although this is biodegradable so it is not a long-term solution. Ground-up car tires and discarded, shredded car bodies are other absorbent coverings. Another is lateritic crusts, which are already available in the natural environment.[72] While some of these measures may work in certain areas, in general it appears that practical logistics, the labor and amounts of material required, expense, miner apathy, ecological impact, and the possibility of introducing additional hazards are factors that would usually render these measures problematic. For instance, selenium is toxic.[73]

There are no federal laws to regulate the use of mercury in Brazil.[74] It would seem that the government could regulate the importation and sale of mercury, which miners can readily purchase in shops that sell gold mining equipment and supplies and even in pharmacies, groceries, and other stores. Most of the mercury now comes from The Netherlands, Germany, and England.[75] However, David Cleary, who has studied gold miners, believes that a ban on mercury would simply make its use clandestine and thus more difficult to regulate.[76] He also asserts that it would be practically impossible to enforce a ban on mercury, given the widespread and mobile distribution of miners in remote and difficult terrain. Indeed, one attempt by the Brazilian government to restrict the sale of mercury to miners simply led to an explosion of smuggling and black market sales.[77]

Ironically, in some ways the gold miners have also been neglected in this crisis, even though their activity precipitated it and is usually illegal. Miners face an alien environment, disease, natural hazards like poisonous snakes, and violence from other miners and also possibly from indigenes. Miners have inadequate or no health care.[78] Sanitation is a problem. Miners are a hundred times more likely to get malaria than other workers in the Amazon because the mining creates ponds of water that provide breeding grounds for mosquitoes.[79] According to Mallas and Benedicto: "Many persons get sick and die in the jungle before having a chance to see a doctor—no doubt there have been many deaths by mercury poisoning and thousands of persons are probably affected."[80] There is no law and order maintained by federal or provincial governmental authorities in this frontier region of the Amazon. Also, most of the miners are not getting rich. Indeed, they are often exploited by others who finance, equip, and supply their activities. Conditions of semislavery, including child labor, exist in some mining camps.[81]

Increased attention to the needs, problems, interests, and rights of the miners might lead to eventually improving the situation for all parties concerned. For example, if both the health and the health care of the miners were better, this would reduce the health problems for peoples with whom the miners interact, like the Yanomami.[82]

Response: Government

There has been a tendency for the government at the federal and provincial levels to simply ignore, deny, or minimize the problems of gold mining in the Amazon. However, on at least one occasion, April 1, 1989, in its Our Nature Project (Nossa Natureza), the federal government of Brazil publicly acknowledged the potential dire consequences for human health and the environment of mining with mercury.[83]

When the government has taken some action, usually as a result of international pressure, it has been completely inadequate. For example, in May and November of 1990, then-President Fernando Collar de Mello of Brazil ordered the military to bomb landing strips used by airplanes transporting gold miners and their equipment and supplies. Some 13 airstrips were bombed, but at least 156 others were not.[84] Several attempts were also made to expel miners from Yanomami territory, but although their number was substantially reduced they have periodically returned in waves. Currently a new invasion of miners is under way in Yanomami territory.[85]

Earlier, some of the measures the Brazilian government could have taken in the case of the Yanomami crisis were succinctly identified by a group of Brazilians, the Action for Citizenship Committee:

> It is obvious to even the most ingenuous observer that the invasion would collapse if the Civil Aviation Authority were to merely enforce the rules for registering landing strips, presenting flight plans, controlling cargo, and maintaining aircraft; if the federal government's environmental agency (IBAMA) were to send inspectors to stop the degradation and devastation of the environment; if FUNAI were to allocate the staff and resources needed to protect the Indians; if the Treasury were to send tax inspectors; and, finally, if a federal police force was posted in strategic positions to stop the invasion of protected areas.[86]

The recent gold rush in the Amazon, like its predecessors in earlier centuries, has been a dilemma for the government to control and regulate. Part of this stems from the diffuse, transitory, and clandestine nature of the informal mining sector. Another reason is that the miners are working deposits in extremely remote and rugged terrain along small rivers in mountains covered with tropical forest. These areas are usually well beyond police and military control.[87] The number of miners is twice that of the Brazilian army.[88] When a government airplane or helicopter is sighted, the miners simply flee into the forest temporarily. When expelled from an area they almost always return later. Thus, even if there were any political will to seriously confront the illegal invasion of miners in indigenous territories, the practical logistics seem to render this difficult if not impossible. Formal mining by companies and in shafts or tunnels would have been somewhat easier to control than the informal, widely dispersed mining.

Also Amazonian countries like Brazil and Venezuela continue to experience severe economic and political problems that render concerns for indigenous and environmental welfare secondary at best for both government and citizenry. In many respects the ultimate problem is inadequate land distribution and economic opportunities. Had Brazil developed effective agrarian reform and economic development programs, then some of the major causes of the poverty and landlessness that drove many into mining would have been absent.[89] In Brazil about half of the arable land belongs to just 1 percent of the landowners, while around 3 percent is divided among 3.1 million small farmers.[90] Such considerations leave little room for any optimism that gold mining will ever be properly regulated and managed. It is not sufficient to treat only the symptoms of the mining crisis; the underlying causes must also be effectively addressed.

Not only have the governments of Brazil and Venezuela been embarrassed internationally by publicity from advocacy organizations concerned with human rights and the environment, but in addition both have failed to maintain security within their own borders as long as the miners are not regulated. Moreover, the government gains relatively little revenue since the miners sell most of their gold on the black market to avoid taxes, a Brazilian tradition.[91] Thus, effective governmental action would benefit the government itself by promoting a better international image, giving it access to more of the profits from the mining, and allowing it to control the security of its border zones.

The increasingly toxic landscape of the Amazon is hardly likely to attract ecological and ethnic tourism in the future, although tourism is the fastest growing industry in the world and has the potential to be a sustainable and green economic activity in many areas. Moreover, fisheries in the Amazon that play an important role in the nutrition and economy of people in riverine villages and towns are being jeopardized. Thus, uncontrolled mining is greatly narrowing the economic options and jeopardizing the health of the workforce for the future development of the Amazon.

Response: Populace

Political, economic, and personal preoccupations render most of the public apathetic to both the mining crisis and its human and environmental impacts in the Amazon. Ignorance, ethnocentrism, and racism regarding indigenous people compound the matter. The populace needs to be better informed of the full human and environmental costs of gold mining, and to learn how this is greatly increased by inadequate responses by the government. In Brazil and throughout the world there is a need to inform consumers, reduce the demand for gold, and even boycott it.[92]

Another dimension of mercury and other pollution is that it tends to impact those who are least powerful economically and politically.[93] In the Amazon many thousands of people who regularly consume fish may well be at risk for mercury poisoning; many have already been poisoned. Poor people are dependent on fish as their cheapest regular source of quality protein in their diet, so they are unlikely to be able to substitute meat for fish.[94] However, in contaminated areas people need to avoid eating predatory fish. Because of biomagnification, contamination levels are highest in predatory fish, intermediate in omnivorous and planktivorous fish, and lowest in herbivorous fish.[95] Obviously, it is especially critical that pregnant women and children avoid eating contaminated fish.

Given the extent and gravity of mercury contamination from mining in Brazil, it seems likely that some of the more than 900 environmental organizations in Brazil may take advantage of the 1985 law for the "diffusion of interests" that allows citizens and organizations to sue polluters without risking the payment of costs or penalties if their case is not successful. However, such initiatives may be discouraged by the widespread corruption of the judicial system.

Response: International

The international community is part of the problem of the degradation and destruction of human societies and environments in the Amazon. Conveniently, the international and national business interests involved in the mining are almost unknown, although they include companies from Canada, the United States, and Europe.[96] For example, what companies supply the mercury for processing the gold? Potentially this could be an important pressure point to try to improve the situation, since mercury is clearly a serious health threat and environmental contaminant. If citizens in the United States and other countries were aware of the mercury disaster in the Amazon, many might boycott all stocks and products of the companies in question—thus pressuring them to take some remedial action.

The international community must also be part of the solution. History provides no reason to hope that the governments of the nation states of the Amazon will suddenly make any profound changes to improve policy and its implementation. Only concerted, systematic, penetrating, and sustained action by the international community will give the Yanomami and other indigenes any chance to survive.

For example, in the case of the Yanomami, one of the greatest needs is for adequate emergency medical assistance by international organizations. On February 11, 1991, then–Secretary General of the United Nations, Javier Perez de Cuellar, wrote a letter to the president of Brazil offering humanitarian assistance from the UN, UNICEF, World Health Organization, and other appropriate agencies.[97] However, assistance was not accepted. CCPY (Commission for the Creation of the Yanomami Park, now Pro-Yanomami Commission), together with agencies such as Doctors without Borders (Medicins du Monde), has provided medical assistance to the Yanomami in Brazil, though much more is needed.[98]

Response: Missionaries

Missionaries working with indigenous groups endangered by mining have responded by providing emergency medical and other humanitarian assistance. For the long term they have also provided some schooling for indigenes to better cope with the national language and society, though any schooling is problematic if it is not bilingual and bicultural to include and perpetuate the indigenous heritage as well. However, the efforts of missionaries have been constrained by limited personnel and resources, yet it would seem that much more could be done given the gravity and urgency of this crisis, particularly in the case of groups like the Yanomami. In this situation missionaries often have the best opportunity to monitor and report on the human rights of indigenes. Missionaries have a long-term presence in the region, compared to most others like anthropologists who are usually short-term transients. Also, missionaries have an organizational affiliation that has tremendous national and international power if activated. This is not to ignore the fact that missionaries, like anthropologists, are a heterogeneous group, and some individuals in either group may behave unethically and jeopardize or even violate the human rights of the people with whom they work.[99]

Response: Anthropology

Many government officials and missionaries, as well as some anthropologists, assume that the cultural extinction of indigenous peoples is inevitable in the face of "civilization" and "progress." From their perspective the Yanomami and other indigenes must change or perish. Others, however, realize that there is nothing inevitable about cultural extinction; rather, it is a moral choice of policy makers. Instead, this position advocates self-determination as the pivotal group-right for indigenous societies.[100]

In the late 1960s, this position advancing self-determination together with moral outrage at atrocities committed against indigenous peoples motivated the development of anthropological advocacy organizations such as the Anthropology Resource Center, Cultural Survival, International Work Group for Indigenous Affairs, and Survival International. Historians may well view advocacy anthropology as one of the major achievements of anthropology in the 20th century.[101]

In the case of the Yanomami, the American Anthropological Association (AAA) took various actions on behalf of the human rights of the Yanomami, including resolutions at the business meeting of the annual convention and the establishment of the special Yanomami Commission chaired by Terence Turner, which had significant success.[102] The AAA also developed an explicit and systematic approach to human rights research, education, and advocacy in its Commission for Human Rights (1992–95), which has become a permanent Committee for Human Rights. Individual anthropologists have also followed their personal and professional conscience in taking action on behalf of endangered indigenous groups in the Amazon and elsewhere. Others who are not directly involved in the Amazon have taken action by educating their students and initiating letter writing or other types of campaigns.[103]

Human Rights

Clearly, human rights are universal, indivisible, and interconnected.[104] Indeed, the entire recent episode of gold mining in the Amazon could be seen as a complex chain reaction of human rights violations extending back to the problems of the economic and social justice of impoverished peoples seeking to achieve economic security. Many of the miners have had their human rights violated through exploitation, oppression, corruption, and violence. They in turn have violated the rights of others to a clean and safe environment, the ancestral land rights of indigenes, and so on. Government actions and inactions have aggravated the whole matter.

In recent years interest has been developing in relating the formerly largely separate domains of human rights and environment.[105] For example, three international conventions currently in the final stages of drafting explicitly treat the linkage between human rights and environment: the UN Declaration of Principles on Human Rights and the Environment (see the appendix to this volume), the UN Declaration on the Rights of Indigenous Peoples, and the Inter-American Declaration on the Rights of Indigenous Peoples of the Organization of American States.

The 1994 draft of the UN Declaration of Principles on Human Rights and the Environment includes the following articles that are clearly relevant to the gold mining situation in Brazil:

2. All persons have the right to a secure, healthy and ecologically sound environment;

5. All persons have the right to freedom from pollution, environmental degradation and activities that adversely affect the environment, threaten life, health, livelihood, well-being or sustainable development within, across or outside national boundaries;

14. Indigenous peoples have the right to control their lands, territories and natural resources and to maintain their traditional way of life;

20. All persons have the right to effective remedies and redress in administrative or judicial proceedings for environmental harm or the threat of such harm.

Recently the United Nations agreed in principle to recognize that "all individuals are entitled to live in an environment adequate for their health and well-being." Furthermore, Brazil was one of the nations incorporating this principle into its national constitution.[106] The 1988 Constitution of Brazil also has excellent and extensive environmental clauses, according to Nickel and Viola.[107]

Written or oral statements, however, are one thing, while actions are too often quite another. At all levels, government actions contradict their statements.[108] Thus, for example, in 1985 the Inter-American Commission for Human Rights of the Organization of American States charged that in the case of the Yanomami the Brazilian government had violated numerous articles it agreed to in the "American Declaration of the Rights and Duties of Man," including the rights to life, liberty, personal security, equality before the law, religious freedom and worship, preservation of health and well-being, education, recognition of juridical personality and civil rights, and property. In particular this commission charged that the Brazilian government was liable for failing to take timely and effective measures to protect the human rights of the Yanomami in the construction of the Northern Perimeter Highway into Yanomami territory in the early 1970s and in allowing the invasion of gold miners into Yanomami territory in the 1980s.[109] The Brazilian government finally allowed this commission to send representatives to assess the Yanomami situation on the ground in late 1995— some 15 years after the original request.[110]

Furthermore, in the Yanomami case the Brazilian government has obviously violated numerous other international agreements it has made—ranging from the UN Convention on Genocide, the UN World Charter for Nature, the International Labour Organization's Convention 107 on Tribal and Indigenous Populations, the ILO Convention on Tribal and Indigenous Peoples No. 169, the 1992 Rio Charter and Agenda 21, and so on.[111]

Gold mining and mercury contamination are clearly one specific case of a linkage between human rights and the environment. The illegal invasion by miners of indigenous territory, together with the resulting degradation and destruction of their interrelated population, society, culture, and environment, involves a multitude of serious human rights abuses. For both indigenous and other human populations in areas contaminated by mercury, this violates the most fundamental of all rights—the right to life.

All international instruments on human rights pivot on this right to life. Obviously this right necessarily depends on a safe and healthy environment, and that is absolutely endangered by mercury contamination, among other actions of the miners.

Although enormous progress has been made since World War II in developing international conventions on human rights, less progress has been made in actually protecting and advancing human rights on the ground. Part of the problem is that nation-state governments are hypocritical, signing human rights conventions as part of their public relations management, while at the same time promoting a hidden agenda that often not only fails to protect human rights but actually violates them. In other words, a major Achilles heel of international conventions on human rights is that the very political body that has the authority and power to protect and advance rights is often the agent of the violation of rights, either directly or indirectly. National sovereignty prevents intervention by other nations or international organizations. Moreover, the human rights framework does not address the relatively recent development of multinational corporations that may abuse the rights of local communities, albeit with the complicity of the nation-state government.[112] There is also a tendency of advocacy organizations to be exclusively reactive rather than also proactive. Another obstacle is inadequate flow of current information from frontier zones. These serious weaknesses of rights are clearly played out in the Amazon Basin. Nevertheless, human rights remains an important weapon against inhumanities. Undoubtedly, there will be court cases against the governments and mining companies for reparations based on mercury contamination and other problems related to gold mining.

Conclusions

Given the hazardous human health, economic, and environmental consequences of mercury use in gold mining, ideally, its use should be immediately and strictly prohibited. However, this appears to be simply impractical given economic and political forces as well as logistic considerations. The most appropriate measures seem to be:

1. Adoption of relatively simple and inexpensive technology by workers on placer mines and in gold shops to reduce mercury emissions
2. Technological remedies to clean up mining sites where contamination is concentrated
3. Avoidance of the consumption of contaminated carnivorous fish (and especially by mothers and children)
4. Continual environmental and health monitoring and treatment[113]

The long-term environmental impacts of mercury contamination in local ecosystems, in the Amazon Basin as a whole, and for the planet are unknown. However, this is yet another serious stress on the Amazon environment that is already suffering from numerous other stresses. There are limits to the capacity of any biological system to sustain stress and recover.

Ann Misch in *World Watch* labels mercury contamination in the Amazon "a public health disaster of frightening proportions."[114] Jed Greer of Greenpeace International observes in *The Ecologist*, "People in the future will remember this frantic search for bullion because they and the global ecosystem will still be suffering its harmful consequences."[115] Contaminated areas are a serious risk to future as well as present generations, since mercury deposited in sediments can be remobilized with erosion and transported by seasonal flooding and other changes in the course of rivers and streams. For example, in both California and Gwynedd (Wales), mercury is still detectable in the sediments, approximately a century after the gold mining. Thus, any economic and social benefits of mining may eventually be far outweighed by its human and environmental costs.[116]

A drop in the price of gold could reduce mining pressure in some areas of the Amazon. The price is related to many factors, including political developments in South Africa, which remains by far the world's largest producer; the value of the U.S. dollar; interest rates; oil price fluctuations; fashions; and so on.[117] However, as long as poverty persists, as long as gold mining is seen as an attractive economic alternative and mercury is available and affordable without government regulation, then small-scale miners are likely to continue contaminating themselves, other human beings, and the environment in the Amazon.[118] Each year miners invade new river areas of the Amazon, thereby extending the human and environmental impacts further. Furthermore, historically, everywhere miners tend to work their way upstream along placers to locate the mother lode. Whereas the rubber boom at the turn of the century focused on lowlands, the gold rush of the last two decades has extended into the middle and upper Amazon to impact on many of the relatively traditional indigenous societies remaining there.[119] Thus, in these and other respects, as Hecht and Cockburn have aptly pointed out, there is more to come:

> Wherever it has occurred, the use of mercury has been associated with human poisoning, and the levels of poisoning that are likely to appear in the Amazon promise to eclipse Bhopal or any comparable case of industrial poisoning. The widespread decentralized scale of mercury contamination of the environment and its inhabitants has no historical precedent. What is known about mercury poisoning is the result of a few "hot-spot" exposures in the industrial world.[120]

Moreover, nearly every mining company in the world is exploring for gold somewhere. A number of companies are considering or already constructing facilities for cyanide-heap leaching of gold-bearing sediments in the Amazon and elsewhere.[121] For example, at Serra Pelada, as much as 60 percent of the gold remains in the tailings,[122] and this could be extracted by companies using cyanide-heap leaching. Of course, cyanide presents an additional array of serious dangers to humans and the environment, and these have already been demonstrated at the Omai gold mine in Guyana and elsewhere.[123]

Mining can no longer be ignored in the last frontiers like the Amazon where it has such devastating human and environmental consequences on tremendously valuable indigenous cultures and ecosystems. As the pioneering work of Shelton Davis suggested, mining should become one of the top priorities for urgent, critical, multidisciplinary research at the basic, applied, and advocacy levels in the Amazon and elsewhere. The above review indicates the high priority that should be given to widespread analytical and clinical long-term research on the detection, monitoring, assessment, and treatment of all aspects of the human and environmental impacts of mercury contamination in the Amazon. Because of the human and environmental variability in mining areas and their hinterlands, results from one place cannot be readily extrapolated to others.[124] Also, research has barely begun on the biogeochemical cycling of mercury in forest and aquatic ecosystems of the tropics.[125] The behavior and ecology of fish is also critical in understanding routes of mercury biomagnification.[126] The kinds of field studies on indigenous and peasant subsistence fishing that anthropologists, geographers, and biologists have pioneered in the Amazon are relevant for understanding pathways of methylmercury contamination in humans through fishing and fish consumption.[127] Anthropological, economic, political, legal, and psychological research is sorely and urgently needed on all the different interest groups involved in gold mining for a more holistic understanding of the situation and in search of ways to try to reduce or resolve aspects of the crisis.[128] Perhaps there might even be a possibility of finding some common ground for conflict resolution. However, fieldworkers must be informed of the dangers and sensitive to them as well.

It may be that the political leaders promoting gold mining will be celebrated in history not for their achievements in national and human progress, but rather for the greedy and ignorant ways in which they stymied true human progress. The real riches of the national heritage of countries of the Amazon are being sacrificed—cultural, linguistic, species, and ecosystem diversity.

Notes

1. Some of the background and information for this essay were kindly provided by Bruce Albert, Nelly Arvelo-Jimenez, Jean Chiappino, Marcus Colchester, Gustavo A. Eskildsen, Rebecca Holmes, Gail Gomez, Marco Antonio Lazarin, Jacques Lizot, Paula Loya, Sergio Milano, Peggy Overbey, Abel Perozo, Linda Rabben, Haydee Seijas, Patrick Tierney, and Terrence Turner. The following organizations were also helpful: Amanaka'a, American Anthropological Association, Brazilian Embassy, Commission for the Creation of the Yanomami Park and its successor The Pro-Yanomami Commission, Cultural Survival, Indian Law Resource Center, Instituto Venezolano de Investigaciones Cientificas, Survival International, and World Rainforest Movement. To these and others I am most grateful; however, only I am responsible for any deficiencies or other problems in this essay.

2. Quoted Marcello M. Veiga, John A. Meech, and Raphael Hypolito, "Educational Measures to Address Mercury Pollution from Gold-Mining Activities in the Amazon," *Ambio* 24:4 (1995) 216–217.

3. Quoted from Terence Turner and Davi Kopenawa Yanomami, "I Fight Because I am Alive: An Interview with Davi Kopenawa Yanomami," *Cultural Survival Quarterly* 15:2 (summer 1991) 1. See also Davi Kopenawa Yanomami, "Letter to All the Peoples of the Earth," *Cultural Survival Quarterly* 13:4 (1989) 68–69.

4. Dennison Berwick, *Savages: The Life and Killing of the Yanomami* (London: Hodder and Stoughton, 1992); J. Butler, "Land, Gold, and Farmers: Agricultural Colonization and Frontier Expansion in the Brazilian Amazon," Ph.D. diss., University of Florida, Gainesville, 1985; David Cleary, *Anatomy of the Amazon Gold Rush* (Iowa City: University of Iowa Press, 1990a); Susanna Hecht and Alexander Cockburn, *The Fate of the Forest: Developers, Destroyers and Defenders of the Amazon* (New York: Verso, 1989); A. Feijao and J. A. Pinto, *Garimpeiros in South America: The Amazon Gold Rush* (Pará, Brazil: Union of Amazon Garimpeiros and Merchants Bank of the Future, 1990); Gordon MacMillan, *At the End of the Rainbow? Gold, Land, and People in the Brazilian Amazon* (New York: Columbia University Press, 1995); Alcida Rita Ramos, *Sanuma Memories: Yanomami Ethnography in Times of Crisis* (Madison: University of Wisconsin Press, 1995); Patrick Tierney, *Last Tribes of El Dorado: The Gold Wars in the Amazon Rain Forest* (New York: Viking Press, 1996).

5. MacMillan, *op. cit.*, note 4, p. 178; Carlos Prieto, *Mining in the New World* (New York: McGraw-Hill, 1973); Amnesty International, *The Americas: Human Rights Violations Against Indigenous Peoples* (London: Amnesty International, 1992); John H. Bodley, *Victims of Progress* (Mountain View, Calif.: Mayfield Publishing Co., 1990); Hecht and Cockburn, *op. cit.*, note 4.

6. David Cleary, "Gold Mining and Mercury Use in the Amazon Basin," *Appropriate Technology* 17:2 (1990b) 17–19; Marshall C. Eakin, "The Role of British Capital in the Development of Brazilian Gold Mining," in Thomas Greaves and William Culver, eds., *Miners and Mining in the Americas* (Dover, N.H.: Manchester University Press, 1985), 1–28; John Hemming, *Red Gold: The Conquest of the Brazilian Indians* (Cambridge: Harvard University Press, 1978), 377–408. Serra Pelada closed in the late 1980s because it became structurally unsound.

7. Marcus Colchester, *Venezuela: Violations of Human Rights, Report to the International Labour Office on the Observation of ILO Convention 107* (Chadlington, England: Forest Peoples Programme, World Rainforest Movement, 1995), 19–27; Veiga *et al., op. cit.*, note 2, pp. 216–217; Cleary, *op. cit.*, note 4.

8. Jed Greer, "The Price of Gold: Environmental Costs of the New Gold Rush," *The Ecologist* 23:3 (1993) 91–96.

9. John E. Young, "For the Love of Gold," *World Watch* 6:3 (1993) 19–26. See also John E. Young, *Mining the Earth,* Worldwatch Paper 109 (Washington D.C.: Worldwatch, 1992).

10. Michael Goulding, Nigel J. H. Smith, and Dennis J. Mahar, *Floods of Fortune: Ecology and Economy along the Amazon* (New York: Columbia University Press, 1996), 50. See also MacMillan, *op. cit.*, note 4, pp. 30, 34–37.

11. MacMillan, *op. cit.*, note 4, pp. 59–60, 76, 162; Berwick, *op. cit.*, note 4; Cleary, *op. cit.*, note 4; Hecht and Cockburn, *op. cit.*, note 4.

12. Shelton Davis, *Victims of the Miracle: Development and the Indians of Brazil* (New York: Cambridge University Press, 1977).

13. Shelton H. Davis and R. O. Mathews, *The Geological Imperative: Anthropology and Development in the Amazon Basin of South America* (Irvine, Calif.: Program in Comparative Culture Occasional Papers No. 5, 1976) 3.

14. Davis, *op. cit.*, note 12, pp. 89–90.

15. Linda Rabben, "Brazil's Military Stakes Its Claim," *The Nation* 250:10 (March 12, 1990) 341.

16. Colchester, *op. cit.*, note 7, p. 29.

17. Neil Hollander and Robert MacLean, "Mud-Caked Amazonian Miners Wallow in Newfound Wealth and Power," *Smithsonian* 15:1 (1984) 89–96. Also see Cleary, *op. cit.*, note 4; Davis, *op. cit.*, note 12, pp. 105–110; J. Mallas and N. Benedicto, "Mercury and Goldmining in the Brazilian Amazon," *Ambio* 15 (1986) 247. For numerous other examples of contradictions and complicity in government practices see Ramos, *op. cit.*, note 4, pp. 271–312.

18. Davis, *op. cit.*, note 12, p. 103.

19. For further discussion of the geopolitics of the Brazilian region, see Bruce Albert, "Indian Lands, Environmental Policy and Military Geopolitics in the Development of the Brazilian Amazon: The Case of the Yanomami," *Development and Change* 23 (1992) 35–70; Elizabeth Allen, "Calha Norte: Military Development in Brazilian Amazonia," *Development and Change* 23 (1992) 71–99; MacMillan, *op. cit.*, note 4; Lucio Flavio Pinto, "Calha Norte: The Special Project for the Occupation of the Frontiers," *Cultural Survival Quarterly* 13:1 (1989) 40–41; Rabben, *op. cit.*, note 15; Marcio Santilli, "The Calha Norte Project: Military Guardianship and Frontier Policy," *Cultural Survival Quarterly* 13:1 (1989) 42–43; Dave Treece, "The Militarization and Industrialization of Amazonia: The Calha Norte and Grande Carajas Programmes," *The Ecologist* 19:6 (1989) 225–228. For a discussion of geopolitics in Venezuela, see Nelly Arvelo-Jimenez, "The Political Struggle of the Guayana Region's Indigenous Peoples," *Journal of International Affairs* 36:1 (1982) 43–54.

20. Eakin, *op. cit.*, note 6, p. 11.

21. Veiga *et al., op. cit.*, note 2, p. 218.

22. *Appropriate Technology*, Special Issue on "Small-Scale Mining" 17:2 (Sept. 1990) 1–35.

23. MacMillan, *op. cit.*, note 4, pp. 156–157; Young, *op. cit.*, note 9, pp. 20, 24.

24. Leslie E. Sponsel, Thomas N. Headland, and Robert C. Bailey, eds., *Tropical Deforestation: The Human Dimension* (New York: Columbia University Press, 1996); MacMillan, *op. cit.*, note 4, pp. 92–97, 157.

25. Olaf Malm *et al.*, "An Assessment of Hg Pollution in Different Goldmining Areas, Amazon Brazil," *The Science of the Total Environment* 175 (1995) 127–140. Useful sources on mercury include Leonard J. Goldwater, *Mercury: A History of Quicksilver* (Baltimore: York Press, 1972); Patricia A. D'Itri and Frank M. D'Itri, *Mercury Contamination: A Human Tragedy* (New York: John Wiley & Sons, 1977); Martin Lodenius, ed., Special Issue "Mercury Pollution and Gold Mining in Brazil," *The Science of the Total Environment* 175:2 (Dec. 11, 1995) 85–162; Jerome O. Nriagu, ed., *The Biogeochemistry of Mercury in the Environment* (New York: Elsevier, 1979); Carl J. Watras and John W. Huckabee, eds., *Mercury Pollution: Integration and Synthesis* (Boca Raton, Fla.: Lewis Publishers, 1994). Also see *Water, Air, and Soil Pollution*, Special Issue on Mercury 56:1 (April 1991) 843.

26. Jerome O. Nriagu, "Legacy of Mercury Pollution," *Nature* 363:6430 (June 17, 1993) 589.

27. Greer, *op. cit.*, note 8, p. 92.

28. Rodolf Reuther, "Mercury Accumulation in Sediment and Fish from Rivers Affected by Alluvial Gold Mining in the Brazilian Madeira River Basin, Amazon," *Environmental Monitoring and Assessment* 32 (1994) 239–258; and A. W. Andren and J. O. Nriagu, "The Global Cycle of Mercury," in Jerome O. Nriagu, ed., *The Biogeochemistry of Mercury in the Environment* (New York: Elsevier, 1979), 1–22.

29. Wolfgang Christian Pfeiffer and Luiz Drude de Lacerda, "Mercury Inputs to the Amazonian Basin," *Environmental Technology Letter* 9 (1988) 325–330.

30. Roald Hoffman, "Winning Gold," *American Scientist* 82:1 (Jan.–Feb. 1994) 15–17.

31. Malm *et al.*, *op. cit.*, note 25, p.128; Jerome Nriagu *et al.*, "Mercury Pollution in Brazil," *Nature* 356 (April 2, 1992) 389.

32. E. Salati, "The Climatology and Hydrology of Amazonia," in Ghillean T. Prance and Thomas E. Lovejoy, eds., *Amazonia* (New York: Pergamon, 1985), 18–48; Emilio F. Moran, *Through Amazonian Eyes: The Human Ecology of Amazonian Populations* (Iowa City: University of Iowa Press, 1993). Olaf Malm, Fernandeo J. P. Branches, *et al.*, "Mercury and Methylmercury in Fish and Human Hair from the Tapajós River Basin, Brazil," *The Science of the Total Environment* 175 (1995) 143; F. M. D'Itri, "What We Have Learned Since Minamata," *Environmental Monitoring and Assessment* 19 (1991) 173–176.

33. Greer, *op. cit.*, note 8, p. 92; Hecht and Cockburn, *op. cit.*, note 4, p. 145; Goulding *et al.*, *op. cit.*, note 10, p. 73.

34. Goulding *et al.*, *op. cit.*, note 10, p. 94; Greer, *op. cit.*, note 8, p. 92.

35. Malm *et al.*, *op. cit.*, note 25, p.135; *op. cit.*, note 32, p.147.

36. Ilkka Aula *et al.*, "The Watershed Flux of Mercury Examined with Indicators in the TuCururúi Reservoir in Pará, Brazil," *The Science of the Total Environment* 175 (1995) 97–107; Petri Porvari, "Mercury Levels of Fish in Tucuruí Hydroelectric Reservoir and in River Mju in Amazonia, in the State of Pará, Brazil," *The Science of the Total Environment* 175 (1995) 109–117.

37. L. D. De Lacerda *et al.*, "Mercury Distribution in Sediment Profiles from Lakes of the High Pantanal, Mato Grosso State, Brazil," *Biogeochemistry* 14 (1991) 91.

38. World Health Organization, *Mercury—Environmental Aspects* (Geneva: WHO International Program on Chemical Safety, 1989); World Health Organization, *Methyl Mercury, Environmental Health Criteria 101* (Geneva: WHO International Program on Chemical Safety, 1990).

39. Hirokatsu Akagi *et al.*, "Methylmercury Pollution in the Amazon, Brazil," *The Science of the Total Environment* 175 (1995) 85–95.

40. Malm *et al.*, *op. cit.*, note 32, p. 148; Olaf Malm, Wolfgang C. Pfeiffer, *et al.*, "Mercury Pollution Due to Gold Mining in the Madeira River Basin, Brazil," *Ambio* 19:1 (1990) 14.

41. Tuika Leino and Martin Lodenius, "Human Hair Mercury Levels in Tucuruí Area, State of Pará, Brazil," *The Science of the Total Environment* 175 (1995) 199; Aula *et al.*, *op. cit.*, note 36.

42. Reuther, *op. cit.*, note 28, p. 239; Malm *et al.*, *op. cit.*, note 40, p. 13; and Luis A. Martinelli *et al.*, "Mercury Contamination in the Amazon: A Gold Rush Consequence," *Ambio* 17:4 (1988) 252–254.

43. Goulding *et al.*, *op. cit.*, note 10, pp. 87, 93. For example, see Janet Chernela, *The Wano Indians of the Brazilian Amazon: A Sense of Space* (Austin: University of Texas Press, 1993) and Leslie E. Sponsel and Paula Loya, "Rivers of Hunger? Indigenous Resource Management in the Oligotrophic Ecosystems of the Rio Negro, Venezuela," in C. M. Hladik *et al.*, *Tropical Forests, People and Food: Biocultural Interactions and Applications to Development* (London: Parthenon, 1993), 435–446.

44. Hecht and Cockburn, *op. cit.*, note 4, p. 145; "Gold-diggers Poison Brazil's Wild Parádise," *New Scientist*, Sept. 12, 1992, p. 8; De Lacerda *et al.*, *op. cit.*, note 37.

45. D'Itri and D'Itri, *op. cit.*, note 25, pp. 118–121.

46. D'Itri, *op. cit.*, note 32; D'Itri and D'Itri, *op. cit.*, note 25, pp. 15–28. Also see E. Smith and A.M. Smith, *Minamata Disease: Words and Photographs* (New York: Holt, Rinehart and Winston, 1975); and Masazumi Harada, "Minamata Diseases and Organic Mercury Poisonings Caused by Ingestion of Contaminated Fish" in E. F. Patrice Jelliffe and Derrick B. Jelliffe, eds., *Adverse Effects of Foods* (New York: Plenum, 1992), 135–148.

47. L. Chang, "Pathological Effects of Mercury Poisoning," in J. O. Nriagu, ed., *The Biochemistry of Mercury*, (New York: Elsevier, 1979), 519–568; and K. Khera *et al.*, "Teratogenic and Genetic Effects of Mercury Toxicity," in J. O. Nriagu, ed., *The Biochemistry of Mercury* (New York: Elsevier, 1979), 503–512.

48. Nriagu *et al.*, *op. cit.*, note 31.

49. Fernando J. P. Branches *et al.*, "The Price of Gold: Mercury Exposure in the Amazonian Rain Forest," *Clinical Toxicology* 31:2 (1993) 295–306.

50. Branches *et al.*, *op. cit.*, note 49. Also see Malm *et al.*, *op. cit.*, note 47, p. 144.

51. MacMillan, *op. cit.*, note 4, pp. 163–166.

52. Marcus Colchester, ed., *The Health and Survival of the Venezuelan Yanoama* (Copenhagen: International Work Group for Indigenous Affairs Document No. 53, 1985), 59–72.

53. Spielman *et al.*, "Regional Linguistic and Genetic Differences among the Yanomama Indians," *Science* 184 (1974) 637–644; R. Brian Ferguson, *Yanomami Warfare: A Political History* (Santa Fe, N.M.: School for American Research Press, 1995); R. J. A. Goodland and H. S. Irwin, *Amazon Jungle: Green Hell to Red Desert? An Ecological Discussion of the Environmental Impact of the Highway Con-struction Program in the Amazon Basin* (New York: Elsevier, 1975); Alcida R. Ramos and Kenneth I. Taylor, *The Yanomama in Brazil 1979* (Copenhagen: International Work Group for Indigenous Affairs Document No. 37, 1979); Colchester, *op. cit.*, note 7.

54. CCPY, Update 83, Dec. 15, 1995.

55. "Censo Indigena de Venezuela de 1982," *Boletin Indigenista Venezolano* XXI, pp. 227–239; 1992 personal communication from Rebecca Holmes.

56. See also Colchester *op. cit.*, note 7, pp. 35–38.

57. M. B. Castro, B. Albert, and W. C. Pfeiffer, "Mercury Levels in Yanomami Indians' Hair from Roraima, Brazil," in Cep Consultants, eds., *Proceedings of the 8th International Conference on Heavy Metals in the Environment* (Edinburgh: 1991), 367–370.

58. Lawrence H. Hecker *et al.*, "Heavy Metal Levels in Acculturated and Unacculturated Popula-tions," *Archives of Environmental Health* 29 (1974) 181–185.

59. MacMillan, *op. cit.*, note 4, pp. 49–50, 155.

60. Bruce Albert, "Gold Miners and Yanomami Indians in the Brazilian Amazon: The Hashimu Massacre," Barbara Rose Johnston, ed., in *Who Pays the Price? The Sociocultural Context of Environ-mental Crisis* (Washington, D.C.: Island Press, 1994), 47–55; Zeze Weiss and Martin D. Weiss, *The Yanomami Massacres and the Role of a Powerful Anti-Native Alliance* (New York: Amanaka'a Amazon Network, 1993).

61. Linda Rabben, "Demarcation—And Then What?," *Cultural Survival Quarterly* 17:2 (1993) 12–14; Nelly Arvelo-Jimenez and Andrew L. Cousins, "False Promises," *Cultural Survival Quarterly* 16:1 (1992) 10–13.

62. MacMillan, *op. cit.*, p. 52.

63. Leslie E. Sponsel, "The Yanomami Holocaust Continues," in Barbara Rose Johnston, ed., *Who Pays the Price? The Sociocultural Context of Environmental Crisis* (Washington, D.C.: Island Press, 1994), 37–46; Leslie E. Sponsel, "The Current Holocaust in the Amazon: Ecocide, Ethnocide, and Genocide Against the Yanomami Nation," in C. Patrick Morris and Robert K. Hitchcock, eds., *International Human Rights and Indigenous Peoples* (Tucson: University of Arizona Press, 1996a, in press); Leslie E. Sponsel, "The Killing Fields of the Brazilian and Venezuelan Amazon: The Continuing Destruction of the Yanomami and Their Ecosystems by Illegal Gold Miners, Future Scenarios and Actions," in Pamela J. Puntenney, ed., *The Knowledge to Act: Coming to Terms with Environment and Human Rights* (Iowa City: University of Iowa Press, 1996b, in press).

64. Bodley, *op. cit.*, note 5, Chapter 10; Davis, *op. cit.*, note 12, pp. 167–168. An excellent firsthand account of the history of the Yanomami crisis is Ramos, *op. cit.*, note 4, pp. 271–312. Berwick, *op. cit.*, note 4; MacMillan, *op. cit.*, note 4; Ramos and Taylor, *op. cit.*, note 53; Survival International, *Yanomami: Survival Campaign* (London: Survival International, 1991); and Tierney, *op. cit.*, note 4, are also important contributions on the Yanomami crisis. For ethnographies of the Yanomami, see Jacques Lizot, *Tales of the Yanomami: Daily Life in the Venezuelan Forest* (New York: Cambridge University Press, 1985); and Ramos, *op. cit.*, note 4.

65. Brian Burkhalter, *Amazon Gold Rush: Markets and the Mundurucú Indians* (Ann Arbor, Mich.: University Microfilms International, 1983); S. Brian Burkhalter and Robert F. Murphy, "Tappers and Sappers: Rubber, Gold, and Money Among the Mundurucú," *American Ethnologist* 16:1 (1989) 100–116; Robert F. Murphy, *Headhunter's Heritage: Social and Economic Change Among the Mundurucú Indians* (Berkeley: University of California Press, 1960).

66. Andrew Gray, *And After the Gold Rush? Human Rights and Self-Development of the Amarakaeri of Southeastern Peru* (Copenhagen: International Work Group for Indigenous Affairs Document No. 55, 1986), 33–35, 57, 62, 104.

67. Hecht and Cockburn, *op. cit.*, note 4, pp. 143, 158. Also see Terrence Turner, "The Kayapo Revolt Against Extractivism: An Indigenous Amazon People's Struggle for Socially Equitable or Ecologically Sustainable Production," *Journal of Latin American Anthropology* 1:1 (1995) 98–121. For other cases of indigenes and gold mining see Kaj Århem, "Dance of the Water People," *Natural History*, Jan. 1992, pp. 46–53; Bruce Albert Bruce, ed., "Bresil: Indiens et Developpments en Amazonie," *Ethnies* 5:11–12 (1990) (Paris: Revue de Survival International), 1–46; Gray, *op. cit.*, note 66; and MacMillan, *op. cit.*, note 4, pp. 29–30.

68. Nelly Arvelo-Jimenez and Keith Conn, "The Ye'kuana Self-Demarcation Process," *Cultural Survival Quarterly* 18:4 (1995) 40–42.

69. Mary Douglas and Aaron Wildavsky, *Risk and Culture: An Essay on the Selection of Technological and Environmental Dangers* (Berkeley: University of California Press, 1983); Veiga *et al.*, *op. cit.*, note 2, pp. 216–220; Albert, *op. cit.*, note 60.

70. Evelyn J. Caballero, "Gold from the Gods: Traditional Small-Scale Mining from Benguet Province, Philippines," Ph.D. diss., University of Hawaii, 1992; Cleary, *op. cit.*, note 4, pp. 225–228; Cleary, *op. cit.*, note 6, p. 19.

71. Veiga *et al.*, *op. cit.*, note 2, pp. 216, 219. Raphael Hypolito, "The Hypolito Retort—Making Mercury Recovery Safe," *Appropriate Technology* 17:2 (1990) 20.

72. Marcello M. Veiga and John A. Meech, "Gold Mining Activities in the Amazon: Clean-Up Techniques and Remedial Procedures for Mercury Pollution," *Ambio* 24:6 (1995) 371–375.

73. Malm *et al.*, *op. cit.*, note 25, p. 138.

74. Mallas and Benedicto, *op. cit.*, note 17, p. 249.

75. Veiga *et al.*, *op. cit.*, note 2, p. 216.

76. Cleary, *op. cit.*, note 6, p. 19.

77. Branches, *et al.*, *op. cit.*, note 49, p. 304. Also see *Appropriate Technology*.

78. MacMillan, *op. cit.*, note 4, pp. 71–72, 79–80.

79. Branches *et al.*, *op. cit.*, note 49, p. 302.

80. Mallas and Benedicto, *op. cit.*, note 17, p. 249.

81. Gray, *op. cit.*, note 66, p. 57. See also A. Sutton, *Amazonian Slavery: A Link in the Chain of Brazilian Development* (London: Anti-Slavery International, 1994).

82. MacMillan, *op. cit.*, note 4, pp. 71–72, 80. These considerations should not in any way be taken as condoning the illegal presence of miners and the human and environmental horrors they cause.

83. Hecht and Cockburn, *op. cit.*, note 4, pp. 119–121.

84. Berwick, *op. cit.*, note 4, p. 234.

85. CCPY, Update 86, "New Law Brings Avalanche of Claims to Indian Lands," May 1996, pp. 1–4.

86. Action for Citizenship Committee, "Roraima, Brazil: A Death Warning," *Cultural Survival Quarterly* 13:4 (1989) 64.

87. Eakin, *op. cit.*, note 6, p. 12.

88. Veiga *et al.*, *op. cit.*, note 2, p. 218.

89. Hecht and Cockburn, *op. cit.*, note 4, pp. 121, 147. See also Macmillan, *op. cit.*, note 4.

90. Monica Bergamo and Gerson Camarotti, "Brazil's Landless Millions," *World Press* 43:7 (1996) 46–47.

91. Eakin, *op. cit.*, note 6, p. 24.

92. Young, *op. cit.*, note 9, 1993.

93. D'Itri, *op. cit.*, note 32, p. 178; Johnston, *op. cit.*, note 60.

94. Leino and Lodenius, *op. cit.*, note 41, p. 124.

95. Porvari, *op. cit.*, note 36, p. 114; Malm *et al.*, *op. cit.*, note 32, p. 149.

96. Colchester, *op. cit.*, note 7, p. 21; Weiss and Weiss, *op. cit.*, note 60.

97. CCPY, July 1991.

98. Survival International, "Yanomami Health Aid," *Survival International News* 10 (1985) 3.

99. Thomas N. Headland and Darrell L. Whiteman, eds., Special Issue "Missionaries, Anthropologists, and Human Rights," *Missiology* XXIV:2 (April 1996) 161–299.

100. Christian Bay, "Human Rights on the Periphery: No Room in the Ark for the Yanomami?," *Development Dialogue* 1–2 (1984) 23–41; Bodley, *op. cit.*, note 5, Chapter 10.

101. Bodley, *op. cit.*, note 5; Ellen Messer, "Anthropology and Human Rights," *Annual Review of Anthropology* 22 (1993) 221–249; Marc S. Miller, ed., *State of the Peoples: A Global Human Rights Report on Societies in Danger* (Boston: Beacon Press, 1993); Leslie E. Sponsel, "Relationships among the World System, Indigenous Peoples, and Ecological Anthropology in the Endangered Amazon," in L. E. Sponsel, ed., *Indigenous Peoples and the Future of Amazonia: An Ecological Anthropology of an Endangered World* (Tucson: University of Arizona Press, 1995), 263–293; Robin Wright, "Anthropological Presuppositions of Indigenous Advocacy," *Annual Review of Anthropology* 17 (1988) 365–390.

102. American Anthropological Association, *Report of the Special Commission to Investigate the Situation of the Brazilian Yanomami* (Washington, D.C.: American Anthropological Association, 1991).

103. Cara Elmore and Leslie Gross, "A Massacre and a Lesson About Life," *NEA Today* (National Education Association) 13:5 (1994) 29; George P. Nicholas, "The Yanomami in the Classroom," *Cultural Survival Quarterly* 16:2 (1992) 28–30.

104. Jack Donnelly, *Universal Human Rights in Theory and Practice* (Ithaca, N.Y.: Cornell University Press, 1989).

105. Andrew Gray, "International Protection of Indigenous Rights: The Subsurface—Forgotten or Ignored?," *International Work Group for Indigenous Affairs Newsletter* 3 (July-Aug.-Sept. 1993) 2–3; W. Paul Gormley, *Human Rights and Environment: The Need for International Cooperation* (Leyden: A. W. Sijthoff, 1976); W. Paul Gormley, "The Legal Obligation of the International Community to Guarantee a Pure and Decent Environment: The Expansion of Human Rights Norms," *Georgetown*

International Environmental Law Review 3 (1990) 85–116; Human Rights Watch and Natural Resources Defense Council, *Defending the Earth: Abuses of Human Rights and the Environment* (New York: Human Rights Watch, June 1992); Johnston, *op. cit.*; James W. Nickel, "The Human Rights of a Safe Environment," *Yale Journal of International Law* 18 (1993) 281–295; Nickel, James W. and Eduardo Viola, "Integrating Environmentalism and Human Rights," *Environmental Ethics* 16 (1994) 265–27; Henn-Juri Uibopuu, "The International Guaranteed Right of an Individual to a Clean Environment," *Comparative Law Yearbook* 1 (1977) 101–120; Arthur H. Westing, "Human Rights and the Environment," *Environmental Conservation* 20:2 (1993) 99–100.

106. Westing, *op. cit.*, note 105, p. 99.

107. Nickel and Viola, *op. cit.*, note 105, p. 266.

108. For example, see Brazilian Embassy, *Brazilian Policy on Indigenous Populations* (Washington, D.C.: Brazilian Embassy, 1993).

109. Inter-American Commission on Human Rights, *Annual Report of the Inter-American Commission on Human Rights 1984–1985* (Washington, D.C.: Organization of American States, 1985).

110. CCPY, Update 83, Dec. 15, 1995.

111. Also see Nelly Arvelo-Jimenez *et al.,* "Indian Policy," in John D. Martz and David J. Myers, eds., *Venezuela: The Democratic Experience* (New York: Praeger Publications, 1977), 323–334; and Colchester, *op. cit.*, note 7 on repeated violations of the ILO Convention 107 in Venezuela.

112. Donnelly, *op. cit.*, note 104. See also Ellen Messer, "Anthropology and Human Rights in Latin America," *Journal of Latin American Anthropology* 1:1 (1995) 48–97.

113. Malm *et al.*, *op. cit.*, note 32, p. 149.

114. Ann Misch, "The Amazon: River at Risk," *World Watch* 5:1 (1992) 37.

115. Greer, *op. cit.*, note 8, p. 96.

116. Cleary, *op. cit.*, note 4 or 6, p. 17; Ronald Fuge *et al.,* "Mercury and Gold Pollution," *Nature* 357 (June 4, 1992) 369. Also see Duane A. Smith, *Mining America: The Industry and the Environment, 1800-1980* (Lawrence: University of Kansas Press, 1987). For benefits see Cleary, *op. cit.*, note 4, pp. 211–222.

117. Gray, *op. cit.*, note 66, pp. 42–46.

118. Cleary, *op. cit.*, note 4, pp. 228–230; MacMillan, *op. cit.*, note 4, pp. 179–180.

119. Goulding *et al.,* Nigel J.H. Smith and Dennis J. Mahar, *op. cit.*, note 10, pp. 50–51.

120. Hecht and Cockburn, *op. cit.*, note 4, p. 143.

121. Greer, *op. cit.*, note 8, pp. 91–94

122. Hollander and MacLean, *op. cit.*, note 17, p. 96.

123. Desiree Kissoon Jodah, "Courting Disaster in Guyana," *Multinational Monitor* 16:11 (1995) 9–12.

124. MacMillan, *op. cit.*, note 4, p. 160.

125. Malm *et al.*, *op. cit.*, note 32, p. 149.

126. Michael Goulding, *The Fishes of the Forest: Explorations in Amazonian Natural History* (Berkeley: University of California Press, 1980); Goulding *et al.*, *op. cit.*, note 10; Nigel Smith, *Man, Fishes, and the Amazon* (New York: Columbia University Press, 1981).

127. For example, see Smith, *op. cit.*, note 126; and Sponsel and Loya, *op. cit.*, note 43.

128. See Al Gedicks, *The New Resource Wars: Native and Environmental Struggles Against Multinational Corporations* (Boston: South End Press, 1993).

CHAPTER 6

War on Subsistence
Mining Rights at Crandon/Mole Lake, Wisconsin

Al Gedicks

Preface

On March 29, 1995, the United States Army Corps of Engineers held a public hearing on the Mole Lake Sokaogon Chippewa Reservation, in Wisconsin, to take comments on Exxon/Rio Algom's proposed underground zinc-copper mine next to the reservation. Tribal members testified about the historical origins of their present reservation and the significance of the wild rice that they harvest from Rice Lake on the reservation.

Fred Ackley, a tribal judge, recalled the history of the creation of the reservation at the hearing:

> The government asked our chief why he wanted this reservation in this spot. Our chief walked over and gave him a handful of wild rice and he said, "This is the food of Indian people. This is why I want my reservation here on this lake. There are six or seven other lakes in this area where my people have been harvesting food for a long time." So he wanted his reservation right here on this lake for the wild rice.

> Through the hard times that we've had to live as Indian people here in Mole Lake, we realized that money and everything else that the white people had, didn't count. Because what the Great Spirit gave us was the food for our people—subsistence to go on another year, to have another offspring, to bury another elder. Also, he taught us how to pray for that every year. We've been doing that every year here in Mole Lake. We still pray for everything we get. We do it our way.

Charles Ackley, the son of Chief Willard Ackley, still harvests and sells wild rice (see photograph). He testified about the threat to wild rice from the proposed mine:

> East of us here, where this mine is supposed to take place, is all spring fed. And if they start fooling around underground, they're going to be a lot of lakes going dry east of us here. And suppose that Exxon taps into our underground water spring? What is going to happen to our water situation in our community? And do we all want to risk that to have a mining company come into our area and do that?

Rose Van Zile is a grandmother and a veteran wild rice harvester:

Al Gedicks is Professor of Sociology at the University of Wisconsin, La Cross, WI 54601. He is a longtime environmental/Native solidarity activist in the upper midwest who has served as the director of the Center for Alternative Mining Development Policy and as the executive secretary of the Wisconsin Resources Protection Council.

Right now I'm saying I don't want this mine here. I don't want it to be part of my everyday life. When I grow old, I'd like to have my grandchildren here to comfort them, the way my grandparents comforted me and gave me the enjoyment of going to school, coming home, having my dinner and relaxing and knowing that I have a safe place to come home to every night. And when I rest I don't have to worry about the water or the wild rice.

I went out there for 23 years of my life and I picked rice. I still do today. And yes, I'm mad. I'm damned mad at this mining. To me, no mining in Mole Lake. That's what I say. That's what my grandson is going to say. That's what my children are going to say. No mining in Mole Lake. Thank you very much.

Introduction

Indian tribes in the northern portions of Wisconsin, Minnesota, and Michigan are seriously threatened by sulfide mining operations in ways that are difficult for non-Indians to perceive. For Indian people, natural resource harvest is more than a means to provide food. It is a cultural activity that renews both the Indian person and the resource that is harvested.[1]

Recent court rulings have upheld the reserved rights of the Lake Superior Chippewa Nation to hunt, fish, and gather on public lands ceded to the U.S. government in 19th century treaties.[2] For the past decade, Chippewa (Ojibwa) spearfishers have had to defend those treaty rights against those northern Wisconsin residents who accused the Chippewa of depleting the fish populations. After disproving the racially motivated charges and peacefully resisting mob violence, the Chippewa now face the prospect of toxic contamination of their fish, deer, and wild rice resources as a result of large-scale mining projects in the Chippewa's ceded treaty lands. The focal point of recent Chippewa resistance to environmental degradation to their traditions is Exxon's attempt to construct a large underground mine next to the Sokaogon Chippewa reservation in northern Wisconsin.

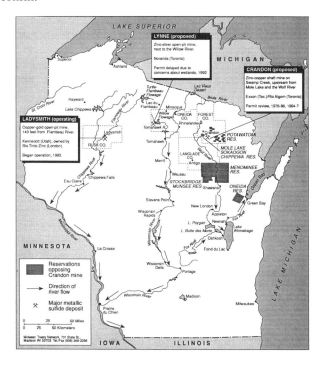

Charles Ackley (left) and his son harvest wild rice in Rice Lake on the Mole Lake Reservation near Crandon, Wisconsin. Photograph by Al Gedicks.

In 1975, Texas-based Exxon Minerals Co. discovered one of the ten largest zinc-copper sulfide deposits in North America, adjacent to the Mole Lake Sokaogon Chippewa Reservation near Crandon, Wisconsin. Situated at the headwaters of the Wolf River in Forest County, Exxon's proposed mine for that deposit is the largest of a series of metallic sulfide mines planned for development in northern Wisconsin. The Crandon/Mole Lake mine would extract approximately 55 million tons of sulfide ore during the 30-year life of the project.

In 1993, after prolonged opposition by environmental and Native American groups, Kennecott Copper (a subsidiary of London-based Rio Tinto Zinc) began an open-pit copper sulfide mine on the Flambeau River outside Ladysmith, Wisconsin. The Flambeau mine is tiny in comparison to the Exxon project. But it represents the "foot in the door" the mining industry has been after since 1968 when Kennecott first discovered the orebody at Ladysmith. "Discovery of the Flambeau deposit," Kennecott geologist Ed May wrote, "has opened the way to the development of a new domestic mining district."[3] In 1982, Exxon Minerals' chief lobbyist James Klauser told the Wisconsin Manufacturers and Commerce Association that the state could host up to ten major metal mines by the year 2000, the Ladysmith mine being one of them.[4] Klauser now heads the Wisconsin Department of Administration, which oversees the mine permitting process.

Exxon's proposed underground shaft mine would disrupt far beyond its surface area of 550 square acres. Over its lifetime, the mine would generate an estimated 44 million tons of wastes—the equivalent of eight Great Pyramids of Egypt.[5] When metallic sulfide wastes have contact with water and air, the potential result is sulfuric acids, plus high levels of poisonous heavy metals such as mercury, lead, zinc, arsenic, copper, and cadmium. After a decade of facing strong local opposition, Exxon withdrew from the project in 1986, citing depressed metal prices.[6] Exxon then returned in September 1993 to announce its intention to mine with a new partner—Canada-based Rio Algom—in their new "Crandon Mining Co." In its report on the Exxon/Rio Algom joint venture, *The Northern Miner,* Canada's mining industry newspaper, noted that "The only objections raised at the Crandon press conference...came from native Americans who expressed concern over archaeological aspects of the site. No objections were heard from environmental groups."[7] The paper's characterization of the objections from Native Americans as insignificant, compared to the possible objections from nonnative environmental groups, is all too typical of the way native cultures have been ignored by the dominant society.

Mining vs. Native Subsistence

The threat of annihilation has been hanging over this community since 1975. The mental stress and mental anguish are unbearable at times.[8] (Wayne LaBine, Sokaogon Chippewa tribal planner)

The planned mine lies on territory sold by the Chippewa Nation to the United States in 1842, and directly on a 12-square mile tract of land promised to the Mole Lake Sokaogon Chippewa in 1855.[9] Treaties guaranteed Chippewa access to wild rice, fish, and some wild game on ceded lands. The Mole Lake Reservation (formed in 1939) is a prime harvester of wild rice in Wisconsin. The rice, called *manomim,* or "gift from the creator," is an essential part of the Chippewa diet, an important cash crop, and a sacred part of the band's religious rituals.[10] The Wisconsin Department of Natural Resources (DNR) emphasized the centrality of wild rice to Chippewa culture in its analysis of Exxon's proposed mine: "Rice Lake and the bounty of the lakes harvest lie at the heart of their identity as a people . . . The rice and the lake are the major links between themselves, Mother Earth, their ancestors and future generations."[11]

Any contamination or drawdown of water would threaten the survival of both fish and wild rice. The Chippewa were not reassured when Exxon's biologist mistook their wild rice for a "bunch of lake weeds." Later, Exxon maintained that any pollutants from the mine would travel along the rim of Rice Lake and cause no harm to the delicate ecology of wild rice. The tribe asked the U.S. Geological Survey to perform a dye test to determine the path of potential pollutants. The results showed the dye dispersing over the entire lake. Exxon's own environmental impact report blandly mentioned that "the means of subsistence on the reservation" may be "rendered less than effective."[12]

Sokaogon chairman Arlyn Ackley responded to Exxon's announcement to resume the mine permit process by recalling Exxon's previous attempt to develop the ore body:

Exxon claimed it would be an "environmentally safe" mine in the 70's. They claimed it wouldn't harm our sacred wild rice beds or water resources. We had to spend our own money on tests to prove their project would in fact contaminate our subsistence harvest areas and lower the water level of Rice Lake. Exxon's claims of environmentally safe mining were unfounded.

I think these companies are willing to lie. Their history is one of pollution, destruction and death. Just last month, more than 70 Yanomami Indians were massacred by miners in the

Amazon forest. As far as we are concerned, Exxon and Rio Algom are of the same mind set. Let it be known here and now that these companies are prepared to plunder and destroy our people and lands for their insatiable greed. They may be more polite in North America, but they are no less deadly to Native people.[13]

Half of the projected mine waste is rocky "coarse tailings," which would be dumped to fill up the mine shafts. The other half is powdery "fine tailings," which would be dumped into a waste pond, covering 350 acres (or about the size of 350 football fields), at least 90 feet tall. The water table beneath these ponds is as close as 15 feet down. As proposed, it would be the largest toxic waste dump in Wisconsin history.[14] To control leakage into wells and streams, Exxon plans to place a liner under the waste pond. The U.S. Environmental Protection Agency (EPA) admits that tailings ponds are "regulated…loosely" and that leaks from even the best of dumps "will inevitably occur."[15] The U.S. Forest Service says that "there are currently no widely applicable technologies" to prevent acid mine drainage.[16] The mining industry cannot point to a single example of a metallic sulfide mine that has been successfully reclaimed (returned to a natural state). This fact was confirmed by a 1995 Wisconsin DNR report.[17]

Besides the mine waste, the half-mile-deep mine shafts would themselves drain groundwater supplies, in much the same way that a syringe draws blood from a patient. The wastewater would be constantly pumped out of the shafts, "drawing down" water levels in a four-square-mile area. If not adequately regulated, this "dewatering" could lower lakes by several feet, and dry up wells and springs.[18] An Exxon engineer once pointed to a terrain map of the mine and said that, from the standpoint of the wetlands, the groundwater, and the overall topography, "You couldn't find a more difficult place in the world to mine."[19]

The potential threat to the economy and culture of the Sokaogon Chippewa from Exxon's proposed mine must also be evaluated in the context of the cumulative environmental threats facing both Indian and non-Indian communities in the northwoods. The Chippewa, along with other Indian nations in northern Wisconsin, already suffer a disproportionate environmental risk of illness and other health problems from eating fish, deer, and other wildlife contaminated with industrial pollutants like airborne polychlorinated biphenyls (PCBs), mercury, and other toxins deposited on land and water. "Fish and game have accumulated these toxic chemicals," according to a 1992 U.S. EPA study, "to levels posing substantial health, ecological, and cultural risks to a Native American population that relies heavily on local fish and game for subsistence. As the extent of fish and game contamination is more fully investigated by state and federal authorities, advisories suggesting limited or no consumption of fish and game are being established for a large portion of the Chippewa's traditional hunting and fishing areas."[20]

The Watershed Alliance to End Environmental Racism

We like where we're living. They put us here years and years ago on federal land and now that we're here—they discover something—and they either want to take it from us or move us away from it. We don't want to do this. This is where I belong. This is my home. This is where my roots are and this is where I'm gonna stay.[21] (Myra Tuckwab, Sokaogon Chippewa tribal member)

If Exxon could have limited the conflict over the mine to a contest between itself and the Sokaogon, the construction of the mine would be a foregone conclusion. Multinational mining companies have a long record of overwhelming native peoples whose resources they have sought to control.[22] In each case, the corporation has sought to reduce its political and financial risks by limiting the arena of conflict so that the victims are completely exposed to the reach of the corporation—while only one tentacle of the corporation's worldwide organization is exposed to the opposition.[23]

The nature of the proposed mine, however, posed a number of environmental and social threats that were of major concern to native residents, environmental groups, sportfishing groups, and other Indian tribes. The nearby Menominee, Potawatomi, and Stockbridge-Munsee nations would be severely affected by the mine pollution and the social upheaval brought by new outsiders. With Mole Lake, they formed the Nii Win Intertribal Council (Nii Win is Ojibwa for "four"). Unlike in the last Exxon battle, the tribes have considerably more revenues available from casino proceeds that can be used to fight Exxon's current proposal. Nii Win immediately began hiring lawyers and technical experts to challenge Exxon/Rio Algom's mine permit application. They also purchased a Nii Win house on a seven-acre parcel, across the road from the Exxon mine site, to monitor all activities at the site. The Oneida Nation, which is downstream from the mine near Green Bay, also joined the opposition. In the distant and recent past, these tribes have survived relocation, termination, and assimilation, against overwhelming odds. They now see the mine as one more threat to their cultures and their future generations.

All five tribes are working in alliance with environmental and sportfishing groups within a campaign called WATER (Watershed Alliance to end Environmental Racism). The Wisconsin conflict over treaty spearfishing pitted Chippewa against some white fishers from 1984 until the anti-Indian protests ended in 1992.[24] Now the mining conflict finds Native Americans and some sportfishing groups on the same side, opposing an outside threat to the same resources. Trout Unlimited's Wolf River chapter says that "the mine as proposed would be a threat to the Wolf River as a trout stream."[25]

Opening Up the Mine Permit Process

Our reservation is directly adjacent to this mine project. The mine water will flow through it. How can the DNR possibly discuss socioeconomic impacts without even notifying our tribe of this meeting? Our people stand to lose our very existence. Our wild rice beds will be devastated. Our cultural and spiritual traditions will be seriously damaged—or destroyed. Yet the DNR has the arrogance to assume we don't need to be invited to the table.[26] (Arlyn Ackley, Sokaogon Chippewa Tribal Chairman)

One of the symptoms of environmental racism, besides the disproportionate impact racial minorities experience from environmental hazards, is the exclusion of racial minorities from participation in the decision-making process. One of the objectives of the WATER campaign is to provide statewide press advisories of any activity by the Wisconsin Department of Natural Resources (DNR) or the Crandon Mining Co. (CMC) relating to the mine permitting process.

In January 1994 the DNR had planned a series of meetings over three days with officials and consultants of the CMC to determine the scope of study for the social and environmental studies that would be part of the company's mine permit application. Although the DNR did not notify any of the affected Indian and non-Indian communities, word leaked out and WATER issued a statewide press advisory that was picked up over the wire services. On the morning of the first meeting, the headline in the state's largest morning newspaper, *The Milwaukee Sentinel*, was: "Indian leaders blast DNR over meetings on mining project." The DNR's mine project coordinator, Bill Tans, said Chippewa leaders were not invited because the meetings were not set up for public comment. "These are strictly preliminary meetings, and everything can change," he said.[27] Tans explained that the tribes would have an opportunity to comment at the time of CMC's publication of a Notice of Intent and a scope of study for its mine permit application in April 1994. However, from the perspective of the tribes, this effectively excluded them from determining the agenda for the proposed studies related to the mine permit. It also contributes to a "psychology of inevitability" about the mine because all the planning is done behind closed doors and presented to the public as an accomplished fact. As a result of the negative publicity generated by this story, the DNR agreed to set up a fax communication system to notify the tribes in advance of any planned meetings with CMC.

Mobilizing the Grassroots Opposition

The women have been entrusted with the Water and the men with the Fire. These are two things that sustain life. If you take care of them, they will take care of you.[28] (Eddie Benton-Benai, Three Fires Midewin Society)

Even before Exxon/Rio Algom filed its notice of intent to seek mining permits for the Crandon/Mole Lake mine, the WATER campaign announced a statewide emergency rally to stop the proposed mine at the state capitol in Madison. In March 1994, over 400 people from all around the state rallied at the state capitol and listened as Frances Van Zile, an *Anishinabekwe* (Chippewa woman), spoke about the role of women as the "Keepers of the Water" in her culture:

This isn't an Indian issue, nor is it a white issue. It's everybody's issue. Everybody has to take care of that water. The women are the ones who are the keepers of that water. I ask all women to stand up and support that and realize that if it wasn't for the water none of us would be here today because when we first started out in life, we were born in that water in our mother's womb. And I'll bet you everybody here turned on that water today to do something with it. And that's what they're going to pollute. That's what they're going to destroy. I'm not going to have any more wild rice if that water drops down three feet from the mine dewatering. That is important to my way of life—to all Anishinabes' way of life.

And they're taking that away—they're going to destroy our way of life.

Following the rally at the state capitol, demonstrators marched to the headquarters of the Wisconsin DNR and to the Wisconsin Manufacturers and Commerce Association. The latter is one of the chief lobbying organizations for the mining companies as well as for the mining equipment manufacturing industry in Milwaukee. By their physical presence, the WATER campaign intended to put corporate and governmental decision makers on notice that the resistance to this mine project could reach into the centers of corporate and governmental power. Sokaogon Chippewa tribal members Fred Ackley and Frances Van Zile dramatically illustrated this determination to confront corporate decision makers when they attended Exxon's annual shareholder meeting in Dallas, Texas, the following month.

The Exxon Shareholder Campaign

We see our shareholder actions as a vehicle to give access to corporate board rooms for communities like Mole Lake.[29] (Toni Harris, Sinsinawa Dominican Sisters of Wisconsin)

In addition to environmental and fishing groups, the WATER campaign also included various church groups that held stock in several mining companies and were willing to raise issues of social and corporate responsibility through shareholder resolutions. Shortly after Exxon announced its intention to seek mining permits at Crandon/Mole Lake, the Sinsinawa Dominican Sisters of Wisconsin, along with six other religious congregations, filed a shareholder resolution on behalf of the Sokaogon Chippewa and the other Native communities affected by Exxon's mining operations. The resolution specifically asked Exxon to provide a report to shareholders on the impact of the proposed mine on indigenous peoples and on any sacred sites within indigenous communities. The resolution also called on Exxon to disclose "the nature of and reason(s) for any public opposition to our Company's mining operations wherever they may occur."[30]

Exxon immediately informed the U.S. Securities and Exchange Commission, which has regulatory authority over shareholder resolutions, that it intended to omit the Sinsinawa resolution from its 1994 proxy statement. The company argued that the resolution is moot because "extensive studies covering the impact on the environment and indigenous people and all other material aspects of the project were prepared by both Exxon and the Wisconsin Department of Natural Resources" before Exxon suspended the project in 1986.[31]

Sister Toni Harris responded that the studies Exxon referred to did not address the specific questions raised in their resolution. "Most significantly," said Harris, "the 446 page Environmental Impact Statement published in November 1986 was criticized as inadequate by the U.S. Department of the Interior and the Environmental Protection Agency."[32] In their letter to the Wisconsin DNR, in response to the environmental impact statement for the Crandon project, the Interior Department said it did not "believe there is sufficient consideration of potential long-term impacts associated with the proposed mine development, or of contingency plans to assure that adequate environmental protection will be provided. We also feel that special attention should be paid to the effect of long-term discharge to the Wolf River, and to the water resources of the Mole Lake Indian Reservation."[33] The SEC ruled that the Sinsinawa resolution was not "moot" and that Exxon could not exclude the resolution from stockholder consideration.

With the SEC victory in hand, the Chippewa were able to challenge Exxon on its home turf. Fred Ackley and Frances Van Zile spoke to the resolution and explained to the shareholders that the very existence of their culture was at stake in this proposed mining investment. The resolution received 6 percent of the vote, or 49 million shares.

Most shareholder resolutions of this type receive less than 3 percent of the vote. While the resolution was defeated, the Chippewa won enough votes to reintroduce the resolution at the 1995 shareholders meeting.[34]

The Wolf River: Ecology and Economics

Crandon Mining Co.'s proposed construction and operation of a hardrock metallic sulfide mine at the headwaters of the Wolf River seriously threatens this magnificent river. Water quality and tremendous ecological diversity is imperiled, including bald eagle, wild rice, lake sturgeon and trout habitat. The Wolf River is the lifeline of the Menominee people and central to our existence. We will let no harm come to the river.[35] (John Teller, Menominee Tribal Chairman)

"The environment comes first," says Jerry D. Goodrich, president of the Crandon Mining Company. "If we can't protect the Wolf, there'll be no Crandon mine."[36] Opponents of Exxon's proposed mine won't argue with Goodrich on this point. The Wolf River is at the center of the northeastern Wisconsin tourist economy and the meeting ground between Indians and sportfishers who have a history of bitter disagreement over Chippewa spearfishing.[37] The Wolf River, in Langlade and Menonimee counties, is the state's largest whitewater trout stream, supporting brown, brook, and rainbow trout fisheries. Over 50,000 tourists are attracted to the area every year to enjoy trout fishing, whitewater rafting, and canoeing.[38] The lower half of the river is designated a National Wild and Scenic River.

During Exxon's first attempt to develop the Crandon/Mole Lake deposit, the Wolf River became a rallying point for both environmental and tribal opposition. The Menominee Indian Nation strongly opposed the mine, partly because the Wolf River runs through their reservation. Exxon's mine proposal called for dumping over 2,000 gallons of mine wastewater per minute into the trout-rich streams that drain into the Wolf River. A biological consultant, hired by Trout Unlimited and other environmental groups, reviewed Exxon's proposal and concluded that "The discharge of waste water from the Crandon Project to Swamp Creek could result in the bioaccumulation of heavy metals in aquatic organisms and changes in the natural species composition of the area."[39] By the time that the DNR held public hearings on the draft environmental impact statement in June 1986, more than 10,000 signatures had been collected on petitions asking the governor, the legislature, and the DNR to oppose any dumping into the Wolf River. The Langlade County board had also passed a similar resolution. The mobilization of public sentiment about preserving the pristine quality of the Wolf River became a major turning point in the first Exxon battle, because the widely perceived economic threat to the Wolf River tourism industry was felt to outweigh any potential economic benefits from the mine project.

Shortly after Exxon announced that it would once again seek permits for the mine the Wolf River Territory Association, a group of business people promoting the area for tourism, passed a resolution against the mine. And Herb Buettner, owner of the Wild Wolf Inn and president of the Wolf River chapter of Trout Unlimited, warned that "If the mine were to go in, it would wipe out the Wolf River trout stream and create a pile of tailings that in 50 years would be a Superfund (hazardous waste) site."[40]

Jerry Goodrich's concern for preserving the pristine quality of the Wolf River has not reassured those who are familiar with Exxon's strong opposition to DNR's proposed classification of the upper Wolf River as an "Outstanding Resource Water" (ORW) under the provisions of the federal Clean Water Act. If this status were granted, any water discharged into the Wolf would have to be as clean as the water in the river, or cleaner. The first indication that Exxon might revive its Crandon project came in May 1988 when James D. Patton, Exxon Minerals' manager of regulatory affairs, wrote to Wisconsin DNR Secretary Carroll Besadny warning that DNR's proposed classification of the Wolf River "could create a significant potential roadblock to any future resumption of the Crandon project."[41] Exxon's intense lobbying against the designation was counteracted by the combined forces of the Menominee Tribe and the Wolf River Watershed Alliance. The Wolf River received ORW status in November 1988.

Besides Exxon's opposition to ORW classification for the Wolf River, the company's record with the 1989 Exxon Valdez oil spill raised additional doubts about the company's ability to manage a high-risk mining venture in the ecologically sensitive Wolf River watershed. Adding to doubts about Exxon's environmental record is the fact that Crandon Mining Co.'s first public relations officer, J. Wiley Bragg, handled public relations for Exxon in Alaska after the Exxon-Valdez spill.[42]

Prior to the first public hearing on Exxon's mine permit application, the WATER campaign ran a series of local newspaper ads that asked: "Will the Wolf River Be Exxon's Valdez? What If It Happened Here?" The ads emphasized that Wisconsin has abundant clean waters but that the history of metallic sulfide mining is one of poisoned rivers, lakes, and groundwaters. The ads urged citizens to attend the DNR public hearing and state their concerns about the proposed mine. More than 300 people, including Native Americans, local property owners, fishers, small business owners, and environmentalists, packed into the Nashville Town Hall in April 1994 to express their concerns. Because of the large number of people who wanted to testify, the DNR stayed past midnight and still was not able to accommodate all those who wanted to speak. Of the 300 people who attended the hearing, only a handful were in favor of the project. Two-thirds of the people who testified mentioned their concern about the Wolf River, local lakes and streams, or groundwater.

Some mine opponents accused the DNR of manipulating the order in which testimony was heard and preventing several knowledgeable antimining citizens from speaking until last, when the media and the majority of the audience had left after waiting five hours. Among those who had registered early in the evening but was not called till last was Wisconsin Public Intervenor Laura Sutherland. The Public Intervenor is an office in the Wisconsin Department of Justice empowered to protect public rights in the natural resources of the state. Despite Exxon's objections, the Citizens Advisory Committee, which oversees the Public Intervenor, unanimously directed the Public Intervenor to review Exxon's mine proposal. One of Sutherland's principal concerns in the permitting process was the fact that "The DNR has never before permitted *any* discharge into ORW waters and this mine proposal, therefore, presents the possibility of a dangerous precedent."[43] Although Sutherland's testimony was not covered in the press reports immediately after the meeting, the *Milwaukee Journal* featured her written testimony in a front-page story the following week, followed by a strong editorial that warned that "The loss of recreation and tourism from a degraded environment could end up outweighing any economic gains from the mine."[44]

Prior to the DNR meeting, Crandon Mining Company president Jerry Goodrich sent out a letter to local residents warning that "Certain groups opposed to mining and other industry development are planning to bus people in from Green Bay, Madison, Milwaukee and other distant locations to pack the hearing with opponents of the Crandon Project (or, at least, people who will say they are opponents of the project)."[45] It was the classic "outside agitator" ploy. It backfired when the WATER campaign took out ads in the local newspapers the following week that asked: "Can We Trust Exxon to Tell the Truth?" The ad pointed out that "There were *NO* busloads of opponents, there were never any planned. In fact, 68% of those who gave oral statements were from Forest County and the area immediately downriver of the project. The only people that came from 'distant locations' were the employees of Exxon temporarily living near Crandon. Mr. Goodrich, where do you get your misinformation?"[46]

In April 1995, the national conservation group American Rivers placed the Wolf River on its list of the nation's 20 most threatened rivers because of the possibility of pollution from Exxon/Rio Algom's proposed mine. The Menominee, along with the River Alliance of Wisconsin and the Mining Impact Coalition of Wisconsin, provided the documentation on the threat from mine pollution. The day after the Wolf's designation as a threatened river, Exxon announced it was abandoning its plans to dump treated wastewater from the mine into the Wolf River. Instead, the company would build a 40-mile pipeline and divert the wastewater into the Wisconsin River near Rhinelander, Wisconsin.

While the timing of Exxon's announcement may have been calculated to divert attention from the American Rivers announcement and the continuing controversy over mine waste discharges to the Wolf River, mine opponents were quick to point out that the new plan threatens pollution of both the Wolf and Wisconsin rivers. David Blouin, a spokesperson for the Mining Impact Coalition of Wisconsin, said the threat to the Wolf would remain because tailings from the mine would still be stored at the headwaters of the Wolf. Because the Wisconsin River is not as clean as the Wolf, the company would not have to spend as much treating the discharge. In addition, the plan could actually increase groundwater depletion in the area of the mine because of the amount of water necessary to pump the wastes to Rhinelander.[47] Whatever the motivation for the change of plans, it was a retreat from Exxon's previously stated position that they could meet the stringent requirements for discharge into a water body rated as an Outstanding Resource Water.

In all of these activities, the WATER campaign is developing a multifaceted counterstrategy to Exxon's ecologically and culturally destructive mine plans. Through intertribal organization, alliance building with environmental and sportfishing groups, mass demonstrations, shareholder resolutions, and mass media publicity, the Sokaogon Chippewa hope to increase the political and financial risks of the project for Exxon and Rio Algom. This was the reason why the Sokaogon and the Nii Win Intertribal Council invited the Indigenous Environmental Network (IEN) to hold their fifth annual "Protecting Mother Earth Conference" on the Mole Lake Reservation in June 1994, in conjunction with a regional gathering coordinated by the Midwest Treaty Network.

International Networking

There'll be decades of fallout regardless of who wins this battle. This is one of the great events. We want to put Mole Lake and Exxon on the map.[48] (Walter Bresette, Red Cliff band of Lake Superior Chippewa)

Previous IEN conferences brought together community-based indigenous activists from throughout the Americas and the Pacific Islands to work together to protect indigenous lands from contamination and exploitation. IEN's previous efforts have helped grassroots activists defeat a 5,000-acre landfill on the Rosebud Lakota Reservation in South Dakota, and a proposed incinerator and an asbestos landfill on Dine (Navajo) land in Arizona.[49]

Approximately 1,000 people gathered on the Mole Lake Reservation during the five-day conference. "This is to put Exxon and (Wisconsin) Governor Tommy Thompson on notice that we can bring people up here to stop the mine," said Bill Koenen, an IEN National Council member and a Mole Lake band member.[50] On the last day of the conference, over 300 native and nonnative people participated in a "spirit walk" to the proposed mine site where they conducted a spiritual ceremony while trespassing on Exxon's property. Exxon called the Crandon police but no arrests were made. The police were reluctant to interrupt the ceremony.

The Mole Lake gathering also featured a Wisconsin Review Commission to review the track records of Exxon and Rio Algom around the world. The commission included groups representing farmers, churches, workers, civil rights activists, women, small businesses, tribal governments, and recreational groups. A similar commission was assembled in the 1970s by the Black Hills Alliance to investigate the track records of uranium mining companies that wanted to mine in the sacred Black Hills of the Lakota (Sioux).

The panel, chaired by Wisconsin Secretary of State Douglas LaFollette, heard testimony from Native people who came from Alaska, New Mexico, Colombia, and Ontario. Testimony focused on people who have been directly affected by Exxon's mining and oil drilling activities and its chemical and oil leaks.

Nearly all the testimony before the commission was delivered by Native peoples from North and South America, which reflects the fact that a disproportionate amount of resource extraction occurs on Native lands. Native Eyak fisher Dune Lankard explained how the Exxon Valdez spill damaged the resource-based cultures of local Native peoples on Prince William Sound:

> I grew up fishing since I was five years old on the ocean. I thought I had the most incredible way of life in the world and I never believed once that anyone could ever kill the ocean. So when it happened, I was in shock. They leave you with the social impacts—the suicide, the alcohol, the drug abuse, the loss of jobs, the loss of a way of life, the loss of language, the loss of subsistence. How do you add all that up? How do you compensate somebody for taking everything away from you?[51]

After the oil spill, Eyak government leaders complained that Exxon simply refused to recognize their Native group. The company took the position that the Eyak were not adversely affected by the oil spill, and it consequently refused to provide food and services that were provided for Natives elsewhere.[52] Exxon was fined $5 billion in punitive damages for economic losses from the spill in 1995. The company is appealing the fine.

Some of the most damning testimony came from Armando Valbuena Gouriyù, a Wayuu Indian from the Guajira peninsula, on the northern tip of Colombia, where Exxon operates the El Cerrejòn open-pit coal mine in a joint venture with the Colombian government. It is the largest coal mine in the western hemisphere. Valbuena worked at the huge coal mine, from 1983 until Exxon fired him for his union organizing activities in 1988. The construction of the mine had a devastating effect on the lives of approximately 90 Wayuu *apushis* (matrilineal kinship groupings), who saw their houses, corrals, cleared ground, and cemeteries flattened for the construction of a road from El Cerrejòn to the new port of Puerto Bolivar, with no respect for indigenous rights.[53] The excavation of the open pit has also caused the adjoining rivers and streams to dry up, along with people's drinking wells. The area affected is roughly 94,000 acres.[54] Colombian army troops and armored tanks were called in three times to break miners' strikes.[55] In 1992, the London-based Survival International, an international Native rights organization, named Exxon to its list of the top ten companies who were doing serious damage to tribal peoples' land in the Americas.[56] The vice president of the El Cerrejòn mine, Jerry Goodrich, is now the president of the Crandon Mining Company. While Goodrich was vice president at El Cerrejòn, more than 30 workers died during work at the mine.[57] Valbuena testified that Jerry Goodrich "promised us jobs and prosperity and instead worked to destroy our traditional ways and forced us from our land. This must not happen again . . . To allow this mine is to disappear from the earth."[58]

The Wisconsin Review Commission released its report on the track records of Exxon and Rio Algom on March 24, 1995—the sixth anniversary of the Exxon Valdez oil spill. In releasing the report, Wisconsin Secretary of State Douglas La Follette urged the state legislature to approve the mining "bad actor" legislation that would require the state to consider a company's past performance before approving state mine permits. "Past violations," La Follette said, "are taken into account for everything from driver's licenses to gaming licenses, but not permits for potentially harmful mining developments."[59] The commission presented its citizens' hearing panel as a model for public participation in the absence of governmental action, as well as for multinational citizens' tracking of multinational corporations.

Exxon was offered the opportunity to respond to the charges in the report prior to the report's publication, but chose not to do so. Instead, Dick Diotte, director of community relations for the company, criticized the report for being "obviously biased," adding that "We're not going to respond point by point." As far as the proposed Crandon mine was concerned, "The mine will be developed with today's technology and shouldn't be judged by things that were done under old technology."[60]

The Movement to Ban Sulfide Metal Mining

Exxon could not have imagined the opposition this project would generate. It has united people from all over the state in defense of our resources. Sportsmen, from the Conservation Congress on down, have joined the tribes, environmental groups of every stripe and taxpayers concerned about the long-term societal burden this mine and others like it would create, in fighting back. Those constituencies individually have power. Combined they are extremely powerful. Thanks to this legislation they are being mobilized.[61] (Bob Hudek, Executive Director, Wisconsin Citizen Action)

The typical industry response to any criticism about mine waste problems was that "new technologies" would solve any potential problems. The WATER campaign decided to create a petition drive that would force the industry and the Wisconsin DNR to disclose how these "new technologies" would solve the fundamental problems of acid mine drainage from metallic sulfide mines. The petitions asked the Natural Resources Board, the citizen board that oversees the DNR, to use its rule-making authority to ban the mining of sulfide mineral deposits because of the well-known releases of acid drainage from sulfide metallic wastes and the responsibility of the DNR to prevent pollution resulting from the leaching of waste materials.

In December 1994, nearly 40 representatives of groups in the WATER Campaign presented more than 10,000 signatures on petitions requesting the ban. While DNR Secretary George Meyer told the board that it did not have the authority to ban metallic sulfide mining, he admitted that his staff could find no examples of successfully reclaimed metallic sulfide mines.[62] When the board denied the petition, mine opponents immediately filed a petition for a judicial review of the board's decision.

Mine opponents won a stunning victory when a Rusk County judge overturned the decision by the Natural Resources Board to dismiss citizen petitions, and asked the DNR to come up with rules to ban metallic sulfide mining. The judge cited state statutes that gave the DNR broad powers to protect, maintain, and improve the waters of the state.[63] The DNR appealed the decision. The Wisconsin Appeals Court ruled in favor of the DNR, saying that the legislature did not authorize the DNR to ban metallic sulfide mining.

Meanwhile, mine opponents worked with state Rep. Spencer Black (D-Madison) to introduce a mining moratorium bill that would prohibit the opening of a new mine in a sulfide ore body until a similar mine has been operated elsewhere and closed for at least ten years without pollution from acid mine drainage. Despite a well-organized grassroots lobbying campaign and an overwhelming Assembly vote (95–4) to bring the bill out of committee for consideration, the powerful mining lobby convinced the Republican-controlled Senate to adjourn a week early to avoid sending the bill back to the Assembly for a final vote.[64] Mine opponents responded to the legislative setback by launching a statewide Mining Moratorium Pledge Campaign. The campaign will ask every candidate for state legislative office to pledge to support the moratorium bill when it is reintroduced during the next legislative session in January 1997.

The Federal Environmental Review Process

Even if the mining company makes substantial financial commitments for restoration of the site, there will more than likely be damages not provided for with financial assurances. The neighbors, particularly the tribes, will receive a relatively meager proportion of the short term economic benefit, but by virtue of the location of their lands, will inherit the brunt of the environmental problems and economic bust cycle. It seems unfair that a large and powerful, but temporarily involved, interested party can reap the benefits, but leave the majority of the costs to less powerful interests who cannot reasonably move from the area to escape long term costs.[65] (Janet Smith, U.S. Department of the Interior, Fish and Wildlife Service, Green Bay, Wisconsin)

The construction of the proposed Crandon mine would involve the filling of approximately 30 acres of wetlands. Under the provisions of the Clean Water Act, the U.S. Army Corps of Engineers (COE) must review such projects. In November 1994, the Fish and Wildlife Service of the U.S. Department of the Interior (DOI) expressed serious reservations about the project:

> The Department is particularly concerned about the proposed permit action because we believe that it could potentially result in a diminishment of Indian interests in exchange for benefits for the general public. The courts have held that federal agencies cannot subordinate Indian interests to other public purposes except when specifically authorized by Congress to do so.[66]

The DOI recommended that the affected tribes play a greater role in identifying environmental impacts and "impacts to Indian trust resources" as defined in the treaties with the federal government. Furthermore, the DOI recommended that the COE be the sole lead agency for the federal environmental impact statement (EIS) "so that the impacts to Indian trust resources can be appropriately assessed in a purely federal forum. The state does not have the authority to assess impacts to Indian trust lands and thus should have no role in doing so."[67] The COE's decision to conduct its own EIS has provided mine opponents with two separate opportunities to argue their case.

The public hearings held by the COE on the Crandon project brought out overwhelming public opposition in the capital city of Madison, in Crandon itself, and on the Sokaogon Chippewa reservation. At the hearing on the reservation, tribal members expressed their determination to stop Exxon's proposed mine. Bill Koenen, a tribal member and environmental specialist, testified as his three sons stood beside him: "Our children will be right behind us to help us defend our sacred land and wild rice beds." And Robert Van Zile, a traditional pipe carrier, reflected the views of many who spoke when he said, "If I have to defend this land with my life, I will."[68]

While Exxon has claimed that its Crandon mine studies are "one of the most thorough environmental studies in state history,"[69] the COE has determined that the groundwater models used by Exxon to predict water drawdown around the mine are scientifically inadequate, and it has proposed additional studies by an independent consultant with no ties to Exxon.[70]

Tribal Sovereignty and Regulatory Authority

This move by the Thompson/Klauser administration to fight clean water comes as no surprise. Klauser was Exxon's chief lobbyist when the mining industry helped rewrite Wisconsin's water quality laws that govern mining. They eliminated the Public Intervenor's Office, made the administration of the DNR a political appointment, and are even appealing the state judicial decision that gives the DNR authority to determine what kinds of mining are to be allowed. Thompson will not let anything interfere with Exxon's proposed mine—not State or Federal law, not the will of the citizens, and not the concern for clean water.[71] (Sandy Lyon, WATER Campaign)

In 1984 the U.S. Environmental Protection Agency (EPA) announced that it would pursue government-to-government relations with tribes.[72] In 1994–95, three Wisconsin Indian tribes asked the EPA for greater regulatory authority over reservation air and water quality. The Forest County Potawatomi asked for tougher air pollution standards on its reservation under the federal Clean Air Act.[73] Meanwhile, the Sokaogon Chippewa and the Oneida were granted independent authority from the EPA to regulate water quality on their reservations. Under amendments to the Clean Water Act, the U.S. EPA can designate tribes as independent regulators of surface water quality in the same way the EPA can give authority to states. Tribal regulatory authority would affect all upstream industrial and municipal facilities, including Exxon's proposed mine in the Swamp Creek watershed. Because Swamp Creek flows into the tribe's Rice Lake, the Sokaogon have to give approval for any physical, chemical, or biological upstream activity that might degrade their wild rice beds.[74]

At public hearings on the tribal requests, local citizens, lake associations, and the Wolf River Watershed Alliance testified in support of tribal regulatory authority. Many of the local lake property owners associations expressed extreme dissatisfaction with the way in which Republican Governor Tommy Thompson and his chief aide, James Klauser, a former Exxon lobbyist, paved the way for mining by making the DNR Secretary a political appointment and eliminating the Public Intervenor's Office. The experts hired by the Public Intervenor had raised serious questions about the scientific adequacy of Exxon's groundwater studies and their waste disposal plans. Many citizens applauded the tribe for trying to preserve clean water for everybody.[75]

Some local business people testified in opposition, charging that the regulations would "shut down northern Wisconsin." This was the same kind of misinformation used by those who opposed Chippewa off-reservation spearfishing during the turmoil lasting from 1984 to 1992. The Wisconsin Mining Association, representing some of the largest mining equipment companies in Milwaukee, warned that tribal water quality authority "could be the most controversial and contentious environmental development affecting the state in decades."[76]

Within a week of EPA approval of Sokaogon Chippewa and Oneida water quality authority, Wisconsin Attorney General James Doyle sued the U.S. Environmental Protection Agency in federal court, demanding that the federal government reverse its decision to let Indian tribes make their own water pollution laws. Several Republican state legislators have called on Congress to change the Clean Air Act to disallow tribal authority over clean-air standards.[77] Once again, mainstream politicians are using scare tactics to suggest that Indian sovereignty over reservation resources is an economic threat to small business owners while they ignore the serious potential for long-term damage to the resources and economic base of northern Wisconsin.

In response to the state of Wisconsin's challenge of the EPA's tribal water quality authority, the Wolf River Watershed Alliance filed an *amicus,* or "friend of the court," brief supporting EPA's approval of requests by the Sokaogon Chippewa and Oneida tribes. "If the state is stupid enough to appeal this thing, we'll certainly write a brief detailing all the instances where the state has been derelict in its authority or abdicated its responsibility," said Robert Schmitz, president of the alliance.[78] Meanwhile, a federal court ruling in Montana has upheld the right of Indian tribes to set water-quality standards on their reservations.[79]

Save Our Clean Waters Speaking Tour

This is collectively the largest, broadest, multiracial environmental alliance ever formed over a single issue in Wisconsin. (Annette Rasch, Wisconsin Greens)

Exxon executives may have believed they could avoid public resistance to their proposed mine by abandoning plans to dump mine wastewater into the Wolf River and instead divert it 40 miles to the Wisconsin River. If so, they seriously underestimated the depth and extent of public opposition.[80] The Wolf River Watershed Education Project was an effort to bring the issue of Exxon's proposed mine to the public that would be directly affected by the mine—whether environmentally, economically, or culturally. The project built on previous joint efforts of grassroots environmental groups, sportfishing groups, and Native American nations. When Exxon announced its plan to divert mine wastewater into the Wisconsin River, the project expanded to include that watershed.

Beginning on Earth Day, two speaking tours simultaneously went up the Wolf and Wisconsin rivers, stopping in communities along the way. Major goals of the tour included building momentum for a rally at the Hat Rapids dam on the Wisconsin River, the site where Exxon/Rio Algom proposes to discharge treated wastewater, and mobilizing public support for legislative passage of a moratorium on sulfide mining. The 12-day tour drew over 1,000 people in 22 cities and towns. The tour culminated in a rally at the Hat Rapids dam and a parade past Exxon/Rio Algom corporate head-quarters in Rhinelander, Wisconsin, on May 4, 1996, which drew some 1,000 people, according to a Sheriff's Department estimate.

Exxon responded to the tour by buying radio and full-page newspaper advertise-ments in cities and towns along the Save Our Clean Waters speaking tour.[81] Company spokespeople accused mine opponents of spreading misinformation and half-truths about the project, without themselves specifically identifying a single example. The WATER Campaign responded with its own radio ads. The text of one ad read as follows: "The DNR couldn't find a single metallic sulfide mine anywhere that had been closed without polluting the water. In light of this fact, it makes you wonder. Why should Wisconsin's water be the proving ground for Exxon's experiment?"

At the same time that Exxon/Rio Algom was accusing mine opponents of misleading the public, two independent experts retained by the Wisconsin DNR raised serious concerns about virtually every aspect of the company's waste disposal plan. "Crandon Mining Co. has been misleading the public," said David Blouin, spokesperson for the Mining Impact Coalition of Wisconsin. "Their claims that the proposal will cause no harm cannot be supported by the inadequate data presented so far." The DNR has asked the company to do further testing to determine the potential for acid generation and toxic metal releases from mine wastes.[82] This research will involve additional costs and will upset the company's permit timetable by at least two years. This will provide ample opportunities to mobilize even greater public opposition to the project.

Whatever the final outcome, the coming together of the five tribes with their non-native neighbors, environmental, and sportfishing groups to oppose Exxon/Rio Algom has transformed this local battle into what the *New York Times* has described as "one of the country's fiercest grass-roots environmental face-offs."[83]

Conclusion

Resource extraction plans . . . proposed for Indigenous lands do not consider the significance of these economic systems, nor their value for the future. A direct consequence is that environmentally destructive programs ensue, many times foreclosing the opportunity to continue the lower scale, intergenerational economic practices which had been underway in the Native community.[84] (Winona La Duke, Anishinabe [Chippewa] activist)

Mining, by its very nature, constitutes an assault on the physical, social, and cultural environment. When this assault occurs in ecologically sensitive areas inhabited by native peoples who rely on traditional subsistence economies, the results can be disastrous. In the past, this corporate assault on Native cultures has frequently gone unnoticed and unreported. Chippewa resistance to Exxon's proposed mine emerged at a time when Native peoples all around the world were actively opposing large-scale destructive development projects on or adjacent to their lands. Their initial efforts to oppose Exxon were favorably viewed by some of their non-Indian neighbors and an effective Native–environmental alliance was born. With the emergence of the Watershed Alliance to end Environmental Racism, a new level of political organization and resistance has emerged to challenge the unquestioned assumptions of global industrialization—and the inevitable disappearance of Native subsistence cultures.

Notes

1. Great Lakes Indian Fish and Wildlife Commission, *Sulfide Mining: The Process and The Price: A Tribal and Ecological Perspective* (Odanah, Wisc.: 1996), p. 17.

2. Great Lakes Indian Fish and Wildlife Commission, *A Guide to Understanding Chippewa Treaty Rights* (Odanah, Wisc.: Sept. 1991), pp. 1–2.

3. Edward R. May and Robert W. Shilling, "Case Study of Environmental Impact—Flambeau Project," *Mining Congress Journal* (Jan. 1977), p. 39.

4. Ron Seely, "Mining Has Strong Potential in Wisconsin," *Wisconsin State Journal,* Jan. 31, 1982.

5. Wisconsin Department of Natural Resources, *Final Environmental Impact Statement, Exxon Coal and Minerals Co. Zinc-Copper Mine, Crandon, Wisconsin* (Madison, Wisc.: Nov. 1986), p. ii. The weight of the Great Pyramids was calculated from figures provided in the *World Book* (1987), vol. 15, p. 810a.

6. Al Gedicks, "The Sokaogon Chippewa Take on Exxon," Chapter 3 in *The New Resource Wars: Native and Environmental Struggles Against Multinational Corporations* (Boston: South End Press, 1993).

7. "Rio, Exxon Team Up in Wisconsin," *The Northern Miner* 79:29 (Sept. 20, 1993).

8. Testimony before the U.S. Army Corps of Engineers, Public Hearing, Mole Lake Sokaogon Chippewa Reservation, March 29, 1995.

9. Edmund Jefferson Danziger, *The Chippewas of Lake Superior* (Norman: University of Oklahoma Press, 1978), 153.

10. Thomas Vennum, Jr., *Wild Rice and the Ojibway People* (St. Paul, Minn.: Minnesota Historical Society Press, 1988); Robert P. W. Gough, "A Cultural-Historical Assessment of the Wild Rice Resources of the Sokaogon Chippewa," in COACT Research, Inc., *An Analysis of the Socio-Economic and Environmental Impacts of Mining and Mineral Resource Development on the Sokaogon Chippewa Community* (Madison, Wisc.: 1980).

11. Wisconsin DNR, *Final Environmental Impact Statement, Exxon Coal and Minerals Co., Zinc-Copper Mine, Crandon, Wisconsin* (Madison, Wisc.: Nov. 1986), 108. The importance of subsistence

activity can be seen in the fact that 86 percent of the Chippewa families rely to a great extent on hunting and fishing for food, while over 90 percent rely on gardening, ricing, and picking wild plants. *Ibid.*

12. Exxon, *Forecast of Future Conditions: Socioeconomic Assessment, Crandon Project.* Prepared for Exxon Minerals by Research and Planning Consultants, Inc. (Oct. 1983), 316.

13. Masinaigan (Talking Paper), "Chippewa Leaders Voice Concerns about Proposed Wisconsin Mine" (Odanah, Wisc.: Great Lakes Indian Fish and Wildlife Commission, fall 1993).

14. Laura Sutherland, "Comments on Exxon/Rio Algom's Notice of Intent," *Wisconsin Public Intervenor,* Feb. 1994, p. 2.

15. Jack Schmidt, "Problems with Tailings Ponds: Incomplete Regulation, Inconsistent Review, Threats to Water," *Down to Earth (*newspaper) (Helena, Mont.: July/Aug. 1982).

16. U.S. Forest Service, *Acid Drainage from Mines on the National Forests: A Management Challenge* (Washington, D.C.: Dept. of Agriculture, 1993), 3.

17. "An Overview of Mining Waste Management Issues in Wisconsin," Bureau of Solid and Hazardous Waste Management, July 1995.

18. Wisconsin Department of Natural Resources, *Final Environmental Impact Statement, Exxon Coal and Minerals Co., Zinc-Copper Mine, Crandon, Wisconsin* (Madison, Wisc.: Nov. 1986), 131.

19. Larry Van Goethem, "Exxon Mine Will Feature Elaborate Waste Water Plan," *Milwaukee Journal,* March 28, 1982.

20. U.S. Environmental Protection Agency, *Tribes at Risk: The Wisconsin Tribes Comparative Risk Project* (Washington, D.C.: Oct. 1992), ix.

21. Cited in Al Gedicks, *The New Resource Wars: Native and Environmental Struggles Against Multinational Corporations* (Boston: South End, 1993), 63.

22. Anthropology Resource Center (ARC), "Transnational Corporations and Indigenous Peoples," *ARC Newsletter* 5:3 (Sept. 1981); Julian Burger, *Report from the Frontier: The State of the World's Indigenous Peoples* (London and Cambridge, Mass.: Zed Books and Cultural Survival, 1987); Michael C. Howard, *The Impact of the International Mining Industry on Native Peoples* (University of Sydney, Australia: Transnational Corporations Research Project, Feb. 1988).

23. Ralph Nader, "Approaching Strategy for Confronting the Corporate Threat," *Akwesasne Notes* (Rooseveltown, N.Y.: Mohawk Nation) 14:6 (winter 1982) 9.

24. Rick Whaley and Walter Bresette, *Walleye Warriors: An Effective Strategy Against Racism and for the Earth* (Philadelphia: New Society, 1993).

25. Trout Unlimited (Wolf River Chapter), "Mining Policy Statement" (Jan. 1994).

26. James E. Causey, "Indian Leaders Blast DNR Over Meetings on Mining Project," *Milwaukee Sentinel,* Jan. 10, 1994.

27. *Ibid.*

28. Cited in Sue Erickson, "Of Women and the Water," Masinaigan (Talking Paper), Odanah, Wisc., Great Lakes Indian Fish and Wildlife Commission, spring 1994, p. 3.

29. WATER Press Release, "Religious Investors Group Wins SEC Action Against Exxon Crandon Project," Feb. 7, 1994.

30. Exxon, Proxy Statement (1994), p. 16.

31. *Ibid.*

32. Sister Toni Harris, General Councilor, to Amy Bowerman, Office of Chief Council, Securities and Exchange Commission, letter of Jan. 4, 1994.

33. Sheila Minor Huff, Regional Environmental Officer, U.S. Department of the Interior, to Howard Druckenmiller, Director, Bureau of Environmental Analysis and Review, Wisconsin DNR, letter of July 31, 1986.

34. The resolution received 5.3 percent of the vote in 1995, falling short of the 6 percent necessary for the resolution to be automatically considered the following year. See "Exxon Asked to Disclose Public Opposition to Mines," *Forest Republican,* May 4, 1995.

35. *Isthmus Newsweekly* (Madison, Wisc.), May 26, 1995.

36. Peter A. Geniesse, "Wolf Key to Mining Fortunes," *Appleton Post-Crescent*, April 24, 1994.

37. Nathan Seppa, "Old Foes Now Allies: Indians, Sports Fishermen Join to Oppose Mine," *Wisconsin State Journal*, Feb. 11, 1994.

38. Larry Van Goethem, "Exxon and the Wild Wolf River," *Wisconsin Sportsman*, 15:2 (March 1986) 39.

39. Dr. Arthur S. Brooks, "Comments on the DEIS' description of water impacts of the Crandon Project." June 1986, p. 10.

40. Seppa, *op cit.*, note 37.

41. James D. Patton, Letter to Carroll D. Besadny, Secretary, Wisconsin Dept. of Natural Resources, May 20, 1988, p. 4.

42. Ron Seely, "Exxon's PR Man: J. Wiley Bragg," *Wisconsin State Journal*, April 25, 1994.

43. Wisconsin Public Intervenor's Comments on Notification of Intent, April 23, 1994.

44. Don Behm, "Proposed Giant Mine Raises Fears: State Official Questions Impact on Water Supply of Zinc, Copper Project," *Milwaukee Journal*, April 28, 1994; "Mining Mustn't Spoil the North" (editorial), May 8, 1994.

45. Jerry Goodrich, letter to Forest County residents, April 15, 1994.

46. WATER newspaper ad, *Forest Republican*, May 5, 1994.

47. Ron Seely, "Plan Changes for Mine Wastes," *Wisconsin State Journal*, April 19, 1995.

48. Cited in Peter A. Geniesse, "Fighting Exxon," *Post-Crescent* (Appleton, Wisc.), June 19, 1994.

49. Bruce Selcraig, "Native Americans Join to Stop the Newest of the Indian Wars," *Sierra* 79:3 (May/June 1994) 47.

50. Peter Maller, "Mole Lake Expect Allied in Mine Fight," *Milwaukee Sentinel*, June 16, 1994.

51. Testimony to the Wisconsin Review Commission, Mole Lake, June 18, 1994. Reprinted in *Report on the Track Records of Exxon and Rio Algom*, March 24, 1995, p. 11.

52. U.S. Department of the Interior, Minerals Management Service, "Social Indicators of Alaskan Coastal Villages, Part 1, Technical Report no. 155 (Anchorage, Alaska: Feb. 1993) 207.

53. Minewatch, "Summary of Material about the El Cerrejòn Coal Mine and the Wayuu in the El Guajira Peninsula, Colombia." Materials collected by Survival International and summarized by Minewatch, London (Feb. 1994) 1.

54. George Vukelich, "Minding the Mine" (Interview with Armando Valbuena Gouriyù), *Isthmus Newsweekly* (Madison, Wisc.) July 8, 1994.

55. Americas Watch and United Mine Workers of America, "Petition before the U.S. Trade Representative on Labor Rights in Colombia" (May 1990), p. 23.

56. Survival International, "Top Ten List" (London: Sept. 1992).

57. Roger Moody, *The Gulliver File: Mines, People and Land: A Global Battleground* (London: Minewatch, 1992), 367.

58. Marla Donato, "To Allow This Mine Is to Disappear from the Earth: Intercontinental Victims of Exxon-Rio Algom Mining Rally behind Mole Lake Anishinabe," *The Circle: News from a Native Perspective* (Minneapolis, Minn.) 15:7 (July 1994).

59. Ron Seely, "Exxon Mine Plans Opposed," *Wisconsin State Journal*, March 24, 1995.

60. Dave Newbart, "Mining Firms' Past Hit," *Madison Capital Times*, March 23, 1995.

61. Cited in "Mining Moratorium Challenges Mining Companies," *Pioneer Express* (Crandon, Wisc.), Dec. 18, 1995.

62. Don Behm, "DNR Board Likely to Reject Petitions for Ore Mining Ban," *Milwaukee Journal*, Dec. 8, 1994.

63. Tim J. Sheehan, "Judge's Ruling Sides with Mining Opponents," *Leader-Telegram* (Eau Claire, Wisc.), Sept. 12, 1995.

64. Julie Wichman, "Elephants Leave Tailings Behind: State Republicans Stampede from Mining Bill," *Shepherd Express* (Milwaukee newsweekly), May 23, 1996.

65. Janet Smith, Dept. of the Interior, Fish and Wildlife Service, Green Bay, Wisc., Field Office, comments to the U.S. Army Corps of Engineers on a Section 404 permit application for the proposed Crandon mine, Nov. 18, 1994, p. 3.

66. *Ibid.*, p. 2.

67. *Ibid.*, p. 3.

68. Public hearing on Exxon's Crandon project, Sokaogon Chippewa Reservation, March 29, 1995.

69. Full-page advertisement in *Forest Republican* (Crandon, Wisc.), Oct. 11, 1995.

70. U.S. Army Corps of Engineers, St. Paul District, "Evaluation of Groundwater Modeling at the Crandon Mining Site," Feb. 21, 1996, p. 1.

71. WATER Press Release, Jan. 26, 1996.

72. Steve Fox, "Taking Us Down to the River: An Indian Pueblo Challenges Upstream Polluters," *Workbook* 17:4 (winter 1992) 153–154.

73. Steven Walters, "Tribe Seeks Air Pollution Protection within 60 Miles of Reservation," *Milwaukee Sentinel*, Dec. 13, 1994.

74. Don Behm, "2 Tribes Hope to Control Reservations' Water Quality," *Milwaukee Journal*, Feb. 5, 1995.

75. Mike Monte, "Indian Tribes: Our New Environmental Conscience?," *Wisconsin Outdoor News*, July 21, 1995.

76. James Buchen, "Delegation of Federal Clean Water Act," *Badger State Miner*, Oct./Nov. 1995.

77. Steven Walters, "Tribe's Request Could Jeopardize Current, Future Jobs, Groups Say," *Milwaukee Journal/Sentinel*, April 27, 1995.

78. "Tribal Water Plan Supported," *Daily Journal* (Antigo, Wisc.), Feb. 1, 1996.

79. "Indian Lawsuit Will Proceed," *Wisconsin State Journal*, April 5, 1996.

80. Ron Seely, "New Opposition Group to Crandon Mine Forms," *Wisconsin State Journal*, March 26, 1996.

81. "Company Starts Publicity Campaign to Support Mine," *Wisconsin State Journal*, April 30, 1996.

82. Robert Imrie, "More Crandon Mine Tests Ordered," *Wisconsin State Journal*, May 22, 1996.

83. Keith Schneider, "A Wisconsin Tribe Tries to Turn Back a Giant," *New York Times*, Dec. 26, 1994.

84. Winona La Duke, "Indigenous Environmental Perspectives: A North American Primer," *Indigenous Economics: Toward a Natural World Order (Cornell University: Adwe:kon Journal, summer 1992), p. 57.*

PART FOUR

Agriculture and Agri-Conflict

Food is essential to life, and as a critical resource it influences all aspects of human society. Human health, biophysical integrity, economic vitality, cultural viability, and political security are all affected by the pattern of food production, distribution, and consumption.

What does food security mean? At the most fundamental level, food security simply means enough food is produced to meet all the needs of society. Yet, while global food production currently meets and at times exceeds food needs, one in five children on the planet go hungry each day. Thus, food security also infers equitable access, not only to food, but also to the means to produce food now and in the future. This means that food security relies on production systems that sustain and support human and environmental systems.

The post–World War II rise of conventional agriculture—capital, chemical, technological intensive monocrop production aimed at meeting national and export market needs—significantly transformed the culture, economy, and health of farming communities around the world. All over the globe, farms grew larger. The ownership of farms changed from family or community ownership to corporate ownership. Different crops were grown using different methods, requiring a massive increase in capital and technology, as well as a mobile, migratory labor force. Intensive production and chemical inputs stimulated degenerative change in the environment, in the health of humans working in that environment, and in the health of those consuming food products.

The chapter by Valerie Wheeler and Peter Esainko critically examines efforts to reshape food production systems by documenting the emergence of an alternative agricultural movement in the United States. They map out the rise of agribusiness (a historical transformation of control over who farms what, how, where, and for what markets) and the emergence of such issues as the purity of food (free of harmful toxins), plus the dangers of the food production process (ecological havoc wreaked by conventional agribusiness methods). In the United States, farmers were active participants in the transformation process and agribusiness developed through legal means. Convinced by government experts and chemical company representatives that new technologies and farming methods will produce higher and higher yields, farmers took out loans, bought more land, applied an ever-increasing load of chemical inputs, and, because of huge capital outlays required each year, became increasingly vulnerable to variations in the market, fluctuations in climate, incidents of new pests, and so forth. A disastrous year meant defaulting on loan payments and taxes. Across the country, farms were seized by banks and the government and resold at auctions to corporations.

Wheeler and Esainko describe efforts to reassert the small-scale, self-sufficient organic farm, efforts that rely on rights-protective mechanisms that encourage and support information dissemination and participation at all levels of the decision-making process (electing representatives, lobbying, organizing public information and political action campaigns, participating in public hearings and on regulatory committees). Cultural notions, language, and beliefs play a significant role in the transformation of food production systems, by encouraging and legitimizing the process of alienation of farmers from agricultural knowledge and shaping and supporting the struggle of organic farmers to reassert their authority in scientific knowledge and decision-making systems. Conflict occurs in the context of control over the production and praxis of agricultural knowledge, and thus the shape and form of national agricultural policy (decision-making systems, in theory, rest on a knowledge base). Despite the rights-protective system in which these struggles occur, Wheeler and Esainko show us how the status quo can co-opt and at times corrupt the movement.

While the global spread of agribusiness required the same sorts of transformations across the world, the political context and social consequences of these transformations are profoundly different in rights-protective vs. rights-abusive settings. In his chapter, James Phillips documents the social impact of this transformation in Honduras where large farms were created by forceful means—farmers who held legal title or the right to prove legal title were ignored, were forcibly evicted, and had their lands seized. The Honduran government worked with national or multinational agroindustries (often with the economic support of multilateral agencies) to convert a subsistence oriented farm production system to an export agricultural system. In some cases the eviction of small-scale farmers occurred under the guise of legal means, with the state declaring their lands "forest area," a category defined by the Honduran constitution as state land.

In Honduras, there are few legal mechanisms that support the rights to question, complain, and lobby for change, and those that exist are rarely enforced. The struggle to reshape food production systems involves efforts by the dispossessed to reassert their rights to land and opportunities to farm, as well as efforts by the broader society to restructure the resource management decision-making system in the country—thereby allowing broader public participation and a voice in the decision-making process. Efforts to negotiate change within the existing system are met in reactive and repressive fashion. As in the case in the United States, cultural notions, language, and beliefs play a significant role in the transformation of food production systems; in the Honduras case, by legitimizing the abuse of human rights in the name of national economic development, abuses that led to confrontational politics and escalating incidents of violent conflict. Cultural notions, language, and beliefs also allow the articulation of linkages between land tenure issues, social justice, environmental quality, and structure of decision-making systems.

Despite the sharp differences in problem and response, both cases suggest that meeting the challenges of a growing population requires substantive transformation in food production systems. Ensuring food security requires transformations that reflect environmental quality and social justice concerns—transformations that inherently depend on rights-protective mechanisms and processes. Change must occur from all levels: top down (national and international policies), bottom up (power, access, and use patterns on the ground), and supportive efforts from all sides (value choices that support progressive change).

CHAPTER 7

Purity and Danger
Regulating Organic Farming

Valerie Wheeler and Peter Esainko[1]

Introduction

Without food, there is no life. Without human culture, there is no human food. But culture varies, as does food and how it comes to be, through access to resources and labor. Control of access to food defines social relations before any other need. Until 10,000 years ago, resources were wild and human social organization was small-scale. Even with localization of wild resources after the last glacial retreat, with sedentary living and the subsequent domestication of plants and animals, communities remained small. In some places on the planet, domestication of storable grains facilitated the rise of tribute-taking, nonproductive political elites, growing populations, cities, and the eventual emergence of states some 5,500 years ago.[2]

In the millennia since, history can be characterized as continually escalating patterns of production, leading to environmental decline, with subsequent conquest of farther geographical realms. Empires rise, deteriorate, die out, or are transformed by technological innovations. New ways to organize labor, land, water, even new "foods," sustain in the short run otherwise threatened economies. In recent history (since the 16th century), the ever-faster engine of change has been commerce in search of profit, generating a global economy. The goal of food production is no longer to feed people but to turn food into money. The strategies employed to that end, especially industrialization in the last 200 years, carry heavy social and environmental costs that we are only beginning to comprehend.[3]

American agriculture since its inception has always been explicitly commercial, producing food to be sold to nonproducers who benefited more than farmers themselves. Agriculture subsidized American towns, cities, industry, nation-states, and "development" generally—at great cost to the farmer and the countryside. Since the 18th century, agriculture has been intensified scientifically: since 1850, chemically through fertilizers; since 1900, mechanically through planting and harvesting machines; since 1920, economically through consolidation and debt, turning farms into factories, first with crops and (in the last third of this century) with livestock; and since 1950, petro-chemically. This model of development has become global, and the chronic response to

Valerie Wheeler is a Professor of Anthropology at the California State University–Sacramento, 95819. Peter Esainko is an anthropologist and independent scholar. They can be reached via email (wheeler@csus.edu).

the resulting overproduction and falling prices has been to increase productivity still more. Small producers are replaced by large ones, as small cultures are replaced by large. And the landscape has become industrialized. Agricultural chemicals pollute surface and groundwater. Without organic matter, soils compact from heavy machinery and erode in wind and water. Irrigation depletes underground water sources, and salts build up in the soil. Wildlife and human food and health are compromised by toxic residues from fertilizers, pesticides, and herbicides.[4]

Yet, since the colonization of the United States, another theme of agriculture as a "way of life" has played counterpoint to the dominant commercial one—a counterpoint that is usually difficult to hear outside of sentimental and nostalgic contexts but that periodically is resonant, sounding out the long-term costs of extractive agriculture and seeking reform.[5] No doubt movements protesting the dominant system's abuses have arisen throughout history, voices that try to turn the cultural tide. One imagines ancient Uruk or Ephesian "Friends of the Land" vainly warning against salinization from irrigation agriculture or siltation from deforested hinterlands, as the ports became landlocked. One such contemporary and unfinished note is the current organic farming movement, a production system that emerged in reaction to the problems of conventional agriculture and that is becoming institutionalized through U.S. federal regulations ("national organic standards").

The National Organic Standards Board has defined "organic agriculture" as:

> an ecological production management system that promotes and enhances biodiversity, biological cycles, and soil biological activity . . . based on minimal use of off-farm inputs and on management practices that restore, maintain, and enhance ecological harmony. "Organic" is a labeling term that denotes products produced under the authority of the Organic Foods Production Act. The principle [sic] guidelines . . . are to use materials and practices that enhance the ecological balance of natural systems and that integrate the parts of the farming system into an ecological whole. Organic agriculture practices cannot ensure that products are completely free of residues; however, methods are used to minimize pollution from air, soil, and water. Organic food handlers, processors and retailers adhere to standards that maintain the integrity of organic agricultural products. The primary goal of organic agriculture is to optimize the health and productivity of interdependent communities of soil life, plants, animals, and people.[6]

Soil fertility and the control of moisture and pests are achieved primarily through crop rotation (biodiversity) and the management of organic matter such as crop residues and both animal and green manures. Supplements must be made from unaugmented natural materials; for example, fish emulsion and rock phosphate are allowed, but not fortified fish emulsion or phosphate treated with sulfuric acid. Cultivation and crop rotation control weeds. Petroleum products are used only to run the machines. An established organic farm is an ecological system tuned by the timing decisions of a knowledgeable farmer who knows that farm and its history intimately. The farmer is an artisan who farms as a way of life—in sharp contrast to the "technicians" in industrial agriculture who work in outdoor factories producing a narrow inventory of homogeneous crops.

In this chapter, we examine some of the problems in American agricultural production, the rise of an organic farming movement in response to these problems, and the social, symbolic, and economic difficulties in achieving a fundamental transformation

Sign in a field on a small farm in northern Ohio advertising "certified organic." Status awarded by the Ohio Ecological Food and Farm Association. Photograph by Valerie Wheeler.

of our food production system. Our discussion is based on research conducted over the past 13 years, including ethnographic research on organic farms in chemical-intensive counties in Ohio, participant observation research in agricultural extension and other agro-policy arenas, and comparative research on the organic movement in both California and Ohio. The questions we consider are: what will be the effect of national standards on organic agriculture? Will it evolve to converge with conventional agriculture in the industrial model? Will the artisans become workers, if they remain on the land at all? What will happen to the right to livelihood of organic farming? And finally, why does it matter?

20th Century "Farming"

Farmers are . . . helpless subjects of the corporate kingdoms of agripower. The lords of the manor in the feudal system of the Middle Ages . . . demanded no more of their subjects than modern suppliers of chemicals, machinery, and fuel demand of theirs. . . . The lord of the medieval manor was rich. The peasants who worked the land were not. The lords of corporate agribusiness who supply the inputs for industrial agriculture are rich. The farmers who work the land are not. The peasants identified themselves willingly with a particular feudal lord and declared their loyalty to that lord. Their modern counterparts who work the land wear hats advertising the corporate lords for whom they work.[7] (Wes Jackson, 1987)

As this century ends, the United States is no longer an agricultural society. Less than 2 percent of the U.S. population are farmers, and that is declining. The rest of us have little connection with food production, and agriculture is just another special interest dominated by multinational corporations. At the beginning of the century, however, most Americans were still on the farm or had just left it for new factories in the cities.

The federal government, through land grant universities and the agricultural extension service, had spent four decades developing scientific (and commercial) agriculture. During the Progressive era (1900–1917), those institutions further sought to tie rural populations to national development by supervising homelife as well, promoting increased production to provide "cheap food" for urban factory workers, thus subsidizing industry. Knowing that commodity prices would fall with increased production, farmers resisted such appeals until World War I, when temporarily high international prices and wartime government control of farm supplies and equipment pulled and pushed farmers into greater production on increased acreage. In May 1920, prices collapsed to prewar levels, leaving farmers bankrupt, debt-ridden, and poorer than ever, since nonagricultural prices were 50 to 100 percent above prewar levels. The only relief offered farmers was expanded credit, the primary "solution" (and method of control) for the rest of the century. Low prices forced persistent high production, which, while not getting farmers out of their predicament, benefited urban populations. The Roaring Twenties were an urban phenomenon; in the countryside, the Great Depression reigned.[8]

In the 1930s, the ecological bill for agricultural extraction came due; the result was a human-made ecological disaster, the Dust Bowl.[9] Although erosion had been a serious effect of European-style farming in the United States from colonial days, the scale of the Dust Bowl could not be ignored, and the federal government formed the Soil Conservation Service under Hugh H. Bennett in 1935. He in turn was a founder of Friends of the Land, a citizen auxiliary to promote a "new agriculture" that included prominent intellectuals, scientists, ecologists, writers, and farmers such as Liberty Hyde Bailey, Paul B. Sears, Edward H. Faulkner, W. A. Albrecht, Gifford Pinchot, Aldo Leopold, and E. B. White. The organization's periodical *The Land*, which First Lady Eleanor Roosevelt thought should be in every home in the United States, included art and poetry, as well as scientific, technical, and philosophical articles on conservation farming. At the same time, member-author Henry A. Wallace, Secretary of Agriculture from 1933 to 1940, transformed the Department of Agriculture's yearbooks from dry annual reports to detailed handbooks for farmers, providing state-of-the-art information for agricultural practice.[10] The most famous member of the Friends of the Land was writer Louis Bromfield, owner of Malabar Farm in Ohio. Bromfield built a thousand-acre showcase of conservation farming from several small, worn-out farms. Tens of thousands of visitors came to his and other conservation farms; most of those visitors were farmers, eager to learn ways to save their soil.

The conservation movement was not necessarily organic, although many of its scientists wrote about organic processes and methods. The first use of the phrase "organic farming and gardening" in the United States may have been by J. I. Rodale, who founded a periodical by that name in 1942. He was concerned about the effects on human health of both chemical fertilizers (which he called "dope" and "medicines") and pesticides (such as arsenic, sulfur, and DDT). Rodale's inspiration and cofounder of the magazine was Sir Albert Howard, who beginning in 1905 observed, experimented with, and invented methods of producing compost to supply large commercial farm soils with the humus he considered essential for soil fertility and plant health. Howard argued that plant pests and diseases were symptoms of poor soil health; that healthy plants were not attacked significantly by pests and diseases; that chemicals—"artificials" as he called them—poison "life in the soil" such as mycorrhiza that make nutrients available to plants; that compost and green manures will put soil "in good heart" and thus suitable for healthy plant life. Howard was a conventionally trained agricultural scientist whose observations of peasant agricultural practices in the West Indies and India convinced him that crop diversity and the return of organic matter to the soil maintained fertility—the foundation of organic practice to this day. He was critical of the separation of agricultural science from practical farming, the methods of conventional scientific research, and large-scale commercial farming. He thought the profit motive was inappropriate in the production of food, which, like water and shelter, should not be expected to pay its way. "The people must be fed," he wrote; "the financial system is . . . but a secondary matter."[11]

Howard and Rodale spoke glowingly of their method's growing number of adherents, but they met criticism, even ridicule. Rodale cited a comment in a fertilizer journal on the importance of organic matter. The writer said that although declining yields in soils with little organic matter gave some "thunder" for the organic matter "cult," depending entirely on crop residues and manure for fertility would not feed a growing population. Rodale retorted that "time will rather call the followers of the chemist Liebig the cultists," not centuries of "good practical farmers from Adam's time."[12] Those in the conservation movement were ambivalent about the organic argument. W. A. Albrecht, a Missouri agronomist whose soil research in the 1940s and 1950s was so important in supporting organic farming methods, referred in passing to "the organic cult and the chemical camp." A reviewer in *The Land* of Howard's book *An Agricultural Testament* says of Howard, "He is a humus man; he is also a nature worshipper," that he (the reviewer) had never heard of the mycorrhizal association, and that Howard, himself a scientist, criticizes other scientists and is not concerned with human health or the large amounts of cheap labor that his composting methods require.[13] Louis Bromfield himself used the crop rotation, cover cropping, green and animal manuring, and tillage methods required in present-day organic farming. Having observed Howard's composting system in India, he modified it to require less human labor at Malabar in Ohio. He insisted that organic matter was essential to erosion control, soil moisture, life in the soil, and—here he parted company with strict organic practices then and now obtaining the greatest benefit from chemical fertilizers (although the fertilizer formula he used seems to have been heavy on natural ingredients and light on chemical nitrogen and potassium). He defended judicious use of some chemical fertilizers because soil restoration would take too long and be too expensive for the ordinary farmer who had taxes and rent to pay. At the same time he was critical of most fertilizer manufacturers for their primitive formulas and expensive but useless fillers.[14]

In the early 1950s in the pages of *The Land*, a heated exchange took place over chemical fertilizer. Its defenders, while granting some benefits from humus, insisted that "organiculture" (another Rodale term) was a religion, and its adherents were "cockeyed cultists" who followed a "ridiculous dogma" and were therefore "organatics." In their mild replies, the practitioners of composting, manuring, and the use of untreated minerals documented successful organic farmers in the East and Midwest and called repeatedly and in vain for testing of organic methods by experiment stations. *The Land*'s editors, worn down by the "extremist" charges and countercharges, preferred a middle ground with a tilt toward organics, but not completely away from chemical fertilizers in cases of severely limited fertility. *The Land* briefly metamorphosed into *Land and Water*, essentially a scientific Soil Conservation Service publication and, after his death in 1956, a wistful memorial to Louis Bromfield. It ceased publication in 1959.

The conservation movement was vital, exciting, and effective in its time—but was quickly forgotten with the petrochemical intensification of agriculture, a "new" new agriculture in the 1950s.[15] Just as the internal combustion engine became the profitable way to use gasoline, agricultural chemicals became the profitable way to use wartime inventions—nitrates and pesticides. Hybrid corn seed, mechanization, and industrial inputs from World War II spread rapidly, generating productivity that was "the envy of the world" while increasing the scale and concentration of agriculture and reducing the number of farmers. In 1962, Rachel Carson's classic *Silent Spring*[16] challenged the wisdom of this chemical age, but postwar social changes—the civil rights movement, the Vietnam war, and the Great Society—put agricultural and environmental issues on hold until the 1970s.

DDT was banned in the United States in 1972, although it is still manufactured for export and residues are still found on agricultural land here.[17] Hundreds of other chemicals replaced it in a new boom. Cheered on by U.S. Secretary of Agriculture Earl Butz, farmers planted "fence row to fence row," tearing out conservation shelter belts and terraces and planting corn destined for the global market up and down the hills of former sheep pastures. They also greatly increased their consumption of machines, fertilizers, pesticides, and land, using loans urged on them by the federal government and financial institutions looking for a high rate of return on petrodollar deposits. Domestic investment in agricultural expansion was analogous to investment loans to third world countries, with a crucial difference: banks could not foreclose on Argentina or Peru if they failed to make their loan payments, but they could and *did* on farmers at home when prices fell with overproduction. The postwar economic expansion ended in 1973, as did the rise in domestic real weekly wages, but this reality was obscured by inflation. After 25 years of increasing fertilizer and chemical use without conservation methods, the soil contained inadequate organic matter to keep it from eroding into watersheds already contaminated with chemical runoff. The scientific solution this time was "no-till" agriculture, or planting a new crop directly into the previous year's crop residue—a method even more dependent on both herbicides for weed control and on toxic chemicals to kill pests in the surface litter.[18] By mid-decade, a new generation of philosopher-scientist-writer-farmers began to critique the environmental and social disaster produced by this latest round of intensification: some of the most notable were Barry Commoner, Jim Hightower, Wendell Berry, Gene Logsdon, and Wes Jackson. Organic farms were rediscovered and found to be both economically viable and ecologically superior.[19] By contrast, chemical agriculturalists defended their technology by raising the specter of starvation if their methods were altered or abandoned; their solution to problems caused by technology was to apply more technology.

Organic Farming

In 1972, Rodale Press, still publishing *Organic Gardening*, converted 290 acres of its Pennsylvania farm into organic production, and in four years had a stable and fully productive system in place (140 bushels of corn per acre—compared to the top county conventional yield of 157 bushels achieved with 190 pounds of nitrogen, 230 pounds of phosphorus, and 673 pounds of potassium).[20] In this case, the organic system was obviously economically advantageous because of reduced input purchases. That year Rex and Glenn Spray, exposed to the idea of organic farming by the National Farmers Organization, put their 600-acre Ohio farm into an organic system, the state's most successful for the next 25 years, with 132 percent of county averages for corn in one five-year period.[21] Their father had begun using the herbicide atrazine in the late 1940s but within a few years annual grasses were a serious pest, requiring more herbicides for control. After eliminating petrochemicals, the brothers used a local slaughterhouse product for fertility but changed to a carbon-based product whose distributors also supplied advice. Thus began a structured program of crop rotations, tillage, and organic matter management that made this farm a stable, fertile, noneroding, and ordered ecosystem—an example to this day to farmers of Ohio that it can be done. Public recognition of that example was a long time coming, however, as the social, institutional, and symbolic pressures against organic farming barred even neighbors from acknowledging what they saw driving by the verdant fields. The organic farmers confessed that they sometimes felt like pariahs.

With the help of Rodale's *Organic Farming and Gardening Magazine*, California Certified Organic Farmers (CCOF) was formed in 1973 with 50 farmer members to define, standardize, and regulate the term *organic* (see photograph). By 1979, it had three chapters. In 1977 the Ohio Ecological Food and Farming Association (OEFFA) was organized. In 1979, Robert Rodale, J. I. Rodale's son, founded *New Farm* magazine, an important source of alternative information for working farmers throughout the United States. (Rodale died an untimely death in 1990; *New Farm* ceased publication in 1995.)

In 1979, during the Carter administration, U.S. Secretary of Agriculture Bob Bergland asked for research into the potential of organic farming for mitigating environmental and economic problems in American agriculture. After surveying 69 organic farms in 23 states, a multidisciplinary team produced a sympathetic, 94-page report in 1980, the same year that land prices ended their inflationary spiral, leading farmers to bankruptcy as their equity fell below their debt. This downward spiral tightened in the early 1980s, and "petrofarming" was exposed as not only an ecological disaster but an economic and social one as well. A new literature appeared on "saving the family farm," as the shakeout of this decade reduced the farming population further.[22]

Organic advocates had hoped that the official and sympathetic USDA report would, at long last, give organic farming authority. Instead, the new Reagan administration eliminated the office that produced the report and announced that the solution to agriculture's problems was the free market, which meant eliminating price supports, subsidies, and thus, farmers. In the Congress, legislation introduced to support "organic" and "innovative" farming failed. Scientific, industrial, and policy personnel involved in conventional agriculture were opposed to change and resisted any loss of their domination of agricultural policy and practice. Finally, "organic" still had an image problem as a primitive, unproductive, and antiscience agriculture practiced by marginal people.[23] Why such a stubborn and stereotyped cultural resistance to a scientifically proven agricultural alternative? A cultural problem requires cultural analysis, which leads here into the realm of symbolism.

The Purity Rule

[University people] act as if contact with farmers would de-professionalize them; they avoid us peasants. (A young organic farmer, 1988)

In human affairs, culture universally defines any relationship to conceptions of food. Humans also universally distinguish between "culture" and "nature," ranking culture higher than nature; for instance, to begin to turn a child into a "human being" means controlling its organic processes. Where the organic of any sort contacts the social—birth, death, sex, sweat, and manure—it creates cognitive impurity, and rituals abound to separate the two again. Social anthropologist Mary Douglas has explicated this principle most clearly:

> The purity rule is a control system to which communicating humans all submit. It imposes a scale of values which esteem formal relations more than intimate ones. The more the society is vested with power, the more it despises the organic processes on which it rests. The more hierarchised the social system, the stronger the control demanded. Social distance measures itself by distance from organic process.[24]

A profound effect of technology in industrialized agriculture, for example, has been to distance the farmer from what is farmed: a 12-row planter machine with air-conditioned cab equipped with a stereo and a cellular phone gives higher status and insulation from nature than smaller tools. Moreover, the whole trend of agricultural technology in the United States has been to eliminate the "farmer," replacing lower-valued acts and artifacts with higher-valued ones (machines, money, prestige).[25]

But the crops and animals produced are "food," and food is organic; without it, there is no life. The more "culturized" food production and processing are, the more that food's organic source is obscured (indeed, "value" has been added symbolically as well as economically). Occasionally, raw foods are culturally elaborated into a cuisine. In the 1970s, the counterculture developed a "natural food" system as an alternative to mainstream corporate food processing and distribution. Although the concept of "natural" was quickly rendered meaningless by a retailing food industry, at least one cuisine from the period survived. Chef Alice Waters' "California cuisine" evolved from private meals for radical friends into Chez Panisse, a Berkeley restaurant and cultural institution whose menu features organically grown foods whose added value comes from color, taste, freshness, and presentation.[26] Although the standing of this new cuisine in the fine cooking community is ambiguous, its consumers are upper-middle class and are likely to remain so. High prices at such places insulate those of high status, and allow the use of normally status-lowering behavior to strengthen differentiation from lower orders who cannot afford to eat there. Organic foods in elite markets are incongruous but profitable, as farmers selling in those markets have observed.

Nonproductive elites become so by distancing themselves from the organic processes of food production, leaving farmers intimately involved with organic processes and thereby assigned a lower position in the social hierarchy. Historically in the United States, the dominant urban perception of those who farm has been contemptuous: rural people are seen as ignorant hicks, comical hayseeds, and stupid yokels. (Thomas Jefferson called himself a farmer, though that is not what gave him status.) In this century, farmers' status has risen with increasing social distance from the organic realm, a distance created by machines and science. Professions create elite status, and beginning in the late 19th century, agriculture grew increasingly (if not thoroughly) professionalized. Scientists in agricultural experiment stations, formed by the 1887 Hatch Act, sought to raise their own status by "basic" research, although their client farmers wanted applied studies. To mute this contradiction while continuing to lift their status, the scientists tried to professionalize farmers, using the simple agriculture criterion of per-acre productivity achieved through technology. (This is still the sole measure of farming success. The use of other measures, such as profit and efficiency would demonstrate the supremacy of lower-status farmers such as the Amish.[27])

The purity rule is manifest throughout a society, whose structure is replicated in its relations with both the natural and the supernatural. People living in a society with relatively egalitarian social relations also have egalitarian relations with nature. Australian aborigines of the Western Desert, for instance, distinguish completely between human and not-human, between culture and nature, yet their relations with the natural world are harmonious and ritually reciprocal.[28] Hierarchical social relations, in contrast, are replicated in hierarchical relations with nature, the maximum expression of which is to break open the secrets of nature with the rituals of science, in order to control it.

In contemporary western science, basic research seeks timeless truths that capture complexity in simple structures, hierarchy manifest in method. Basic research has consistently had higher social status than applied research and is most cognitively and socially distant from everyday reality. Applied research, by definition immediate and intimate, has lower status and is therefore avoided or regarded with ambivalence. Furthermore, applied science means involvement with people, fields, and farms that the narrow hierarchical view considers disorderly—researchers complain that farmers cannot be controlled in experiments. On-farm research, which contradicts the "purity" rule, has low status, is avoided, and is even rejected as scientifically invalid. The ecological perspective on agriculture, however, requires looking at variables interacting in a whole system. While it is less work to look at only one or two variables at a time with all others controlled by elimination, and while it is difficult to keep many concepts in mind at once, the "laws of nature" are inherently complex, evolving, and unpredictable. Organic farming research must be on-farm, even on-*a*-farm, because that is where the system is—diverse, site-specific, and intimately managed by humans. That such complex research has been limited is explained by greater costs in money and time, and lesser rewards (publications, credit, grant money) for such research. Symbolic barriers are not discussed.[29]

Sustainable Agriculture

The term "organic" is not in vogue. Because the proponents of organic gardening and farming have been accused of being too pure, too religious, too evangelistic, many people are substituting "ecological," "practical," "low input," for "organic." (Dana Jackson, 1986)[30]

In an interesting transference of the "purity" rule, organic agriculture was accused of being "too pure" because its rejection of chemical-intensive agriculture was unequivocal. It was explicit and uncompromising about practice and who did it: *farmers* did it, not scientists or manufacturers. The complex symbols of purity and primitivity seemed to be insurmountable barriers to dissemination, and thus new concepts were invented. Instead of organic, the new agriculture should be ecological, biological, or regenerative. The term that caught on was "sustainable agriculture," coined by Wes Jackson in 1980 to describe an agricultural program run on solar energy that saved soil through perennial food crops.[31] The term, if not Jackson's meaning, quickly supplanted the problematic "o"-word. It sounded progressive, self-evident (who would want agriculture or development or the environment to be unsustainable?), broad, and sufficiently safe that diverse professional groups could at least start to talk to each other about real change.[32] And its agenda keeps getting bigger, even moving away from ecological issues, as Patricia Allen outlines:

> What do we want to sustain—food production, food consumption, groundwater levels, profits, gender relations, current patterns of property ownership and income distribution? Who should benefit from sustainable agriculture—farm owners, agricultural workers, consumers, transnational food industries, the hungry? How can we best work toward sustainability—technological development, policy changes, economic reforms, educational developments? Such questions have been obscured by the current emphasis on farming practices, which overlooks problems such as hunger, poverty, racial oppression, or gender subordination that many experience in current agrarian structures (for example, family farms, rural communities, and wage labor).[33]

The goal of a radical social reorganization of the food production system explicit in these questions marginalizes organic farming as a mere production method and niche market rather than exploring its potential for sustainability.[34] The value of organic systems is diminished further by questioning their sustainability if they do not explicitly address these social issues.

Sustainable agriculture is a big concept—difficult to operationalize, an undefinable feel-good term that attracts everyone, that neutralizes challenges, and that has so far changed little. To correct the definitional weakness, it has been proposed that basic scientific research will provide the facts to make the concept real,[35] a rededication of the model of science as the source of authoritative knowledge, which organic agriculture is still not permitted to have except under the rubric of the broader, socially acceptable, concept.[36] Finally, sustainability is an upper-middle-class movement of officials and academics,[37] an elite that seeks to construct its authority for top-down innovation through science on one hand and ambitious national policy initiatives on the other. Meanwhile, out in the countryside, symbolic barriers have not been removed; some conventional farmers, even if willing to experiment with change, do not like the term "sustainable" any more than they do "organic." Both seem too far from the mainstream, though the first more closely adheres to forms of agriculture that have been found wanting. Its structural and cultural contradictions make its future look cloudy.

As the professionals were developing their sustainable agriculture, farmers and their local organizations continued to develop the organic agriculture system on their own. They rediscovered and invented nonchemical production methods, disseminated information and supported each other through conferences and field-day demonstrations, constructed local certification organizations to inspect and credential crops as "organically grown," developed markets, and built relationships with consumer and environmental groups concerned about the destructiveness of chemically dependent global agriculture.

In 1981, farmers, activists, faculty, and students from the University of California–Davis, and other interested persons, established the Steering Committee for Sustainable Agriculture and held the first of what have continued to be annual conferences on alternative agriculture. Now known as the Ecological Farming Conference, this is the largest annual gathering of the organic/sustainable community in the United States. By 1984, California Certified Organic Farmers certified 150 growers, 300 in 1987, 540 in 1989; it certified 518 growers, 9 processors, and over 49,000 acres in 1994. Major crops in acres are wine grapes, rice, table grapes, apples, and cotton. State-wide standards were set in the Organic Foods Act of 1990, including mandatory registration of all organic producers and handlers.[38]

The Ohio Ecological Food and Farming Association began to certify organic farms in 1981. In 1989, Ohio passed legislation defining organic foods and approving certifying agencies in the state. By 1994 the Ohio Ecological Food and Farming Association certified 131 farm operations and processors, making it the seventh largest program in the United States; in 1995, it certified 164, and it also currently certifies for the national Organic Crop Improvement Association.[39] The major crops are soybeans, corn, and small grains. By 1990, 22 states had certification standards. Initial pressure on farmers for national standards seems to have come from European organic groups concerned about international trade, but despite urgings from some state leaders concerned about larger markets, American producers in the 1980s seemed content with their local organizations.

During this period, institutions promoting conventional agricultural science and extension and exercising their structural authority ignored the organic movement or warned off curious conventional farmers. Organic farmers continued to develop alternative extension systems and informal empirical research, periodically attempting to get the attention of the agricultural establishment but being rebuffed as unscientific, old-fashioned, regressive, uneconomic, and misguided. The clash of paradigms was physical as well as ideological: with few exceptions, agricultural scientists and extension agents would not set foot on organic farms to see for themselves.[40]

The Big Change

In 1989, everything changed. That spring, the Natural Resources Defense Council (NRDC) publicly charged that alar, a growth regulator used on apples, was a public health hazard the federal government could no longer ignore. During a media extravaganza, the government insisted that foods were safe and objected to the preemption of its guardian role. Meanwhile, conventional apple growers, forced into bankruptcy as demand for their product disappeared, filed suit against the NRDC, and organic producers sold a normal year's supply of apples in three weeks. A family-owned supermarket chain in California introduced residue testing to market its produce as free of pesticides and tried marketing organically grown food. Other California supermarkets charged that the firm was engaging in unfair practices by implying that food in other stores was contaminated. The California Department of Agriculture insisted that its testing of 1 percent of fresh fruit and vegetables was sufficient to protect the public, which therefore did not need private residue testing. Other supermarkets tentatively offered organic produce to customers. Prices went up.

In the autumn of 1989, after four years of data collection and negotiation, the National Research Council's Board on Agriculture published an extensive report on "alternative" agriculture, calling for fundamental reforms. The report blamed federal commodity support programs for environmental and economic degradation and put together case studies of 14 farms that fit the category "alternative," ranging from one certified organic (the Spray farm in Ohio) to one in subtropical Florida that was heavily dependent on chemicals but used less than recommended application rates. Response to the report varied. The sustainable agriculture movement began to congratulate itself for having won. The Fertilizer Institute claimed that starvation would result from the report's recommendations, that animal manures could contaminate human food, and that, besides, consumers valued appearance and taste more than nutrition or purity. An extension specialist in Michigan claimed that sustainable agriculture "is roughly equivalent to unilateral disarmament" and showed slides of well-fed and starving children overseas, crediting agricultural chemicals for the state of the well-fed ones. A press release from the Cooperative Extension in Ohio warned that "farming organically has too many drawbacks for most farmers," that without pesticides most crops would fail overnight, leaving Americans dependent on foreign food containing unknown dangers. Highly placed agricultural administrators warned the public against "emotion" in decisions about food and farming, and suggested that materials used in organic farming would make people sick.[41]

While Americans told household surveyors that they were willing to pay higher prices for organically grown produce, those who shopped in supermarkets did not, and prices dropped. In contrast, business increased dramatically in community-based natural food stores and cooperatives, at least in California, selling mostly locally grown produce. The "bust" was for large-scale growers who had opportunistically converted part of their large holdings in vegetable, tree, and vine crops into organically grown— made possible because at that time California certification standards required only a one-year transition period. These growers had expected to move their organic products into supermarkets throughout the country as a simple addition to their conventional marketing; instead, they were disappointed.[42] Organics had the most success nationally as processed nonstaple foods: baby food, breakfast cereal, and snacks such as popcorn and chips, all of them value-added items that are still important in the processed organic foods inventory. Baby foods and snacks themselves stand for focal points in the American diet: what good parents feed their infants, while they themselves graze on conventional treats, all highly processed and highly profitable in conventional or organic form to food manufacturers (if not to farmers).

National Standards

Not wanting to see the term "organic" be made meaningless, as "natural" was in the 1970s, the "organic food industry"—retailers, processors, manufacturers, and farmers—sought to protect and develop the budding market by making a push to legislate a single national labeling standard as to what could and could not be called organic for easier interstate and international commerce in raw and processed foods. For example, a jar of organic pasta sauce may include tomatoes from California and Ohio, mushrooms and onions from other states, and herbs from yet another source. To be certified organic, the sauce must be made of ingredients from certified sources. If different states have different standards for labeling an item as organic, the status of the processed food could be compromised. The manufacturer must be able to document the source for each ingredient, as the farmer must be able to document the method of production. Handling, transport, and storage of both fresh and processed foods must also comply with standards that state that food cannot be contaminated by contact with forbidden substances, such as fungicides during storage.

In early 1989, a proposed U.S. Senate farm conservation and water protection act included a two-sentence definition of organic food and instructed the Secretary of Agriculture to do a feasibility study of a national certification program. Alarmed by their exclusion in developing such a bill, representatives of 35 independent state and regional certification groups organized with consumer and environmental public interest groups to capture the move to include national organic standards in the 1990 Farm Bill, turning the focus of regulation from the purity of the product to how it is produced. In nine months, while the House Committee on Agriculture and the U.S. Department of Agriculture (USDA) recommended study of the matter, members of the "organic trade" successfully lobbied Congress to include national certification in the bill. Organic supporters claiming "a historical moment" and a "legislative miracle" felt validated by the new structure. Others thought the oppressive structures imposed by distant bureaucrats and the mass-marketing of big business would corrupt the organic philosophy.[43]

The virtually all-volunteer grassroots organic farming and marketing organizations, having invented the production methods and enterprises, thought they had a good chance to influence the makeup of the National Organic Standards Board (NOSB), a body appointed in 1992 to advise the Secretary of Agriculture in drawing rules for how food and fiber were to be grown, handled, and processed if they were to be labeled as organic. Their influence, however, turned out to be minimal. Absent from the initial board was any farmer with experience in vegetables, fruits, or nuts (major organic crops); any small farmers; and any farmer from California, which has the largest and most diverse group of organic growers in the United States, producing about one-fourth of the national total. Instead, those with ties to conventional agricultural science and commodity groups, and corporate food manufacturers, dominated. Many in the organic movement felt co-opted: they had worked hard for the legislation but were then excluded from the formal regulation process. Some individuals were so disappointed with the outcome that they did not want to be part of regulation; others warned that organic practitioners must continue to be involved through lobbying and testimony, or risk the future altogether.

Developing regulations for organic farming has taken so much more time than expected that the original board members' terms have expired. Their replacements have tended to include more members and supporters of the organic community. The NOSB and volunteer technical support persons have put in thousands of person-hours to write standards for organic crop and livestock production, materials, processing, and certification. The work has been slow because of severely limited budgetary support, the many steps required in drawing federal regulations of any kind, shifting political administrations, and institutional ambivalence on the part of the USDA. Hundreds of pages later, the proposed standards are not yet written into regulations, though they are on their way to having the force of law in 1997. The manager of the USDA's National Organic Program observed: "No program that the Department has put together has had as much public comment and public input as this one has . . . will have . . . will continue to have. . . . We think this is a model for how future regulations should be developed."[44]

Business or Way of Life?

We are not an industry—we are a community with shared values that cannot be imposed by the regulatory process. We value stewardship of the land, cooperation, conservation of resources, and independence. We are a very diverse group . . . we are not in it for the money. There are very few organic farmers who could not make a lot more money at some other kind of work. . . . (Elizabeth Henderson, 1992)[45]

Is this where we are being led? Is this where we want to go? Will institutionalization kill everything that is good and reasonable and sane and just about the approach we advocate?" (Caroline Carr, 1992)

Organic farmers felt they won a victory when the . . . farm bill made a provision for a national organic certification program, but that is when I sadly said goodbye to the Organic Movement." (Gene Logsdon, 1992)[46]

For over half a century, organic farmers have been a rebuke to the dominant agricultural system. Current practitioners value American agrarian ideals of community, self-help, and cooperation, and have resisted alienation of their considerable labor. They are sophisticated about cooperation among themselves and exploitation by scientific, political, and economic elites. They farm for at least some profit but do so without subsidy, subject to the market's full effect . . . which may force them back toward specialization (as a "niche" market) or industrial methods (large-scale use of land, labor, and energy) about which they are profoundly ambivalent.

Such a population, although small, by its very existence exacerbates the uncertainties of conventional agricultural institutions in crisis precipitated by their own values and policies. As long as organic agriculture was on the fringes of American consciousness and culture, it could be stigmatized as backward and uneconomic, and dismissed. Under the umbrella of more respectable sustainable agriculture in the 1980s, however, and aided by increasing public interest in the quality of food, organic agriculture became a voice in agricultural reform. The movement generated its own parallel farming, research, extension, and marketing functions, including local self-regulation to protect farmer and consumer from those who would violate organic principles and practices, fraudulently labeling their product "organic." Under pressure by some segments of the movement to develop national regulations to facilitate commerce, farmers managed to keep certification focused on the ecological purity of farming practice rather than on the dietary purity of food. If the consumer's desire for pesticide-free food could be met without altering farm practices, neither the organic farmer nor the environment would benefit.

Before national standards, contrasting visions of organic agriculture as a business or as a way of life could coexist. With national standards, business wins. Organic farmers and advocates worry about having to bear the full costs of implementing national regulation and the loss of local participation if private organizations eventually are not allowed to be certifying agents and are replaced by state agriculture departments, themselves controlled nationally. Opportunists who have no interest in organic philosophy or long-term practice are entering the market, maximizing production to take advantage of premium prices, which in turn will drive prices down, reproducing the conventional history of conventional agriculture. Those who support the goals of organic farming but want organic food to be "more affordable" for a mass market reproduce equally conventional 20th century cheap food policy, which did and will drive out small producers, and the industrial processes of specialization and routinization.[47]

The organic people have other reasons to worry. Under industrial capitalism, agricultural reform has been difficult and short-lived where it has happened at all. Attempts to change can revert to the original trend, and winning can turn into losing. For example, a recent citizen attempt in Michigan to control the nuisance of huge hog-containment operations that pollute air, water, and land was nullified by legislative extension of the state's "right to farm" laws to these operations rather than bringing them into the domain of industrial regulation.[48]

The Iron Law

Increasingly, the organic foods marketplace is beginning to look and feel much like the conventional marketplace. Price, rather than the total costs of production and stewardship, is once again reigning supreme. Overproduction . . . is depressing farmgate prices, while marketing efforts are inadequate to absorb the growing production. Investment bankers…now prowl organic trade shows eager to incorporate emerging organic manufacturers into larger food multinationals or venture capital driven marketing plays.[49]

CCOF used to be made up of farmers and the cost was affordable; after all, we just wanted to make sure that the folks with the CCOF labels were in fact organic. The costs now are getting very high because as I see it the inspectors are charging way more for inspections. My last one was so high and I was so broke I thought I was going to have to quit myself. . . . I started getting a bill from the state . . . charging everyone that called themselves organic. . . . What did we do that is so wrong that we have to pay off the gov[ernment] to let us farm organic?[50]

Conventional agriculture has been insulated by subsidies for major crops since 1933, when prices were supported at "parity" with indexes of farm costs based on pre–World War I figures. Organic agriculture, however, has always been subject to market forces, since the premium usually given organically grown crops is higher than the support price.

Classical economics developed the Iron Law of Wages, which states that wages tend to fall to subsistence levels in a free market.[51] This law has been neglected, not only because its implications were unpleasant, but more likely because it was not understood that subsistence is defined within a culture and differs with social status and time. For example, an office worker must spend money for clothes that a factory worker need not consider; here "subsistence" must include what is expected in office dress.

Violations of the Iron Law can occur for a limited period like post–World War II United States through most of the 1960s, when living standards rose. They can also result from union action, again for a time and only for some workers; or under conditions where failure to offer more would cause too much social unrest.

Even less noted is the entrepreneur's corollary to this law: that any successful enterprise attracts competition that brings profits close to zero, unless new markets open or some noncompetitive advantage is gained, usually with government assistance or subsidy. Larger firms with better access to such advantages can delay their moment of truth for quite some time, but at last (as in the United States since 1970) are squeezed and must in turn squeeze and downsize their workers. The popular invocation of "supply and demand" obscures this law's action.

Both wages and profits thus yield their fruits, first to owners of land from which wealth is produced (who in practice may be the entrepreneurial firm), and after that to those in charge of assignment of rights. In the case of organic farming, landlords (or their proxies, banks) can reap only that part of profits that conventional farmers would also have to yield. This leaves a potential windfall for private or state agents selling rights to the name "organic." A national certifying agency, by extracting part or all of this surplus, can thus reduce the farmer to a subsistence livelihood.

The organic farmer also risks continued transfer of wealth to other nonfarmers: manufacturers of materials and knowledge for which the farmer has to pay. Will organic agriculture simply substitute expensive "natural" external inputs for petrochemical ones? Will the prohibition against synthetic materials be weakened? The centerpiece of concern over reproducing the very system the organic community has sought to reform is the materials list in the national standards, that is, substances approved for fertility and pest control. The latter class of materials also reintroduces the problem of food purity: plant-based pesticides, such as neem, pyrethrum, rotenone, and sabadilla, can be highly toxic, although biodegradable, in biological systems. Furthermore, inert ingredients in manufactured materials may themselves be toxic but are excluded from evaluation because of trade secret protections to business. Decisions regarding inclusion of such materials by National Organic Standards Board have not been unanimous; specifically, the consumer representative on the board dissassociated herself from the botanicals review because she thought other members did not sufficiently evaluate these substances before listing them as allowed materials.[52] Where fertility and pest control are achieved through crop rotations and cultivation, as on the Spray farm in Ohio, inputs are not an issue.

Conclusion

You can do anything short term, but the long term is going to tell. (Rex Spray, Ohio farmer, 1996)

It is clear to me that if we are to have any hope of creating an ecological food system, with anything like democratic control, that food system has to be local and organic. (Bill Duesing, 1995)

What the law actually does is turn the tables in favor of the farmer. Instead of only being a marketing tool as in the current system, certification now becomes a license that is necessary to continue the business of organic farming. USDA certifying agents cannot place an undue burden on someone's right to obtain a license to conduct their business. (Bill Reichle, California farmer, 1995)[53]

National standards for an agricultural production system are unique in American history. Their development is a dramatic story, even a heroic one, of commitment and endurance. Their existence fills some farmers with dread, some with hope. As a method, organic farming successfully produces food; as an economy, however, it is vulnerable. A large question looms about the extent to which this institutionalization of alternative farming methods will actually change the large and powerful structures of American agriculture as a whole or simply be absorbed by those structures as another market opportunity. In Ohio, for instance, more-conventional farmers are beginning to grow some of their soybeans organically, not because they are interested in the long-term practice of a less extractive agriculture but because of the $18 each bushel brings—far more than the mere $5 for conventionally grown beans. All such farmers want to know is the minimum they must do to be certified by an international organic trade organization; they are not interested in participating in the educational or certifying activities of the state organic farming community. Such opportunism is repellent to established organic farmers, and the chronic worry of smaller farmers that they will be squeezed out economically as large producers drive down prices means that standards themselves will not create security. It is "business" as usual.

Is there an alternative?

Currently, organic growers may combine several economic strategies: selling wholesale to distributors and stores, direct selling in farmers' markets, and subscription farming. The last form is the least commercial and the most outside conventional economic institutions. Community-supported agriculture, realized in a voluntary association called a "CSA," relates farmers directly to subscribing or member households, which give the farmer at the start of the growing season or monthly an estimated share of costs of production and livelihood for the farmer. In exchange, each household receives a weekly portion of the production available that week or a market-defined portion equivalent to the money paid in. In some CSAs, members are expected to contribute labor, and the idea of equitable sharing of both benefit and risk is established morally, not by the market. In others, the CSA is a business enterprise with a "familiar face" created through newsletters and occasional visiting days to the farm. As farmer Paul Underhill notes, however, CSAs are not the answer for all farms; they seem to work best for small farms located in or near communities with a relatively tight social structure:

We have taken the industrial model of farming and removed just one element—synthetic chemicals and the monocrop farming they allow. But Wendell Berry, who believes that much of farming technology alienates the farmer from the land, would cast a stern eye at our diesel bill, our tractors and truck, our debts, our intensive cropping, and our reliance on hired farm workers. Unfortunately, California's farm economy makes it difficult, if not impossible, for a farmer to succeed without imitating many of the worst practices. Unless you have a largely self-sufficient farm, you must stay competitive in selling your produce. This means that the most conscientious, fair, ecologically minded organic farmer has to compete with the people who are in just for the money and do as little as they can while still being able to get the higher prices for organic food. Family farms and the mutual assistance that they tend to provide for each other have never been the rule in California. And while Community Supported Agriculture seems like a solution to this problem for small organic farmers, the wholesale market gets more competitive each year. Neighbors and friends in the close knit organic community have found themselves set against each other in recent years as the market grows and brokers and produce managers continue to push for lowering prices and "making organic more affordable." (Paul Underhill, 1996)[54]

A CSA is an "imagined community" that urban dwellers find attractive; if they do not see it in this way, however, their commitment may be tenuous, no less self-interested than any other commercial transaction, which in turn forces the farmer to recruit replacements to keep the CSA alive. Commitment may be more of an issue in California where the year-round season requires greater consumer support and where much of the population is nonnative, lives in urban settings, and has few social ties to the California agricultural community.[55] On the other hand, CSAs in a Midwestern context, with their 20-week season and more balanced rural/urban settlement patterns, might prove more viable. CSAs *can* exist outside the organic certification system, especially smaller ones whose members are involved in production practices and have confidence in them. Where "organic" is a feature of membership, and the membership is large, participation in a certification system may be necessary. Organic farming methods work. They have been successfully tested in the modern world for over half a century. Methods will continue to evolve, taking account of ecological and other complexities. The movement is too big to disappear or act as a mere niche market, and it is international. Austria, for example, has about 25,000 organic farms on 1 million acres; 12 percent of its land area is certified organic or in transition, probably 15 percent by the end of 1996. While this case is "unique in the world," Germany, Greece, Italy, Portugal, Spain, and Switzerland have shown comparable or greater growth since 1990, and Switzerland and Sweden are approaching 4 percent of their agricultural areas, the latter officially planning for 10 percent by the year 2000. These changes are occurring as a result of top-down and bottom-up efforts: farmers, communities, and consumers actively seeking alternative food production strategies, and national governments establishing policies that encourage growth in organic food production.

In the United States, if National Organic Standards actually becomes law and is implemented, if the 1996 Congressional mandate to phase out all agricultural subsidies by the year 2003 is implemented, if Congress in the present period of relentless conservatism does not revoke the Organic Food Production Act, if farmers can and will pay the full cost of regulation, we can expect the organic movement to bifurcate. These changes at the national level will make organic production strategies much more attractive to conventional farmers, who may gradually come to adopt the holistic social as well as ecological values of organic food and farming. However, given the economic structure of conventional agriculture, the shift to organic production does not necessarily mean we will see a rise in the number of small, self-sufficient farms. Large growers will continue to be large growers—part of the hegemonic global food industry. In the meantime, the survival of small growers is dependent on their ability to make a living locally, and this depends on the willingness of their American customers to pay the full cost of food.

Notes

1. Our thanks to Richard N. L. Andrews and Laura B. DeLind for their helpful comments on an earlier draft of this paper.

2. John H. Bodley, *Anthropology and Contemporary Human Problems*, 3d ed. (Mountain View, Calif.: Mayfield Publishing, 1996), 1–5.

3. *Ibid.*, p.1.

4. National Research Council, *Alternative Agriculture* (Washington, D.C.: National Academy Press, 1989), 97–130; Ann Misch, "Assessing Environmental Health Risks," *State of the World 1994* (New York: W. W. Norton/Worldwatch Institute, 1994), 117–136.

5. Ralph Borsodi, "The Case Against Farming as a Big Business," *The Land* 6:4 (1947–48) 446–451. The latest decline in farm population has, paradoxically, been paralleled by the growth of farm motifs, including black-and-white cows and antique farm implements and even barnwood, in suburban home decor and of mass magazines with "country" in the title or content.

6. National Organic Standrds Board, "Definition of Organic" drafted and passed in Orlando, Fla., April 1995. The U.S. Dept. of Agriculture estimates that in 1994 there were about 5,550 organic producers in the country (estimated to be 0.3 percent of all farms), 4,050 of them certified by at least one and sometimes more of the 33 private and 11 state organizations. Although those organizations will continue to certify under the Organic Production Act, they will do so to a single national standard that supersedes all others. Organic sales for 1994 were estimated at $2.3 billion, perhaps 1 percent of the total agricultural economy, up from $1.9 billion the previous year; $332.7 million of the 1994 total was from produce, up 32 percent, and $393 million came from direct sales (Committee for Sustainable Agriculture, *Organic Food Still Matters*, summer 1995, p. 12). California, the eighth-largest agricultural producer in the world, sold $20 billion in agricultural goods in 1994. The estimated gross sales from its organic agriculture in 1992–93 were $75.4 million or 0.4 percent (Douglas D. Weidman, *California's Organic Growers: An Export Market Profile*, master's thesis, California State University–Sacramento, 1995; K. Klonsky and L. Tourte, *Statistical Review for California's Organic Agriculture 1992–1993*, Cooperative Extension, Dept. of Agricultural Economics, University of California–Davis, 1995). Because agricultural statistics vary and are often incomplete and not strictly comparable, it is difficult to generate a reliable national figure for the organic share of the agricultural sector. We have concluded that for 1992 it must have been 0.3 percent; for 1996, it is of the order of 0.6 percent, a growing but tiny David against the Goliath of conventional agriculture. The cultural and political effect of organics, however, is much larger.

7. Wes Jackson, *Altars of Unhewn Stone: Science and the Earth* (San Francisco: North Point Press, 1987), 97–98.

8. David B. Danbom, *The Resisted Revolution: Urban America and the Industrialization of Agriculture, 1900–1930* (Ames: Iowa State University Press, 1979). 19th century agriculture was a series of booms and busts, chronic debt, overproduction, low prices, financial failures, and national depressions. We are focusing on the second century. These data lend perspective: in 1900, 42 percent of Americans lived on 5.7 million farms averaging 147 acres; by 1936 less than 25 percent remained, by 1970 less than 5 percent, and by 1992 less than 1.8 percent on 1.9 million farms averaging 490 acres. Prices per bushel, measured in constant (1967) U.S. dollars, for wheat and corn in 1900 were $2.48 and $1.40; they peaked, along with soybeans, in 1919 ($4.17, $2.92, and $7.92 respectively), and

have since gone below levels of the Great Depression, in 1990 dropping to $0.67, $0.58, and $1.47. For each dollar paid American farmers, domestic consumers paid $2.17 for food in 1947, $3 in 1959, $4 in 1985, and $4.50 in 1993. Sources: *U.S. Bureau of the Census, Historical Statistics of the United States, Colonial Times to 1970*, Bicentennial Edition (Washington, D.C.: Government Printing Office, 1975); *U.S. Bureau of the Census, Statistical Abstracts of the United States* (Washington, D.C.: Government Printing Office, 1981, 1991, 1995); U.S. Dept. of Agriculture, National Agricultural Statistics Service, Agricultural Statistics (Washington, D.C.: Government Printing Office, 1967 to 1993).

9. Donald Worster, *The Dust Bowl: The Southern Plains in the 1930s* (New York: Oxford University Press, 1979).

10. After 1962, the centennial year for the Morrill Act that established land grant universities, the yearbooks became trivial exercises in self-promotion at the fourth-grade level—perhaps because the petrochemical industry provided instructions for using its products, and because the knowledge base thought necessary for successful farming was sharply reduced.

11. Sir Albert Howard, *An Agricultural Testament* (London: Oxford University Press, 1940), 198.

12. J. I. Rodale, *Paydirt* (New York: Devin-Adair, 1945), 134–135; J. I. Rodale, *The Organic Front* (Emmaus, Pa.: Rodale Press, 1948).

13. George Mitchell, "Review of An Agricultural Testament," *The Land* 2:4 (1943) 347.

14. Louis Bromfield, *Malabar Farm* (New York: Harper and Row, 1947); Charles E. Little, ed., *Louis Bromfield at Malabar* (Baltimore: Johns Hopkins Press, 1988).

15. See Worster, *op. cit.*, note 9, for a less enthusiastic assessment.

16. Rachel Carson, *Silent Spring* (Boston: Houghton Mifflin, 1962). The book was violently attacked, and Dow Chemical published a rebuttal, *Silent Autumn*, threatening world hunger without use of pesticides.

17. H. L. Boul *et al.*, "Influence of Agricultural Practices on the Levels of DDT and Its Residues in the Soil," *Environmental Science and Technology* 28:8 (1994) 1397–1403. See also National Research Council, *Alternative Agriculture* (Washington, D.C.: National Academy Press, 1989) for a summary of productivity and chemical use in American agriculture from the 1960s to the 1980s. For data on soil loss and water quality, see National Research Council, *Alternative Agriculture* (Washington, D.C.: National Academy Press, 1989), 97–119.

18. National Research Council 1989, *op. cit.*, note 17. For a historical view of organic matter and erosion control, see James F. Parr and Sharon B. Hornick, "Agricultural Use of Organic Ammendments: A Historical Perspective," *American Journal of Alternative Agriculture* 7:181–189 (1992); for a case study of no-till use in the Midwest, see Michael Chibnik, "Saving Soil by Abandoning the Plow: Experimentation with No-Till Farming in an Iowa County," in Michael Chibnik, ed., *Farm Work and Fieldwork: American Agriculture in Anthropological Perspective* (Ithaca, N.Y.: Cornell University Press, 1987), 90–117.

19. R. Klepper *et al.*, "Economic Performance and Energy Intensiveness on Organic and Conventional Farms in the Corn Belt: a Preliminary Comparison," *American Journal of Agricultural Economics* 59 (1977) 1–12; J. A. Langley *et al.*, "The Macro Implications of a Complete Transformation of U.S. Agricultural Production to Organic Farming Practices," *Ecosystems and Environment* 10 (1983) 323–333 [of 10 areas, only Texas and the Southeast lost net income; gains elsewhere ranged from 14 to 80 percent]; T. Cacek and L. L. Langner, "The Economic Implications of Organic Farming," *American Journal of Alternative Agriculture* 1:1 (1986) 25–29.

20. Wendell Berry, *The Unsettling of America: Culture and Agriculture* (San Francisco: North Point Press, 1977), 196–197.

21. National Research Council, 1989, *op. cit.*, note 17, p. 262.

22. USDA Study Team on Organic Farming, Report and Recommendations on Organic Farming (Washington, D.C.: U.S. Dept. of Agriculture, July 1980). For discussion of the loss of family farms see Gary Comstock, ed., *Is There a Moral Obligation to Save the Family Farm?* (Ames: Iowa State University Press, 1987); Peggy F. Barlett, *American Dreams and Rural Realities: Family Farms in Crisis* (Chapel Hill: University of North Carolina Press, 1993); Amory B. Lovins *et al.*, "Energy and

Agriculture," *Meeting the Expectations of the Land*, Wes Jackson *et al.*, eds. (San Francisco: North Point Press, 1984), 68–86.

23. Garth Youngberg et al., "The Sustainable Policy Agenda in the United States: Politics and Prospects," in Patricia Allen, ed., *Food for the Future: Conditions and Contradictions of Sustainability* (New York: John Wiley & Sons, 1993), 295–318. In the USDA Study team report (*ibid.*, p. xii), the authors observed: "Contrary to popular belief, most organic farmers have not regressed to agriculture as it was practiced in the 1930's. While they attempt to avoid or restrict the use of chemical fertilizers and pesticides, organic farmers still use modern farm machinery, recommended crop varieties, certified seed, sound methods of organic waste management, and recommended soil and water conservation practices." Note that this defense of organic farmers depends on tying them to outside hierarchical sources of authoritative knowledge that is "modern," "recommended," "certified," and "sound."

24. Mary Douglas, "In the Nature of Things," *Implicit Meanings* (London: Routledge & Kegan Paul, 1975), 216, 214.

25. Marty Strange, *Family Farming: A New Economic Vision* (Lincoln: University of Nebraska Press, 1988).

26. Warren J. Belasco, *Appetite for Change: How the Counterculture Took on the Food Industry 1966–1988* (New York: Pantheon Books, 1989). Belasco offers an excellent discussion of the "food wars" of the 1970s: the development of the natural food industry and the fierce reaction against it by food scientists and manufacturers, including the symbolic rendering of nature as impoverishing, ruthless, dangerous, and even deadly—interestingly enough, similar in structure and content to attacks on organic farming.

27. David B. Danbom, "The Agricultural Experiment Station and Professionalization: Scientists' Goals in Agriculture," *Agricultural History* 60:2 (1986) 246–255.

28. Robert Tonkinson, *The Mardu Aborigines: Living the Dream in the Western Desert* (Ft. Worth, Texas: Holt, Rinehart and Winston, 1991).

29. See also Lawrence Busch and William B. Lacy, *Science, Agriculture and the Politics of Research* (Boulder, Colo.: Westview Press, 1983). William Lockeretz, "Removing Applied Agricultural Research from the Academy," *American Journal of Alternative Agriculture* 10:1 (1995) 19–24; Peter Esainko and Valerie Wheeler, "A Little More than Kin and Less than Kind: Organic Practice vs. Institutional Theory," Paper given at the Varieties of Sustainability Conference, Agriculture, Food and Human Values Society, Asilomar, Calif., 1991.

30. Dana Jackson, "Sustainable Agriculture: A Concept Catching On," *The Land Report* 26 (1986) 7–9.

31. Wes Jackson, *New Roots for Agriculture* (Lincoln: University of Nebraska Press, 1981 and 1985).

32. Youngberg *et al.*, *op. cit.*, note 23.

33. Patricia Allen, "The Challenges of Sustainability in Food and Agriculture," *Organic Farmer* 4:1 (1993) 20–21.

34. Youngberg *et al.*, *op. cit.*, note 23, p. 310.

35. Youngberg *et al.*, *op. cit.*, note 23, pp. 311–312.

36. Since 1988, the U.S. Dept. of Agriculture has spent some $6 to 7.5 million in a competitive grants program originally called LISA (Low Input Sustainable Agriculture), then SARE (Sustainable Agriculture Research and Education program). Small grants are given for research, demonstration, and extension projects by public- and private-sector professionals, farmers, and business persons. SARE funds on-farm research, though very few projects deal with organic systems. Profitability is a primary concern. SARE also has a sophisticated system for disseminating the results of its projects.

37. Frederick H. Buttel, "The Production of Agricultural Sustainability: Observations from the Sociology of Science and Technology," in Patricia Allen, ed., *Food for the Future* (New York: John Wiley & Sons, 1993), 19–45.

38. *California Certified Organic Farmers*, Statewide Newsletter 11:4 (1995) 19; CCOF information brochure, 1994.

39. *Ohio Ecological Food and Farming Association*, News 15:3 (1995) 3; 15:5 (1995) 4.

40. Valerie Wheeler and Peter Esainko, "Structural Power and Authoritative Knowledge in Alternative Agriculture," Paper at the Society for Applied Anthropology, Charleston, S.C., 1991.

41. National Research Council, 1989, *op. cit.,* note 3; Institute of Food Technologists, "Organically Grown Foods: A Scientific Status Summary," *Food Technology* 44:12 (1990) 123–130; Preston Smith, "Why Does Jack Hate LISA?" *New Farm* 11:7 (Nov.–Dec. 1989); Martha Carroll, "Organic Growing Still Has Many Drawbacks," press release, Ohio Cooperative Extension Service, Ohio State University, OARDC, Wooster, 1989; Charles Hess, "Sustainable Agriculture: The Power of Thought," *Sustainable Agriculture in California: A Research Symposium* (University of California–Davis: Sustainable Agriculture Research and Education Program, 1990), 1–20; Gerald W. Thomas, "Sustainability: Striking a Balance Between Economic and Ecological Constraints," *Sustainable Agriculture in California: A Research Symposium* (University of California–Davis: Sustainable Agriculture Research and Education Program, 1990), 1–5; John E. Kinsella, Speech at the Student Farm Field Day, University of California–Davis, 1990.

42. Desmond Jolly, "Consumer Willingness to Pay Price Premiums for Organic Apples and Peaches," University of California–Davis: Sustainable Agriculture Research and Education Program, 1989; Desmond Jolly *et al.*, "Organic Food: Consumer Attitudes and Use," *Food Technology* 43:11 (1989) 60–66; S. Lynne Walker, "Organic Food Still Seeks Its Niche," *Sacramento Union*, Sept 10, 1991, p. A1+; David Lively, "Organics Boom Not Bust," *In Good Tilth* 1:6 (1991) 1–2.

43. Thomas Forster, "OFAC Lobbying Efforts Triumph," *Organic Farmer* 1:4 (1990) 26; Gene Logsdon, "Kiss of Death? Federal Organic Standards Are Not What the Doctor Ordered," *New Farm* 15:3 (1993) 12ff.

44. Harold Ricker, "National Organic Program Update," Eco-Farm Conference, Asilomar, Calif., January 1996.

45. Elizabeth Henderson, "Some Comments and Concerns About the NOSB," *Organic Farming* fall 1992, p. 21.

46. Caroline Carr, "Follow-Up: National Organic Standards Board," *Ohio Ecological Food & Farm Association News* fall 1992, pp. 16–17; Gene Logsdon, "Organic Overload?," *Farmer to Farmer* (Ozark Small Farm Viability Project), Sept. 1992.

47. Fred Kirschenmann, "The Organic Food Industry: Where We've Been, Where We Are, and Where We're Going," Speech delivered at the 10th Annual Organic Trade Association Dinner, Sept. 14, 1995, Baltimore, Md.

48. Laura B. DeLind, "The State, Hog Hotels, and the 'Right to Farm': A Curious Relationship," *Agriculture and Human Values* 12:3 (1995) 34–44.

49. Frederick Kirschenmann *et al.*, "Towards a Sustainable, Organic Food Marketing System," *Organic Farmer* 4:2 (1993) 19–20.

50. Sal Schettino (sals@rain.org), "Sustainable," Organic Gardening Discussion List GL@UKCC.uky.edu, Feb. 11, 1996; http://www.rain.org/~sals/my.html.

51. Named by Ferdinand Lassalle, this law was derived by David Ricardo from pioneer work by the French physiocrats. Other schools of thought favored the just wage, the wages fund, marginal productivity of labor, bargaining theory, purchasing power theory, and equal wages.

52. "The Special Review of Botanicals," *Farmer to Farmer* 3:10 (Jan. 1995) 7.

53. Bill Duesing, "Is Organic Enough?," The Natural Farmer (NOFA), winter 1995–96; Bill Reichle, "Fairness in Certification—the Rules Have Changed," *Farmer to Farmer* 3:7 (Jan. 9, 1995) 12.

54. Paul Underhill, CSA Newsletter, Terra Firma Farm, Winters, Calif., Aug. 16, 1996.

55. In a western CSA whose several hundred members receive a detailed and friendly newsletter with each weekly box, the farmers were taken aback when 14 of those who had reserved the 15 slots offered for a specially planned workday on the farm canceled at the last minute.

56. Nicholas Lampkin, "Austria" (Doc 550) and "Organic Farming Statistics" (Doc 563), April 23 and 26, 1996 (http://ekolserv.vo.vlu.se/Docs/www/Subject/Organic-farming/550-599). See also N. H. Lampkin and S. Padel, *The Economics of Organic Farming: An International Perspective* (Wallingford, England: CAB International, 1994).

CHAPTER 8

Resource Access, Environmental Struggles, and Human Rights in Honduras

James Phillips

Introduction

On May 3, 1991, five peasants were shot and killed as they slept on a piece of land they had peacefully occupied in northern Honduras. The Honduran government had awarded them title to the land 15 years before, but an army colonel and other large landowners had continued to occupy it. The army colonel was later convicted in the 1991 peasants' murder, and he served two years in prison before being released. Known throughout Honduras as the El Astillero massacre, this incident and others like it gave rise to many popular songs in peasant communities, including one with these words: "The land is for sustaining life, not just for the powerful. The life of a peasant is worth the same as a rich man's."[1]

In Honduras today, the preservation and advancement of basic human rights, the equitable use of land and resources, and the preservation and sustainable use of the country's natural environment are three inextricably connected aspects of a single historical process. In the experience of many Hondurans, a powerful connection is being forged between environmental degradation, inequitable systems of land tenure and resource control, and the erosion of a variety of basic rights. This connection derives its power from the current sense of insecurity and crisis in Honduran society.

Control of Resources, Environmental Degradation, and the Crisis of Insecurity

Large landowners have existed alongside peasant farmers in Honduras for much of the country's history, and especially since the arrival of the banana companies in the early 1900s. Typically, Honduran landowners who could afford to expand production of profitable export crops did so by expanding their own landholdings, often annexing the land of peasants.[2] The process of consolidating large holdings by eliminating small holdings or pushing peasants to marginal lands was quickened by the expansion of export markets for Honduran fruit, beef, and wood after World War II and into the present. In

James Phillips is an anthropologist who has worked for over 25 years on social change and development issues in the Caribbean and Latin America. He has been a staff member of several international development agencies, and has taught anthropology at several universities in the United States. Comments can be sent to 1130 Toman Creek Road, Ashland, OR 97520.

recent years, this process has been clearly documented in southern Honduras, as well as in the northern fruit-company areas.[3]

The country's unequal land tenure patterns have successfully restricted access to natural resources for rural Hondurans, while contributing to a growing sense of insecurity about resources and needs. Insecurity has been sharpened by clear signs of accelerating environmental degradation and dwindling resource, felt especially (but not exclusively) in the daily lives of the poor majority.

Deforestation is generally cited as the most apparent environmental problem in Honduras.[4] Soil erosion and depletion, water contamination, and lack of urban waste management are other important concerns. In Honduras deforestation has continued at such a pace that in 1988 the director of COHDEFOR (the Honduran Forestry Department) warned of emerging and irreversible desertification.[5] The following year, a report issued by the Honduran Ecology Association calculated that ten hectares of forest were being destroyed in the country every hour.[6] In summary:

> . . . there is overwhelming evidence from Honduras . . . that rates of loss of forests, soils, fisheries, and other crucial natural resources exceed rates of regeneration and that ensuing consequences such as land degradation, watershed deterioration, and destruction of coastal resources have reached critical levels in many areas.[7]

Throughout the 1980s, climatic symptoms of environmental deterioration became apparent. Much of the country suffered drought. Peasant farmers in the northern department of Yoro endured such a drought that many were forced to change their diet by replacing the traditional corn, which the drought destroyed, with wheat flour sent as drought aid from the United States.[8] Punctuating the drought were major floods such as that which occurred in parts of Choluteca department in 1988, and in the Aguan Valley in 1990. Both of these areas are centers of agro-industry. With their homes or plots of cultivation perched precariously on marginal lands above rivers or on steep mountainsides, poor people died or lost their homes and crops in mud slides and washouts. Floods also affected thousands of landless rural families who migrated to rapidly growing cities such as Tegucigalpa, the nation's capital, where they lived in flimsy shacks along riverbanks and canals or on mountainsides considered too steep for urban development.

During the past 30 years, the availability of basic foods consumed by most of the population—maize, beans, sorghum—has declined, even as export agriculture has expanded. From 1952 to 1986, the number of kilograms of corn produced per person declined from 140 to 107, with similar declines in beans and sorghum. The number of hectares per person planted in these crops also declined.[9] Some of the effects of this declining production were clear by the 1970s: the price of maize in the local market increased by 107 percent from 1972 to 1979, with an increase of 117 percent in the price of beans during the same period.[10] Prices have continued their upward trend, and the level of per-person daily caloric consumption, already the lowest in the hemisphere, has declined further. As noted by anthropologist Susan Stonich, "despite thirty years of economic growth, a majority of Hondurans find themselves less able now than in the mid-1960s to obtain their basic food requirements. Food security continues to elude them."[11]

A leader for CODDEFFAGOLF, an environmental justice group fighting for resource access and use rights on the Honduran coast. Photograph by Susan Stonich.

Largely controlled by foreign agribusiness corporations and a local elite of large landowners, access to land and resources has been further compromised, in popular perception and in experience, by accelerating environmental deterioration. The combined effects of environmental deterioration and limited access to land and resources on the daily diet, income, physical security, and other life-quality indicators of many Hondurans have sharpened a sense of insecurity and crisis.

Forces Blamed for Environmental Deterioration

In Honduras, assigning blame for the country's environmental problems, deforestation in particular, is an exercise fraught with political implications.[12] During the past 30 years environmental degradation, especially deforestation, has intensified as a result of the interplay between the export-oriented market strategies of agro-industries and large landowners (fruit, sugar, cotton, beef, and wood) and the survival/subsistence strategies of hundreds of thousands of small-scale peasant farmers.

Since the arrival of the Spaniards 500 years ago, cattle ranching has been a significant aspect of life in Central America. Traditionally, the owners of large cattle ranches formed a politically powerful local and national elite in Honduras. In this century, as corporate fast-food chains in the United States and elsewhere expanded and the demand for beef grew, ranching expanded in Honduras and came under increasing foreign corporate control. Foreign fruit companies have been even more dominant landowners, clearing thousands of acres of forest and planting banana, pineapples, and other export crops.[13] Aside from the initial deforestation involved in converting forest to agribusiness, the company plantations and cattle ranches have tried to take advantage of cycles of market expansion or higher consumer prices in the importing countries by expanding production in Honduras, which has often meant expanding landholdings by displacing peasant farmers.

Logging has also contributed to this process of peasant marginalization and deforestation in Honduras, as elsewhere in Central America.[14] Historically, Honduras has been a lumber-exporting country. The earlier export logging for precious tropical hardwoods (mahogany) has been largely replaced by the growing demand for oak, highland pine, and other woods used in construction and fine furniture to satisfy local elite and export markets. With worldwide demand for paper and paper products burgeoning in this computer age, foreign companies have targeted forests of lowland pines in eastern Honduras for paper and pulp production.[15] Logging roads have opened up access into previously remote regions, drawing marginalized peasants, ranchers, and others.[16] Peasant farmers displaced by corporate agribusiness plantations and ranches often went to more marginal, forested areas, where they cleared land and farmed until the tropical soils gave out or they were displaced again by plantations and ranches. Then they moved on to yet another marginal forest area, tried to find work on the plantations or ranches, or migrated to the city. This process has shaped the current crisis in Honduras, and it continues today.

Progressive marginalization of peasant farmers contributes to destruction of forests and depletion of topsoils not suited for farming; however, it is the poverty and landlessness of peasants that drives them into areas marginally suited for cultivation, and pushes them to intensify their cultivation beyond what the soil and resources might sustain. In addition, the poor rely on the forests for firewood, in one form or another, including charcoal. Gathering firewood in the forest is cheaper than having to buy energy for domestic use, and the availability of "free" firewood helps sustain many poor families. (COHDEFOR estimated in 1988 that 6 million cubic meters of firewood are extracted from Honduran forests annually.)[17]

Two additional causes of environmental destruction in Honduras are also regularly mentioned. Forest fires from natural and human causes destroy thousands of hectares of forest annually, although some of this area may eventually return to forest.[18] War and its attendant activities has also had a major impact on the country's natural environment. As the primary base for U.S. military presence in Central America during the 1980s, Honduras had more miles per person of airstrip runway (most of it military) than any other country in the world. Peasant groups regularly complained that many peasants were displaced when military bases were built or expanded to accommodate an increased U.S. military presence, and that the joint war games and training maneuvers of the U.S. and Honduran armies resulted in forest damage and environmental pollution, as well as other physical and social disruptions to the rural population in some areas. Church workers in southeastern Honduras estimated that 10,000 Honduran peasants and rural dwellers were displaced from their homes and lands by the presence of Nicaraguan Resistance forces ("Contras") on Honduran soil during the 1980s.[19]

"Honduras is an Occupied Country . . . Run by the U.S. Embassy"[20]

Most of the major causes of environmental destruction in Honduras can be understood in a context of national dependency within an international system—a perspective shared by many Hondurans. The impact of the U.S. military presence during the 1980s makes this clear, but Honduran peasants, to say nothing of the country's environmental resources, are also at the mercy of expansions and contractions in the foreign markets served by the fruit, beef, and logging companies. In times of market expansion, these large companies become more aggressive about expanding into peasant lands. In times of foreign market contraction or economic downturn, however, peasants who own land are tempted to overexploit it to survive; those who rent land from others often see their rent raised; and poor urban dwellers return to rural areas seeking land to grow food in order to escape hunger in the cities. External economic cycles drive the environmentally destructive actions of both large-corporate and small-peasant land users.

The history of Honduras, with its intimate connection to and dependency on foreign economies and policies, has conditioned Hondurans to understand both internal repression and inequitable access to and control over resources as products of (or at least conditioned by) their external dependency. The dominance of foreign fruit companies and their involvement with local military and police power in quelling labor protests and dislodging peasants, for example, is a central experience in the country's popular history.[21] This understanding of basic rights violations as tied to external dependencies and external control of land and resources has also prompted a popular sense that the natural resources of the country are constantly in danger of being sold to foreigners by the country's own power elite.[22]

Responses to the Crisis

The two processes of increasing land and resource monopolization by a relative few and accelerating environmental degradation have acted in tandem to produce increasing insecurity for Honduran peasants, rural workers, and ultimately the entire society. Hondurans have responded to this history of rising insecurity, inequity, and environmental deterioration in ways that link social conditions (especially the abuse of fundamental human rights) to the environmental integrity in their country—as, for example, illustrated in the struggle over agrarian reform.

Agrarian reform in Honduras has been a slow process of considerable struggle since the 1950s. When a modern, full-scale agrarian reform law was passed in 1975, years of partial and temporary measures and considerable conflict had preceded it, and more conflict and frustration were to follow.[23] Ironically, it was 1974, the year before passage of the agrarian reform law, which was the peak year for land distribution to Honduran peasants. In 1974, a total of 287 peasant groups and almost 10,000 peasant families received some 47,000 hectares through the agrarian reform apparatus. Distribution of land to peasants and the rural poor declined after 1974, and it has never kept pace with peasant expectations or the government's own declared goals. Much of the land that government agencies—in particular the National Agrarian Institute, or INA—classifies as distributed to peasants in some years has involved no new land transfers, but only confirmation of title to land already worked by peasants.[24] Many plots are too small to sustain self-reliance, and many recipients receive little or no credit or other supports.

Some analysts argue that the agrarian reform, weak as it is, has been chiefly responsible for sparing Honduras the bloody revolutions and civil wars experienced by other Central American countries in the 1970s and 1980s.[25] The fact that an agrarian reform law remains on the books and functions at a minimal level has provided peasant organizations with a legal standard against which to measure the inequities of land and resource access in Honduran society, together with some channels through which to apply political pressures. This ongoing struggle is what Honduran peasants mean when they say, "*We* are the agrarian reform," and it highlights the importance of peasant unions and organizations.[26]

The peasant organizations have increasingly rejected colonization schemes and movements by marginalized peasants to "new" lands in forested areas as a solution to land hunger. Their opposition sprang, at first, from their intention, first, to force government authorities and agencies to take seriously the responsibilities mandated by the agrarian reform laws, and, second, to protect the rights of peasants unjustly and illegally pushed off their lands by large landowners and corporations. In a word, the unions chose to fight for what they believed was theirs rather than to support the flight of their members to marginal areas.[27] Seen in this way, the unions' policy amounts to an organized demand for accountability from government officials, large landowners, and agribusinesses.

As this policy has developed, union leaders and members have become increasingly articulate about other reasons for their refusal to support peasant movement onto marginal lands. They want to avoid conflicts among peasant groups seeking the same marginal lands. They also want to avoid supporting peasant invasions of lands claimed historically by indigenous tribal peoples who are seen as natural allies in the struggle for land rights and resources. The unions also are increasingly aware of the environmental damage caused by unchecked land marginalization, for many of their own members have had bitter experiences farming marginal lands where soils failed after a few years and families faced soil erosion and depletion, decreasing yields, and increasing poverty. Others have worked hard clearing and cultivating marginal forest areas only to see their land taken over by large landowners once the clearing is done. In addition, this policy of claiming land they have already been cultivating, rather than seeking marginal lands, keeps their actions within the scope of agrarian reform processes.

For all these reasons, peasant unions have supported their members' continuation on lands they have traditionally cultivated, rather than their removal to marginal lands. To exercise political pressure for continued agrarian reform and to dramatize and reverse the injustice that they believe is involved in the way peasants have been pushed off their lands, the unions support annual nonviolent land occupations throughout the country by groups of peasants at the start of the planting season. Rejecting the less confrontational route to marginal lands, they prefer to risk the hazards of open confrontation with large landowners who, from the peasants' perspective, have illegally seized peasant lands.

For peasants, the hazards of such confrontation are many and serious. In Honduran law, land occupations have been classified as acts of terrorism, although harsh measures against peasant occupiers are not always enforced. In Honduras, land occupations are like Russian roulette: you can succeed or you can die. During the 1980s and early 1990s people died in land occupations. The El Astillero massacre of 1991, in which five peasants were killed by armed agents of a large landowner, was only one of many such incidents.[28] The repression has not been confined to those directly involved in land occupations. Peasant union leaders and supporters have been threatened, imprisoned, tortured, "disappeared," and killed.[29]

The El Astillero killings were especially troubling to many Hondurans because the landowner in question was an army colonel, a man in a position of power and relative impunity in Honduran society. Although massive public pressure resulted in his conviction and imprisonment, he was released and returned to his rank in two years. The case seemed to underscore for the peasant unions and others the need for accountability from the nation's power elite in matters of land and resource control and fundamental human rights. All the survivors of the El Astillero massacre went into hiding—as far as possible. Two survivors eventually left Honduras to seek asylum in the United States. They based their asylum claim on a reasonable fear for their lives and safety if they should be forced to return to Honduras. Their claim was granted in 1995.[30]

The El Astillero incident, and others like it, illustrate two other kinds of responses to the crisis of insecurity: repression and exile. Violent repression is perpetrated by private persons and public figures who can count on their power and impunity. Exile is a response to the inaccessibility of resources (economic survival) but also to the threat of physical violence, for in Honduras the two are often closely related. Such cases of asylum raise questions about the relevance of the distinction in U.S. immigration law and policy about economic immigrants and political refugees, as well as about the plight of those who may be called "environmental refugees."[31]

The response of some indigenous groups in Honduras provides an example of the indivisibility of rights and how people are beginning to articulate it. At least six major self-defined groups of indigenous peoples live in Honduras today, including about 18,000 Tol-speaking Xicaque people who live in villages and settlements in the mountains and hills of the northern department of Yoro.[32] The Xicaque hold forested lands in the mountains that they regard as theirs by reason of formal treaties with the Honduran government going back to the 1860s.

Prior to 1974, individual caciques (local community leaders) granted permits to outsiders (non-Xicaques) to log areas of the tribal forests. After the 1974 establishment of COHDEFOR (the Honduran Forestry Development Corporation), the Xicaques found themselves increasingly at the mercy of bureaucrats who had to approve contracts and who were in a position to reward caciques whom they liked and punish caciques whom they regarded as too independent. This politicization from the outside was disruptive and destabilizing for the Xicacque.

In 1979, after a period of tensions, killings, and other problems, the Honduran government joined with the Xicaques in forming the Yoro Indigenous Cooperation Project (PROCOINY) to provide a vehicle for dialogue. While engaged in speaking and other activities through PROCOINY, Xicaque leaders came into dialogue with other organized groups, including labor and peasant unions, grassroots Church groups (Christian based communities), foreign aid donors, indigenous groups outside of Honduras, and many others. Eventually, a movement among younger Xicaque to redefine their Indian identity and to become a clearly recognized political force led to the formation of the Federation of Xicaque Tribes of Yoro (FETRIXY) in the late 1980s. FETRIXY gradually assumed the functions of a pan-tribal governing council, replacing the local caciques as speakers for the Xicacque people. FETRIXY drafted a set of objectives and guidelines for use and preservation of the tribal forests, and prompted the search for new ways to combine traditional sustainable forest management and use with modern methods and markets for forest products.

But as they worked to redefine and strengthen their cultural, political, and economic identity, the Xicaque faced various external pressures and challenges, including threats, intimidations, and killings perpetrated by large landowners and occasionally Honduran army personnel, as well as land invasions by landless, marginalized peasants. In 1988, for example, the Xicaque formally complained to the National Agrarian Institute, which had permitted a group of non-Xicaque peasants calling themselves Los Invencibles to occupy one of the "best regions" of the Xicaque land.[33] In another incident, peasants were accused of killing a Xicaque in a land dispute. In the period from 1988 to mid-1993, five tribal leaders were killed. The best-known of these, Vicente Matute, killed in September 1991, was president of FETRIXY.[34]

These incidents provoked the independent Committee for the Defense of Human Rights in Honduras (CODEH) to denounce what it perceived as a systematic campaign by large landowners and the military against fundamental rights of the Xicaque and other indigenous peoples of Honduras. CODEH defined those rights in terms of rights to life and physical security, rights to continued tenure and use of tribal lands, and rights to free expression of tribal cultural identity and lifeways. All of these, CODEH declared, were inextricably related.[35]

In the context of these conflictive histories of peasant and indigenous response to the insecurity of decreasing access to land and resources and increasing environmental deterioration, it is easier to understand the importance of massive popular protests such as such as those that greeted a proposed logging agreement in 1991. In that year, agencies of the Honduran government entered into negotiations with a U.S.-based transnational corporation, one of the world's largest producers of cardboard. They were negotiating an agreement that would have given the cardboard-maker 40 years of logging rights to 320,000 hectares of tropical lowland pine forest in the Mosquitia region of eastern Honduras (about one-third of the country's territory and home to thousands of Mosquito Indian people) as well as rights to log certain forested regions within a 150-mile radius of the northern Honduran Caribbean port of Puerto Castilla. The corporation promised to create 15,000 new jobs and pay Honduras US$20 million.[36]

Most of the Honduran public, even members of the National Congress, knew little or nothing of the negotiations until a tentative agreement was announced in September 1991. Massive public protest demonstrations followed, with marches and rallies in several cities. Typical statements heard during the protests express the concerns, demands, and hopes of many Hondurans, while they provide insight into the evolution of environmental rights in that Central American country:

> The state bureaucracy which oversees forests in our country has grown while the forests have dwindled. Those who control forestry here are politicians and private interests instead of trained technicians and forestry professionals. Personal gain replaces national interest . . . (A

member of Colegio de Profesionales Forestry de Honduras [Honduran Organization of Forestry Professionals])

Once again, after a long silence, we students are speaking up to defend our rights. In Honduras, students have always been among the first to defend rights, and many have died for this. But we are defending the future as well as the present. So for me, this is really like a big celebration . . . (A university student)

I am here protesting with these others because, once again, the government is trying to sell our country to foreigners. They want to sell the future of my children and the country for their own profit. I have struggled all my life to have enough land to grow my food, and things are still hard. I don't want my children and grandchildren to have the same, or worse, problems . . . (A peasant farmer)

We don't want to be left in the middle of a desert or without any natural resources which are the habitat of many animals and with which our people sustain themselves. . . . We don't like being treated like people who don't think. . . . Our people have never asked the government for our necessities. . . . (The president of Miskito Asla Tankana, an indigenous organization)

Such protests are another form of response, one that unites various organizations representing different sectors of Honduran society. This fact, considered with many of the statements of participants, illustrates a process of identifying environmental sustainability, access to resources, and various basic rights as closely related aspects of a single historical process.

Conclusion

An integrated understanding of the connections between equitable access to land and resources, environmental sustainability, and human rights has been emerging in Honduras, together with an increasing sense of the indivisibility of rights.[37] This integrative insight has been the product of a long history that has moved many Hondurans through successive levels of understanding about human rights in relation to the country's natural environmental resources. Different groups in Honduras have experienced these levels of human rights understanding in different ways.

The struggles of the peasant unions have moved them further toward a wider sense of the connections between inequitable systems of land tenure, environmental degradation, and deterioration of human rights. Peasant marginalization is a result of both unjust and restricted control of land and resources. Marginalization is a cause of environmental deterioration from which the peasants themselves immediately suffer. Trying to end marginalization can precipitate gross violations of peasants' rights. In fact, the whole process is one of progressive violation of increasingly more fundamental rights. The violation of one type of right sets in motion a process for violation of other kinds of rights. One fruit of the Honduran situation over the past 20 years has been a clearer empirical recognition of this essential indivisibility, a recognition gradually articulated by wider sectors of Honduran society.

The history of human rights activism in Honduras began with denouncing gross violations of the rights of individual peasants, indigenous peoples, and environmental activists, usually violations involving killing, disappearance, or torture by large landowners, the military, and others. The right to life and physical security was the most fundamental issue, and it was at first incidental that those threatened were so threatened precisely because of their involvement, in some way, in struggles over natural resources.

But in the logic and dynamic of Honduran experience, the centrality of the struggle over the land and its resources could not remain an incidental, secondary-rights consideration. Human rights groups—especially CODEH, the largest one, and the one with the highest public profile—increasingly understood the gross violations of life and physical safety as manifestations of systematic repression, itself a symptom of pervasive structural injustices—in particular, the system of inequitable and insecure access to land and other natural productive resources. Human rights extended to equitable access and reasonable use of these resources.

Finally, these rights were meaningless unless they were sustainable and could be exercised by future generations as well. It was necessary to safeguard the natural environment. Underlying the indivisibility of all these rights were both philosophical considerations about the integral nature of human life, and practical and historical experience of how they reinforce each other. One practical thread uniting them was accountability. The same impunity and lack of accountability that permitted some to control and use land and resources however they pleased also permitted them to eliminate or contain any possible threat to their control in whatever way was most effective.

In the context of Honduran history, accountability raises questions about democratic process and national sovereignty. Government and military officials, politicians, and those with economic power in Honduran society may find it increasingly difficult to make decisions about environmental resources, to cede resource rights to foreigners, or to resort to violent repression—without accounting to other sectors of society in the future. The Honduran experience invites conclusions that parallel recent writings about the connection between sustainable development and levels of popular participation.[38] At a celebration after the suspension of the logging agreement discussed above, a leader of Fundacio Cuero y Salado, the country's largest environmental group, was quoted as saying:

> This has been an incredible event in which all sectors of the Honduran people united against a government plan that was seriously flawed, justifying their position to the government to the point where the government accepted the voice of the people. This has been a great example of democracy working in the country.[39]

Notes

1. Elias Ruiz, *El Astillero: Masacre y Justicia* (Tegucigalpa: Editorial Guaymuras, 1992).

2. Centro de Documentacion de Honduras, *25 Anos de Reform Agraria* (Tegucigalpa: Centro de Documentacion de Honduras, 1988).

3. Susan Stonich, "The Political Economy of Environmental Destruction: Food Security in Southern Honduras," in *Harvest of Want: Hunger and Food Security in Central America and Mexico*, Scott Whiteford and Anne E. Ferguson, eds. (Boulder, Colo.: Westview Press, 1991).

4. Deforestation can be assessed in various ways ranging from statistical measurements (for example, 40 percent conversion of forest to other uses) to assessments that emphasize "the reduction of the capacity of a forest to fulfill a particular (social, cultural, or economic) function," a perspective advocated by Miriam Schmink, "The Socioeconomic Matrix of Deforestation" (paper presented at Workshop on Population and Environment, Hacienda Cocoyoc, Morelos, Mexico, Jan. 1992). This

latter approach raises issues of political control and accountability, and implies that conflict is possible, even likely, among apparently divergent functions deemed important by different groups in a society.

5. Jorge Arevalo Carcamo, quoted in the Honduran daily *El Tiempo*, Sept. 7, 1988.

6. Mayra Lisset Funez Martinez, *Problematica ambiental en Honduras* (Tegucigalpa: Asociacion de Ecologia, 1989).

7. Susan Stonich, *op. cit.*, note 3, p. 46.

8. This aid occurred within the context of an ongoing campaign by U.S. businesses to develop in Honduras a market for imported wheat-based products as permanent replacements for locally grown corn.

9. Stonich, *op. cit.*, note 3, p. 52.

10. Economist and Central Bank advisor Edmundo Valladares, quoted in "La miseria financiando el modelo de desarrollo," *El Tiempo*, Jan. 5, 1981.

11. Stonich, *op. cit.*, note 3, p. 46.

12. Carcamo, *op. cit.*, note 5, reported that 811,000 hectares of forest were destroyed by fire in an 11-year period, 80,000 hectares were degraded through slash-and-burn agriculture, and 6,000,000 cubic feet of firewood taken. The three causes singled out in this report—forest fires, peasant farming methods, and collecting firewood for fuel—emphasize activities of peasant farmers and poor rural dwellers. Funez Martinez, *op. cit.*, note 6, provides more insight into the forces at work by mentioning the role of cattle ranching for beef export (creating pasture out of forest). Her list of factors contributing to environmental deterioration includes: overcultivation and overgrazing; indiscriminate cutting of trees for wood; inappropriate agricultural technologies; fires; firewood as the major energy source in households and small businesses (bakeries, for example); natural disasters; migratory agriculture (slash-and-burn and short-term colonization of forest areas); and urbanization. Such a list is still inadequate for understanding the causes of environmental degradation.

13. Walter LaFeber, *Inevitable Revolutions: The United States in Central America* (New York: Norton, 1983), 43–46.

14. James D. Nations and Daniel I. Komer, "Indians, Immigrants and Beef Exports: Deforestation in Central America," *Cultural Survival Quarterly* 6:2 (1982) 8–12. Mario Ponce Cambar, "Honduras: Politica agricola y perspectives," in *Honduras: Realidad Nacional y Crisis Regional* (Tegucigalpa: Centro de Documentacion de Honduras, 1986), 249–278.

15. Cambar, *op. cit.*, note 14.

16. In 1988, a Honduran government proposal to build a road through part of the eastern department of Olancho (in the heart of the area targeted by paper and pulp companies) spurred protests by groups in Honduras, including a coalition of indigenous peoples. In a statement, the United Committee of Indigenous Peoples of Honduras said that the road would "provoke irreversible destruction of the virgin grassland (selva) in the biosphere reserve of Rio Patana," and that "large landlords have already penetrated twelve kilometers into the area to exploit the stands of precious wood and cattle-grazing land, to kill wildlife with explosives in the river, and to take our archaeological heritage" (reported in *El Tiempo*, Aug. 26, 1988).

17. Carcamo, *op. cit.*, note 5.

18. Carcamo, *op. cit.*, note 5; Funez Martinez, *op. cit.*, note 6.

19. Information about the environmental and other effects of war and military presence in Honduras was gathered by the author during three months of fieldwork in Honduras in 1988 and reported in James Phillips, "Deforestation as Symbolic Catalyst for Protest Toward Change: Honduras," a Paper presented at the Thirteenth International Congress of Anthropological and Ethnological Sciences, Mexico City, Aug. 1, 1993. See also Environmental Project on Latin America (EPOCA), *Militarization*, Green Paper No. 3 (San Francisco: EPOCA, 1989).

20. A comment by a prominent Honduran lawyer to the author in 1984. Foreign scholars also point to the country's foreign dependency as a cause of rural poverty. See, for example, Alison Acker, *Honduras: The Making of a Banana Republic* (Boston: South End Press, 1988), 11. Also LaFeber, *op. cit.*, note 13, pp. 9–10.

21. Mario Posas, *El Movimiento Campesino Hondureno* (Tegucigalpa: Editorial Guaymuras, 1981).

22. Phillips, *op. cit.*, note 19, pp. 13–15.

23. Douglas Kincaid, "'We Are the Agrarian Reform': Rural Politics and Agrarian Reform," in *Honduras: Portrait of a Captive Nation*, Nancy Peckenham and Annie Street, eds. (New York: Praeger, 1985), 135.

24. Centro de Documentacion de Honduras, *op. cit.*, note 2, pp. 3–5.

25. Kincaid, *op. cit.*, note 23, p. 135.

26. Kincaid, *op cit.*, note 23, p. 136.

27. Elvia Alvarado, *Don't Be Afraid, Gringo: A Honduran Woman Speaks from the Heart,* Medea Benjamin, trans. and ed. (San Francisco: Institute for Food and Development Policy, 1987); "Land Takeovers Planned," *Latin America Daily Report*, July 16, 1991.

28. Ruiz, *op. cit.*, note 1; *c.f.*, Committee for the Defense of Human Rights in Central America, "Massacre at Aguas Calientes," *Accion Urgente*, May 10, 1991.

29. There are many reports of killings of peasant leaders, detentions, tortures, and threats. Here are a few: Amnesty International Urgent Action, UA 298/87, Oct. 30, 1987; "Unequal Distribution of Land Is Social Time Bomb in Honduras Countryside," *Central America NewsPak* 6:8 (1991) 138 (trans. of an article in the Mexican daily *Excelsior*, May 24, 1991, part 3:1); "Peasants Killed," *Latin America Daily Report,* July 16, 1991; and Centro de Documentacion de Honduras, *Conflictos Agrarios en Honduras: Cronologia 1982–1986* (Tegucigalpa: Centro de Documentacion de Honduras, 1986).

30. In her written opinion, the presiding judge noted a close connection between legal and non-violent struggle for land rights and the oppression and lack of official protection or responsibility that attended this struggle in Honduras. She also noted the inability of the civilian government of Honduras to ensure personal safety and basic rights to all the country's citizens. Case Immigration Court, San Antonio, Texas, April 10, 1995, hearing, Case nos. A-73-084-587 and A-73-084-595.

31. James Phillips, "Are There Environmental Refugees?," a Paper presented at the Annual Meeting of the Society for Applied Anthropology, Albuquerque, N.M., April 1995.

32. Jose Maria Tojeira, *Los Hicaques de Yoro* (Tegucigalpa: Editorial Guaymuras, 1982).

33. Reported in the Honduran daily *La Prensa*, March 3, 1988.

34. Anthony Stock, "Land War," *Cultural Survival Quarterly* 16:4 (1992) 16–18; Comite para la Defensa de los Derechos Humanos en Honduras (CODEH), *Boletin* 80 (Sept. 1991) 2.

35. Comite para la Defensa de los Derechos Humanos en Honduras (CODEH), *Boletin* 80 (Sept. 1991) 8–9.

36. Comite para la Defensa de los Derechos Humanos en Honduras (CODEH), *Boletin* 85 (Feb. 1992) 8. Hannah C. Riley and James K. Sebenius, "Stakeholder Negotiations Over Third World Resource Projects," *Cultural Survival Quarterly* 19:3 (1993) 39–43. Riley and Sebenius analyze the failure of communication and integration between the formal negotiations in this case and the "informal" popular expression discussed here. Their list of references chronicles the coverage accorded this incident by the *Chicago Tribune*.

37. The 1994 Draft Declaration of Principles on Human Rights and the Environment, written by an international group of environmental protection and human rights experts under the sponsorship of the United Nations, states: "Human rights, an ecologically sound environment, sustainable development, and peace are all interdependent and indivisible." It also states: "All persons have the right to a secure, healthy and ecologically sound environment. This right and other human rights, including civil, cultural, economic, political and social rights, are universal, interdependent, and indivisible." See the appendix to this volume.

38. Craig R. Kirkpatrick, "Ecology, Government Legitimacy, and a Changing World Order," *Bioscience* 42:11 (Dec. 1992) 867–869; Sharachandra M. Lel, "Sustainable Development: A Critical Review," *World Development* 19:6 (June 1991) 607–621; Riley and Sebenius, *op. cit.*, note 36, pp. 42–43.

39. Quoted in Greg Grigg, "Honduran People Say No to Stone," *Focus on Honduras* summer 1992, pp. 1–3.

PART FIVE

Development, Degradation, Misery, and Conflict

Mexico: warm climate, sparkling white beaches, lush tropical rain forests, beautiful handicrafts, great souvenirs. For millions and millions of people, Mexico is a land of exotic vacations. For others, it is the source of desperately poor migrant workers. And for still others, it is home. Mexico is a country in chaos. The economy has crashed, the political system is rocked by scandals, and revolutionary leaders are once again public heroes. How has this come to pass? Is the current political situation the inevitable result of degradation, inequity, and misery, and are these conditions simply Mexican problems?

The following two chapters look at the origins and anatomy of human environmental crises from multiple lenses: considering the effects of inequity in culture and power relationships between the United States and Mexico, between wealthy tourists and their impoverished "hosts," between the Spanish-speaking elites and the indigenous minorities, between the many complex divisions in Mexican society. Oriol Pi-Sunyer and Brooke Thomas illustrate cultural and biological impacts of tourism on Mayan communities in the Yucatan, mapping out the varied changes and identifying some of ways people respond to these changes. The story they present is one of complexity, with residents engaging modernity to a greater or lesser degree, and step by step, losing the flexibility and resilience that allowed their communities to survive through the centuries. David Stea, Silvia Elguea, and Camilo Perez Bustillo take us further into the geographic and political landscape of Mexico, asking what are the conditions and contexts that gave rise to revolution in Chiapas: what was it that made revolution on January 1, 1994, appear to be a viable option to resolving local problems?

Both chapters illustrate the ways in which previously peripheral regions are transformed through a process that utilizes cultural notions (to justify the fundamental abuse of human rights by taking lands and resources and by contributing to the demise of a cultural way of life); conceptual mechanisms (which compartmentalize the complex aspects of reality and see as significant only those facets that appear in the cost/benefit sections of an accounting spreadsheet); and, physical distancing mechanisms (which separate those who decide on and experience the benefits from those who pay the price of change). In both cases a "dual periphery" is at work, between the United States and Mexico, and between Mexico and its underdeveloped states Quintana Roo and Chiapas.

As noted in the introduction and illustrated in the following chapters, the social context of development is often one of co-optation of traditionally held lands and resources, with little or no recognition of resident peoples' rights and little or no compensation for their subsequent environmental health problems. People living in targeted areas are described as living in extreme poverty. Their subsistence or barter-based economies are ignored or belittled, their cultures deemed primitive. They are called lazy, backward, ignorant, illiterate, stupid. Their situation of inequity is their own fault. Surrounding lands are seen as unoccupied, empty, or "wilderness" areas that can be claimed and used by the state. Legally, state co-optation of peripheral population territory and resources is supported by western notions of property rights: the contention that resources held in common—common property—do not in fact constitute "actual" property rights.

Pi-Sunyer and Thomas ask, Is tourism the socially beneficial and environmentally benign development alternative, as commonly presented? Answering this question, the authors suggest, requires examining the lesser-quantifiable aspects of tourism development on a long-term scale. The data presented indicate that Maya communities, especially those adjacent to and dependent on resort development for employment, are seeing their culture, community, health, and thus their future erode, even as their dependency on wage labor increases. Pi-Sunyer and Thomas map out a human environmental crisis in the making.

Stea, Elguea, and Perez Bustillo examine what happens when human environmental crises are historically ignored and recent events—framed in a language of positive change—exacerbate conditions or stimulate fears of worsening conditions. They describe the chain of events leading up to and following the January 1994 revolt in Chiapas, events that link the Zapatista revolt to a history of human rights abuse and dysfunctional governance. The pattern of response by the revolutionaries suggests a broad spectrum of tactics used to sustain the confrontation while minimizing violent conflict. Government response similarly includes a range of tactics aimed at minimizing violent conflict, though not necessarily with the Zapatistas, but rather in the hopes of inhibiting the spread of violent confrontations elsewhere in the country. Perhaps the most significant feature of the Chiapas engagement has been the central role played by information flows and communication technology. Human environmental crises are no longer experienced in singular, silent fashion. Global access to computers, fax machines, modems, satellite communications, and solar-powered battery packs has provided the powerless with a voice. Information influences and shapes cultural belief systems and legitimizes political authority. Thanks to cyberspace, *absolute* control over information access is no longer possible, as evidenced by the daily communiqués from Commander Marcos during the initial conflict, and the continued updates in the months since.

The emergence of human environmental crises in the Yucatan and Chiapas are not simple matters of internal relations and events in Mexico. Tourism, international investment, NAFTA—these factors, and others, play a role in the genesis of crisis. International forces, relations, and conditions also play a role in the resolution of crisis.

CHAPTER 9

Tourism, Environmentalism, and Cultural Survival in Quintana Roo

Oriol Pi-Sunyer and R. Brooke Thomas

Introduction

We don't want to end up like the Maya of Tulum: street vendors in a town owned by outsiders. (An elderly Mayan, Cobá, 1993)

NAFTA will kill us. (A vendor at an archaeological site, Tulum, 1993)

Reminds you of Vietnam, right? (A Mayan youth, Akumal, 1994)

This chapter presents the initial findings of a larger research project aimed at providing an in-depth, multidisciplinary analysis of the consequences of rapid tourism development on Maya communities in Quintana Roo.[1] Change has been not only rapid, but also dramatic and disturbing; as Theron Nuñez first observed with reference to tourism in Mexico, "In the newly developed countries of today's world, when the larger society (particularly the formal apparatus of the state) takes special interest in previously overlooked rural communities . . . the anthropologist should be alert to the consequences."[2]

In the course of the last 25 years, the state of Quintana Roo, which occupies the eastern portion of the Yucatán peninsula, and which until 1974 had been a thinly settled federal territory, has been experiencing the massive penetration of tourism and collateral processes. This has transformed the area, and particularly the coast, from one of the most isolated regions of Mexico to a veritable tourist factory. Quintana Roo, for all the vast sums of money poured into the construction of resorts and supporting infrastructure, continues to offer beautiful beaches and reefs, Mayan pyramids and tropical forest environments—all a short jet-flight from Florida and the eastern United States. Cancún has become an architectural fantasy city with its grandiose hotels and full range of distractions and attractions vying for tourists' attention and money. Sun-and-sea resorts have now have spread southward to almost every available lagoon and beach; archaeological tours, including New Age pilgrims in search of ancient knowledge, disgorge bus after bus at Maya sites; and ecotourism has sought out remote locations deep in the interior forests.[3] (See photograph.)

By standard economic measures, tourism development in this part of Mexico has been an unqualified economic success for the Mexican government and major investors,

Oriol Pi-Sunyer and R. Brooke Thomas are both Professors of Anthropology at the University of Massachusetts–Amherst, Amherst, MA 01003. They can be reached via email (oriol@anthro.umass.edu) and (rbthomas@anthro.umass.edu).

international and national; the Cancún model has even been replicated in other parts of the country and beyond. This tourist-driven transformation has been minimally studied, and it is not clear how it is affecting the Maya: their health and diet, the environment and resources upon which they depend, their social organization and collective identity. We should recall that these are the native people of the Yucatán, the descendants of the builders of the pre-Hispanic cities and ceremonial centers. Furthermore, although the Maya now find themselves a numerical and ethnic minority in Quintana Roo, the Maya-speaking people constitute one of the largest indigenous groups in Mesoamerica. These collectives are pressing—as has become very evident in Chiapas—for cultural recognition, autonomy, dignity, and social and economic justice.[4] The history of resistance stretches back centuries. Since colonial times, the forests of Quintana Roo have served as a refuge area and region of resistance for the Maya as they fled the exploitation of Spanish and Mexican landowners and administrators. Here, in relative isolation, they lived in small communities dependent on slash-and-burn agriculture, beekeeping, hunting, and the utilization of forest resources.

Today, as Mexican and Mayan history collide once again along the Caribbean coast, this way if life is being severely challenged. The customs, rituals, and language that have held Mayan communities together, binding them to their ancestors, the spirit world, their land, and one another, are being challenged externally by agents of change, and internally by members of their own communities. A grid of all-weather roads crisscrosses the state, bringing with it a growing degree of demographic, economic, and political penetration. Tourism, government services, and commercial activity directly and indirectly touch all Maya settlements. Flowing out of the hamlets and villages are young men and women in search of work on the coast. Ideas of "progress" return with them, following the lines of electrification and the Coca-Cola trucks. Generations in the community seem split as the elderly attempt to hold on to traditional usages while younger people confront modernity. The questions "Who are we, where are we going,

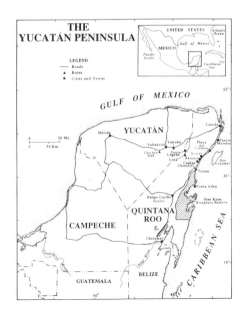

Billboard advertising a resort along the Cancún–Tulum Road. The themes of adventure and the Maya are common in tourism propaganda. Photograph by R. Brooke Thomas.

and what will become of us?" are at the core of a continuous discourse that takes many specific forms.

Our research attempts to give voice to these concerns, placing them within the broader political economic context of tourist development and the encompassing dependency relationships that characterize this industry. Tourism in locations such as Quintana Roo faces enormous competition from similar destinations, and tourism policy is only partially within the control of host countries. In a very real sense, Quintana Roo can be thought of as constituting a "double periphery": it lies at the margins of a national state that is itself highly dependent on its powerful neighbor to the north, the United States. Within this structure of dependency, indigenous peoples—and certainly the Maya of the Yucatán—are the most subordinated.

The perspectives and opinions of the Maya concerning such issues remain largely unheard as they move through the tourist world as silent and invisible waiters and domestic workers, groundskeepers, construction workers, petty vendors, and hammock weavers. Experience, age, gender, and levels of education all play a role in influencing their hopes and perceptions. For the most part there is little outright resistance to the technological and material aspects of consumer society; however, there appears to be a growing awareness of the costs of shifting from subsistence agriculture to a cash economy. Most obviously, the wages of the average Maya worker are pitifully low. As a higher percentage of the population experiences some formal education, and television becomes the entertainment of choice in the majority of Maya households, attitudes toward modernity become marked by ambivalence. Money—or lack of it—is a factor, but also the caution and resentment of becoming a marginalized people in their own land. And with what or whom can they identify in the mass-mediated messages they receive through television? Fundamentally, their actions reflect patterns of accommodation and resistance appropriate to very confusing times, when the institutions of the state are under siege. And what it means even to be Maya is constantly being negotiated, as everyone in Mexico is poised between the uncertain present and a future filled with hope and risk. In listening to the Maya, one learns to examine many things—including tourism— from the bottom up.

The story presented here is a compelling one of the multiple forces and processes that converge on Yucatán. First, we become aware of the power of tourism to create a spectacular economic boom in a formerly remote and isolated tropical shore by reconstructing nature and fabricating illusion. An examination of how these strategies work on the ground indicates that the quick profits that propel the industry relegate the well-being of the people and the security of the environment to very secondary considerations. This is an endemic flaw of much tourist development, and it often leads to the degradation of the very cultural and physical spaces to which tourists are initially attracted. In due course, the industry can bring about its own demise; in Richard Butler's words, "there is almost inevitably the overreaching of some or all capacity limits and degradation, decline, and change in the tourist product, which includes both environmental and human elements."[5]

A second issue, given economic and political realities, is what role the Maya can and should play in tourist development, and whether a significant restructuring of tourism is indeed possible. If the Maya continue to be kept on the economic and social fringes, one may ask what forms their resentment is likely to take, and how heightened Maya militancy may impact the tourist industry.

Finally, since most readers have been tourists—and anthropologists share significant characteristics with tourists—we can place ourselves within the dilemma of development as privileged consumers whose actions may leave behind real consequences. In the specific case of Quintana Roo, "benign" one- or two-week vacations of relaxation and indulgence add up to millions of visitors flowing through Cancún, moving down the coast, and penetrating deep into the interior. Largely unnoticed, and certainly taken for granted, is the stream of people, goods, capital, and information needed to keep this quantity of visitors in appropriate "vacation mode." Among these we may note the flow of service personnel from all over Mexico seeking better employment; the movement of food, equipment, and construction materials originating in other parts of Mexico and the United States; and, not least, the quantities of solid and liquid wastes that now accumulate in vast quantities and often leach out to pollute the seashore. All this pressure is straining a fragile land that is already showing evidence of severe environmental stress.

Working in a Very Real World

While our primary concern is an examination of the ways that ordinary people react and respond to tourism, we should remember that this local world is inextricably linked to another world that encompasses not only the opaque workings of Mexican politics, but also the mystique of international development plans and other global forces—including the drug trade. In short, Quintana Roo may be Mexico's remote southeastern frontier, but it is hardly a distant Eden.

The short epigraphs at the head of the chapter are meant to remind us of these relationships. The first is from an elderly man in the farming community of Cobá expressing concern about the possible privatization of common land (the *ejido*) and development of another tourist hotel in town. He makes his point by addressing the marginalized condition of the Maya of nearby Tulum who have sold their property to people from outside the peninsula and have, in his words, "lost their community."

The second is excerpted from a series of conversations we had in 1993 with union officials representing the vendors who plied their trade near the archaeological site (and major tourist attraction) of Tulum. Their prediction proved accurate, and a year later they had been evicted from their "irregular" stores to make room for much fancier tourist boutiques. Whether the North American Free Trade Association (NAFTA) was in some way responsible for the dismantling of their shops is open to question, but these storekeepers were in no doubt that the coming NAFTA would benefit only the rich and the foreigners, and would cause distress to small-scale operators. By early 1995, Mexico had been confronted by a catastrophic financial crisis, an insurgency in Chiapas, and the spectacle of former President Carlos Salinas de Gortari (who had negotiated and signed the NAFTA) hiding in exile. President Salinas's administration had also undertaken to change both Article 27 of the constitution and agrarian reform legislation. These changes not only negated any legal possibility of peasants obtaining land, but also put in extreme peril the land already in their hands. Without question, tinkering with the key Article 27 was bound to increase tension and reduce incentive for peasants to work with institutions of the state.

The third statement comes from a young Maya interpreter who often led us through the back lanes of the service community of Akumal's beach resorts. In all probability, the palm-thatched village houses and the periodic military patrols along the beach in search of drugs washed up from the Caribbean reminded him of American movies and television shows (all readily available). But regardless of the stimulus, his comment catches the element of tension and uncertainty that often lies beneath the placid veneer of everyday pueblo life. In fact, the military have become a growing presence in the Mexican countryside.

We might add one other episode. In spring 1996, while accompanying her husband, Brooke Thomas, on a trip to discuss our findings with community leaders, Shirley Thomas went for a swim in the Akumal lagoon. Just beneath the surface ("What *is* this?") she found two sealed plastic containers—the by now familiar "kilo" packets of cocaine—which the village police refused to touch until higher authority arrived. Politics, money, and drugs are just part of the complex and often dangerous "real world" within which local events and concerns are played out.

The Structure of the Touristic System

Is tourism a "life and death matter" as we approach the end of the millennium? Perhaps not in a literal sense, but for many inhabitants of Third World societies, and especially for indigenous groups in such countries, tourism represents a particular face of both development and forced social change. Fundamentally, this externally driven process works to dismantle corporate identities and reduces the ability of individuals and communities to survive economically and culturally. For some groups it is thus not an overstatement to speak of a "crisis" engendered by tourism: a crisis variously of identity, employment, and security.

Tourism has received limited attention from anthropologists and other social scientists. There is little in the classical tradition of either anthropology or sociology that discusses the phenomenon, and even today it is sometimes difficult for academics to take the subject seriously.[6] Yet, as Erik Cohen observed more than a decade ago, tourism deserves to be treated as something other than an exotic and marginal topic derived from a superficial activity.[7] The economic case can be argued with little difficulty. Travel is now the single-largest item in international trade. Some 425 million visitors generate US$230 billion in expenditures per year.[8] Since the 1960s tourism has grown at the rate of some 10 percent per year, a trajectory that is likely to continue for the rest of the century.[9] A phenomenon of this type—global in scope, touching societies of different types, manifesting itself in sundry forms and scales—is not inherently all good or all evil. Much depends on the context, and in our opinion the key analytical question is the degree to which mass tourism may work to reinforce and perpetuate relations of dependency and inequality. Dependency, as we use the concept, is a historical process that changes the internal functioning of economic and social systems in such a manner that local economies are weakened and thereby forced to serve the needs of external markets.[10]

Tourism in Mexico has become a major source of foreign exchange, a new kind of tropical export product. But tourism is also a highly competitive industry, since tourists and tour operators have numerous alternative destinations at their disposal.[11] Consequently, attracting foreign tourists and foreign capital is a difficult process that has meant austerity (particularly for the poor), a labor force under increasingly rigid discipline, and other "belt-tightening" measures. What is harder to understand is how the state itself has become a partner in this process of exploitation. At least part of the answer must be sought in the influence of a general myth of development (shared by Mexican and international technocrats alike) that holds that the poverty of poor countries arises from an inadequate spread of market forces. It follows that the recommended solution to poverty is increased capitalist penetration. An economic transformation along these lines typically entails massive inputs of capital from rich countries and a restructuring of local-level economic relations. The guiding myth is also—indeed, *has* to be—uncritically optimistic: any demonstrated failures are attributed to local aberrations, not to the model, and real social costs are always played down.

Writing of what he refers to as the ideology and practice of "developmentalism," Arturo Escobar observes that:

> Wherever one looked, one found the repetitive and omnipresent reality of development: governments designing and implementing ambitious development plans, institutions carrying out development programs in city and countryside alike, experts of all kinds studying underdevelopment and producing theories ad nauseam.[12]

Escobar could easily have been discussing the plans, first formulated in the late 1960s, drawn up to develop the coast of Quintana Roo into a major tourist destination dominated by the new resort city of Cancún.

The putative rewards of tourism are many, including international and cultural understanding, but the tangible benefits, it is claimed, are chiefly economic and easily demonstrable. Tourism, as we have noted, is essentially a sort of internal export industry. What are sold are the various "attractions" of the country, be these natural or cultural. In the process, a flow of foreign exchange is generated and one can balance the money coming in against the money going out. In the case of Mexico, the figures are strongly favorable: in 1988, the 5.69 million foreign visitors entering the country brought in $1.35 billion more than Mexicans spent abroad, a balance that had risen to $1.79 billion by 1992.[14] Furthermore, the claim is often made that tourism is the ideal "smokeless" industry—a relevant selling point in this era of ecological anxiety.

Tourism differs from other export sectors in that production and consumption both take place at home—an appealing feature for countries such as Mexico that suffer high rates of unemployment and underemployment. Again, to turn to specifics, some estimates for Mexico assert that the hospitality industry is responsible for about 3 percent of the gross domestic product and generates almost 2 million direct and indirect jobs.[15]

Tourism not only employs many people, but it does so in ways significantly different from most other industries. Many tourism-related occupations call for little formal education or specialized training. In addition, tourism in general, and resort tourism in particular, often hires people from surrounding semirural environments, thus presumably helping to stem migration to the overcrowded cities.[16]

Finally, a number of indirect advantages are commonly attributed to the expansion of this sector. Given that tourism in less-developed countries caters to many guests from wealthier societies, a whole series of improvements in services and infrastructure can be expected to benefit both visitors and residents. Roads must be built and maintained, systems of sanitation and potable water installed where these are not present, and access made available to health providers, communications systems, and the like. This piggyback effect again seems unproblematic to planners and bureaucrats in distant offices.

A related argument is linked to the needs of tourists. Not only do they consume "services" in the abstract, but they must be fed and housed, and provided with all those tangible tokens—the straw hats, the textiles, the carvings—that make the visit memorable. Tourist expenditures, therefore, should bring direct benefits to local shopkeepers, farmers, craft workers, and even prostitutes. The tourist dollar, once spent, is assumed to touch and benefit many people through what is termed the multiplier effect.

The Other Side of the Tourist Coin

This is necessarily a brief overview of the most common arguments presented in favor of the type of touristic development that has taken place in Quintana Roo, but anyone with minimal experience of tourism in the Third World is bound to recognize that it does exact a price, although it is harder to say what form this price takes. At the level of popular discourse and media reporting, the costs of tourism are commonly expressed in cultural and aesthetic terms. Tourists are often perceived as altering host societies in ways that are negative, generally by bringing about some loss of "authenticity." Sometimes it seems that local life was inevitably better in the past, that villagers were more contented, less mercenary, more "traditional." Blame for this turn of events is put on the deluge of visitors and, in lesser measure, on natives who, somehow, should not have permitted themselves to be seduced by the forces of modernity.

The cultural costs of tourism are often painful and deserve a nuanced and sympathetic analysis. It is nevertheless true that much of the discussion of "loss" probably reflects, more than anything else, a contemporary western distress that small-scale societies and "remote" peoples will, in the words of Errington and Gewertz, become "demoralized and disoriented with the shattering of their formerly beautiful customs by modernity."[17] Such concerns may tell us more about "our" fears of anomie and disorientation than about "their" priorities in the contemporary world.[18]

Granted that there is often a cultural price to pay for tourism, the most powerful argument against the type of tourism we are discussing is a variant of the critique of development.[19] Not only have Mexican economic policies in general failed to narrow the enormous gap between the rich and the poor, but also one can reasonably claim that the expansion of tourism has further reinforced the dualistic structure of Mexican society.[20] Today, income distribution in Mexico is so skewed that the top 10 percent of the population accounts for 39.5 percent of the national income—leaving the bottom 20 percent to manage with a share of 4.1 percent.[21]

Our position is not simply that mass tourism is likely to reinforce preexisting socioeconomic structures, but rather that inequalities will impact most severely on the lives and prospects of just those populations with whom tourists come into contact, people who are often characterized by extreme material poverty and minimal political influence.[22] Clifford Geertz, discussing economic development in Southeast Asia, observes that modernizing states "do not bring all their citizens equally with them when they join the contemporary world of capital flows, technology transfers, trade balances, and growth rates," a problem that was already apparent a generation ago.[23] In 1974, the British ambassador to Panama wrote in a dispatch to the Foreign Office:

> Unless the Kuna can perform a miracle unique in our world, of teaching themselves to accommodate to and manage a 20th Century explosion of tourists, industrial development and cash nexus, it seems impossible that they will not be obliterated.[24]

Fundamentally, when peripheral regions, such as Quintana Roo, are brought into the process of modernization, local populations (commonly regarded as "backward" by the national elites) are assigned very subordinate roles in the development process—sometimes to the point of invisibility. A recognition of these asymmetries helps us to engage a whole range of questions and issues. For example, it is significant that tourism development in Mexico commonly takes the form of distinct enclaves, resorts such as Acapulco, Puerto Vallarta, and Cancún. More recently, the shift has been to packaged tours and self-contained "gated" complexes that provide accommodation and recreation within highly controlled environments. Fundamentally, what we have in all such settings are pieces of the First World ensconced in Third World environments. There is no process of "convergence"; on the contrary, arrangements of this type work to keep *apart* the worlds of tourist and native, a gap likely to be filled by various forms of "staged authenticity."[25]

Leaving aside the question of what might have been done for local people with even some of the resources earmarked for hotels, roads, and airports, there is no question that the majority of those who work in the tourist sector live under very difficult conditions and enjoy little in the way of job security. To this we can add the phenomenon of an ethnic division of labor. Concretely, in Quintana Roo the Maya are defined as cheap manual labor, quite unsuited to positions of responsibility and authority.[26] This results in Mexicans and foreigners occupying the public relations positions and managerial roles. In conclusion, the realities of luxury tourism in Quintana Roo can be summed up as a system in which the poor subsidize the rich. "Tourism," in the words of Cynthia Enloe, "is not just about escaping work and drizzle; it is about power, increasingly internationalized power."[27]

Quintana Roo

A generation ago, Quintana Roo was one of the most inaccessible locations in Mexico, a frontier where the institutions of the state were barely represented. In 1950, the total population numbered only 26,967 inhabitants, a figure that would increase to 50,169 by 1960.[28] Thus, until the advent of mass tourism in the early 1970s, it remained little changed from what it had been for centuries: an extensive region with a very low population density inhabited by Maya farmers in the interior and small mestizo populations in a few coastal locations.

From the 16th century to the 20th, Quintana Roo was what Aguirre Beltran[29] has so aptly termed a "zone of refuge," first for Indians fleeing Spanish control and secondly, following independence, for Maya villagers no more inclined to come under Mexican rule. The 1847 native uprising in Yucatán known as the Caste War, and the other insurrections that followed, further isolated the region. Campaigns by the Mexican army well into this century reinforced a Maya distrust of state authority.

It was not until the late 1960s that this high degree of isolation—and autonomy— began to change. First came the roads, then the airports; and with them a mounting influx of outsiders, both Mexicans and foreigners. What is particularly interesting about these changes is that up to two or three decades ago the region had hardly registered on the mental maps of urban Mexicans. When they thought about the territory at all, it was usually in terms of a backward area associated with the questionable activities of smugglers, chicle gatherers, and forest-dwelling Indians.

With the expansion of tourism the region, and particularly its coast, rapidly became redefined as a tropical paradise, a land of broad, sandy beaches and pristine forest. Tourism propaganda often contrasts the modernity of Cancún and other resorts with the theme of a changeless natural world of "still crystal-clear waters and virgin beaches," a land "that still belongs to nature, where ocelots, kinkajous and spider monkeys still roam wild in their native habitat."[30]

The reality is rather different. In the 1960s, Cancún was a village of some 600 people. Today it is not only a city of more than 300,000 inhabitants, but it is growing at an annual rate of 20 percent, a truly frightening statistic. This huge resort with over 140 hotels attracts more than 2 million visitors a year, of which 1.5 million are foreigners.[31] More than this, the whole coast from Cancún south to Tulum has been converted into a string of resorts, theme parks, and hotels, effectively transforming what had been space of public access into the highly controlled world of the managed resort.

Cancún dominates Quintana Roo, and it is very much a child of 1960s development thinking, a mega-project requiring massive investment for a colossal plan of construction. It has certainly become a major international tourist destination, one particularly attractive to North Americans.[32] But it would be wise to remember the cyclical and uncertain character of global tourism, and particularly the decline of Acapulco, once the major Mexican playground for the rich. By the 1970s, a number of factors, including the opening up of new resort areas with more modern facilities, a deterioration in the Acapulco physical environment, and the fact that the resort was no longer seen as an elite location, led to a marked drop in Acapulco's popularity and profitability.[33] Some observers claim that Cancún is already confronted by similar problems of image and security.

Ecological Anxiety

It is perhaps the realization that Cancún's long and massive line of hotels no longer quite responds to contemporary needs and tastes that has helped to bring about a diversification of the market in the direction of environmental and cultural tourism. We don't find the romanticization of a simpler, more "authentic," way of life such as has been described for cultural tourism in Mexico's state of Chiapas and in Guatemala. More than anything else, alternative tourism in Quintana Roo plays on the theme of the grandeur that was the Maya civilization (now safely in the past) and the quest for the particular kind of dream world associated with jungles and exotic animal life. Not surprisingly, one encounters many latter-day Indiana Joneses indulging their fantasies, as well as more serious ecological tourists. The impressive Maya sites of the area, particularly Tulum and Cobá, receive a large influx of visitors—and Tulum is showing clear signs of wear and tear.

A major problem related to all forms of tourism stems from the inherent fragility of the biogeographical system on which the touristic system has been erected. The tourist boom has had both anticipated and unforeseen consequences on environmental quality, consequences that, unless remedied, are bound to impinge on the profitability of the industry. At the same time, the growing environmental awareness—as well as an emerging market for ecologically friendly tourism—has directed attention to the uniqueness of the peninsula and to the crisis it faces. But these issues—problems posed by the limits of growth—hardly form part of the traditional experience-perceptions of the Maya. Prior to the advent of tourism they had seen no need to undertake programs of environmental preservation, nor had they had disputes surrounding land use practices or the utilization of their natural resources.

A Fragile, Living Rock

Generally unnoticed by the tourist, and certainly little heeded by developers, is the fragile nature of Quintana Roo's linked environments. The 16th century Spanish bishop Diego de Landa described this land thus: "Yucatán is the country with the least earth I have ever known, since all is a living rock." Contemporary Maya farmers describe much of this terrain as zekel: "land very stony or full of stones."[34] Precipitation from tropical storms falls on the interior forest percolating through thin pockets of topsoil; it then rapidly makes its way into the porous calcite bedrock that underlies the peninsula. From here it flows through a complex network of underground rivers to the coast where it surfaces in freshwater vents in the mangrove swamps behind the beaches, in cuts or lagoons, or beyond the beach itself. In many cases, resorts along the tourist zone are built on a lens of beach built up between the swamp and the sea, and are protected under calm conditions by the offshore barrier reef running the length the peninsula's eastern coast. Connecting these terrestrial and marine ecosystems is the underground flow of water that makes its way across the limestone platform.

In the area there has been remarkably little land-use planning or environmental impact analysis for most projects, and that which follows is a brief review of some of the more apparent consequences. Cancún now suffers from problems of urban congestion, including a decline in air quality; there has also been a substantial deterioration of the lagoon behind the beach resorts as a consequence of erosion and water pollution. The surrounding mangroves, which might counteract these processes, are being filled in for further development, and a golf course encroaches on the city's most important archaeological site.

The main highway south from Cancún to Tulum (136 km long) is lined with an assortment of billboards advertising resorts with such alluring names as Secret Beach and Shangri-La. The tourist is invited to visit Puerto Aventuras, touted as "A new civilization on the Maya Caribbean" combining experiences that are both "primitiva" and "sofisticado." These supposedly remote and beautiful locations are often the source of very tangible environmental problems. The complexes consume great quantities of potable water and release nutrient-rich waste materials that in due course reach the fragile reefs.

Debris, seemingly from cruise ships, litters unsupervised beaches, while sea turtles seeking beaches on which to lay their eggs are distracted by resort lights. Likewise, cuts and lagoons that gave refuge to fishers and even an occasional manatee, have been transformed into marinas and charter-boat anchorages. Conch have largely disappeared from the inshore waters, while sharks, around which a short-lived industry was formed in the 1980s, have become a rare catch. A lively underground trade exists in exotic animals, and resorts frequently display caged birds and melancholy spider monkeys as if to verify their rarely-seen existence.

Finally, cattle ranching has become a prestigious enterprise, and with it has come the extensive clearing of forest. This change of the natural cover often degrades the quality of the soil (already poor), as it simultaneously reduces habitats and hence biodiversity. In contrast, the small-scale farming of forest patches—"making milpa"—is much less disruptive, owing to the fact that once the plot is abandoned the forest rapidly regenerates. Cattle is a cash crop, reared by those with connections to urban markets, and consequently a product that does not normally benefit the average Maya.

In conclusion, an obvious contradiction exists between the theme of unmarred nature and the reality of an increasingly impacted environment. A number of sincere and meaningful efforts are under way to counteract these trends, but all too often ecology has been co-opted by the market. It takes only paint and a little imagination to turn standard transportation into "ecobuses" and "ecotaxis," a marketing technique that does little more than gesture at ecological sensitivity. These problems and shortcomings are inevitable in an industry that measures success by its ability to fill airplanes, hotel rooms, and the rosters of tour operators. The underlying reality is that both nature and people—including the visiting anthropologist—are constantly asked to define everything in terms of price: "How much does it cost to fly to Miami?"; "How much is that camera in dollars?"; "Is that an expensive backpack?" The visitor off the plane engages in a rather similar discourse: "Beer, cold beer, cerveza, cuanto?" This mediation of relationships by the cash nexus is not simply a consequence of tourism but also reflects the several parallel processes that have functioned to incorporate the region into a world where everything seems to have a price.

Some final observations. All tourism, it has often been pointed out, is a form of play and fantasy. Surely, it will be argued, if tourists want to identify with jungle adventurers (ecological or otherwise), this is strictly their business. It would be that, except that the shift toward environmental and "adventure" tourism, as well as the transformation of archaeological sites into tourist attractions, carries material and cultural consequences for local people. Most obviously, whatever land and resources are taken out of local control reduces local economic options. Cultural options are precluded as well when sacred spots such as cenotes (water-filled sinkholes), caves, and ancient temples (where Maya still go to pray and converse with the spirits) become tourist attractions. Even when the Maya are not barred from using these sites by admission fee, they explain that the spirits are reluctant to come—because of the intrusion of alien influences.

Whose Land, Whose Nature?

The not unreasonable fear of some Maya that their universe—including their spiritual world—is being drastically altered has a bearing on the general question of rights to land and resources. That Quintana Roo was a thinly settled territory is beyond argument, but this did not make it an "empty land" or its peoples incompetent guardians. Here, as in so many other locations with an indigenous population, the assertion by those in power that local people were not using their lands "properly" has been used to "redefine" resources—specifically, beaches, extensive archaeological sites, and forest land—as state or private property.[35] Now the Maya find themselves in the middle of an international debate on ecological preservation. Already, the Sian Ka'an Biosphere Reserve, to the south of Tulum, constitutes the largest such protected area in Mexico.

If the Maya use of resources is stigmatized as destructive ("They kill everything around and have no regard for the forest"), traditional Maya life is commonly categorized as backward and primitive. What was most evident from our conversations with both managers in the tourist industry and long-established residents is how little most of them knew about their Maya neighbors. We were told many times that the Maya were "happy"; happy in nature, but also happy to find work as maids and gardeners. A number of non-Maya residents, including North Americans, saw the Maya as exotic archetypes with many admirable "qualities," as interesting elements of local color who harked back to the region's frontier past. But whether the stress was on barbarism or natural nobility, these depictions were remarkably free of any sense that the subjects in question constituted a subordinated group: a people with genuine grievances. It is not remarkable that members of a dominant group deny that they are subordinating those holding positions of structural inferiority. Such denial, however, works to maintain inequality, perhaps even transform it into a marketable asset.

Research Design

Our aim in Quintana Roo was to study a sample of Maya communities that were experiencing tourism in significantly different ways and varying degrees of intensity. We recognized that "tourism" was a kind of shorthand, part of a more general process of incorporation into national life and national economy. Yet people *did* discuss tourism and clearly recognized it as an important element in their lives. Specifically, we looked at the structure of group relations, ongoing changes in diet and health, natural resource use, and general cultural perceptions—in sum, how Maya villagers saw themselves and the increasingly complex world they inhabit. To date there has been no comprehensive or systematic evaluation of how almost a generation of change has affected both Maya culture and Maya health.

Our sample consisted of two service communities, Akumal and Ciudad Chemuyil, attached to beach resorts; Cobá, a village adjoining a major inland archaeological site; and a hamlet deep in the interior, Punta Laguna, which supplements "traditional" agriculture with ecotourism. The four sites differ in size and composition of population, resources under their control, degree of articulation with tourism, and their isolation— always relative—from state institutions and market forces. We use "community" with caution, not only because the term often implies a high degree of boundedness, but because populations in Quintana Roo fluctuate in response to many factors, including the availability of work, agricultural prospects, security of tenancy, and government plans and policies.

We collected community aggregate data and used an extensive household question-naire to sample 82 households, a figure that represents some 25 percent of the population of these settlements. We also undertook in-depth interviews, carried out dietary and store inventory surveys, and conducted nutritional and anthropometric surveys in two elementary schools. Finally, we gathered information from several other sources ranging from official documents to interviews with tourists.

Differing Faces of Tourism

Sun and Sea Tourism

As sun-and-sea resorts spread down the coast, service communities developed in their vicinity. These are composed of people drawn from towns and villages across the Yucatán peninsula, and increasingly from other parts of Mexico. Since few inhabitants have access to agricultural land, they are completely dependent on stores and vendors for basic needs.

Akumal was selected because of its dependency on resort employment and the pressures faced by its residents. The 400 villagers live directly outside the boundaries of a resort and recreation complex of the same name, and the contrast between the resort and the service community could not have been starker. The resort is pleasant, spacious, and well-maintained, and it faces a sandy beach. It is filled with contented visitors and the owners of holiday properties. The village houses of the service community were built of natural materials, scrap or cinder blocks—more shantytown than tropical hamlet. Although electricity was available, the community had to manage without garbage removal, a sewage system, or potable water. While the main water line to the resort passed through the village, residents had no access to it and were forced to rely on a series of shallow and unsanitary wells.

Already in 1993, pressure was mounting to evict the people of Akumal. The resort management and condo owners declared it an eyesore and an actual or potential health hazard. They also hypothesized that runoff from the village might damage the lagoon or reef (we only heard a few of these people express concern for the health of the villagers). By the summer of 1994, approximately half the homes in the community had been razed: the remains of the demolished houses are still visible. Finally, in the summer of 1996, assisted by a hurricane that damaged many of the structures, the government ordered all houses and businesses vacated. This action was facilitated by the circumstance that the Akumal people lacked titles to their house lots and were technically squatters on federal land.

It is unclear whether the vacated land will become an ecopark or, as is now rumored, be turned into a tastefully landscaped extension of the resort. Whatever the outcome—and in spite of the efforts by the Akumal management and others to relocate residents to more "suitable" locations—resentment and resistance to these actions ran high. Akumal provided low-cost housing for service workers and, equally important, a space of relative autonomy from the growing controls of the industry and government.

Ciudad Chemuyil, the second service community that we looked at, is a new development that, at the time of the study, contained 250 houses. This community was established by a consortium of hotels and the government in order to concentrate, and presumably the better to control, the growing labor force attracted by the expanding tourism. Its location, several miles inland from the resort area, appears designed to segregate workers from clients, a hypothesis reinforced by the fact that nearly half of the inhabitants of Ciudad Chemuyil had been evicted (some left voluntarily) from Akumal and other "irregular settlements."

Promotional literature describes Ciudad Chemuyil as a "new Maya city," and plans for an eventual expansion to 250,000 inhabitants. Even if this target is not reached, such a massive development is bound to transform the human geography of the coast and to reinforce racial and ethnic separation. The new settlement (presented as superior, healthier, and more modern) consists of small, poorly ventilated, cement block houses—all identical—on minimal lots. Company minibuses pick up maids, gardeners, waiters, and cooks in the morning, take them to their places of work, returning them in the evening. Most employees work a grueling seven-day week for four weeks and then receive a break of five days. Ciudad Chemuyil is essentially a company town, totally dependent on resort employment, lacking natural resources of its own, and with a population tied to 30-year mortgages underwritten by employers. It is hard to escape the conclusion that this is an arrangement designed to sap self-reliance and meant to transform hotel workers into the modern equivalent of plantation labor.

Archaeological Tourism

Unlike Akumal and Ciudad Chemuyil, the village of Cobá did not come into being as a result of tourism. Settled some 50 years ago by a small group of Yucatán farmers, Cobá has grown over the years to approximately 900 inhabitants. What makes Cobá a tourist destination is its location at the edge of one of the largest archaeological complexes in Mesoamerica: the Classic Maya site from which the community takes its name.

The development of the ruins into an attraction for the "adventurous" tourist followed the completion in the 1970s of a road connecting Cobá to the coastal highway. This link brought not only tourists, but also in due course electricity, easy delivery of commercial goods, potable water, a health clinic, and a school. By the time of our study, the men and women of Cobá were increasingly dependent on different types of wage work, including resort construction. As our colleague Ellen Kintz notes, this growing dependence on wage labor "provides cash but strains social ties."[36]

Today, some 60,000 annual visitors, mostly foreigners, make their way to that archaeological site and the protected forest trails that surround it. Tourists arrive by car and bus and, except for those booked into one of the two small hotels (one of which is a Club Med "Villas Arqueológicas"), most leave by the end of the day. Although tourism has stimulated the sale of handicrafts and the establishment of a handful of stores and restaurants, most townspeople complain that the tourist trade leaves them nothing, and many insist that it represents a net loss.

From the very beginning, tourism was placed in contention, since the newly designated archaeological zone contained some of the community's prime agricultural land. This initial loss of resources was followed by other destabilizing changes, including a heightened awareness of class and ethnic inequalities, plus pressures to privatize the *ejido* communal holdings (this tends to split the community generationally). The strains also manifest themselves in the religious sphere. A generation ago, religious practice was a variant of folk syncretism that joined elements of Catholic ritual to a Mayan cosmology in which the milpa, the forest, and the community represented a model of the universe, and the task of ritual practitioners was to maintain these components in proper harmony.

Something of this belief remains, but Cobá is now an arena for competing congregations, and about two-thirds of the population identify with different Protestant and Evangelical denominations. Sectarian balkanization has reinforced individualism and undermined the old ties of reciprocity sanctioned by custom and ritual. The new religious ideology tends to privilege the individual over the community, much as the market constructs the individual as consumer and autonomous economic agent.

Ecotourism

At the opposite pole of dependency typical of the communities along the Cancún-Tulum corridor is the hamlet of Punta Laguna. This is a forest community deep in the interior, composed of a handful of interrelated families and subsisting almost entirely from its milpas, kitchen gardens, and the products of the surrounding forest. Unlike the situation in nearby Cobá, ritual practices remain largely intact, and community bonds, essentially links of kinship, remain strong. Honey represents one of the few cash crops, and this helps explain why the residents have long protected a large stand of the canopy forest. The forest, in turn, offers food and shelter to a colony of spider monkeys.

Tourists come in small numbers to see the monkeys and are escorted by teenage boys who act as guides. These youths speak with enthusiasm about the local flora and fauna and use tracking skills to locate the monkeys. Most tourists are fascinated by the experience, even if initially disconcerted by a certain looseness of organization. Still, having to wait some minutes while a small child searches for an available guide may increase the value of the experience; it certainly reflects the homespun nature of Punta Laguna ecotourism.

Interesting as the experience is likely to be for the visitor, such tourism does not contribute much to the local economy. The tips collected by guides put little extra money into circulation, and the guest waiting in the entrance shed is invited to buy postcards and honey. In recent years, the environmental organization Pronatura has provided funds for improving trails and offered other forms of support, but perhaps its most valuable contribution has been to underscore the importance of protecting the environment.

Punta Laguna, although not many miles from the main road, remains very quiet and traditional. It lacks telephone service or electricity, and harbors no resident outsiders. All our ethnographic visits had to be negotiated well in advance and required community approval. In our interviews we found that most people did not think that the Maya language was in danger of disappearing, but that they were worried about possible challenges to religious practices and a decline in the systems of reciprocal assistance. An important concern, and certainly the chief concern of the young, was a lack of money. This little hamlet is about as self-sufficient in basic needs as any place in the state, but people feel poor and young men are beginning to leave to search for work on the coast. However, the jobs open to clearly rural, and often monolingual, Maya-speaking workers are the hardest and most menial—"slave labor," as one young man expressed it.

Surviving in a Changing World

What is happening to the Maya as they confront the spectrum of changes and challenges that has engulfed them? The Maya have been termed a resilient people, and certainly they have been able to survive 500 years of domination, by resisting, by accommodating, by fleeing. But it can be argued that nothing on the present scale has ever occurred. What seem different about this tourism-driven transformation are not only its rapidity and overwhelming scale, but also its capacity to seduce local populations.

The gap in material wealth between the tourist and the chambermaid is immense, but they are not people inhabiting totally separate, conceptual universes. Maya peasants and workers perceive tourists and rich residents as special and privileged, but also as representing a more general cosmopolitanism associated with contemporary life. This perception is reinforced by the now ubiquitous presence of television, which on a daily basis reinforces the impression that the world beyond the peninsula—where the tourists come from and rich people live—is similarly organized. Needless to say, this is a world of consumption, where worth is measured by acquisitive power. The messages are indeed contradictory: they stress that the whole world is a marketplace, but also make it clear that not all customers are equal. Finally, when a Maya works day after day within the power inequalities of an industry that privileges class and ethnic stratification, one's Maya background, with its emphasis on reciprocity and community, is bound to be challenged as "backward."

In the paragraphs that follow, we outline some of the principal changes, cultural and biological, which the Maya are experiencing, and say something about their responses to them. In comparing similarities and differences between the communities, we have found the contrasts to be rich and at times unexpected. One can reasonably speak of a gradient in questionnaire responses and general opinion moving from Punta Laguna to Cobá, and on to the coastal service communities of Akumal and Ciudad Chemuyil. Thus, there is a strong fear of loss of ritual and mutual assistance in the inland communities where they are most needed in "making milpa." The inhabitants of coastal communities, which have no milpa lands, are not much concerned about rituals that they associate with country life.

Dietary Delocalization and Nutritional Status

One of the most visible changes is in food consumption patterns, and especially in the high dependence on commercial soft drinks and sugar-fortified fruit juices. Mexico has one of the highest Coca-Cola consumption rates in the world: slightly over one Coca-Cola product per person per day. Since Coke accounts for 50 percent of market, the average Mexican drinks about 16 ounces of soft drinks daily. As one Mayan teenager remarked, "We drink it for breakfast, lunch, and dinner, and when we're hot or cold." Our surveys indicate that in the service communities consumption is higher than the national average, and in the inland village somewhat lower. Soft-drink consumption is often associated with snacking, and the snacks in question tend to be high in fats, salt, and sugar. Coke and junk foods constitute merely a part of a more general pattern. As people, particularly those on the coast, become removed from their milpas and kitchen gardens, they find access to a variety of fruits and vegetables to be problematic. Vendors of these items come only once a week, and their produce is expensive and of poor quality. The more durable vegetables such as tomatoes, peppers, and onions have become staples, while processed and prepared foods, especially canned meats, are heavily relied on. Work schedules also incline householders toward more prepared foods and such take-out meals as pizza.[37]

The consequences of this changing diet are most apparent in the ubiquity of dental caries. These are pervasive throughout all age groups, and dental rot and missing teeth are pronounced in the service communities. Babies are given Coke in a bottle as early as six months of age (after two years is most common), and come to prefer this to mother's milk. Compared to children from the United States, the elementary school children of Akumal and Cobá are substantially shorter and stockier, which hardly augurs well for health and fitness of the next generation.[38]

Household Demography

A pattern of early marriage and large families has been typical of the Quintana Roo Maya who, until recent times, lived in a thinly settled region where land for milpa agriculture was readily available. This too is changing. Daltabuit reports that in the rural community of Yalcoba, 12 percent of women give birth before 16 years and 58 percent between 16 and 19 years: mean completed fertility was 7.2 children.[39] In our household questionnaire we asked people (generally heads of family), "What is the best age to start having children?" Responses varied in relation to the community's dependence on wage labor and integration of the cash economy. Whereas Punta Laguna still showed a strong preference toward teenage motherhood, Cobá—more closely tied to tourism and facing problems of a shrinking resource base—was only slightly in favor of early motherhood. In contrast, most respondents in the coastal communities thought that marriage and childbirth should be delayed, commonly that "waiting beyond [the age of] 20 years was best." Reasons given in support of the delay included both the decline in kin-base support and the compromised health of the young mother.

These opinions mesh well with other findings. Thus, younger and older households unanimously (100 percent) expressed a desire for smaller families in all communities except Punta Laguna (a still substantial 75 percent). Also, there was a general agreement (75 percent of the total sample) that young couples wanted to live separately from their parents. These statistics no doubt reflect what are to be taken as ideal situations, but they also have a bearing on practice. Education, for example, is increasingly viewed as necessary for employment and advancement, and this includes the education of girls (who still trail boys in years of school attendance). Cost is another factor. The increasing burden of raising children was constantly cited as the reason underlying the desire for small families. In the service communities, a high number of young householders responded that two children—"the pair"—constituted the ideal complement—a figure that they recognized as a clear departure from the household structures they themselves had grown up in.

Obviously, this is still an emerging pattern, but the direction is unmistakable. It is not surprising that changes in economy and livelihood, the shift from rural to quasi-urban, and the perceived importance of education will all influence household demography: it has happened elsewhere as part of a general process of modernization. But we suggest that there is more to it than merely responding to outside pressures. Basically, it also shows that where the Maya—often depicted as highly "traditional"—are in a position to make decisions that actually influence their lives, they are not averse to doing so.

Scarce Resources and Kitchen Gardens

As discussed earlier, historically, Maya farming communities were essentially self-sufficient and needed only a few outside items. Until recent times, trade was carried on solely through traveling merchants who went regularly through the region carrying their merchandise on muleback.[40] Loss of access to land and forest, together with the growth of population in recent decades, has brought added pressures on community resources. When we asked what forest resources were becoming most scarce, people consistently drew attention to the difficulty of obtaining the hardwood upright posts and the palm thatch needed to make traditional houses.

This is a problem that particularly concerns inland communities. We learned that in Cobá it is necessary to go at least four kilometers from town to search out these materials. To build a single house now requires as many as 50 round trips (a total of 400 kilometers) into the forest, a cost in time and effort that is becoming prohibitive. Only half in jest, some of our friends suggested that on our return we should bring a sturdy, all-terrain vehicle: "You will see how easily visits and interviews can be arranged!" Incidentally, both hardwood posts and thatch are very much in demand for tourist construction, since they give the resorts the necessary exotic touch. The scarcity of wood and thatch for house building has led to an increase in the use of cinder blocks, a very expensive substitute.

In a less direct manner, the necessity of seeking outside employment and links to the cash economy have affected the number of households that maintain kitchen gardens. These are relatively small plots adjacent to dwellings and are tended and controlled by women. They produce an array of valuable foodstuffs including vegetables, herbs, fruits, and medicinal plants; it is not unusual to find small domesticated animals, even a household pig. These kitchen gardens have to be seen as part of a large agricultural complex—a complement to milpa agriculture—and it is very significant that they fall within women's sphere of control. The exchange of produce from these gardens helps to underpin the ethos of reciprocity. Kitchen gardens are rare in and around the coastal service communities and are even declining in Cobá. Taken together, these shifts indicate how difficult it has become to maintain both a degree of community self-sufficiency and the underlying social networks.

Cultural Perceptions

Tourism, together with the political, ideological, and economic restructuring of the region, has brought about the penetration of national and international values, of models of self and society that are not always internally consistent and that in fact often conflict with customary Maya forms. We have diverse religions that integrate custom and ritual and compete for the Maya soul; a national educational system that fosters a societal model based on assimilation; and clinics that undermine the legitimacy of curers and, by extension, the validity of the Mayan cultural universe.

The most powerful pressures are derived from changing economic relations. As tourism has grown, consumption norms (and expectations as well) have soared. In addition to the aforementioned dependency on commercial foods, construction materials, and household items, the Maya increasingly demand articles and commodities that do not remotely substitute for traditional items. Televisions and appliances are now seen as virtual necessities. Younger people have become particularly concerned with style, especially in the service communities where some contact with tourists is common. Laborers returning to inland villages following a stint on the coast are likely to arrive with new clothes and hairstyles, electronic gadgets, and Mexicanized mannerisms. Sometimes, they deride their stay-at-home peers as hicks. Behavior of this type creates tensions within households and between generations.[41] As it is, three-quarters of the older people think of the young as lazy, unwilling, and unable to make milpa: "fat bellies" in the local idiom.

Yet still, the vast majority of Cobá's respondents agreed that there was really no alternative to nonagricultural employment, preferably in town but if necessary in a more distant location. A good deal of the literature on Mesoamerican peasant societies interprets wage labor as a mechanism that helps maintain rural communities. While it is true that peasants with their limited resources have little choice but to hire themselves out, the strategy exacts a toll. Typically, such employment pulls the youngest and strongest from the village, the very people most able to make milpa and undertake house construction. In reality, it is virtually impossible for a man both to be a successful farmer and to engage in regular employment outside of his community. Temporary work is a possibility, though this is becoming scarce.

Talking to dedicated farmers—and there are still a number of them around—we learned that farming continues to offer a satisfaction, a deep sense of belonging, that they could not find elsewhere. But there is a catch. Consistently, these same farmers remarked that while milpa generally provided all the food the family needed, even in the best years it brought in little cash.

TV: The Outside World Invited Home

Except for Punta Laguna, which has yet to receive electricity, television is omnipresent in the localities we studied. In the two service communities, almost 90 percent of the households have television sets, and even in the much more rural Cobá TV ownership is 70 percent. A black-and-white set costs US$200, equivalent to a well-paid waiter's monthly wage. An additional $230 is needed for hookup costs, and cable fees come to $6 to $7 per month. For a minimum wage or part-time laborer, the cost of a set and installation may well represent half the annual cash income—and yet television has almost become a necessity.

Attitudes toward television are decidedly ambivalent. Many people report the TV is on six hours a day; all day on weekends. Parents complained that their children do not do their homework, and many adults readily admit that they watch too much television and it interferes with their work. Nevertheless, the nightly soap operas, whose plots and incidents seem to be known to everyone, are watched by the whole family, and parents commonly use the television as a handy baby-sitter. In fact, television viewing has become a social occasion, a daily ritual. The people of Punta Laguna, who can only see programs in other places, are the most enthusiastic about the positive value of the medium.

What is being watched? Televised programming is mostly a combination of light entertainment, cartoons, soap operas, and movies. In terms of content, it depicts a world that is often the antithesis of the values, social roles, and patterns of behavior typical of established Maya culture. Cynthia Miller, who has studied the impact of television in the nearby community of Yalcobá, writes of the challenges to Maya norms and behaviors, "challenges which involve changing perceptions and performances of social roles among genders and generations, language change, changes in community members' ideas about traditional occupations and basic needs; and the ways in which emotions are constructed, performed and talked about."[42] Henry Geddes, a member of our research team, is of the opinion that the media contribute to the fragmentation and commodification of Maya communities.[43]

There is no question that television (in the form of both commercial advertising and regular programs) depicts a world oriented toward consumption, a place of metropolitan settings inhabited predominantly by well-to-do, white (often blond) individuals. Along with the ads for cigarettes, processed foods, and beverages—items usually available in the local *tienda*—is the less explicit message that those who are portrayed are the legitimate representatives of the national culture. Needless to say, Mexican television is no more a mirror of actual Mexican life than television elsewhere, but Maya viewers are seldom in a position to make such informed judgments. Our impression is that the message of consumption and its relationship to modernity does get through clearly. What of the underlying ideological premises? When asked about specific settings depicted in programs, several of our informants placed them "very far away" in a world that we gathered was not quite real, or connected to their own tangentially if at all. This "distancing" may help protect the Maya from the sense of cultural marginality that has been so destructive to many small-scale societies; while the "outside" world of televised images is invited to enter the house, history and experience have also taught the Maya to be very cautious.

Resistance

Resistance comes in countless forms and measures, and the Maya have proved themselves masters at it for almost half a thousand years. In the past, when pushed too hard they withdrew into the forest, and if this didn't work they took up arms. Our informants were very much conscious of what was taking place across the state border in Chiapas, in part, at least, due to media coverage—however slanted. While people did not actually volunteer political opinions, their common response was their statement that the indigenous inhabitants of Chiapas had been forced into armed rebellion by loss of land and by increasingly oppressive political and economic conditions. One feature of the Zapatista revolt that is very pertinent to Quintana Roo is the degree to which the Zapatista leadership consistently links the plight of native peoples to broader issues of poverty and inequality. As economic and political forces have transformed the countryside, peasant communities have not only lost resources, but become less egalitarian, more demarcated by class and differential access to political patronage. Furthermore, an important segment of the Zapatista agenda addresses the concerns of women; as a Zapatista woman delegate expressed it, "The women are completely oppressed and exploited. We (women) demand respect, true respect as Indians."[44]

The Zapatista movement is the most visible new social movement in Mexico, though there are numerous others. All such movements have the potential of joining together a varied constituency in the interests of political change and greater economic equality. The platform for indigenous rights has become a symbol of what needs to be addressed in the whole society. It did not surprise us, therefore, when a woman in Ciudad Chemuyil responded to the question whether she was a Maya with the following words: "I can't really say that I am a Maya. My grandparents came from Spain, poor people looking for a better life. But I feel Mayan. As a mother and a working woman I support their struggle and I identify with their demand for dignity."

Recommendations

Obviously, tourism in Quintana Roo is part of a much bigger picture, and any "recommendations" that we offer are conditioned by two recognitions: that one can hardly change the part without addressing the whole, and that certainly there are no quick fixes. One statistic stands for many others: excluding Africa, Mexico now ranks sixth from the bottom of the world's nations in income inequality.[45] Today, seven out of ten Mexican wage earners—9 million people—earn $300 or less each month.

A whole literature has merged analyzing and explaining the Mexican crisis, and while a discussion of their work falls outside of our purview, our first recommendation is one of greater awareness.[46] It is in the nature of tourism that those who travel abroad leave their cares and concerns at home. But Quintana Roo, exotic though it may appear, is basically an economic extension of the United States. The American dollar functions as a parallel currency; hotel rooms, airfares, and items in luxury stores are dollar denominated. Maids, waiters, taxi drivers, beach attendants, and other service personnel prefer to receive tips in dollars—particularly following the devaluations of recent years.

This relationship is well known to all working in Quintana Roo. One of our middle-class Mexican informants commented that the state had much more in common with South Florida than it did with Mexico City. Fundamentally, what we suggest is that economically Quintana Roo is akin to northern Mexico. It is equally dependent on U.S. trade, and the bulk of the area's investment is from the United States. The maquiladoras, the 2,500 border factories, produce almost exclusively for the American market and are in physical proximity to the United States. As such, they have been the subject of numerous studies and plans. People in the United States, we believe, should also be made aware of the role of multinationals in developing tourism among our neighbors to the south, something that the tourism industry has no interest in doing.

It is, we believe, possible to exert considerable pressure on the industry (and the Mexican government) to meet minimal standards of employment and labor practice. The model here is one that already is having some impact on corporations that engage in cut-throat "outsourcing" in the Third World: apparel companies, toy manufacturers, and so forth. What is being outsourced in Quintana Roo (and Mexico as a whole) is a particular kind of commodity: fantasy and leisure. The working conditions of those who make these breaks possible should certainly concern different kinds of organizations, including trade unions and pension funds. Similar tactics can be applied to environmental issues and questions of indigenous rights as well.

The goal of such efforts is not to destroy or cripple tourism—which is bound to prevail as the mainstay of the state's economy—but rather to help defend those who have become dependent on it. This is a responsible agenda that ensures that the conditions attracting tourists in the first place are protected and reinforced. Among these conditions is social tranquility, an absolutely indispensable component of any successful tourist policy. Our argument is that the long-term prospects of the industry are intimately tied to the well-being and security of the local populations, and that these can only be realized when ways are found to redistribute some of the immense profits earned by the sector.

It should also be possible to increase Maya involvement in tourism. The current structure of tourism—the massive wall of hotels along the Cancún beachfront and the gated complexes further down the coast—denies opportunities to small businesses (wood carvers, blouse- and huipil-makers, roadside stands, handicraft shops, and so forth). Such enterprises would bring a little more money into the village economy, but, equally important, they would signal a much-needed *Maya* involvement in tourism. For the same reasons, community-run operations such as those at Punta Laguna should be supported. None of this entails large-scale investment. The ideal sponsors for such work are specialized foundations, nongovernmental organizations, and environmental groups.

For the same reasons, it is vital to overcome the current employment policies that presently relegate the Maya to the lowest-paying jobs and place Mexicans and foreigners in virtually every position that entails contacts with the customer. We have been told by managers that the issue is one of skills and education, not discrimination; this seems a very questionable explanation. Even a generation ago, it might have been reasonably suggested that the Maya would make their own decisions on how to articulate with the modern world. Today, though, options have become reduced and the poor people of Quintana Roo—Maya and non-Maya alike—must find solutions in solidarity with other groups, other organizations. The Zapatista uprising in Chiapas has highlighted the plight of indigenous communities in Mexico and the shortcomings of the government's economic and social policies. The degree of popular support enjoyed by the Zapatistas has helped protect them from repression; for its part, the Zapatista director- ate has been highly conscious of the importance of good publicity and good public relations—both in and out of Mexico. As anthropologists, we see our task as dual: first, to work as interpreters of cultural systems; second, to act as advocates, to our best ability, for a people that badly needs help and support. We have not appropriated a role, yet still have been asked to fill it.

Notes

1. Research presented here was primarily carried out in 1993 and 1994. The specific design is based on numerous discussions as to how a multidisciplinary approach to tourism in Quintana Roo could be conducted. Participants in these discussions, including the authors, were Magali Daltabuit, Alan Goodman, Guillermo Iranzo, Tom Leatherman, Debra Martin, and Alan Swedlund.

We are indebted to the people of the four study communities, Akumal, Ciudad Chemuyil, Cobá, and Punta Laguna for kindly allowing us into their homes and patiently answering our many questions. In Akumal and Ciudad Chemuyil we were assisted by Roger Tun Pacho, Miguel Pani, Brenda Detering, and Rodolfo Lopez. Michael and Linda Mulgrew of the *Centro Ecologico de Akumal* kindly provided lodging for our volunteers, and Charles Shaw and Hilario Hiler provided valuable advice. In Cobá, Francisco May Hau and Ramona May Cen served as interpreters, as did Serapio Canul in Punta Laguna; Francisco Itza assisted us with lodging.

Five student volunteers, Marne Ausec, Guillermo Iranzo, Catherine McGarty, Marketa Sebelova, and Ellie Zucker, were most effective research assistants. Henry Geddes and Cindy Miller worked along with us studying the effects of mass media on cultural perceptions, and Alan Goodman and Kelly Keenan analyzed the anthropometric school data. Laurie Greenberg, Ellen Kintz, and Tom Leatherman, whose work preceded ours, provided valuable advice in designing questionnaires. Finally, we are indebted to our friend and colleague Magali Daltabuit for introducing us to the communities and the problems of tourism in Quintana Roo, and for working along with us on this project.

We are grateful for the support provided by the Wenner-Gren Foundation for Anthropological Research (Research Grant # 5618) and for a University of Massachusetts Faculty Research Grant (Summer 1994).

2. Theron A. Nuñez, "Tourism, Tradition and Acculturation: Weekendismo in a Mexican Village," *Ethnology* 2:3 (1963) 347–352, quote from p. 348.

3. Veronica Long, "Tourism Development, Conservation and Anthropology," *Practicing Anthropology* 14:2 (1992) 14–17.

4. Gary H. Gossen, "Maya Zapatistas Move to the Ancient Future," *American Anthropologist* 89:3 (1996) 528–538.

5. Richard Butler, "Alternative Tourism: The Thin Edge of the Wedge," in Valene L. Smith and William R. Eadington, eds., *Tourism Alternatives, Potentials and Problems in the Development of Tourism* (Philadelphia: University of Pennsylvania Press, 1992), 35.

6. Malcolm Crick, "Representations of International Tourism in the Social Sciences: Sun, Sex, Sights, Savings and Servility," *Annual Review of Anthropology* 18:44 (1989) 309.

7. Erik Cohen, "The Sociology of Tourism: Approaches, Issues, and Findings," *Annual Review of Sociology* 10 (1984) 373–392.

8. Smith and Eadington, eds., *op. cit.*, note 5, p.2. These figures are taken from a 1991 World Travel Organization report and, as is often the case with WTO statistics, they fail to distinguish between leisure and business travel. Increasingly, though, much business travel includes a tourist itinerary.

9. "Third-World Tourism," *The Economist,* March 11, 1989, p. 19.

10. For a discussion of tourism and dependency, see Colin Michael Hall, *Tourism and Politics, Policy, Power and Place.* (Chichester and New York: John Wiley, 1994), 122–132. A whole literature on dependency theory, Marxist or neo-Marxist in orientation, emerged out of the Latin American experience in the 1960s. See, for example, Andre Gunder Frank, *Development and Underdevelopment in Latin America* (New York: Monthly Review Press, 1968); Samir Amin, *Unequal Exchange* (New York: Monthly Review Press, 1976); Fernando Enrique Carduso and Enzo Faletto, *Dependency and Development in Latin America* (Berkeley: University of California Press, 1979); Ronald H. Chilcote and Joel C. Edelstein, *Latin America: The Struggle with Dependency and Beyond* (New York: Schenkman Publishing Company, 1974).

What is important for our purpose is the stress on the inequality of relationships in international trade between First World and Third World countries. This critique very seldom addressed questions of cultural or ethnic domination related to the development process. The premises of developmentalism did not go entirely unchallenged in anthropology. In 1967, one of us drew attention to the dangers of designating a particular economic model as the goal of research or policy, and cautioned against drawing almost exclusively on the "experience of the capitalist countries of the Western world" and taking these as "ideal forms and events. See Oriol Pi-Sunyer, *Zamora: A Regional Economy in Mexico* (New Orleans: Middle American Research Institute, Tulane University, 1967), 170.

11. Charles L. Geshekter, "International Tourism and African Underdevelopment: Some Reflections on Kenya," in Mario D. Zamora *et al.,* eds., *Tourism and Economic Change* (Williamsburg, Va.: Dept. of Anthropology, 1978), 57–88.

12. Arturo Escobar, *Encountering Development* (Princeton: Princeton University Press, 1995).

13. Pierre L. van den Berghe, *The Quest for the Other: Ethnic Tourism in San Cristobal, Mexico* (Seattle: University of Washington Press, 1994), 72.

14. Secretaría de Turismo, *El Turismo en México Durante 1992* (Supplemento de La Gaceta del Sector Turismo, vol.7, año 2, Mexico City, 1993), 3.

15. Daniel Hiernaux Nicolás and Rodríguez Woog, *Tourism and Absorption of the Labor Force in Mexico. Economic Development.* Working Paper 34 (Washington, D.C.: Commission for the Study of International Migration and Cooperative, 1990).

16. The population pressures in Mexico are real enough. The workforce is expanding at 3 percent per year, and more than one-third of Mexicans are under 15 years of age; a full 80 percent are under

40. United Nations projections indicate that by the year 2015, metropolitan Mexico City will have a population of 18.7 million.

17. Frederick K. Errington and Deborah B. Gewertz, *Articulating Change in the "Last Unknown"* (Boulder, Colo.: Westview Press, 1995), 162.

18. The myth of the shattered Eden is often juxtaposed with one that emphasizes the inevitability of change and "modernization." Fundamentally, "traditional societies" are depicted as *resisting* change, a transformation that can only come about when pressure is applied. In its 19th century form, it underpinned colonialism and explained human diversity; more recently it was (and continues to be) a key component of development ideology. Especially in the 1950s and 1960s, planners insisted that economic progress was impossible without painful adjustments that would dismantle established systems of belief and community organization.

19. Oriol Pi-Sunyer, "The Cultural Costs of Tourism," *Cultural Survival Quarterly* 6:3 (1992) 7–12.

20. Crick, *op. cit.*, note 6, p. 44; Emanuel de Kadt, "Making the Alternative Sustainable: Lessons from Development for Tourism" in Smith and Eadington, *op. cit.*, note 5, p. 54.

21. *World Development Report 1994* (Washington, D.C. and New York: World Bank and Oxford University Press), 221.

22. John E., Kicza, ed., *The Indian in Latin American History, Resistance, Resilience and Acculturation* (Wilmington, Del.: Jaguar Books, 1993).

23. Clifford Geertz, "Life on the Edge," *New York Times Review of Books,* April 7, 1994, pp. 3–4.

24. Julian Burger, *Report from the Frontier, The State of the World's Indigenous Peoples* (London: Zed Books, 1987), 2.

25. See Dean MacCannell, "Staged Authenticity," *American Journal of Sociology* 79:3 (1975) 589–603; and *Empty Meeting Grounds: The Tourist Papers* (London: Routledge, 1992).

26. We would argue, on the basis of both observation and literature, that tourism tends to reinforce prejudice and racism, particularly when the objects of the tourist gaze are exoticized "others." That this prejudice is typically rendered in the language of paternalism is hardly surprising.

27. Cynthia Enloe, *Bananas, Beaches and Bases* (Berkeley and Los Angeles: University of California Press, 1989), 40.

28. Dirección General de Estadística Octavo Censo General de la Población (Resumen General) (México, D.F.: Estados Unidos Mexicanos, Secretaría de Economía, 1962), 7.

29. Gonzalo Aguirre Beltran, *Regions of Refuge,* Monograph 12 (Washington, D.C.: Society for Applied Anthropology, 1979).

30. *Passport Cancún,* 20th ed. (Cancún: Apoyo Promocional, 1994), 9.

31. Secretaría de Turismo, "El Turismo en México Durante 1992," Supplemento de La Gaceta del Sector Turismo, Mexico City (vol. 7, año 2, 1993).

32. Michael Collins, *Ecotourism in the Yucatan Peninsula of Mexico* (Syracuse, N.Y.: SUNY, ESF-IEPP, 1991).

33. Gustavo Lins Riberiro and Flávia Lessa de Barros, *A Corrida por Paisagens Autênticas: Turismo, Meio Ambiente e Subjetividade na Contemporaneidade* (Brasília D.F.: University of Brasília) Anthropology Series No. 171, 1994, p. 8.

34. Rayfred L. Stevens, "The Soils of Middle America and Their Relation to Indian Peoples and Cultures," in *Natural Environment and Early Cultures,* Robert C. West, ed., Handbook of Middle American Indians, 1. Robert Wauchope, gen. ed. (Austin: University of Texas Press, 1964), 265–315; see p. 303.

35. Magali Daltabuit and Oriol Pi-Sunyer, "Tourism Development in Quintana Roo, Mexico," *Cultural Survival Quarterly* 14:1 (1990) 9–13.

36. Ellen Kintz, *Life Under the Tropical Canopy* (Fort Worth, Texas: Holt, Reinhart and Winston, 1980), 80.

37. Catherine A. McGarty, "Dietary Delocalization in a Yucatecan Resort Community in Quintana Roo, Mexico: Junk Food in Paradise," Honors Thesis (School of Nursing, University of Massachusetts–Amherst).

38. The anthropometrics used to compare nutritional status show that these children are almost 2 SD (standard deviations) below NCHS levels in height for their age, -1SD below in weight for age, and +1.6 SD above in weight for height. (Analysis by Alan Goodman and Kelly Keenan.)

39. Magali Daltabuit, *Mujeres mayas, trabajo, nutricion y fecundidad* (Mexico, D.F.: UNAM, Institute de Investigaciones Antropologicas, 1992), 144–151.

40. Alfonso Villa Rojas, *The Maya of Quintana Roo* (Washington, D.C.: Carnegie Institute of Washington, Publication 559, 1945), 68.

41. Kelly A. Keenan, "Conversations with *Le Nukuch Maac'obo:* Elderly Mayan Perceptions of and Adaptations to Tourism-led Changes in Occupation, Diet, and Health in Cobá, Quintana Roo, Mexico," Division III thesis (School of Natural Sciences, Hampshire College, Amherst, Mass., 1996).

42. Cynthia Miller, "The Social Impacts of Televised Media Among the Yucatecan Maya" (unpublished manuscript, 1994).

43. Henry Gonzáles Geddes, "Mass Media and Cultural Identity Among the Yucatecan Maya: The Constitution of Global, National and Local Subjects." forthcoming in *Studies in Latin American Popular Culture.*

44. George A. Collier, *Basta! Land and the Zapatista Rebellion in Chiapas* (Oakland, Calif.: Food First, 1994), 60.

45. Jorge Castañeda, "Mexico's Circle of Misery," *Foreign Affairs* 75:4 (1996) 92–105, see p. 63.

46. *Ibid.* See also Andres Oppenheimer, *Bordering on Chaos: Guerrillas, Stockbrokers, Politicians and Mexico's Road to Prosperity* (Boston: Little Brown, 1996).

CHAPTER 10

Environment, Development, and Indigenous Revolution in Chiapas

David Stea, Silvia Elguea, and Camilo Perez Bustillo

Prologue

by Camilo Perez Bustillo

I have traveled to Chiapas as a human rights observer for the National Lawyers' Guild on five occasions since the Zapatista uprising began (January 21–23 and August 23–28, 1994; March 7–9, 1995; and in April and July/August 1996). The first trip was during the immediate aftermath of the uprising itself, including four visits to four of the six highlands towns seized by the Zapatista Army of National Liberation, or EZLN, earlier the same month (San Cristobal, Ocosingo, Oxchuc, and Huixtan), interviews with eyewitnesses of combat in Ocosingo's marketplace, and visits to sites of combat along the highway outside San Cristobal near Rancho Nuevo military base, including the site of an apparent mass grave in the forest near the base. The second trip was as leader of a delegation of 15 lawyers and journalists from the National Lawyers Guild and the Mexican-American Bar Association in Los Angeles and the San Francisco Bay Area, during the week immediately following Mexico's 1995 national presidential and congressional elections. The third trip, during March 1995, was as a part of the first "Mission Civil de Informacion" (Citizen's Information Mission) organized by Bishop Samuel Ruiz as part of his mediation role at the head of CONAI, the nongovernmental mediation body in the on-again, off-again negotiation process between the government and the EZLN. This trip took place following the government's February 8–9, 1995 military offensive (the first military offensive since the January 12, 1994, cease-fire). On the last two trips I again acted as human rights monitor for the National Lawyers' Guild, and most recently attended the "Intercontinental Encounter for Humanity" held in Zapatista territory between July 27 and August 3, 1996.

During the February 1995 offensive, the military conducted raids on alleged EZLN safe-houses at three sites in Mexico City; raided various places in the neighboring states of Mexico and Veracruz; and supposedly "unmasked" the rebel's best-known leader, chief spokesperson, and military strategist—subcommander "Marcos." Most of the

David Stea is a Professor of Environmental Studies and International Affairs at the United States International University–Mexico. Silvia Elguea is a member of the faculty at the Universidad Autonoma Metropolitana–Azcapotzalco. Camilo Perez Bustillo is a member of the faculty of the United States International University–Mexico. Comments can be sent to David Stea, International Center for Culture and the Environment, Puebla 423-502, Colonia Roma, 06700 Mexico, D.F. Mexico.

territory that had been under EZLN control since the January 1994 uprising was retaken in the February 1995 offensive, driving the EZLN leadership and thousands of its unarmed supporters even deeper into the Lacandon jungle and up against the Guatemalan border. The Mexican military offensive was matched by a military buildup on the Guatemalan side of the border, with the evident intent of catching the EZLN in between. Thousands of indigenous and mestizo peasants who had fled Zapatista territory during the initial January 1994 military offensive (with its indiscriminate bombardment of civilian populations) were escorted back to their communities by the military's advance in February 1995. Deep splits—between those resettled and those displaced as a result of the military's clumsy response to the uprising—divided many of these communities down the middle.[1]

I was assigned, together with six others, to visit the small mestizo *ejido* (collective farm) community of Flor de Cafe near the Guatemalan border, along the southeastern edge of the Lacandon jungle in the municipality of Las Margaritas (also taken by the EZLN in January, 1994). We never got to Flor de Cafe because the Mexican army got there first, occupying that community and the neighboring community of Maravilla Tenejapa, driving into the surrounding jungle hundreds of those communities' residents who had been identified by returning community members accompanying the military as EZLN sympathizers. Entire extended families with members on the wrong list fled in terror with whatever they could carry. In most instances those fleeing were indigenous, and those returning mestizo. Several of these families in flight, accused of being EZLN supporters (often simply because they had refused to move during the military's initial offensive in January 1994), had been refugees in the mestizo *ejido* community of Monte Flor, about 25 minutes' walking distance from the Guatemalan border.[2]

We had stopped at Monte Flor on the way to Flor de Cafe at the suggestion of our guides—two nuns from San Cristobal diocese, based at Comitan. On arrival we were informed by community leaders that refugees from other neighboring communities

A mounted detachment of Zapatistas at an unidentified location in Chiapas.

were present, gathering supplies in preparation for their flight into the jungle. They had received word that the Army, which had been gradually occupying the entire surrounding region, was on its way.

Refugees from neighboring communities that had already been occupied by the military informed us that "it was those civilians being resettled who were the most problematic, behaving much worse than the soldiers." At first in communities such as Amatitlan and Maravilla "it was the soldiers who were most aggressive, asking lots of questions, ransacking homes, asking about guns and radios." The most significant impact of the military's occupation was fear—terrorizing everyone, especially the women and children. On February 14, when the Army first arrived in Amatitlan, residents counted 32 helicopters within the first two or three hours, swooping down on the community, scaring the animals into breaking the ropes that were supposed to be restraining them, and causing them to flee into the surrounding brush. Federal agents were pursuing them, "persecuting all those who'd stayed behind," commented a father as he tried to calm down his three weeping daughters aged 7, 5, and 3 years old.

Many of those fleeing identified themselves as supporters of the center-left Party of the Democratic Revolution (PRD). Their main problem was that they had struggled a lot for land "but the government won't give it to us . . . it pays no attention to us, it doesn't take us into account, so what the hell are we supposed to do? . . . " "We had no problems with the EZLN . . . joining them is voluntary, and besides they taught us some important words about unity among indigenous people, words that came to us with the EZLN."

Other refugees were members of ISAAM, the Indigenous People's Organization of Sierra Madre of Motozintla. They talked with us about their ten years of struggle holding ISAAM together, "gradually beginning to understand things, even though they accused us of being communists. . . ." In these communities, unlike in the highlands, there were few problems among indigenous people because of religious divisions since the EZLN—by contrast with some "outside" religions—"respected the traditional authorities in our community." The refugees' concern was that those being resettled by the Army "want to take our lands back." But "we are not animals to be hunted down, we are humans that think and feel . . . but we don't speak Spanish well, we don't understand what they're saying to us sometimes . . . what we want is that the soldiers leave, and leave us alone. We don't want soldiers here. Help us get them out."

"We want help because we're afraid," explained a couple with nine children gathered around them, hiding in between their legs and behind the mother's skirts. "What do we want? We want a life of truth and justice so that all of us have everything we need, that we as indigenous people can be able to speak with a single voice . . . that we have no needs, but enjoy all our rights."

Refugees from Amatitlan told us that over 2,000 troops had been stationed in the town since mid-February, and that there were Guatemalan troops mixed in with the Mexican Army detachments. The Guatemalans were identifiable, they said, because there are significant differences between the Guatemalan dialect of the Tojolabal language and the Mexican variant. According to these refugees, some of the Guatemalans were involved in interrogating community residents. There were even rumors of soldiers from Spain being involved "like in the days of the Conquest."

The main complaints about the soldiers, besides the generalized fear they engendered, was that they were disrespectful, failing to ask permission for things they took, entering into and ransacking houses at will, "grabbing what they want." In Amatitlan they were accused of stealing seeds and sugarcane, threatening one man's wife, saying "they were going to fill her with lead if she didn't let them take what they wanted." As a result two or three of the families that felt most threatened took refuge in a single home, huddling together out of fear, children refusing food in silent terror. "These soldiers don't pay or say thank you."

Life had changed for these refugees irretrievably. "We can't live calmly anymore. Our women are going to die from worrying so much."

Others remembered rifle barrels being jammed under their doors, soldiers taking their chickens, other soldiers taking photographs. Those taking photos of suspected Zapatistas warned that still others would arrive the next day and would make things unpleasant for them, which was the immediate reason for several deciding to leave that night.

For some, such experiences only strengthened their convictions and desire to resist. "We are going to defend ourselves; we're not going to stand by and let these things happen. Maybe the laws don't work for us, maybe there is no law anymore to protect us, because otherwise such things couldn't happen."

The leaders of the Monte Flor *ejido* asked us to spend the night with them because they were afraid the Army's arrival there was imminent, that same day. In the evening a special assembly of the *ejido* was called to welcome us and to ask us to explain why we were there, and how we could help. After our attempt at an explanation was over, the community asked us to be their spokespersons, "to Mexico and to the world . . . and to Bishop Ruiz," each person present signing a formally sealed petition that a human rights observer mission be permanently established in the community to assure their safety if and when the Army came.

We decided to keep the community's identity secret in any public statements until we knew for sure about the military's arrival there, fearing that publicly singling out Monte Flor for "harboring" suspected Zapatistas would only bring more difficulties on them. But we did raise the issue they themselves had raised, of a pattern of reprisals by the Army against communities of political refuge and of human rights violations in the region. We also gave Bishop Ruiz and members of CONAI a private, detailed briefing about the situation in Monte Flor and its neighboring communities, and gave them the original signed copy of Monte Flor's petition that a civilian encampment be established there.

Before the promised peace camp could be installed, however, the Army occupied the Monte Flor sector. By August 1995, there were 800 troops around Monte Flor itself, another 1,500 in nearby Flor de Cafe, and 2,000 still in Amatitlan, but troops had finally left Maravilla Tenejapa.[3] This meant a ratio of about five soldiers per resident in Flor de Cafe. The average ratio in the rest of Chiapas is one soldier for every three inhabitants, a total of between 36,000 and 40,500 troops concentrated among 37 different communities. As of this writing (April 1996) a peace camp of observers from nongovernmental groups (both Mexican and foreign) has been established there, and the community was at least no longer alone in its fears and hopes. We have not been able to confirm what happened to the informants cited above, although there are reports that most are safe, but in precarious conditions, deeper in the jungle.

Introduction

. . . the EZLN, an army nurtured in the cañadas between 1984 and 1994, may be the first force for revolutionary change in Latin America that is rooted in the conflict between preservation of the planet's diminishing biomass and the gut desire of the poorest of the poor, for what passes as progress under the banner of development. The Zapatista rebellion represents an initial skirmish in the coming resource wars of the 21st century.[4]

Why did the uprising in the Chiapas region of Mexico—which began on New Year's Day, 1994—receive so much attention in world media? It was not a civil war of the magnitude now besetting the former Yugoslavia, the death toll was less than 1 percent of that in Rwanda, and it lasted but a fraction of the time of the guerrilla wars in Guatemala and El Salvador. Indeed, for more than 90 percent of its duration it has been "on hold."

What made it significant were a number of factors:

1. First, it was the first major indigenous uprising in the Western Hemisphere since the collapse of the socialist states of Eastern Europe.
2. The Zapatista uprising (see photograph) began the day the North American Free Trade Agreement (NAFTA) took effect—it explicitly targeted the structural readjustment policies represented in neoliberal economics, in the form of "free trade" agreements.
3. The uprising was intimately linked to a context of environmental degradation throughout the forested regions of Chiapas, especially in the Lacandon Biosphere Reserve.

4. Unlike most other Latin American struggles throughout history, this revolt was bottom-up rather than top-down—not a cause looking for a constituency, but a constituency that had found its cause. As the French anthropologist Andres Aubry, a long-time resident of Chiapas, has said: "Unlike the guerrillas in Guatemala, (the Zapatistas) are not seeking out bases of support among the campesinos, but coming up from them."[5]

5. The revolt espoused no traditional ideology. The discourse of the movement in its communiqués and public statements was unusually creative and literary in character, with pronounced indigenous content.

6. This was the first "online" revolution, tying social revolution to the communications revolution through Internet e-mail, providing the EZLN with instantaneous information (and the rest of the world with instantaneous information about the EZLN) and with support networks around the globe.[6]

7. The Chiapas revolt was not just another in a series of uprisings in a poor country beset by turmoil. Mexico is one of the wealthier and more developed members of the "Third World," at least as measured by its gross domestic product; and its recent history, until 1994, had been marked by incredible political stability with uninterrupted rule by a single party (the Institutional Revolutionary Party, or PRI) since 1929. After the former Soviet Union, Mexico has the second-longest reign of a single political party in world history. While many mostly peaceful demonstrations have occurred over the past three decades, the only incident of extreme violence to air in the world-press prior to the Zapatista revolt was the 1968 Tlalteloco massacre, which crushed a strong but short-lived popular movement.

8. Finally, the Chiapas uprising in January 1994 was the first in a series of social tremors shaking Mexico's self-image of placidity and stability, ushering in a period of unprecedented violence and socioeconomic upheaval. Prior to the March 1994 assassination of Luis Donaldo Colosio, the ranking presidential candidate, no top-ranking political figure had been fatally attacked since 1928: 66 at least superficially placid years on the political scene. In the more than two years since 1994 began, fear of assassinations of major figures has become widespread. Due to the timing of the revolt (the day NAFTA went into effect), the Chiapas situation easily became a scapegoat for the disastrous economic events that followed. Newly elected President Ernesto Zedillo used the Chiapas conflict as an excuse for Mexico's catastrophic economic collapse of December 1994—a collapse, in fact, due more to the rapid, ill-considered, and badly-planned "neoliberal" restructuring set into motion during the previous administration of President Carlos Salinas de Gortari.

The purpose of this chapter is to place the Chiapas revolt in broader context—examining the origins of human and environmental crises in Chiapas, the historical patterns of abuses, and the cumulative effect of these problems: leaving people with no choice but to bear arms and forcefully negotiate change. Before considering the Chiapas story, we first describe aspects of the national context.

Neoliberalism, Indigenous Peoples, and the Environment

Mexico is ill-understood by non-Mexican economists, whose models of development do not fit societies characterized by both high levels of urbanization and high levels of subsistence agriculture. The proportions of urbanized population in the United States and Mexico are virtually identical, differing by less than 1 percentage point: both hover at about 75 percent. Yet, while less than 1 percent of Americans are engaged in agriculture, almost 20 percent of Mexicans are so employed. In Mexico, however, few rural farmers are agrobusinesspeople: most mestizos and indigenous people eke out an existence producing a combination of subsistence and market crops.

Confronted with the post–Cold War new world and new hemispheric orders, Mexico has not fared well. After a half-century of import substitution policies, once well-protected domestic industries are now unable to compete in the neoliberal free market spawned in North America by the hastily-conceived NAFTA and globally by the World Trade Organization (GATT's successor). Inevitably, multinational corporations are taking over. As mobile national capital continues to wash in and out of the country, foreign investment is what is sought. A combination of devaluation and inflation has cut the purchasing power of the minuscule minimum wage by more than half over the 20 months since December 1994. More than 1 million workers became unemployed during the first four months of 1995, and by mid-1996 this number had reached 2.2 million. Reduced in size and in its ability to consume, the shrinking Mexican middle class provides few customers for the products of the multinationals now establishing themselves in Mexico; the latter, in their turn, increasingly produce only for export, fueling fears that all Mexico may become a huge maquiladora.

With increase in GDP (the sole index of growth and the implied equation of growth with development), indicators of real improvement in the quality of life—rather than standard of living—become distorted. Measured by number of billionaires, Mexico was, until December 1994, the fourth richest nation on earth: the number of billionaires ballooned from two at the start of the Salinas regime in 1988 to two dozen when he left office in 1994. The income of these two dozen billionaire extended families was more than the combined income of the poorest 25 million of Mexico's people. There is some suggestion that the gap between the richest and the poorest in Mexico is now even greater than that in Brazil.

The negative impacts of structural readjustment (galloping privatization and decimated public spending) have been heaviest in the poorest areas of Mexico—areas with the greatest indigenous population. Salinas's trickle-down arguments justifying neoliberalism resembled those of U.S. President Reagan a decade earlier, but with even less substantial results. In Mexico misery is trickling *up*. The losers in this scenario have been both Mexico's indigenous peoples and its indigenous environment.

El Mexico del sotano	Mexico is at its roots
es indigena . . . pero para	the indigenous person . . .
el resto del pais no cuenta,	but for the rest of the
no produce, no vende,	country he/she does not
no compra, es decir,	count, does not produce,
no existe . . . Revise usted	does not sell, does not

> el texto del Tratado del
> Libre Comercio y vera que,
> para este gobierno, no
> existen los indigenas.
> —Marcos, EZLN

> buy, in sum does not
> exist . . . Review the text
> of NAFTA and you will
> see that, for this
> government, the indige-
> nous people do not exist.

Mexico has the largest indigenous population in Latin America: up to 40 percent of the 40 million or more indigenous peoples who live in the Americas, depending on who's counting, and how. Who is considered indigenous depends on governmental definition. The Mexican government's low estimate of 6 million indigenes includes only those whose primary language is indigenous, who are age 5 or older, and who live on indigenous lands. Small children and town-dwelling Indians who speak predominantly Spanish are thus excluded.[7]

Following a brief period of "indigenismo" at the conclusion of the Mexican Revolution, the national attitude began to take a strange turn: dead indigenes (pre-Conquest Aztecs, Mextecs, Teotihuacanos, Zapotecs, and the like) were venerated and even idolized at the same time as live indigenes were increasingly despised.[8] In the post-Revolutionary nation-building process, Mexico has searched for a national identity. In this search, cultural diversity has *not* been positively valued. Mexico does not see itself as a pluralist country. Thus, the presumed indolence, indifference, and stupidity of the indigenous who "stand in the way of progress" are invoked both to explain environmental destruction and, in the case of Chiapas, to condemn the Zapatistas.[9] It has been disturbingly easy to blame the devastation of the Chapaneco tropical forest on the Mayans themselves, presumed by many to be ignorant of their own environment, rather than on cattle ranching, commercial forestry, large-scale hydroelectric projects, and extractive industries, such as mining and petroleum.[10]

Environmental issues are of relatively low official priority in Mexico: a recent survey on Mexico's problems, conducted by the center-left newspaper *Reforma*, for example, contained no questions whatever on the environment.[11] As of this writing, in mid-1996, it is no wonder that the economic crisis eclipses all other concerns. However, when asked about the most important problem of the country, whose capital city—with almost 25 percent of the nation's population—boasts the world's worst air quality, just 1 percent of the respondents mentioned pollution. The section of this survey on health also contained nothing specifically directed to environmental health, yet it revealed that registered cases of amebic dysentery—whose principal cause is polluted water—had increased by a factor of almost 40 between 1970 and 1990, from under 27,000 to over 1 million registered cases, and that registered respiratory infections had increased more than 2,000 times during the same 20-year period, from under 4,250 to over 9 million. Even correcting for population increases and estimated increased accuracy of reporting, these are still disturbing statistics in a country in which *contaminacion* has long been a taboo word.[12]

Nor is public apathy matched by apathetic legislation. In fact, Mexico has some of the toughest environmental laws in the world. These have simply not been enforced. NAFTA "sidebars" have been hailed for their potential positive effect on the Mexican environment, but what few effects have been felt to date have been along the U.S.-Mexican border, where catastrophic environmental pollution—especially that affecting the U.S. side—has been widely publicized.[13]

A peculiar dialectic seems at work here. Despite the absence of substantive environmental movements in Mexico before 1978, despite the relative ineffectiveness of organizations formed since then, and despite the internal apathy described above, Mexico has presented itself to the world as a country marked by environmental concern. President Salinas was the recipient of the 1991 Earth Prize, jointly conferred by the Nobel family and the United Nations for outstanding environmental statesmanship. Mexico was also the first country to ratify the Vienna Convention and Montreal Protocol agreements for the protection of the ozone layer, and, at the 1992 Earth Summit, it was a signatory to the Treaties on Climate Change and Biological Diversity (which the U.S. delegation, led by then–President George Bush, did not sign).

Mexico has also claimed considerable success in its wildlife programs, including protection of marine turtles (of the world's seven species of marine turtles, six nest on Mexico's beaches),[14] creation of (currently threatened) breeding sanctuaries for gray whales, reduction of dolphin mortality in tuna fishing by 70 percent since 1988, and establishment of world-renowned monarch butterfly reserves.

More recent revelations, however, have cast shadows over ex-President Salinas' self-congratulatory environmental record. For example, the forest cover of the Reserva Mariposa Monarca has been reduced some 40 percent by incursions of local farmers (often coerced), symptomatic of one of Mexico's most insidious environmental trends.[15] An article in the March 28 edition of *Reforma*[16] cited a report by the Secretaria del Medio Ambiente, Recursos Naturales y Pesca, conveying on Mexico the dubious distinction of having the highest rate of deforestation in the world. According to this report, Mexico is losing, annually, a million hectares of forest (2.5 million acres, or more than 4,000 square miles: which means that a square mile of Mexican forest will have disappeared during the 1.5 hours you might take to read this article). More than 50 percent of the largely coniferous northern temperate forests are gone, but fully 95 percent of the tropical rain forests, many once covering large portions of Chiapas, no longer exist. Compounding the disappearing forests have been the disappearing wetlands. Particularly notable has been the loss of the mangroves of Tabasco, Veracruz, and Chiapas, seriously damaging a once-thriving fishing industry.[17]

Chiapas: The Place, the People, and the Problems

Among the most striking disparities confronted in Chiapas is the presence of pervasive poverty in a state abundantly endowed with natural resources. Owing to its fertile soil and dependable rainfall, Chiapas is one of the country's most bountiful agricultural states, ranking first in coffee cultivation . . . third in both corn and avocado production (and) second in cattle raising. . . . Perhaps even more impressive are the state's energy resources. Its rivers have been harnessed for the generation of electricity, and it leads the nation in this category. . . . Owing to its considerable deposits, the state ranks third in petroleum production after . . . Tabasco and Veracruz.[18]

Chiapas: The Place

Chiapas, the southernmost and most biodiverse of Mexico's states, is culturally and ecologically a part of Central America. The predominant cultural groups are Mayan-speaking Mayans, many contiguous with those of Guatemala; the highland and lowland flora and fauna, including the rain forests, are mainly tropical. The Mexican Republic, with 12 of the world's 14 ecosystems, is fourth among the countries of the globe in the number of species within its frontiers, first or second in the number of species per square kilometer of land area, and the most ecologically diverse area in the world bordering on an industrialized nation.[19]

As the most biodiverse part of a country characterized by biodiversity, Chiapas, with its 74,000 sq km, has less than 1 percent of the land area of the continental United States, but as many plant and animal species as the U.S. and Canada combined. The highest density of plant and animal species is found in the Lacandon rain forest, in and around which are located a large portion of Chiapas's highland Mayan communities. The Lacandon is "part of one continuous rainforest (once) extending all the way from Campeche and the Yucatan to the Gran Peten of Guatemala, across the Usumacinta—a swatch of green biomass second only in the New World to the Amazon Basin (and home to) jaguar and ocelot and herds of tapirs, crocodiles and wild boar and howler monkeys."[20] The Lacandon originally constituted more than 20 percent of Chiapas, over 5,000 square miles in extent. All but ignored until the first "boom" in 1859, about 70 percent of the Mexican Lacandon, with its uncounted potential pharmaceutical resources, has been destroyed since 1950 through highway construction, timber harvesting, oil drilling, cattle grazing, export-oriented agriculture, resettlement projects, and, most recently, plowing airstrips for illegal drug and arms traffic.

In addition to its rich biodiversity, Chiapas is rich in energy resources. Accounting for less than $1/25$ of Mexico's land area, Chiapas receives more than 10 percent of the nation's rainfall and generates some 45 percent of Mexico's hydroelectric resources. Chiapas also overlays or is adjacent to a large portion of Mexico's oil reserves: PEMEX, the national petroleum company, extracts 92,000 barrels of oil and 516 million cubic feet of natural gas daily.

In this resource-rich state, large-scale mining, forestry, and cattle-grazing efforts have degraded the environment. Environmental conservation efforts in Chiapas have thus far been limited largely to the Lacandon rain forest. Here and in the remainder of the Mayan region a grand—but as yet largely unrealized—scheme has been hatched for a multinational effort at eco-cultural tourism between Mexico and its Central American neighbors: "La Ruta Maya." Its business counterpart, "El Mundo Maya," much less environmentally concerned, promotes other forms of tourism, together with neoliberal economic development.[21]

Chiapas: The People

Chiapas is also Mexico's most culturally diverse region. Between one-third and one-half of the indigenous languages of Mexico are spoken here. Many of Chiapas's 3.2 million people are "boom time" immigrants (most of whom are mixed-race mestizos). Of the remaining population, the one-third who are indigenous Maya are concentrated in Los Altos and the Lacandon, the two economically poorest of the eight geographical areas of Chiapas. These were for many years the "forgotten people" of Chiapas. Bypassed in the reforms of the Revolution of 1910, and by the Constitution of 1917 for at least two decades (and some more than four), these poorest of Chiapas's poor have for the most part remained in a state of submissive poverty, little touched by land reform and subject to the whims of landlords whose estates steadily increase in size, and also to the whims of cattle ranchers who covet Mayan lands.

The ranks of the Zapatista Army of National Liberation (EZLN) are composed primarily of those who now dwell in and around the Lacandon: the Tzotzil, Tzeltal, Chol, Tojolabal, Mam, and Zoque Mayans who are culturally more a part of Guatemala than of Mexico (Chiapas was still part of Guatemala at the time of Mexican independence). Not all of these are indigenous to the area. Many Chol arrived from Palenque during an earlier "boom"; some Tzotziles are from Chamula; other indigenes are "expulsados" (for example Tushones), many of these, converts to evangelical Protestanism, were driven out of their rigidly traditional villages. The three groups of Lacandon made famous through the activities of Chiapas's Na'Balom Institute—notably, one never Christianized—are not entirely indigenous to the area, either. The original Lacan-Tum were largely extinct by 1769, and many of the present Lacandones were Mayan rebels from Campeche and Yucatan who arrived in the second half of the 18th century.[22]

In addition to indigenous inhabitants and immigrants from other parts of Mexico, refugees, notably Mayans from Guatemala, represent a significant force in the social and environmental landscape. According to nongovernmental agencies, some 45,000 Guatemalan refugees have established residency in Mexico, fleeing a series of repressive governments (backed by the United States) and genocidal acts. (This figure excludes those seeking asylum who have not registered with the United Nations High Commissioner for Refugees, Guatemalans en route to the United States, and Guatemalans who enter Mexico as seasonal workers in the coffee harvest. Some estimates suggest that the number of Guatemalan refugees in Mexico may be as high as 200,000).[23]

About half of the 45,000 or more Guatemalans in Chiapas refugee camps were relocated to Campeche and Quintana Roo, 1,000 km away on the Yucatan peninsula, following an attack by a Guatemalan army unit in April 1984, which killed six refugees. Earlier, in May 1983, President Miguel de la Madrid had picked Chiapas as the site for launching his regional investment program. This program involved few indigenous Mexicans, however, and no refugees, since the latter had been refused permanent asylum. Even children of refugees, denied birth certificates, could never attain the citizenship to which, under the Mexican Constitution, they were entitled. In sum, "Mexico (did) not want to make land available to Guatemalan refugees because that would encourage them to become self-sufficient and give their status a more permanent character."[24]

Given their precarious situation, the more than 20,000 refugees who remained in Chiapas were less concerned with future-oriented sustainable agriculture and forestry practices than with feeding themselves, toward which end they cleared even more of the Lacandon forest. Many of these refugees hailed from other areas of Guatemala than the Lacandon, and were less familiar with the local ecology and its appropriate management, increasing conflict both with local populations and the local environment itself.[25]

Given this situation, and effectively faced with a problem of its own making, de la Madrid's administration, as much to head off socioenvironmental conflict as anything else, thereupon embarked on an unprecedented welfare improvement program, investing, in 1983, nearly $1 billion in an effort that should have resulted in new schools, health clinics, nutrition, and roads.[26] Unfortunately, much of the money ended up elsewhere than intended, resulting in many uncompleted projects and dashed expectations. *Ejido* Morelia, for example, which is located near the pivotal town of Altamirano and was once a property of the Castellanos Dominguez family, "has a basketball court but no net, a government clinic but no government doctor, no potable water, a . . . schoolhouse but only one teacher (three days a week), even a church without a priest."[27]

After the Guatemalan military incursion of April 1984, President de la Madrid's policy changed direction: emphasis on tightened security replaced efforts at environmental protection and reduced conflict. A "strategic highway" almost 450 kilometers long was cut through the Lacandon forest bordering Guatemala. Not coincidentally, perhaps, the road also opened up the area to oil exploration and to the eventual construction of hydroelectric dams.[28] It also undoubtedly helped the resettlement into Chiapas of even more out-of-state colonists, invited by the government to "help fill the vacuum of settlement near the border with Guatemala and thus prevent the incursion of Guatemalan refugees, whom the government confined to border camps."[29]

Chiapas: The Problems

Chiapas, one of the three Mexican states with the lowest socioeconomic development, has the highest illiteracy rate (30–50 percent) of Mexico's 31 states and the Federal District.[30] Wages are one-third the national average: in late 1994, 40 percent of farmers earned under US$50 per month, half of the then-prevailing Mexican minimum wage; almost 60 percent receive less than the minimum wage; and, in line with figures reported in *Reforma* for the general plight of Mexico's indigenous people, more than three out of four in Chiapas earn less than twice the extremely low minimum wage.[31] Some 80 percent of those dependent on cash-cropping earn less than $250 per month. Most disturbing, however, a large number of working Mayans receive no wages at all. An estimated 64,000 families are small-scale coffee growers, marginal producers of a crop that has lost 60 percent of its value on the international market since the price crash of 1990. Nearly all families grow (or grew) corn, some of which has been exported in the past: but the market for Mexican corn has been decimated by cheap hybrid varieties imported, under NAFTA, from the United States.

Mayan women are responsible for a great many of these agricultural activities, as well as for the preservation and transmission of associated environmental knowledge. They must carry out these tasks while bearing large numbers of children: mean fertility is 2.8 children in Chiapas overall, but 7.0 among the Lacandon. Adolescent girls are often sold into marriage before age 15, and the Mayans of Chiapas suffer Mexico's highest maternal mortality rate. While multilingualism is common among the more mobile male population, 30 to 40 percent of the women are monolingual (speaking no Spanish), and their literacy rate of 40 percent compares poorly with the national average of 88 percent.

Chiapas has the highest death rates in Mexico: its infant mortality rate is at the very least twice the national average. One-third of adult deaths are due to curable infectious diseases. Comparisons with Cuba's medical system may be gratuitously unfair, but Mexico is a much richer country, and the ratio of one doctor for every 2,000 patients in Chiapas compares rather unfavorably with one for every 270 in Cuba.

In a sense, Chiapas has been operated (literally "mined") as an internal colony. With 4 percent of Mexico's land area and population, Chiapas is the source of 20 percent of national income. While the state generates nearly one half of Mexico's energy, it is variously estimated that 63–70 percent of homes have no electricity, and 70–90 percent have no access to potable water (accounting in part for the high number of infant deaths due to dysentery). Chiapas produces nearly $1/3$ of Mexico's meat supply, but 90 percent of indigenes rarely eat meat. In the past, protein needs were partially met through a subsistence diet of corn, beans, and squash.[32]

Health conditions reflect chronic problems with food security as well as an inadequate health care delivery system. In turn, these problems derive from inequitable and insecure land tenure. The Constitution of 1917 (the major product of the Mexican Revolution) initiated, through Article 27, a program of land redistribution establishing a system of collective farms called *ejidos*. This land redistribution program was never completed, with Chiapas being one of the regions to receive the promise of reform—though it has never completely experienced the reality of reform.

The Cardenas administration of the 1930s implemented land reform policies in parts of Chiapas, and since then the processing of land claims has been an extremely difficult, tortuous, time-consuming process. Prior to the early 1990s, some success had been achieved. This proved, however, to be a mixed blessing since much of western Chiapas was in the hands of ranchers and other large-scale landowners, and the only land available to settle claims was in the forested eastern part of the state.

In 1992, the much-publicized "reform" to Article 27 of the Constitution of 1917 brought "an end to the land reform policies that have shaped the government's relation to the peasantry for half a century."[33] Not only did this end hopes for the secure land tenure that encourages environmental stewardship, but it also created an atmosphere of cynicism toward those agrarian authorities that had once been perceived as allies. The government replaced large landowners as the hated enemy by taking over their role:

First, the state came to act as a self-interested proprietor of national lands rather than as a facilitator of peasant needs. Governmental action in the creation and administration of biosphere reserves in Chiapas were seen as completely arbitrary. Local populations were involved neither in decision-making concerning these reserves nor in their subsequent management. Bioreserves were deemed off-limits to peasants, exacerbating the pressures on remaining lands. As a result, the reserves were seen as challenges to be overcome rather than as essential elements in the lifeways of all the area's inhabitants.

Second, the government, by rewarding peasants loyal to the ruling party, set peasants against peasants, just as hated landlords had once conceded marginal lands to "their" peasants as a bulwark against the claims of other peasants in the earlier phases of agrarian reform.[34]

Finally, the government played a significant role in the demise of sustainable agricultural practice. Prior to 1982, the male members of many Chiapaneco families had become accustomed to spending time elsewhere as laborers in the public sector. After

1982, when the government slashed employment, workers were told that "the President wants you to go back to farming."[35] This worked a severe hardship on many Chiapaneco families. Some inhabitants of Zinacantán, however, living near or along the Pan American highway, were able to return to farming without giving up nonfarm work. Their additional income enabled them to purchase herbicides and artificial fertilizers, reducing both fallow periods in the Zinacanteco *ejidos* and the number of family members and hired laborers required for weeding, and the like. Family members of these more affluent farmers could thus work in the nonfarm economy, further increasing the family's wealth, while those who could not afford fertilizers and weed sprays became relatively poorer, often forced to rent their *ejido* plots to their richer neighbors. As a result, in some areas, preexisting systems of sustainable agriculture simply disappeared.

Thus, the end of land reform, absence of public participation in ecological preservation efforts in biosphere reserves, and unsustainable agricultural practices seem destined to exacerbate existing environmental problems of Chiapas. When ex-President Carlos Salinas de Gortari, in 1992, "reformed" Article 27 by eliminating land redistribution and allowing the private sale of *ejido* lands, it became clear that subsistence agriculture was doomed for many, if not most, Chapaneco indigenes and peasants, and that promises of social change were unlikely ever to be fulfilled.[36]

The Zapatista Uprising: Origins[37]

The events that led to the Zapatista rebellion did not begin in the 1990s, nor are they a product of the 20th century alone. The Yucatan peninsula and Chiapas, areas of the largest Mayan population in Mexico, have never enjoyed serenity. Historically, Yucatan was the site of a struggle for independence that did not end until the beginning of this century. Chiapas witnessed the Tzotzil-Tzeltal uprising of 1712, the Caste Wars, and several actions by the Chamula, among these the siege of San Cristobal de las Casas in 1869 and the Jacinto Perez ("Pajarito") rebellion of 1911–12.[38]

However, while the social and political antecedents of the Zapatista rebellion stretch back to the time of the Conquest, the environmental crises are of more recent, and more international, origin. In an way, these environmental crises are rooted in two phenomena that blossomed in the United States during the post–World War II era, both associated with surburbanization: escalating demand for houses, and the fast-food industry. Houses implied furniture and fast food implied hamburgers: with demand for houses came demands for increased supplies of tropical hardwoods; and with demand for fast food came demands for cheap meat. The supply of North American lumber was adequate for construction but not for home furnishings, while North American beef was priced out of the fast-food market. Beginning to fill the gap were the countries of Latin America, as the oddly related demands for wood and beef began to exert increased pressure on tropical forests.

Shortly after World War II, and even before governmental decrees of 1957 and 1960 officially opened the Lacandon to colonization, informal invasion of the Chiapas forest region had begun. Starting in 1954, people from other parts of Mexico arrived in Chiapas in increasing numbers. In a 1972 mass gathering in Tecate, Baja California, to which one of the authors had been invited, then–President Luis Echeverria announced grand plans for development of Mexico's northern and southern frontiers. In the same year as the Tecate meeting, President Echeverria "gave" almost $2/3$ of a million hectares of the Lacandon forest to the indigenous heads of 66 Lacandon families, its supposed "original owners," expelling thousands of Tzeltal and Chol settlers: all, in fact, but 1,100 other inhabitants. Members of the Lancandon families had unexpectedly been changed into large-scale landowners overnight. Bribed with religion, material goods, and alcohol, they shortly thereafter signed long-term contracts giving widespread timber-cutting rights to concessionaires such as the Castellanos Dominguez family. In an extraordinary about-face, Echeverria then canceled most private contracts, turning over forestry rights to a quasi-governmental logging corporation.

The evicted settlers, under the leadership of priests and volunteer laity sent by Bishop Samuel Ruiz, began to organize in the Lacandon. A guerrilla organization called "Las Fuerzas Populares de la Liberacion Nacional," formed in Ocosingo, was effectively destroyed by federal troops in 1974. But the torch had been lit.

Twelve days into 1978 and two years into the next presidential term, Jose Lopez Portillo created the Montes Azules Biosphere Reserve, carving 1,250 square miles out of the heart of the Lacandon forest. This, the first international ecological reserve in Mexico, duly recognized by the United Nations (but *not* by the inhabitants of the forest, who were forcibly evicted), was created in the absence of any Mexican public participation whatsoever. *Ejidatarios* in the cañadas bordering the reserve, prevented for a time from expanding *ejido* lands into the forest, soon learned to move the boundary posts when no one was looking. As few funds had been allocated to patrolling the area, nocturnal boundary-shifting posed no great problem.

As the *crisis economica* deepened, so did both pressure on the Lacandon and concern for its potential destruction. The "Ruta Maya" concept was intended to call attention to Mexican efforts at cultural and environmental preservation in its southernmost states of Yucatan, Quintana Roo, Tabasco, and Chiapas. During 1992, in another apparently conciliatory move toward both environmental protection and indigenous interests, President Salinas canceled a hydroelectric project in the heart of Chiapas and redirected a road to avoid its passing through an important nature reserve.[39]

During the energy crisis of the 1970s, Mexico experienced an oil boom, and President Lopez Portillo uttered his now-famous "Edsel" statement: "In the future, the only thing Mexicans will have to worry about is how to spend their money." By 1982, the energy crisis had turned into an energy *glut*, to which Lopez Portillo's response was: "The Mexican mother can always be counted upon to add more water to the stew." The "Mexican Miracle" was over; in the *crisis economica* that followed, the fledgling middle class it was credited with producing had started slipping downhill. For the rural poor, and especially the indigenous poor who had never participated in the "miracle," it was more of the same. The rich, for their part, were about to discover Reaganomics—and about to get much richer.

In the Mexican economic malaise of the 1980s, the southern states slipped into invisibility, and even greater poverty. The pace of deforestation increased. Established cycles of clearing, invasion, and eviction continued at an accelerated rate. Cattle ranchers in Chiapas continued to expand their lands into forest lands earlier cleared for farming by neighboring Mayans, who were forced to move onto increasingly steep, less fertile, and more erosion-prone mountain slopes. As the 1980s opened, just 19 families controlled more than 70,000 sq km of Chiapas's best land.

Much of this cultural and environmental damage was aided and abetted by General Absalon Castellanos, designated as governor of Chiapas by President de la Madrid in 1982 during a time of Guatemalan army incursions; he was named supposedly because of his experience as former commander of the military zone including Chiapas. Castellanos, however, had added to the woes of Chiapas's indigenous population even before he became governor of the state. During the 1960s he had sold land to Tojolobal sharecroppers, which, in the 1970s, payment having been completed, he repossessed on the grounds that no papers had been signed. In 1980, as commander of the Chiapas Military Zone, he ordered his troops to open fire on a peaceful gathering of Tojolobal in Golonchan, killing at least 50. In 1982, because of his military record, he was selected by newly installed President Miguel de la Madrid as the man best able to cope with the waves of refugees entering from Guatemala to escape the genocidal regime of Efrain Rios Montt. The Guatemalan army followed, often penetrating into the Mexican side of the border zone.

The repressiveness of the Castellanos regime is well-documented. Its acts of terrorism—torture, murder, and "disappearances"—are still coming to light. Castellanos used state funds to build roads connecting the 14 ranches owned by family members and (unofficially) encouraged his brothers to establish sawmills in the Lacandon forest. One brother, who chose to set up his lumbering enterprise in the Chimilapas forest reserve on the Chiapas-Oaxaca border, was captured, with his crew, and briefly detained by Zoques in 1987.[40]

Meanwhile, a resistance force, destined to break out seven years later, was beginning to organize in the inner reaches of the Lacandon. Aided by groups of volunteers from northern Mexico—*Torreonistas* (among whom may have been the young man who later became "Subcomandante Marcos")—Mayans began taking control of their lives and their environment. In 1989, then-governor of the state of Chiapas and later Secretary of the Interior Patrocinio Gonzelez Blanco Garrido (ostensibly for environmental reasons, and a year in advance of federal orders) established a state Forestry Patrol and issued a decree imposing a complete ban on logging in Chiapas. Wood already cut by Chiapaneco *ejidos* and used in cooking was supposed to have been exempt from the decree, but Judicial Police and the Forestry Patrol seized farmers' trucks carrying cut wood in Ocosingo, Margaritas, and Altamirano.[41]

In August 1989, newly inaugurated president Carlos Salinas de Gortari, in a symbolic act designed as much as anything to reduce more than a century of hostility between Guatemala and Mexico, embraced Guatemalan President Vinicio Cerezo on the Suchiate bridge connecting the two countries. The occasion was the signing of a cooperative agreement on the management of border lands, environmental planning, and the possible establishment of international parks: "La Ruta Maya." The business community, beginning to recognize the tourist potential of areas away from Mexico's traditional beach resorts, organized their counterpart organization—"El Mundo Maya"—to exploit the opportunities. Mayan labor in Yucatan and Quintana Roo had been employed in beach resorts only at the lowest levels: nothing different was anticipated for inland areas. There, economic pressures continued to mount. During 1989 and 1990, the International Coffee Organization floated the price of coffee on the world market, ruining some 64,000 Chiapaneco peasant farming families.

Not long thereafter, then–U.S. President George Bush expanded his promotion of "the new hemispheric order" to include what has come to be called "NAFTA" (North American Free Trade Agreement). He persuaded President Salinas de Gortari to the idea, which, because of its "fast-track" provisions, would mean initiating radical structural readjustment in Mexico in an incredibly short period of time.[42] Added to the misery of coffee-growing families was another misery now imposed on farmers growing *other* crops, as Salinas began to remove subsidies on corn, which then could not compete with imported hybrid varieties on the "free" market.

Indigenous Action

The political, economic, social, and environmental events outlined above prompted a variety of local responses. Armed uprising was not the beginning point—merely one point in a broad spectrum of struggles aimed at fashioning sustainable survival.

Mayan community groups, aided by "Torreonistas" from northern Mexico, became involved in a variety of sustainability projects that were indigenously initiated, organized, staffed, and implemented. Small-scale Mayan forestry cooperatives, by processing lumber on site, reduced the damage normally caused by extensive road construction. Finished lumber is made into furniture in small local factories. Other sustainability projects have involved various modifications of indigenous agricultural practices, combining subsistence and cash cropping, animal husbandry, and small-game hunting. In response to international threats to the marketing of Chiapas's agricultural products, some coffee growers have turned to producing and exporting organically grown and processed coffee.[43]

Several nongovernmental organizations are now cooperating closely with each other as members of the "Consorcio para la Conservacion y el Desarrollo Sostenible del Sureste de Mexico" and with the Mayan communities. These include ECOSFERA (Centro de Estudios para la Conservacion de los Recursos Naturales); PRONATURA-Chiapas; CISC (Centro de Investigaciones en Salud de Comitan); and PROCOMITH (Programa de Colaboracion en Medicina Tradicional Herbolaria). Programs sponsored include the management and conservation of natural resources in the zones of the greatest biodiversity in Mexico's southeast (principally in "El Ocote" and Lacandon forests, Calakmul, and Sian Ka'an); environmental education for rural and urban communities; protection of migratory birds; reforestation; agricultural, reproductive, and psychosocial health; and identifying and classifying (for nonindigenes) Mayan traditional herbal and medical knowledge. CIES (Centro de Investigaciones Ecologicas del Sureste) is involved in promoting the mental health of Guatemalan refugees and in agroforestry programs, the latter funded by the Rockefeller Foundation.

In another part of Mexico outside Chiapas, a 350,000-hectare tropical forest is managed by a group of Huasteca, a Mayan people.[44] This experiment is notable in that it applies ancient, sustainable forest management techniques to another area of the country. These Huasteca harvest 90 percent of the plant species found in natural forest groves called te'lom, some for subsistence or nutritional supplements, others for the market (incrementing the income of women). With this system, an average Huastec family can subsist on 4 hectares (10 acres) of tropical forest. Low-input, high-productive uses characterize traditional Mayan forest management practices, which (1) are more land-efficient (than conventional uses), (2) use resources very efficiently, (3) have low ecological impact, and (4) provide diversified sources of income.

As yet another example, a union of *ejidos* in the Motozintla region of the Pacific coastal range of Chiapas has dedicated itself to sustainable, organic agricultural production of such cash crops for Mexican and foreign markets as apples, beans, coffee, corn, honey, and mushrooms. Its organization could well have been the administrative model for the EZLN: like the Zapatistas, its general assembly is made up of ordinary farmers who hold greater authority than the administrators and officers, who are at the bottom.

Neither the Mexican government nor local caciques and cattle ranchers have looked very favorably on these attempts to develop environmentally sustainable self-help activity. Land-poor Mayan families have been accused of invading neighboring ranches, especially those on land the Mayans believe was illegally appropriated. The ruling party, for its part, has been promoting the "National Solidarity Program," under which local "sweat equity" is contributed to community betterment programs ostensibly approved and managed by governmental agents. However: "Depending on local conditions, traditions of collective action (or the lack thereof), leadership, and other variables, Solidarity Committees have led in some places to a reinforcement of traditional authoritarian practices . . . Solidarity has been a quintessential 'presidentialist' program. It represents a reassertion of centralized control over resource allocation."[45]

Attempts at unaided self-help, and especially the formation of independent cooperatives, have met with some hostility. Examples are numerous: one community, where a first cooperative coordinates 800 artisan women in 15 neighboring communities and a second trains the same women in accounting and administration, has accused the Mexican army of cutting off their water supply. In the El Prado *ejido*, army elements "destroyed the community pantry, leaving coffee, beans and corn spread all over. They destroyed a motorized saw that was used by the community, the windmill and tortilla makers. . . . They used the community's medicines, broke the hoses used for potable water (and) burned the only documentation for their land and the 'presidential resolution' (title insurance), the only things they have to certify their agrarian rights. . . ."[46]

The Zapatista Uprising

The U.S. Constitution is short, relatively simple, and very difficult to change. The Mexican Constitution is long, complex, and easy to change by presidential fiat. This was amply demonstrated in 1992 when President Salinas changed Article 27 of the Constitution, one of the centerpieces of the Revolution of 1917, effectively abrogating two of the major results of that Revolution: land redistribution and the establishment of *ejidos*. The word "reform" is strange in that it has been used to label changes both toward and away from social justice. In this case, as described earlier, the "reforms" initiated by Salinas eliminated the never-completed process of redistributing land to peasants, except for *ejido* land, which was to be privatized and made available for sale.

At the end of 1992, the newly formed Zapatista Army of National Liberation (EZLN) clandestinely made a decision to go to war. On May 22, 1993, the army clashed with the Zapatistas, just two days before Cardinal Posadas's assassination in

Guadalajara. On May 26, the army withdrew. In December, rumors reached the Zapatistas that the army was ready to strike again, with the excuse of eliminating drug traffickers in the area. This was not entirely unexpected, given that one of Salinas's tickets into the North American free-trade games being refereed by then–U.S. President Bush was his agreement to assign 20 percent of the armed forces to drug enforcement. But it was not welcome news in Chiapas, either, and probably contributed to the decision to rise up in force on January 1, 1993, the day NAFTA was to take effect.

In the one-and-a-half weeks that followed, between 150 (official estimate) and 500 people (based on reliable, unofficial sources) died. On January 2, Absalon Castellanos, the ex-governor loved by ranchers and despised by Indians, was taken prisoner by the EZLN: he was freed, unharmed, on Ash Wednesday, February 16, when the on again–off again peace talks began (and which dragged on for more than two years). The ten days of war in Chiapas that shook the official image of calm, passive, serene, obedient Mexico, made the front pages of the world's press—and made Mexico no longer an invisible player, an "extra" on the world stage.

Initially, there appeared to be considerable public support for the Zapatistas in Mexico as a whole. Their struggle was seen by many as national, rather than regional: a call for social justice by those who cried *¡Ya basta!* The central figure of the Zapatistas, Subcomandante Marcos was the epitome of the charismatic guerrilla leader: crisp, strong, determined, even poetic. EZLN visibility, however, was reduced by the string of assassinations that began in March 1994; and public support was undermined by the devaluation of the peso in December and accusations on the part of the incoming president, Ernesto Zedillo, that the Zapatistas, by driving away foreign investment, were the prime cause of Mexico's economic collapse. The Zapatistas chose to demonstrate how little the army controlled the Lacandon by seizing 38 municipalities in December 1994, and then melting back into the forest.

Zedillo's accusations had drawn some attention away from the role undoubtedly played by the United States; however, banner headlines on the front page of the newspaper *La Extra* on January 15, 1995, accused Wall Street and the CIA of supporting Subcomandante Marcos. Shortly thereafter, Zedillo first moved military forces into the areas of the Lacandon forest openly controlled by the EZLN since the January 1994 uprising; then, in a classic display of indecision, withdrew these in mid-February. The withdrawal may have been in part an attempt to avoid potentially negative publicity resulting from the airing of a Chase Manhattan Bank consultant report, issued on January 13, 1995, but not made public until February 13, stating: "While Chiapas, in our opinion, does not pose a fundamental threat to Mexican political stability, it is perceived to be so by many in the investment community. The government will need to eliminate the Zapatistas to demonstrate their effective control of the national territory and of security policy."[47]

During this brief period of accelerated activity by Mexico's military, between 20,000 and 30,000 peasants and indigenous people of the area, fearing military action against their villages, withdrew into the forest, putting further pressure on the battle-scarred Lacandon to provide them with firewood and land for cultivation. While precise figures are unavailable, observers claim that recent damage to the forest has been considerable; thus, in early 1995, the environment appears to have been one prime victim of this undeclared war. Although the government seemed to have reached the beginnings of an accord with the EZLN in early 1996, environmental degradation continues.

While the Zapatista uprising has caused some villagers to flee deeper into the forest, others have left the region entirely, migrating to areas of Yucatecan tourism or swelling already overpopulated cities. Prompting people to move are armed conflict and the increasing poverty resulting in part from environmental devastation and in part from government policy (the Mexican Secretary of Agriculture recently declared that 17 million rural farmers are simply too many and that at least some must become urban wage-earners). One result is that homeless Chiapaneco children between ages 2 and 10 are appearing on the streets of Cancun.[48]

Epilogue

There is no conclusion to this Zapatista story. The Consulta (an unofficial public referendum promoted by, among others, the national government), organized by the Alianza Civica, was held in late August 1995 and drew between 1 and 2 million Mexican voters and a large number of foreign ballots. This national plebiscite on peace and democracy indicated considerable support for the Zapatistas.[49] Prolonged and often-interrupted dialogue between the Mexican government and the EZLN resulted, on February 13, 1996, in the signing of the first accords, on indigenous rights and culture. This accord, however, represented only one point in a much larger call for reform. The Zapatistas continued to tie their human rights agenda to questions of environmental justice:

> . . . the sixth point of the Declaration of the Lacandon Jungle calls for the end to the plunder of "our natural wealth" in zones controlled by the Zapatistas . . . the rebels' Revolutionary Agrarian Law calls for an end to contamination of water sources in the jungle, the preservation of virgin forest zones, and reforestation of logged-out areas. The lands they demand, say the rebels, should not be carved out of what's left of the Lacandon, but, rather, confiscated from the finqueros.[50]

The Mexican government, on the other hand, confronted by the country's worst economic crisis in half a century, has relegated both environmental issues and social justice to low positions on its current agenda. In May 1996, in an apparent attempt to defuse the situation, President Zedillo made the unprecedented announcement of an intention to revise the Mexican Constitution to recognize explicitly, for the first time, the rights of indigenous people. The Zapatistas responded cautiously to what seemed, at least superficially, a positive move on the government's part. Perhaps the EZLN was right in its concern. The later announcement that units involved in the "war" against narcotics traffic were to be militarized reinforced the fears of some, reported in early June 1996, that antinarcotics action might be used as a pretext for further military repression of the EZLN, thereby reheating what has become Mexico's "cold war" in Chiapas.

As of late September, 1996, no further substantive agreements have been reached since those on indigenous rights in early 1996, and even these have not been translated into binding Mexican law as promised. The EZLN's greatest success during the last year has been to turn the deadlocked peace talks into an ongoing national seminar bringing together the best and brightest of Mexico's "civil society" (the burgeoning community of nongovernmental organizations and independent scholars). It has also sparked activism and involvement in the formulation of its negotiating stance—organizing and utilizing input from the hundreds of grassroots "Comites Civiles de Dialogo" (Citizen's Committees for Dialogue), and sponsoring a successful series of regional gatherings around the world, put together by its solidarity network. This latter effort culminated in the first Intercontinental Congress for Humanity and Against Neo-Liberalism held in five different Zapatista communities between July 27 and August 3, 1996, with more than 3,000 attending from 43 countries. This gathering served both as an international Zapatista solidarity conference and as the point of departure for an ongoing, transnational, decentralized network of activists in anticorporate struggles. A second Intercontinental Congress in 1997 is planned at a European site (location still to be determined).

Sixteen "presumed" Zapatistas continue to be held for charges originally brought as part of the Zedillo government's failed crackdown on the EZLN in February 1995. In August 1996 seven of these prisoners were sentenced to prison terms of 6 years and 9 months. There are other clear indicators of a prevailing "hard line" emerging from the divided governing circles, including the appointment of military commanders in charge of "public security" in 19 of Mexico's 33 political entities (including the Federal District of Mexico itself). This latest surge in militarization was sparked by the June 28, 1996, emergence in Guerrero state of a new armed revolutionary insurgent group known as the People's Revolutionary Army (EPR). The EPR is reported to have other armed contingents in the states of Hidalgo, Veracruz, and Oaxaca—states that join Chiapas in the ranks of the poorest of the poor.

Peace talks with the government were suspended unilaterally by the EZLN on September 4, 1996, amid mounting tensions over the lack of progress in the latest round of negotiations. Evidently, the sharp divisions within the ruling party have affected the Zedillo government's will or ability to pursue substantive negotiations regarding issues of "Democracy and Justice" (which touch on fundamental issues of political and electoral reform). These divisions are reflected in the exile of former President Salinas and the imprisonment of his brother on charges of conspiracy in the assassination of the head of the ruling party while Salinas was still president, as well as mounting evidence of the Salinas family's vast, illicit enrichment through alliances with some of the country's most powerful industrial groups (including those controlling the television industry, the production of tortillas, the construction of newly privatized major highways and office buildings throughout the country, the largest telephone company, and various major retail chains, among others). Rumors persist as to Salinas's complicity and/or cover-up of the assassination of his originally anointed successor, ruling party 1994 presidential nominee Luis Donaldo Colosio. The two major additional precipitating factors in the breaking off of the peace talks by the EZLN include: (1) the impact of the emergence of the EPR, which has followed up its initial appearance on June 28 with spectacular simultaneous attacks on military and police targets in seven states (including key resorts such as Acapulco in the state of Guerrero, and Huatalco in the heavily indigenous state of Oaxaca) during the night of August 28–29, 1996, and further isolated attacks in early September 1996; and (2) the continuously intensifying militarization in the state of Chiapas, especially near the Zapatista bases, but also throughout the country in the wake of the EPR's emergence.

The current fear is that the government is planning a lightning strike against Zapatista strongholds in the near future in an attempt to capture or kill the movement's identified leaders, and as part of an overall crackdown sparked by the challenge posed by the EPR. All this is happening in the context of vastly increased ties between the U.S. and Mexican military, ostensibly for purposes of joint efforts in the drug war, but with few if any real restrictions on the conditions of use for military material provided for antidrug operations (for example, the Mexican military may use drug-war materials to supply its massive national counterinsurgency operations). The popular impression is that now, more than ever, U.S. tax dollars are buying death and repression for Mexico's popular movements and organizations, especially in areas such as Chiapas, Guerrero, Oaxaca, Tabasco, Veracruz, Hidalgo, Morelos, Chihuahua, and around Mexico City.

Notes

1. Twenty-five "presumed" Zapatistas of various alleged ranks were rounded up in the simultaneous early morning raids in February 1995. Meanwhile, it was widely rumored that Marcos's capture was imminent or had already taken place and was being kept secret until his initial questioning had been completed. A witch-hunt atmosphere was quickly generated by press reports of arrest warrants being sought for an "enemies" list of over 2,000 names developed by Mexican military intelligence, including Bishop Ruiz himself. Other names included leftist leaders, people involved in trade union movements, and people who were supportive of the EZLN's demands such as the radical lawyer-activists Ricardo Barco and Benito Miron. The March Citizen's Information Mission was intended to provide a representative cross-section of Mexico's nongovernmental organizations and citizens' groups with an unmediated look at the situation in Chiapas—at first hand—in order to assess the impact of the military's February crackdown.

2. It was notable that the *ejido* assembly of Monte Flor had agreed to give these families refuge because the *ejido* was distinctively mestizo, primarily consisting of settlers from towns such as Comalapa and Motozintla, and because those seeking refuge were indigenous. But Monte Flor, a community of some 300 people that had been cleared out of the jungle 23 years ago, was clearly a well-organized, politically conscious community that felt an obligation to assist their "persecuted brothers," "sharing the same bread with them, each helping the other" as they told us the evening of Wednesday, March 9, as the night—and the Mexican Army—closed in around us.

3. *La Jornada*, Aug. 11, 1995, pp. 1, 9.

4. John Ross, *Rebellion from the Roots* (Monroe, Maine: Common Courage Press, 1995), 263.

5. *New York Times*, Jan. 17, 1995, p. A4.

6. For example, one of the authors was receiving complete daily online reports about the EZLN while in New Zealand in mid-1994.

7. Fernando Benitez, *Los Indios de Mexico* (Mexico: Ediciones Era, 1989).

8. *New York Times*, op. cit., note 5.

9. The classic work on the current situation of indigenous peoples in Mexico is Guillermo Bonfil Batalla, *Mexico Profundo: Una Civilizacion Negada* (Mexico, D.F.: Grijalbo, 1987).

10. For example, the sentiments of former President Carlos Salinas de Gortari, quoted in *International Wildlife Magazine*: "It's not automatic that with growth the environment will improve, but it is automatic that with poverty the environment will worsen." It has been equally easy to deny that such

assumedly simple, docile people could launch their own revolution, and thus to assert that it must have been fomented by outsiders.

11. Rossana Fuentes Berain and Rafael Jiminez, "Pais de Contrastes,"*Reforma*, June 4, 1995, pp. 12A–13A.

12. The evident dearth of interest and involvement on the part of the general public is not paralleled by an dearth of nongovernmental organizations devoted to environment: Cruz Ecologica Mexicana, an informational clearing house based in Mexico City, lists more than 300 environmental NGOs, in addition to the famed "Committee of 100," with offices in the capital's metropolitan area. What is most remarkable is that so many organizations have had so little apparent effect.

13. See, for example, Francisco Vidal, "Fronterra Sucia," *Reforma*, Aug. 26, 1996, p. 14A.

14. Tom Barry, *Mexico: A Country Guide* (Albuquerque, N.M.: Interhemispheric Education Resource Center, 1992).

15. David Barkin, personal communication, 1996.

16. Claudia Ramos, "Preocupa Deforestacion; es la Mas Alta del Mundo," *Reforma*, March 28, 1996, p. 1A. A view of the social conflicts involved in the deforestation specifically of the Lacandon is provided by Lourdes Arizpe, Fernanda Paz y Margarita Velazquez, *Cultura y Cambio Global: Percepciones Sociales Sobre la Deforestacion en la Selva Lacandona* (Mexico: Centro Regional de Investigaciones Multidisciplinarias, 1993).

17. Indeed, deforestation and wetlands destruction are two prime examples—albeit negative examples, in the Mexican case—of the needed interaction between environmental preservation and economic development. The solution proposed by the Mexican government to deforestation, similar to that already tried in other parts of the developing world, is plantation forestry (see, for example, Miguel Perez and Andres Resillas, "Presenta Zedillo Programa Sectoral: Impulsan Inversion en Sector Forestal," *Reforma*, March 28, 1996, p. 3A). This will certainly increase wood product, but will have little or no effect on restoring biodiversity, the centerpiece of the deforestation controversy.

18. See Sergio Aguayo Quezada, *Chiapas: Las Amenazas a la Seguridad Nacional*, Estudios del CLEE (EST-006-86), Centro Lationoamericano de Estudios Estrategicos, June 1987. And, Michael J. Dziedzic and Stephen J. Wager, "Mexico's Uncertain Quest for a Strategy to Secure its Southern Border," *Journal of Borderlands Studies* 7:1 (spring 1992) 19–48. Data from *Mexico Social (1985–1986)*, Indicadores Sociales, p. xxviii, and Agayo, *op. cit.*, note 16, p. 23.

19. Only 2.5 percent of Mexico's land area is protected in its natural form, in 44 national parks, 22 biosphere reserves of one form of another, as well as several specially designated areas. While new areas are currently coming under protection, it is unlikely that Mexico will ever rank with Costa Rica, where by 1988 27 percent of the land area had been placed under some formal protection.

20. Ross, *op. cit.*, note 4, p. 251.

21. For a critical look at the effects of "La Ruta Maya" tourism on the Mayan peoples in Quintana Roo, see Chapter 9 in this volume. A more popular (and more positive, if somewhat questionable) view is provided by Wilbur D. Garrett, "La Ruta Maya," *National Geographic* 176:4 (Oct. 1989) 424–479.

22. One positive effect of the Zapatista movement has been to unite previously disparate Mayan groups under a single cause. Another was to empower women. Unquestionably, with few exceptions, Mayan women have been subservient to men, in reproduction and other spheres, over the half-millennium since the Conquest. The Zapatistas, through the promulgation of the "Revolutionary Law of Women" as its first act on January 1, 1994, are attempting to change this situation, and it is thus not very surprising that one-third of Zapatista fighters are female, as well as several of their most prominent leaders.

23. Beatriz Manz, *Refugees of a Hidden War: The Aftermath of Counterinsurgency in Guatemala* (Albany, N.Y.: SUNY Press, 1988).

24. Fernando M. Olguin, "Guatemalan Refugees in Mexico: International Legal Standards," *Fletcher Forum of World Affairs* 13:2 (summer 1989) 327–355, 345.

25. Duncan Earle, personal communication at the annual meeting of the Association of Borderlands Scholars, 1996.

26. Alan Riding, *Distant Neighbors: A Portrait of the Mexicans* (New York: Vintage Books, 1989), 293–294.

27. Ross, *op. cit.*, note 4, p. 114.

28. Riding, *op. cit.*, note 24, p. 293.

29. George A. Collier and Elizabeth Q. Lowery, *Basta! Land and the Zapatista Rebellion in Chiapas* (Oakland, Calif.: Food First Books, 1994), 43.

30. *Reforma*, June 4, 1995.

31. *Ibid.* The Mexican minimum wage varies slightly by region, but is currently under US$60 per month in most parts of the country.

32. Ross, *op. cit.*, note 4, p. 72.

33. Collier and Lowery, *op. cit.*, note 27, p. 45

34. *Ibid.*, p. 51.

35. *Ibid.*, p. 101.

36. Paradoxically—and in spite of the above statistics—Chiapas has, of all Mexican states, always cast the largest proportion of votes for the PRI, the party that has ruled Mexico since 1928, and under which the problems of the people of the state have been largely ignored.

37. Some popular accounts have appeared in nonacademic journals of the dramatic events in Mexico's southernmost state. These include Medea Benjamin, "On the Road with the Zapatistas," *Progressive* 1995 (May) 28–31; Marc Cooper, *The Zapatistas* (Westfield, N.J.: Open Magazine Pamphlet Series, 1994); and Saul Landau, "The Challenge of the Chiapas," *Progressive* 1995 (April) 41–43.

38. Many argue that the roots of the Zapatista revolt can be traced back to the Spanish Conquest, almost 500 years ago. The monuments that have been erected, such as those to Mendoza in Yucatan and Mazariegos in Chiapas, commemorate the cruelest of the conquistadors. To celebrate the Columbian Quincentennial in 1992, local Mayans pulled down and destroyed the statue of Mazariegos in the center of San Cristobal de las Casas, as the culmination of a march in which over 50,000 indigenous activists participated—this is considered to have been the largest demonstration in southern Mexico in recent history and a key forerunner to the 1994 uprising.

39. In 1994, in the wake of the Chiapas uprising and as NAFTA was coming into effect, Salinas first reversed his 1992 decision, and then closed two natural gas wells, making PEMEX, the national petroleum company created after the nationalization of oil, a net importer of natural gas. This had small effect on most Mexican households, as little piped natural gas is available for domestic use; most is for industry. It had even less effect on indigenous inhabitants of the Lacandon, most of whom cannot afford gas, even bottled gas, for any purpose. More important impacts came from petroleum drilling; thus, shortly after the rebellion began, Zapatistas forced oil exploration crews to abandon test-drilling operations and to flee the Lacandon forest.

40. Ross, *op. cit.*, note 4, p. 160.

41. *Ibid.*

42. President Salinas, a tiny man, threw himself into this task with such enormous zeal that he acquired the nickname "*La hormiga atomica*" ("the atomic ant").

43. Barry, *op. cit.*, note 14.

44. John O. Browder, "Alternative Rainforest Uses," in Susan E. Place, ed., *Tropical Rainforests: Latin American Nature and Society in Transition* (Wilmington, Del.: Scholarly Resources, Inc., 1993).

45. In other words, solidarity efforts have typically been concentrated in those areas in which the PRI is most interested in getting votes. See Wayne Cornelius, "Mexico's Delayed Democratization," *Foreign Policy* 95 (summer 1994) 53–71.

46. Bulletin, Fray Bartoleme de la Casas Human Rights Center, San Cristobal de las Casas, March 3, 1995.

47. Chase Bank, "Political Update," quoted in Ken Silverstein and Alexander Cockburn, "The Killers and the Killing," *Nation* 1995 (March 6) 306–310.

48. *Proceso*, March 20, 1995, p. 30.

49. An analysis of a profile of those voting, however, casts doubt on the representativeness of the sample. In the months that followed, the broadsheet *Aguascalientes* announced that what would emerge from the base of the EZLN would not be a political party in the traditional sense, as some speculated, but rather an FZLN, or Frente Zapatista de Liberacion Nacional, which would claim, as its goal, the formation and development of a "civil organization"—a political force in which all citizens could participate. The ranks of the FZLN will presumably be more broadly based.

50. Ross, *op. cit., note 4, p. 265.*

PART SIX

Postwar Matters

Much of this book has focused on the genesis of human environmental crisis, the varied experience of crisis, and the range of responses. In the following two chapters, we turn our attention to the aftermath. What happens when crisis and misery give way to violent conflict, and when this in turn gives way to substantive change?

Lucia Ann McSpadden takes us to Eritrea, where peace has returned, after decades of war, drought, and famine. With the aid of various international agencies and NGOs, refugees are also beginning to go home. McSpadden examines the tension between the new Eritrean government and the international organizations that play increasingly problematic roles in the repatriation agenda by restricting the flow of aid and usurping power in the rebuilding process. Aid has, for the most part, been used to fund the resettlement of refugees, rather than to improve or enhance the environment to which they return (a war-torn landscape, and an impoverished population who remained, fought, survived, and now must watch those who fled return home in a well-financed manner). McSpadden demonstrates that repatriation means more than moving people across borders, and more than giving them food and aid to tide them over. Repatriation means helping to rebuild the structures that sustain the country, and this requires measures that allow food production systems to thrive again.

Ben Wisner takes us to South Africa, where apartheid has been abolished and the country is struggling to rebuild all aspects of society—identity, economy, political structure, infrastructure. Problems include the need to build infrastructure and opportunity (economic flows), but also at a more fundamental level the problems involve confronting and transforming the culture of violence. Thus, one of the key questions in building the nation is how to rebuild and reinvigorate respect for local structures. Wisner gives us some sense of the immensity of the difficulties, and suggests that defining, shaping, prioritizing, and implementing response (with the aid of government) on a neighborhood-by-neighborhood basis will empower the community, which, in turn, will empower the nation.

Both chapters emphasize the difficulties involved in dealing with the legacies of war. With the galvanizing power of an enemy now placed in the past, one of the major problems confronting these reemerging nations is how to handle the social, political, economic, cultural, and psychological vacuums created when the culture of violence is removed, and when little remains to fill the gap. What happens when the bottom succeeds and becomes the top? Will the successors in radical transformations of power become that which they fought against, shaped by the power and needs of governance to conform and create an established, entrenched elite? Both McSpadden and Wisner argue that building sustainable sociopolitical and economic systems requires engagement at all levels—not just bottom up (in the context of struggle for change) or top down (in the context of rebuilding).

CHAPTER 11

Life and Death Matters in Eritrean Repatriation

Lucia Ann McSpadden

On the Road to Mendefera, South of Asmara, Eritrea, May 1995

I used to play in the woods here when I was a child," Woldemichael said in a soft, sad voice.[1] Surprised at the apparent impossibility, I ask him, "How could this be true?" The land stretches out in front and back, on the right and left of us, in undulating open plains, mostly dirt and scrub grass. Here and there are small, desert-like plants and one or two lone scraggly trees. The earth is dry and dusty—the rainy season has not yet started. It is "open sky" country; one can see far in all directions except where the view is jarred by a rusting tank left by the retreating Ethiopian army in 1991, making graphic the presence of 30 years of village-to-village warfare (see photograph).

Woldemichael's angry response, shocking in its truth, brought home the deep wounds to the earth, to the people, and to the future of Eritrea. "The land has been destroyed by the war—the Ethiopians bombed the countryside; they cut down the trees—for construction, for fuel, to remove cover for the liberation fighters, to destroy us, I think. People were not able to farm, to care for the land. People needed fuel; they cut trees and shrubs too—anything they could find. Now you see what we must work with, what we must rebuild. Now you see that we are beggars! We will not allow you to treat us like beggars!"

Introduction[2]

First, we are dealing with people. There is an attachment, a closeness. This is the most important. Repatriation is not just statistics. It is to give back to people who have been denied their universal rights, people who have been ousted from their home because they are from a certain area—nothing else.[3]

Peace has, therefore, created new needs. We can repatriate refugees, but they need basic resources. People should be able to go back to their home countries or places of origin. . . . The Eritrean experience gives us the example—perhaps a model—and the successful carrying out should give us the experience to carry to other countries. People in many countries are going back home. Countries must be rebuilt and the reintegration of returnees is of the utmost

Lucia Ann McSpadden is an anthropologist and the Research Director at the Life and Peace Institute, Kuarnbogatan 35, S-752 39, Uppsala, Sweden. She can be reached via email (lamcspadden@nn.apc.org).

importance. Now we have the opportunity to do development programs. Therefore, we have an opportunity to consolidate peace for all the region, not just in Eritrea.[4]

The longest-standing armed conflict in Africa, the Eritrean struggle for liberation from Ethiopia, produced hundreds of thousands of refugees between 1961 and 1991. Over one quarter of Eritrea's population fled to save their lives. Although these Eritrean refugees ended up in many different countries, some being resettled in western countries, the majority, over 500,000, have been in asylum in neighboring Sudan—some for up to 20 years.[5]

The retreat of the Ethiopian army from Eritrea, in May 1991, brought this war to an end. The April 1993 referendum established Eritrea as a sovereign nation in the world of nation-states. The government of Eritrea is formed from the liberation fighters; it is not the government that caused the refugees to flee.

The return of 450,000 to 500,000 refugees from Sudan to Eritrea quickly was a salient issue for the new government of Eritrea, for the United Nations High Commissioner for Refugees (UNHCR), and for international donors. The negotiations for this repatriation were particularly prolonged and difficult, revealing the international and national complexities of repatriation and the contradictions within the international refugee system itself. In the context of a country as devastated as Eritrea, these negotiations make painfully clear the vulnerability of the refugees, of the environment, of the people and the nation. Care for the earth, care for the people who stayed behind, care for people who fled and now will return—these are all intertwined with and affected by the system of international response to refugees and their repatriation to their country of origin, a system in which power and control are central concerns. Repatriation is embedded within political, economic, environmental, and social realities. How refugees are repatriated provides the foundation for the challenge to build and sustain true peace with justice.

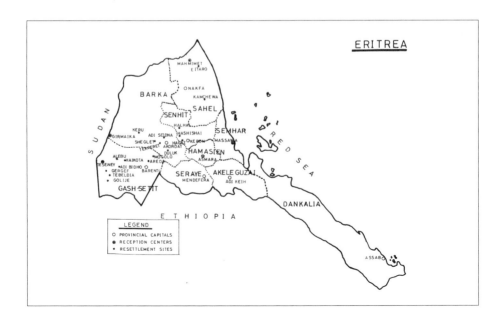

Tank abandoned in a war-torn field. Before the war, this was a lush and fertile landscape. Photograph by Lucia Ann McSpadden.

Repatriation, Peace, and Human Rights: Power and Control

> True peace is inseparable from dignity, honour, righteousness and justice, in short right relationships and honourable conditions.[6]

This quote from a Ghanian theologian lays down the qualities of a sustainable peace as well as the essential conditions for peace. Peace is not limited to the absence of war, although surely it requires the absence of armed conflict. It is not "peace at any price." The critical conditions are grounded in the basic human rights of an individual and of the community. Peace has many aspects: safety, the lack of fear, the availability of basic life necessities, the overcoming of hostilities and/or dehumanization, the elimination of barriers between peoples, between communities and nations, the balancing of power.[7]

Repatriation, the spontaneous or organized returning of refugees from countries of asylum and resettlement back to their native land, is at once a "peace issue" and a "power issue." This is especially true when the numbers are large, the groups of refugees identifiable, the physical and social environment fragile, and the populations economically vulnerable. These are the real conditions for *all repatriations* during this decade.

Repatriation is about the insertion of groups of vulnerable persons into populations that often are also living a precarious existence. Repatriation is about rebuilding a nation after armed, usually long-term, conflict. Repatriation is typically about bringing together peoples who not only have been physically separated but who frequently represent opposing forces. Repatriation is about allocating scarce resources and reinserting people into the life of the land. Repatriation is about economics, politics, and social conditions. Thus, in the specifics of repatriation, terms such as honor, dignity, justice, reconciliation, righteousness, and right relations are not abstractions. These become the results of specific policies, specific decisions. Repatriation negotiated and implemented without concern for honor, dignity, justice, and right relations lays the conditions for future conflict and even for future war. Repatriation is a challenge for building peace with justice.

Repatriation, at least the organized, large-scale kind, is an arena where humanitarian intervention in the processes of reintegration and reconciliation is negotiated by a complex array of governmental, intergovernmental, and nongovernmental actors.

> Large scale repatriation—considered the best permanent solution to refugee situations—forces relief agencies involved to address the question of how short term considerations of relief (food, shelter, water, and medicine) link up with issues of human rights protection, demilitarization, reconciliation, political reform, containment of ethnic conflict, regional reconstruction, and the wide range of development issues.[8]

One of the defining qualities of "refugeeness" is that of being controlled by state powers and authorities. Refugees are subject to specific measures and restrictions because, in fleeing, they have crossed national borders.[9] Power is central to effective repatriation and reconstruction.

> Since assistance to processes of repatriation involves questions of "reinsertion" of people, "reactivation" of local and regional economies, and (re-)construction of civil administration, assistance becomes deeply engaged in the development of technologies and *distribution of power.* (emphasis added)[10]

Repatriation involves the question of the reinsertion of people, the rebuilding of the economy, the reconstruction of political structures—all issues of power and the allocation of and access to social, economic, and political resources. If the agreements on entitlements and obligations are not well worked out, the process of repatriation will be inadequate to the challenge of reinserting large groups of people into a devastated environment.

Eritrean Colonialism and Liberation: Setting the Context for Repatriation[11]

The history of the Eritrean liberation struggle sets the context and shapes the approach of the government of Eritrea to the repatriation negotiations. Eritrea, lying along the northern coast of the Red Sea, became a colony of Italy in 1889. As one consequence, Eritrea became in important ways distinct from Ethiopia. During World War II the defeat of Italy in the Horn of Africa led to Eritrea's being placed under British trusteeship until 1952. After World War II the UN General Assembly recommended the federation of Eritrea with Ethiopia, a federation in which Eritrea was to be in control of its domestic affairs. Basic human rights for Eritreans were granted. However, in 1962 the federation was dissolved unilaterally by Ethiopia, which made Eritrea its province. The United Nations, in spite of its unique responsibility for Eritrea, did not intervene.[12] "Eritrea, therefore, still hosts bitterness against the United Nations and does not have faith in UN integrity."[13]

Armed resistance with the goal of independence was launched by the Eritrean Liberation Front (ELF) in 1961, thus beginning 30 years of a brutal trench warfare. The battle was waged in the rural areas, with Ethiopian offensives especially aimed at civilians. A second liberation front, the Eritrean Peoples Liberation Front (EPLF), was formed in 1970 as a split from the ELF. In 1980 the EPLF drove the ELF out of Eritrea into neighboring Sudan and became the only liberation force carrying on armed struggle inside Eritrea. The ruthlessness of the Ethiopian attacks sent hundreds of thousands into Sudan as refugees.

In May 1991 Eritrea achieved the goal of its struggle, liberation. There is a clear and pervasive sense on the part of the former fighters, government officials, and Eritreans generally that Eritrea won its independence alone, without help from any other nation or international body.[14]

In April 1993 an official referendum was held with over 99 percent of eligible Eritrean voters around the world affirming their wish to have Eritrea be a separate and independent nation. Until the referendum, the Eritrean Peoples Liberation Front (EPLF) was to be the Provisional Government of Eritrea (PGE).

Eritrea and the Repatriation Context

Political Context

The government, currently operating on the principle of the one-party state, is by all accounts clearly the legitimate government of Eritrea[15] and has widespread, although not unanimous, support within Eritrea. It has broad ethnic and religious representation at the official levels. The leaders and most of the civil servants are drawn from the ranks of the EPLF. The government of Eritrea has proven itself, according to western governments and nongovernmental (NGO) sources, to be honest and "clean" in its governing. Confidence in the integrity of the leadership is widespread and high.

This confidence is strengthened by the fact that since liberation, thousands of former fighters have been working in the government without salary, including those at the highest level.

> This is a government which is taking a serious approach to national problems. This is a government which has the interests of the people as central. This is a government in which the leaders themselves are sacrificing. Many are supported by relatives in diaspora. This is a government which is not corrupt.[16]

Importantly the country is at peace. This is a political reality—that is, the war is over and the country is liberated. The factors that caused the refugees to flee no longer exist. Peace is also a social and community reality. One can safely walk the streets day and night. The absence of armed soldiers or armed police from every street corner is a remarkable experience. The human rights record of the government has not been seriously questioned.[17]

Environmental and Social Context

Eritrea is a devastated country. The physical infrastructure has been almost totally destroyed. Churches, mosques, schools, hospitals are gone. Roads must be repaired. The railroad from the port of Massawa on the Red Sea to Asmara in the highlands was ripped up by the Ethiopian forces. Urban areas were depleted as part of the retreat of the Ethiopian army—for instance, the university and schools were stripped of equipment and furniture.

The natural resource base is fragile and degraded; its carrying capacity is problematical. The countryside was severely bombed. Mines are a significant problem, and there is at a minimum 800 tons of steel, including, tanks, left in the countryside.[18] The formerly wooded highlands where the majority of the population lives have been severely deforested.[19] This deforestation increases both erosion and drought in areas dependent on rainfall for agriculture. The lowlands, historically populated by nomads, are drought-prone. The current capacity of the land to absorb 500,000 refugees (15 percent of the population) from Sudan is doubtful.

Providing adequate food for the population of 2.7 to 3 million persons is an enormous problem. Before the war, Eritrea was basically self-sufficient in food.[20] Today approximately 80 percent of the population is dependent on food aid.

The population of Eritrea—approximately 50 percent Muslim and 50 percent Christian—represents nine ethnic groups. The Christians live mainly in the more prosperous highlands while the Muslims live predominately in the lowlands. Arabic and Tigrinia are the official languages. In the process of developing the constitution[21] as well as in the government structures, there is an intentionality to include representatives from the various ethnic groups as well as both Muslims and Christians. However, some people, in discussing the repatriation program, expressed concern that government officials come predominately from the highlands while most of the returnees will be resettled in the lowlands.

The fact that the majority of refugees in Sudan are Muslims, many with a previous relationship to the ELF, poses a significant challenge to the goal of nation building based on ethnic/religious inclusion. There are reports of anti-Eritrean government activities by the National Islamic Front (NIF) in the camps in Sudan.[22]

Thus the Eritrean political, economic, and social context provides a unique and remarkable reality in which the international community can refine repatriation processes and procedures. There is no ongoing conflict; the government is trustworthy. The political causes of the refugees' flight have ceased to exist. The environment is devastated; development needs are pervasive. The government has little if any financial resources and no capacity for absorbing large-scale loans. There is a high level of esprit de corps and commitment to the future of the nation. There is no leader or cadre of leaders assuming dictatorial power over the people. The independence of the nation was won at a high cost, and the reconstruction and rehabilitation needs are evident and pervasive.

From several UNHCR officials' perspectives, Eritrea was the one ray of hope in Horn of Africa. As a Swedish government official also remarked,

> We were eager to get going with the repatriation. We had supported the Eritrean people,[23] and now this was an excellent situation in which to really do repatriation quickly and well. But it didn't happen. It got all bogged down in misunderstandings.

So, how did the negotiations get "bogged down," and what happened to the concerns for the rights of people and for the sustainability of the environment—natural, physical, and social? It seems that what really happened is clouded by everyone's opinions, particularly regarding specific details and intents. However, the consistent issue of who, finally, controls repatriation and for what purposes appears persistently.

Repatriation Negotiations: Conflict Between UNHCR and the Provisional Government of Eritrea (PGE)

After liberation in May 1991, the PGE Commission for Eritrean Refugee Affairs (CERA) began formal contacts with UNHCR. UNHCR opened a permanent office in Asmara in November 1991.

During the early months of the UNHCR's presence in Asmara, considerable difficulties emerged regarding the negotiations for the repatriation. These misunderstandings were embedded in the historical distrust of the United Nations by the Eritrean government. Also, the Eritrean government as a liberation movement, well organized within itself, had little exposure to international agencies, their mandates, their established methods, their expectations, their limitations.

Quickly, misperceptions, misunderstandings, as well as contradictions within the international repatriation system emerged; and these were to influence these negotiations for several years. A former Commissioner of CERA described the experience as a "fierce battle of four years."[24]

Initially the relationship between UNHCR and PGE seemed positive. However, as the government presented its repatriation budget of $600 million for a comprehensive program of return and reinsertion, it became clear that UNHCR and CERA were divided over the amount of funding and what was to be included within repatriation. From the government perspective, refugees were languishing in camps and not able to return because of the lack of development in Eritrea. The PGE insisted on placing repatriation within a total development approach for the entire country. UNHCR stated that donors would not fund UNHCR to do development. It was "a matter of degree and what the traffic would bear;" for example, UNHCR would not build a hospital but would dig a small number of tube wells.[25]

The relevant standard for UNHCR was one that aimed for no lower living facilities than in well-established camps having basic facilities. Refugees could not be given a higher standard than those who stayed behind, that is, a "prize for leaving." One example a UNHCR official noted was the disagreement about the shelter component of repatriation. The government was offering a plan for concrete block houses with an estimated price tag of US$900–$1,200 each. UNHCR, on the other hand, perceived that the donors would question such a high amount of funding going to shelter and would ask why the returnees needed concrete block houses when the rest of the Eritrean people lived in huts, both in Sudan and in Eritrea.[26]

In December 1991–January 1992, the first international appeal for Eritrea went out. UNHCR estimated an amount of US$50 million[27] as a beginning figure. They stressed that they did not expect to get all of the $50 million at one time. Recognizing that UNHCR has moved beyond the old days of "seeds, tools, and a handshake," UNHCR said it didn't know where international donors draw the line. They noted that donors have made it clear that they expect UNHCR to prepare for the return; donors won't fund development through UNHCR.[28] Therefore, their advice was to implement a small and specific project, go to donors, and show how the money was spent. UNHCR stressed that when donors see a good project, UNHCR would get more money for more projects in Eritrea.

This was unacceptable to PGE, which said that this amount of money would only cover logistic and transport costs and not reintegration of the returnees. CERA/PGE insisted that repatriation must not begin until sufficient funds were guaranteed for reintegration and reconstruction. CERA also stressed the social consequences of the proposed repatriation scheme.

> This [limiting repatriation to return of the refugees and not including reintegration/development] would have meant that Eritrea would be drowned in a sea of returnees who had no suitable accommodation. The Eritrean government explained at the time that this would cause major social and economic upheaval as the country did not have the necessary resources for assimilating the returnees.[29]

The basic dilemma was understood as follows:

> One has to see the refugees as part of the community. They are in the same area with those who remained, former fighters, former displaced. We have to target the community, not target the refugees as a separate group. It is a matter of community development not group development.[30]

The UNHCR Chief of Mission in Asmara during that time gave an illustration of the effect on UNHCR programming of insisting on a total reintegration approach:

> The environmental aspect was large in this repatriation. UNHCR had an offer from a German NGO to do a reforestation project in anticipation of repatriation. The project included a study, was able to be funded, and the NGO was ready to start immediately. An American forestry expert said it was a sound and useful project. The plan was to have a seedling project done by the returnees. We went to the Agriculture Department to ask if we could go ahead with this, starting with the study. The answer was, "No, we have to have a complete agreement on repatriation before anything goes ahead."[31]

Throughout the negotiations, the issue of how to determine the amount of funding was a critical disagreement. The PGE, citing the very high cost per head for certain repatriations, such as South Africa and Namibia, perceived that UNHCR was discriminating against Eritrea. UNHCR responded that repatriation funding was not solicited on a cost per head basis but admitted that it was a "bedeviling argument."

UNHCR, citing its experience with international donors, insisted that it could not get funds up front, and could not sit on funds it did get. "If we can't spend it, it gets taken away either by the donor or in-house for other emergencies."[32] The way the repatriation funding works, UNHCR explained, is that financial resources follow successful repatriation, not the other way around; therefore, one must start with a visible, small project. The PGE/CERA refused a sector-by-sector approach, insisting that the entire country had suffered in the liberation struggle, and therefore that one area should not receive assistance while another area does not. They refused to allow UNHCR to begin discrete projects, saying that "it would just open the pipe, and we would not be able to close it."[33]

Increasingly, the Eritrean government stated that an *issue of principle* was involved, that UNHCR was proposing inadequate reintegration funds and clearly wanted to "dump refugees." In interviews donor government representatives stated that it was important for the PGE to bring people back to a good standard of living, taking into account the conditions in the camps in Sudan.

In August 1992 the High Commissioner, Madame Sadako Ogata, sent her special delegate to Asmara. However, this proved to be of no avail. Talks with UNHCR were suspended by the PGE; the UNHCR office in Asmara was downsized to a one-person administration. Clearly the situation between UNHCR and the government of Eritrea had deteriorated to such a point that, although the specifics of the moment are confused, the distance both in procedures and in relationships is clear.

Through all this time both UNHCR and the PGE insisted that what they each wanted was to get the refugees in Sudan back to Eritrea in safety, honor, and dignity, and further to establish them in such a manner that they could become self-sufficient and could contribute to the development of Eritrea. The vast majority of refugees remained in Sudan awaiting an organized program of return and some guarantees as to the conditions awaiting them on return. The most vulnerable were affected by the decisions of the powerful.

Besides the direct effect on those involved in the deliberations, that is, UNHCR and the PGE, the constant negotiations wore out the patience of many people. Public attacks did not create a climate of confidence by either donors or international agencies.[34]

Efforts did continue, however, by both the government of Eritrea and the UN for the organized return of the refugees from Sudan. The UN Department of Humanitarian Affairs (DHA) took over the up-front intergovernmental efforts and organized a planning process for an organized repatriation program, resulting in the "Joint Government of Eritrea and United Nations Appeal for Eritrea," which was presented to an international donors pledging conference held in Geneva, July 6, 1993.

The planning process for this appeal included the UN, NGOs, and, most importantly, international donors. It resulted in an 11-component repatriation and reintegration program, PROFERI (Programme for Refugee Reintegration and Rehabilitation of Resettlement Areas in Eritrea), to return 430,000 refugees during three years and seven months at a cost of US$262.2 million, of which Phase One for 150,000 refugees would require US$110.9 million. A specific objective of PROFERI is to link repatriation of refugees to the rehabilitation of the country, avoiding the creation of a privileged class of returnees within a deprived local population. The goal is that the total population be able to sustain itself after PROFERI ends.[35]

Despite the fact that PROFERI "seemed to present an ideal example of a coordinated response between governmental and non-governmental agencies to bridge the gap between rehabilitation and development," the results of the donors conference were extremely disappointing, some would say disastrous. Pledges amounted to $32.4 million of which only $11 million was "new money." The remainder was represented in food aid through World Food Program (WFP) and would have been available in any case.

> We were misled by DHA and UNHCR. If they had known that donors would not fund such a big project, why did they work with us to develop it? It was not intentional, but it happened. . . . It was a bitter lesson.[37]

In response to questions of why the donor response was so unenthusiastic, several issues were presented:

1. The program isn't a "pure" repatriation; it is rural development plus repatriation. It is too big and will take 50 years; refugees need to be returned now.
2. Being a partner in development means long-term involvement, which donors do not want.
3. Interest in Eritrea (media pressure) was not there.
4. There was an uncertainty about the capacity of a dedicated but inexperienced Eritrean administration to manage such a large and varied program.
5. The government (GOE) was insisting on national project management and execution.
6. The government won't permit international NGOs to work there; this is a great inhibition to getting money.[38] More and more international donors are funneling their money through NGOs.

The point regarding the policy of national execution—which also relates to the restrictions on international NGOs—is a basic principle of the government of Eritrea. The PROFERI document states explicitly that most of the program activities will be implemented and coordinated by the GOE. Donations are welcomed as long as they are consistent with the *goal of building up national capacities, and not substituting for them*.[39]

Pilot Phase of PROFERI: January 1994–May 1995

With the failure of the PROFERI appeal of July 1993, the government of Eritrea, UNDP, DHA, and UNHCR came back together to plan on the basis of the limited funds available. However, the larger donors refused to release money unless the government made an arrangement with UNHCR.[40]

In March 1994, with a new Chief of Mission, UNHCR began to function locally in the repatriation process. The new Chief of Mission stated his intention to work closely with the government:

> I could say "You are a sovereign government. You decide." . . . The government credibility is based on having liberated the country on their own; it is their own achievement. They are legitimate and that creates credibility. However, winning the peace is much more difficult. The real fight is ahead. They are starting below zero. The government will have to deliver . . . back to the people. . . . I did not come to tell the Eritreans this or that. We have a common goal, to get the refugees back.[41]

In this more positive climate, the government allocated 45 million birr (nearly US$7 million) for a Pilot Phase to repatriate approximately 25,000 returnees (some 4,500 households) from Sudan.[42] The Pilot Phase was underfunded. It was a commitment by GOE and UNHCR to "get the show on the road."[43]

According to reports received in May 1995, approximately 20,000 persons were repatriated and received initial reintegration support during the Pilot Phase of PROFERI from November 1994 to May 1995.[44]

A Fragile Environment Reveals On-the-Ground Challenges in the Pilot Phase of Repatriation

An evaluation of the Pilot Phase served as a basis for the Donor Workshop, May 19–20, in Asmara, Eritrea. The aim of the workshop was to encourage support and secure funding for Phase One, the next stage of PROFERI, which aims to repatriate some 135,000 Eritreans from Sudan with a budget of approximately US$111 million.[45] The two days of presentations, with questions and answers, were basically aimed at informing and motivating donors.

Both the government and UNHCR emphasized that the problems between them "were of the past."[46] UNHCR stated its support for the PROFERI plan for repatriation and reintegration. However, tensions and contradictions within the repatriation program and the process for implementing it were quite clear:

> It is evident that a repatriation programme of this nature in a country like Eritrea, devastated by 30 years of war, is not without problems and challenges ... there still are gaps and shortages. ... Neither UNHCR nor CERA will accept to dump returnees in an area and leave them alone. *The real task for the Eritrean Government and all international partners, is the reintegration process,* to give the returnees the tools and means to help themselves, their families and their communities. So we need to work harder, need to improve our delivery. This we can not do without your support. Initial relief and infrastructure like water, health, shelter, basic education, land-distribution and agricultural and livestock-support are all key elements for a real reintegration-process which should be planned for and started immediately. (emphasis added)[47]

Two issues were central: (1) funding by and relationship to international donors, and (2) the effect of the environmental conditions on the total planning and process. These were shaped by and embedded in the two overarching and unanswered questions: (1) whether donors would fund development within repatriation, and (2) who controls the process.

Funding by International Donors

The need for international funding was obvious. Lack of funding and/or delay in receiving funds compromised the implementation as refugees returned to the fragile environment of the lowlands.

> It must be said that the PROFERI programme has found itself in a contradictory position, in a Catch 22 situation. Clearly, donors will not continue to support relief to Eritrean Refugees in the Sudan forever. Yet, limited [financial] support for reintegration has contributed to the inability to fully implement the comprehensive pilot phase, thus making it difficult to meet donor expectations as to quality and adequacy of preparation in settlement sites. In addition, due to delays between pledges and the actual time of payment, CERA has been expected to meet requirements with insufficient funds. Despite these limitations, CERA has by 20 May 1995 received 20.000 returnees, and provided settlement sites with a minimum infrastructure so as to be able to cater for them.[48]

In funding discussions CERA officials consistently stated that the PROFERI program was transparent. Nothing was being hidden, they stated. Donors could come to the sites or to the offices and inspect, see what was happening with their funds, and evaluate.

However, donor representatives stated that the government was *not* transparent because it did not provide adequate written records regarding the use of funds. In response CERA officials noted the detailed planning including issues previously raised by donors. The invitation to "come and see" was consistent.

A Development Solution to a Humanitarian Problem[49]

PROFERI is dealing with more than "tools, seeds, and a handshake." Its mandate includes rehabilitating the region affected by the return and resettlement of the refugees. It is community development, not group relief. The services being identified are basic ones that will benefit all the people in a region.[50]

The Commissioner of CERA outlined the concern that in this emergency situation the process of reintegration must be sustainable after PROFERI is finished. The discussions revealed that a devastated and ecologically fragile environment sets the basic conditions for the return and also reveals significant challenges within repatriation.

Environmental Conditions

Shelter

There were particularly intense exchanges between donors, NGOs, and government officials regarding appropriate shelter in the lowlands, given the reality that "the woody biomass resources in the lowlands of Eritrea cannot be expected to meet the shelter needs of [the returnees]."[51] Environmental concerns (for example, not cutting trees for construction—the position of the government[52]) were in tension with concern for humane, livable conditions in extraordinarily hot climates (for example, not using corrugated metal roofs as suggested by the GOE—the position of many donors and NGOs). Issues of experience with alternative construction materials, funding, fuel needs and environmental protection, timing—as well as the need to move quickly so that sites are prepared, plus the involvement of the community (bottom up vs. top down) in the planning for shelter—were constantly raised in the discussion. Many of these require sufficient funds to be available quickly. CERA noted that it had developed its shelter plans, including using metal roofs, partly in response to the opinion of donors at the 1993 donors conference that the previously planned costs for the shelter component were too high.

Water and Sanitation

Given the low amount of rainfall in the lowlands, the challenge of providing safe drinking water for the returnees is huge. One suggestion was to collect rain water runoff from metal roofs, a suggestion that presented the contradiction regarding humane living conditions in high-temperature climates (see above). Environmentally and humanely functional construction of pit latrines—since a waterborne option is not viable—presented similar polarities of opinions.

Energy

How much fuel will be needed for cooking and heating was unclear, depending on the locations the returnees choose and on which studies one wishes to believe. However, there was no argument as to the ongoing deforestation stemming from fuel-wood demand. Given the low percentage of forested land, this is clearly an extremely short-term possibility. Energy needs are, therefore, a critical element in the interrelationship between resettlement and environment. Fuel-saving alternative stoves and the planting of tree seedlings were being recommended by the GOE.

Food Security

With 80 percent of the population dependent on food aid, the ability of the returnees to feed themselves is problematic. Land availability, adequate tools and materials, and access to water are basic. As subsistence, settled agriculture is expanded in an area historically utilized by agro-pastoralists, there is a direct effect on the environment, which may not be able to sustain such a rapid and marked population increase. There is also competition for scarce or threatened resources.[53]

Funding, Environment, and Social Destabilization: Ethnic, Religious, and Class Relationships to Resource Access

Competition for scarce or fragile resources not only increases tensions directly related to such resources, it also sets in motion conflict that can be orchestrated along ethnic and religious lines. The government's awareness of this danger results in a commitment to prevent the linkage between resource competition and ethnic/religious issues, a commitment that underlies the government's insistence on linking national and community development to repatriation. The reports about the activities of Islamic fundamentalists in the refugee camps in Sudan are particularly worrisome in this context.

The government is clear that returnees must have access to adequate resources to be self-sufficient. It is also explicit that the returnees must not become a separate, privileged class within an impoverished population. Therefore, the community as a whole—not returnees as a group—must be the focus of development.

These issues, which were not resolved at the workshop, point to the hard choices and contradictions within repatriation—for example, time constraints, money limits, differing donor and government perspectives, ecological realities, resource availability. Although there were no questions as to the immensity of the development needs, there were concerns about the capacity of the GOE to carry out such an extensive program, as well as concerns about plans for and funding of capacity building. The most basic question was whether the donors were in fact willing to fund development connected to repatriation. This was compounded by disagreements regarding control of the process.

At the workshop, donors were clearly uncomfortable with the national execution approach, which may be one reason for the sluggish donor response to PROFERI.[54] Capacity building is closely tied to the approach of national execution. Donors queried the GOE's capacity to carry out PROFERI plans. CERA responded with an interest in capacity-building linked to national execution. It was aware, for instance, of the need to improve its record-keeping. And it was cautious about becoming dependent on "experts:"

We don't want "lend me your watch, and I will tell you the time."[55]

CERA and UNHCR were united at the donors workshop on the necessity of getting the refugees out of Sudan and getting them settled back in Eritrea. Their message to the donors was to make this repatriation and reintegration possible by funding PROFERI.[56]

Who Controls Repatriation?

The issue of *control* was critical initially in the early negotiations; for example, early proposals to develop alternative fuel projects, initially accepted and shaped by Eritrean women's groups, were later rejected and not implemented, apparently because they came with funding from UNHCR. Control continued to be pervasive in the donors workshop prior to Phase One of PROFERI. Arguments about building materials, such as concrete block houses, mud brick houses, and metal roofs, were framed in environmental terms, but the issue became trust and control. Importantly, environmental concerns are inherently development issues not encompassed within "traditional repatriation."

On the part of the government, control was expressed through emphases on self-determination, independence, being in charge of one's own country, and reserving implementation for the government. Control by the international donors was expressed through restrictions on funds, emphasis on particular procedures of reporting, and/or by the actual withholding of funds. Control by UNHCR was through an emphasis on operational mandates and procedural limitations.

Protecting People and Protecting the Environment: Will the International System Lead to a Sustainable Peace?

How can countries, scarred by the effects of war, insecurity, land mines and poverty, burdened with the problem of demobilized soldiers [combatants] and displaced civilians, be realistically expected to reabsorb those who return, when they are hardly able to sustain those who remained? The Horn of Africa is but one example of many. Are we not simply creating new and more tragic emergencies? And at what cost to the peace process in these countries? As conflicts are resolved, countries must be rebuilt, so that they can begin to support once again their own population, including the returning refugees and displaced persons. . . . The link between the reintegration of refugees and national post-conflict reconstruction is thus of paramount importance.[57]

Madame Ogata's impassioned statement, cited here, makes clear that the negotiations for the repatriation back to Eritrea of the 450,000-plus refugees in Sudan, while raising issues specific to the Eritrean situation, point to *essential challenges within the international refugee system*, especially as it relates to repatriation. These challenges are embedded in the contradictions within the institutionalized international response to refugees.

Repatriation and Development

The linking of repatriation to development conceptualizes repatriation as part of the nation-building challenge that links diverse and vulnerable groups of people within a devastated reality. There is the very real issue of absorptive capacity and the availability of adequate resources to begin, carry out, and complete the reintegration process. Reconstruction of the country is essential to the successful and secure reintegration of the returnees. Without such reconstruction, there is no sustainability—and likely no lasting peace. Development, however, is a long-term process necessitating a long-term commitment with donors.

Repatriation, Community-Building, and Land Issues

Countries in which agriculture is the basic livelihood, issues of land availability, basic resources, and (re)developing cooperative communities are central within repatriation. The economic and social sustainability is directly related to land and environmental issues. Almost all the returnees are agricultural people and must have land to farm. However, the returnees are only one group within the society, and all groups can be understood as "vulnerable groups."

Although each repatriation situation is unique, the Eritrean example is illustrative. Returnees are being resettled in the same area with former fighters, an area that is already inhabited by agro-pastoralists who, as nomads, must have access to large tracts of land for their animals. The land is fragile. Returnees, who have been sustained in Sudan by the cooperation of the Sudanese government and international donors, are obviously weighing the comparative costs and benefits of that existence against the challenges of starting a new life in Eritrea. The potential for dissatisfaction, and subsequent political instability, is real. Gaim Kibreab, in his study of the refugees' decisions about whether to return to Eritrea, reports:

> Most of the factors that are discouraging the . . . refugees from returning home are directly linked to lack of social, physical (infrastructural) and economic capacity of absorption in their country of origin. The evidence shows that . . . the only way voluntary repatriation can be an attractive and a lasting solution under such conditions is by creating a stable socio-economic base in the areas of return.[58]

The failure to achieve such a stable base can have dire human, national, and international consequences:

> Unless the capacity of communities and areas of return to absorb additional populations is addressed, mass repatriation may spur new forms of human deprivation, social tensions and migratory movements.[59]

The intense conflict in the Eritrean repatriation negotiations reveals the damage that results from the difficulty internationally of linking relief to sustainable development within the context of repatriation.

> . . . it is now clear that relief assistance [to refugees being repatriated] and longer-term development programmes are separated by a wide gap, which threatens the successful reintegration of returnees and the viability of their communities.[60]

This lack of a "seamless continuum" is due to several factors: (1) the donors understand repatriation as moving refugees from "here to there," not as development; donors' repatriation money comes out of different budgets than development money;[61] and (2) the legendary "mandate dilemma" within the UN system.[62]

UNHCR has been struggling for years with the fact that its mandate for repatriation has not historically been considered to include development. Its responsibility is "to register refugees, transport them . . . and provide initial relief."[63] UNHCR's Quick Impact Projects (QIPs)—community-focused, one-time, small budget projects intended to be a bridge to longer-term development done by other UN agencies or NGOs—require close coordination between UNHCR and such agencies. From the frustrations expressed, it seems that this coordination has not usually been successful:[64]

> The humanitarian "Market of Mercy" is a hard market, everyone is struggling for their share, fight to the death. . . . We all define our own small little sectors. That is more important than helping people![65]

Some UN staff asserted that the competition is based on a need to get funds. Funding is a basic contradiction within the international refugee system. Donors, the United Nations, and governments all insist that their goal is self-reliance and independence for the returnees. However, the goal of self-reliance appears to be of less importance when donors are dealing with recipients. In that context, donors put conditions on their aid, and "strings" are attached to the receiving of funds. Typically "Whoever pays the bill calls the tune."[66]

The Eritrean negotiations provide an example. The need for international aid to Eritrea is recognized. However, the Eritrean government insists that the giving and receiving of the aid must not jeopardize national sovereignty or the building of self-reliance and national capacity. At the Summit for Social Development, March 6–12, 1995, President Isaias Afwerki insisted:

> certain assumptions and relationships must change . . . donor-recipient relationships based on dictation of unsuitable antidotes will just not do. . . . Symmetry should be the linchpin of relationships between rich and poor countries. And while donors should insist on rigorous monitoring of their funds, "our independence of decision should not be encroached by conditionalities of aid.[67]

Eritrean government officials noted the presence of approximately 250 NGOs in Ethiopia (in contrast to the 10-plus in Eritrea) and emphasized that they did not intend to turn the development of Eritrea over to outside forces, even humanitarian ones.

> The jobs are for Eritreans. . . . If a gap in capacity is identified . . . the international NGO is welcome to bring in someone from the outside. The expectation [is to have] an Eritrean working alongside . . . so that when the expert leaves, there is an Eritrean who is now knowledgeable to carry on. We want to increase our own capacity . . . not empower international NGOs.[68]

Funding of the international refugee response system contributed to the repatriation negotiation conflicts. UNHCR receives over 90 percent of its funds from donor governments. It has relatively little funds of its own and is thus totally dependent on a small group of western nations.

Quite often the donor governments have a political agenda tied to their contributions so that particular situations fade out of interest for them. An NGO staff noted that although development funding is hard to come by, money for Bosnia comes quickly. A donor country representative asserted that they were sitting on funds for Croatia, Bosnia, and Somalia. They knew things were going to "blow up" there.

Every person I interviewed—whether in the UNHCR, donor governments, NGOs, or Eritrean government officials—stated that preventive work such as reconciliation and confidence building gets no attention. Money is given for symptoms, for visible and graphic crises—not to address causes, not to prevent future destabilization.

> Now things are quiet and stable here [in Eritrea]. What you are doing is conflict prevention. This needs significant support from the international community. But the international community only responds when there are guns and blood.[69]

Since development as part of the total repatriation process is such a long-term process and so expensive, it requires considerable political will on the part of donor countries and the entire international community.[70]

In discussing donor perspectives with donor representatives, several key issues surfaced that are typically present in the broader international context: (1) the political agenda of donor countries as mentioned above; (2) linking of aid to the utilization of services from the donor country;[71] (3) linking continued aid to careful reporting as a measure of government accountability and transparency; (4) sometimes a general distrust of Third World governments, not making distinctions between them;[72] (5) having donor-specific reporting requirements, which can be overwhelming and nonproductive for the recipient.

In the midst of the negotiations, planning, and programs required for repatriating people, it is also easy to lose sight of the human dimension, of the need for effective working partnerships.

> True partnership is based on equality. There is no equality when there is disparity in possessions. But I have possessions—my experience and my skills. Recipients have possessions and know how to use them. We want to be in a situation of mutual responsibility.[73]

Paying attention to the human dimension means addressing the hard questions of repatriation in a context of patience, dignity, and respect.

Sustainable Development, Human Rights, and the Environment: Implications and Recommendations

Threat to Human Rights

A government that is truly the legitimate government of the people, as is currently true for Eritrea, can only maintain that legitimacy by providing for the basic needs of its people. To do that, there must be sufficient resources within a reasonable length of time, a willingness of the government to listen to and respond to the people, and a cooperative, problem-solving relationship between the local community/people and the government. A government is enabled to do that if it can "deliver" basic social and economic services. When the people experience meaningful progress, they will likely be patient, will cooperate with the government toward common goals, and will work intently and intentionally toward the development of their own country.

If the government is not able to deliver such services after a reasonable length of time, a likely outcome is increasing discontent, the turning of one group against another group (seeing "the other" as a threat), and eventually antigovernment organizing. In such a context not only are the people deprived of their basic needs, threatened, and dispossessed, but the likely response of a government is to become oppressive, to attempt to stifle dissent, to be a government against the people rather than for the people. Human rights come under attack, and people become victims.

Relative to Eritrea, the challenge is for the international community to move quickly to bring the refugees back from Sudan. It is morally and politically time to act, and is in the best interests of the donors and the UN. The fundamental challenge is for the international community to work together to combine returning refugees—repatriation—with community and national development—reintegration. These are opportunities to work proactively for peace.

> If voluntary repatriation is to be truly "anchored" as a durable solution to refugee problems, *peace and an opportunity to return home are not enough*. Unless the capacity of communities and areas of return to absorb additional populations is addressed, mass repatriation may spur new forms of human deprivation, social tensions and migratory movements. (emphasis added)[74]

UNHCR, caught between governments, donors, and its own mandates, guards against an expansion of its mandate. Sensitive to the danger of outside control and of losing that for which so many have struggled and sacrificed, refusing to allow others to dictate conditions, the government of Eritrea guards against being overwhelmed while working toward the outside limits of possibilities. The donors, facing multiple and increasing demands as crisis follows crisis and wanting to ensure the responsible use of funds, fall back on rules, regulations, and procedures. They guard against being pulled in beyond their normal limits.

There is a need for new mechanisms and greater flexibility. There is a need to raise funds faster, for the UNHCR to have access to adequate and sufficient funds to negotiate from a position of being able to act. There is an urgent need for effective coordination mechanisms between UN agencies, as well as between those agencies, the donors, the NGOs, and the recipient government.

The government of Eritrea is moving from a liberation movement to a constitutional government. The challenge of winning the peace is complex. Cooperation for development is a new experience for the government and for the society that has been at war for 30 years. The military style of decision-making necessary and effective during the liberation struggle is challenged to shift to a more participatory, delegatory style in response to the demands of building a nation at peace.[75]

Donors as funders of repatriation and of development are finally the main actors, setting the level at which they will contribute funds and the conditions on which they will do so. There is a pressing need for donors to be open to new ways of doing repatriation, to be aware of and responsive to the specific realities of particular situations, to find creative ways to release and combine funds for relief as well as for development for repatriation. Much of the difficulty during the negotiations was due to the lack of adequate funding. The international donor community has, as of spring 1995, pledged less than 30 percent of the requested budget for PROFERI.

Analyzing the Eritrean repatriation negotiation, some recommendations emerge. Some of the recommendations are specific to the Eritrean context; some are general.

Repatriation and the UN Family

The "mandate dilemma" urgently needs continued attention. This requires close coordination and cooperation between UNHCR and other UN agencies as well as between these agencies and governments. Flexibility on the ground in order to respond quickly is necessary. *UNHCR cannot do repatriation alone.* There is a need (1) to define who in the UN should be working with UNHCR in the country of origin and in what capacities, and (2) to equip them—with appropriate mandates, with necessary funds, with on-the-ground support.

Mechanisms of consultation should be developed. Ongoing consultation is needed between UN agencies, as well as among UN agencies, the government, the donors, and the NGOs. A structured format in which the government and NGOs can discuss and dialogue about repatriation with the donors as observers might increase the intentionality of dialogue and the insights of the donors.[76]

Assuming that conflicts between the UN agencies and governments will occur in other situations, trusted intermediaries can be extraordinarily helpful. Mechanisms to identify, to train if necessary, and to utilize such intermediaries would be an important contribution.

Capacity building is a central feature of long-term sustainability in development-based repatriation. UNHCR's and UNDP's supporting and encouraging this with donors could be effective in developing flexible funding and program plans for capacity building.

Government of Eritrea

The demands on the government to carry out successful repatriation of such a large number of refugees in a short time are extraordinary. Structures of cooperation and coordination are needed at various levels: with the UN agencies and international donors—both of whom have a wealth of knowledge about repatriation and about development; with local communities and leadership as they face the incorporation of such large numbers of returnees; with refugee/returnee leadership as they struggle to develop a hopeful life; and with international and indigenous NGOs that can link the local communities to the national structures. In all of this, the development of communities that can be sustained socially within a fragile and compromised ecological environment is at the heart both of the development challenge and of the prospects for peace.

International Donors: The Main Actors

Repatriation clearly must combine return with reintegration, immediate aid with long-term development. This requires a more expanded approach to funding by international donors, an approach that addresses the following challenges: (1) Accepting and supporting the legitimacy of the government of Eritrea (GOE) as it responds to the enormous challenges of reintegrating 450,000 to 500,000 refugees; (2) welcoming the GOE's direct and active role in development, including PROFERI; (3) recognizing the real time pressures, funds appropriate to the needs should be contributed and released in a timely manner; (4) given the unquestioned importance of adequate reporting, recommending that all the donors and the government of Eritrea agree together on one format and one procedure for reporting that would be acceptable to all parties and that would serve the program needs through ongoing program evaluation aimed at increased competency; (5) since the separation of short-term relief/aid funds from longer-term development funds within governments' administration is a block to effective funding of repatriation, seeking more internal cooperation in funding projects that include both relief/aid and development; (6) welcoming the GOE's commitment to develop national capacity through local staffing and building capacity within funding packages; (7) separating the funding of technical support (often provided by expatriate experts) from the provision of direct aid.

Over and above the specific concerns about and recommendations regarding—among other issues—mandates, delegation, mobilizing resources, and developing communication, one faces the very real need to develop cooperative partnerships in response to an important opportunity to empower people at the grass-roots level and undergird the conditions for peace. The words of the Eritrean Ambassador to Sweden and the UNHCR Chief of Mission Asmara capture the essence of this challenge:

> We are asking for so little. We are asking for stability. We are asking for a contribution to stability. Protective measures is the approach that is needed rather than waiting for a disaster.[77]

> For decades, we have seen the Horn of Africa as a theater of war, violence, famine and death. Not only have suffering and destruction been the order of the day, but political instability has threatened the whole region.

> Today, we have a historic possibility to create the basis for lasting peace and prosperity, not only in Eritrea, but in the region. For the first time in 30 years, people return home. Let us not miss this opportunity. The efforts we witness in Eritrea for creating a sustainable peace will be to the advantage of the whole Horn. I know of no better investment.[78]

Notes

1. The name has been changed; the statement is accurate. Woldemichael is a former fighter and later refugee to Germany. He has recently returned to Eritrea to help rebuild his country.

2. This study is based primarily on personal interviews with Eritrean government officials, representatives of donor countries and international NGOs, Eritrean former fighters, Eritrean civilians, UNHCR, Geneva staff and UNHCR, Eritrea staff, other UN agency staff (UNDP and DHA), and participants in the earlier Cross Border Operations. The interviews were conducted in Eritrea, Sweden, the United States, Ethiopia, and Geneva, in November and December 1994; January 1995; May and June 1995.

Documentation was graciously provided by the Refugee Studies Programme, Oxford University; the UNHCR Documentation Centre; the Commission for Eritrean Refugee Affairs (CERA); the Eritrea Relief and Rehabilitation Agency (ERRA); the Eritrean Embassy, Stockholm, Sweden; the Swedish Foreign Ministry; the German Development Institute (GDI); and UNHCR Asmara and UNHCR Geneva. Various international NGOs provided background material.

3. Ambassador Tseggai Tesfazion, Stockholm, Sweden.

4. Arnulv Torbjornsen, UNHCR Chief of Mission, Asmara, Eritrea, May 19–20, 1995, oral statements at the workshop on the Programme for Refugee Reintegration and Rehabilitation of Resettlement Areas in Eritrea (PROFERI), Asmara, Eritrea.

5. The exact number of Eritrean refugees in Sudan is not possible to obtain. The Sudanese government Committee on Refugees (COR) figures, 450,000 to 500,000 at the time of liberation, May 1991, are used by UNHCR and the government of Eritrea.

6. J. Pobee, "'Peace, with Justice and Honour, Fairest and Most Profitable of Possessions'," *Power and Peace* (Uppsala, Sweden: Life & Peace Institute, 1992), 93.

7. See Pobee, *ibid.*, for a fuller discussion of these points within the African context.

8. F. Stepputat, "National Conflict and Repatriation: An Analysis of Relief, Power and Reconciliation," *CDR Project Proposal 93.4* (Copenhagen: Centre for Development Research, Oct. 1993), 5.

9. See J. Clifford, "Traveling Cultures," in *Cultural Studies*, L. Grossberg *et al.,* eds. (New York: Routledge, 1992) and H. Moussa, *Storm and Sanctuary: The Journey of Ethiopian and Eritrean Women Refugees*, (Dundas, Ontario: Artemis Enterprises, 1993), for further discussions of this point.

10. Stepputat, *op. cit.*, note 8, p. 5.

11. The history of Eritrea's liberation struggle is a long and complex one. It is not the intention here to explore the many and interrelated particulars, which are well-elaborated in many writings, but instead to focus on factors that have a contemporary relationship to the negotiations for repatriation.

12. UN Resolution 390-A(V) explicitly stated that the provisions of the federation would not be amended or violated by any body other than the General Assembly. The autonomy of the Eritrean government was guaranteed by the United Nations.

13. M. Fahlen, *UNHCR Mission Report, Eritrea*, 1995-05-26, p. 2.

14. From 1976 to 1991 "unofficial" food aid funded by Northern European countries was channeled into the liberated areas of Eritrea through the efforts of Swedish Church Relief, Norwegian Church Aid, and the Sudan Council of Churches—the Emergency Relief Desk in Khartoum. See M. Duffield and J. Prendergast, *Without Troops and Tanks: Humanitarian Intervention in Ethiopia and Eritrea* (Lawrenceville, N.J.: Red Sea Press, 1994), for a description of the Cross-Border Operation.

15. Chief of Mission, UNHCR Asmara, May 1995.

16. Elias Habte Selassie, UNDP/UNDO, May 1995, Nairobi, Kenya. He recounted that a small number of former fighters were punished by the government for financial corruption. When Selassie asked if they were really "corrupt," given the economic pressures on them, the government said that these former fighters were indeed corrupt and that it therefore had to fight against this temptation.

17. "Countries of the Horn: 3—Eritrea," *New Internationalist* 238 (Dec. 1992) 17.

18. John McCallin, UNHCR Horn of Africa Desk, Geneva, Switzerland, Jan. 1995.

19. As discussed in "Environmental Aspects of Resettlements," by Naigzy Gebremedhin, Coordinator of Eritrea's National Environmental Management Plan, May 1995, only 0.40 percent of Eritrea is now forested. Thirty years ago it was 15 percent forested. According to an FAO report (*Environment Eritrea*, 1:3 [Feb. 1995]), fuel wood demand in Eritrea exceeds supply by 150 percent.

20. Fahlen, *UNHCR Mission Report, Eritrea*, p. 3.

21. A Constitutional Commission, officially independent of the government and committed to the protection of citizens' rights and a pluralistic form of governance, is implementing a two-year participatory process to involve all regions and sectors of Eritrean society in the development of the constitution. If this process is successful, Eritrea has a good chance of becoming a peaceful model in the Horn of Africa.

22. E. Habte Selassie, UNDP/UNDO, Nairobi, Kenya, May 1995; G. Kibreab, 1995, UNHCR officials.

23. The Swedish government had provided funds for food aid delivered through the Cross-Border Operation from Sudan during the liberation struggle.

24. Ahmed Tahir Badouri, May 1995, Asmara, Eritrea.

25. UNHCR Geneva staff, Jan. 1995.

26. UNHCR Geneva staff and "Eritrea," *World Refugee Survey* (Washington, D.C.: U.S. Committee for Refugees), 56.

27. Throughout the interviews and in relevant documents there are differences in the specific amounts mentioned; for example, US$24 million, $50 million, $68 million. Finally, the absoluteness of the amount is not as important as the fact that, in comparison to the PGE's budget estimates, the amount was very small. It was this difference that was salient.

28. This point was also made in interviews by representatives of several international donor countries. They stressed that repatriation (humanitarian emergency relief) funds are administered separately from development money. These funds are not comingled administratively.

29. Ahmed Tahir Badouri, *Eritrea Profile*, Jan. 7, 1995, p. 7.

30. Elias Habte Selassie, May 1995, Nairobi, Kenya.

31. UNHCR Geneva, Jan. 1995.

32. Karin Landgren, UNHCR, Jan. 1995, Geneva, Switzerland.

33. Elias Habte Selassie, UNDP, May 1995, Nairobi, Kenya.

34. Nils Arne-Kastberg, Swedish Mission to the UN, October 1994.

35. "Joint Government of Eritrea and United Nations Appeal for Eritrea," vol. 1, PROFERI, Executive Summary, June 1993, p. i.

36. *Eritrea Profile*, Jan. 14, 1995, p. 7. This opinion was echoed by the NGO staff and UNHCR staff who participated in the planning process.

37. Dr. Nerayo Teklemichael, Director of ERRA/GOE, May 1995, Asmara, Eritrea.

38. "Eritrea," *World Refugee Survey*, p. 56.

39. GOE, "Joint Government of Eritrea and United Nations Appeal for Eritrea," vol. 1, PROFERI, June 1993, pp. i–ii.

40. Arnulv Thornbjornsen, UNHCR Chief of Mission, May 1995, Asmara, Eritrea.

41. Asmara, Eritrea, May 1995.

42. CERA/GOE, "Progress Report on Repatriation and Initial Relief and Food Aid Components of the Pilot Project and Statistical Information on Returnees," May 1995, p. 1.

43. Norwegian Church Aid staff, Nov. 1994, Asmara, Eritrea.

44. Fahlen, *UNHCR Mission Report, Eritrea*, May 15–23, 1995, p. 1. Spontaneous returnees receive less material support than those who return under the organized repatriation program.

45. UNHCR, *Country Operations Plan*, State of Eritrea, May 29, 1995, notes that the actual number able to be repatriated depended in part on truck availability. UNHCR and CERA have experienced major delays in the delivery of nine large trucks for refugee movement and logistics/construction activities. This required CERA to make other, quite costly trucking arrangements.

46. This was also the message I received in individual interviews with UNHCR, CERA, ERRA, and various NGOs.

47. Arnulv Torbjornsen, Chief of Mission, UNHCR, Asmara, May 19, 1995, presentation at Donor Workshop, Asmara, Eritrea.

48. *Ibid.*

49. Herbert P. M'Cleod, UNDP Resident Representative, May 20, 1995, statement at PROFERI Workshop, Asmara, Eritrea.

50. The PROFERI development and integration approach is similar to the national Recovery and Rehabilitation Programme for Eritrea (RRPE) of ERRA but is targeted solely to returnees. RRPE is targeted to the broad population. There are plans to combine CERA and ERRA into one agency, although that had not occurred at the time of the Donors Workshop, May 1995.

51. N. Gebremedhin, "Environmental Aspects of Resettlements," GOE, report to Donors Workshop, Asmara, Eritrea, May 19–20, 1995.

52. The GOE's environmental report, "Environmental Aspects of Resettlements," estimated that approximately 42,000 housing units—five persons per household—will be required to house 420,000 returnees. A traditional *Hidmo* would require 100 fully grown trees, an impossibility in Eritrea. There was concern that even the materials for ordinary huts would not be available.

53. See A. Hansen, *Current Conditions in Returnee Camps in Gash & Setit Province*, report prepared for GTZ Integrated Food Security Programme (IFSP), Gash & Setit, Tessenei, Eritrea, March 1995, for an elaboration of these concerns.

54. As an example, FINIDA negotiated over a year with the GOE regarding cooperation with the university. FINIDA agreed to a lot of give-and-take but would not give in regarding having two Finns at the university to sign checks. When the GOE would not agree to this, FINIDA pulled out.

55. Gerense Kelati, Commissioner of CERA, May 19, 1995, Donors Workshop, Asmara, Eritrea.

56. The UNHCR Chief of Mission, discussing the need for donors to support the repatriation process, reflected that all the donors have asked if CERA has the capacity to receive 100,000 people. He said, "The answer is NO, but they learn by walking. UNHCR will work for basics. They will do it, wait and see. *Believe us—give CERA a chance, support them.* If you are not happy, then you have a base for criticism."

57. Madame Sadako Ogata, UN High Commissioner for Refugees, June 8, 1994, Washington, D.C.

58. G. Kibreab, *Ready, Willing, and Waiting* (Uppsala, Sweden: Life & Peace Institute, 1995).

59. UNHCR, "Policy & Methodological Framework for Quick Impact Projects (QIPs) as a means of facilitating durable solutions through integration," June 30, 1994, pp. 1–2.

60. UNHCR 1993:173.

61. H. Bjuremalm, Swedish Foreign Ministry, Oct. 1994.

62. See E. G. Ferris, *Beyond Borders: Refugees, Migrants and Human Rights in the Post Cold-War Era* (Geneva: World Council of Churches, 1993) for a detailed exploration of the international refugee response system.

63. UNHCR Chief of Mission, Asmara, Eritrea, May 1995.

64. See also Kibreab, *op. cit.*, note 58.

65. UNHCR Chief of Mission, Asmara, Eritrea, May 1995.

66. U.S. refugee resettlement agency staff.

67. International Peace Service, n.d.

68. Elias Habte Selassie, May 1995, Nairobi, Kenya.

69. Member of the German parliament speaking at the Donors Workshop, May 19, 1995, Asmara, Eritrea.

70. Helene Bjuremalm, Swedish Foreign Ministry, Oct. 1994. Also, see Ferris, *op. cit.*, note 62.

71. A German representative recalled that when Germany gave DM3 million to a particular Eritrean project it was likely that only DM1 million would finally be available for the direct implementation of the project. The remainder would be used for salaries, materials, and consultations from Germany. Frequently technical support was included within direct aid.

72. This is especially ironic in the Eritrean context since all the donors informally agreed that the Eritrean government was an honest, legitimate government—in clear contrast to a government such as that of Nigeria.

73. Dr. Nerayo Teklemichael, Head of ERRA, government of Eritrea, May 1995, Asmara, Eritrea.

74. UNHCR, "Policy & Methodological Framework for Quick Impact Projects (QIPs) as a means of facilitating durable solutions through integration," June 30, 1994, pp. 1–2.

75. Part of the responsibility of the Constitutional Committee is to structure mechanisms for such participation into the governance of the country.

76. I am grateful to Nils-Arne Kastberg, Swedish Mission to the UN, Geneva, for this suggestion.

77. Ambassador Tessegai Tesfazion, Nov. 1994, Stockholm.

78. Arnulv Torbjornsen, UNHCR Chief of Mission Asmara, presentation to Donors Workshop, May 19, 1995, Asmara, Eritrea.

CHAPTER 12

Environmental Justice, Health, and Safety in Urban South Africa

Ben Wisner[1]

Introduction

Elsewhere in this volume the concept of environmental rights is equated with the human right to a healthful environment and to sustainable livelihood. In the context of urban South Africa in the postapartheid era, this definition is useful. It focuses attention on the activism of township dwellers in struggling for such rights. It also highlights the limitation of reform and incrementalism in situations that have been rendered nonviable by spatial logic of racial separation and the control of labor power.

This paper sets out to review the situation in South Africa's four largest metropolitan areas at the end of the first year of the new Government of National Unity (GNU). Urban policy in South Africa since the National Party came to power in 1948 was to control "nonwhite" access to and residence in urban areas. In the course of implementing this plan for racial separation and the control of the nonwhite labor power needed in cities, the apartheid regime was in nearly constant conflict with African, colored, and Asian communities. Attempts to "clear black spots" from "white" cities by resettlement were resisted by the residents. Other groups of migrants from rural areas or outlying peri-urban zones set up illegal shack communities on vacant land as near to jobs as they could get. The regime often fought back by further rounds of forced removal and resettlement.

In the course of nearly 50 years of such urban struggle, many lives were lost in violent confrontation. In addition, a far greater price was paid by the affected communities because of increased health and safety hazards to which its peoples had been subjected. The demographic and spatial instability of nonwhite urban areas has made community assessment and mitigation of hazards difficult. Always short of economic means for investment in infrastructure, the locus of planning control was always outside these communities. Squatters and shack dwellers, especially, fell outside even the meager attempts by townships to supply water, sanitation, electricity, drainage, roads, traffic regulation, and health services.[2] Spatial apartheid produced extreme densities and hence subdivision of structures for relatives or renters.

This spatial pattern of extremely dense urban settlement with insufficient services has led to critical health and safety hazards. In addition to public health, fire, and traffic

Ben Wisner is a geographer and the Director of the International Studies Program at California State University–Long Beach. He can be reached via email (bwisner@igc.apc.org).

hazards, these areas often became the site of illegal dumping of hazardous waste. Other common hazards are flooding, mass erosion of slopes, and air pollution caused by mineral coal fires used for warmth and cooking where electricity is commonly absent or unaffordable.

Resistance to apartheid gave rise in the 1980s to campaigns of ungovernability. Residents were urged by political organizers to refuse to pay for utilities and or for rent owed to the townships, because these forms of local government were seen as nonrepresentative and the services they provided were poor. In the period of reconstruction following the April 1994 national elections, which produced a government of national unity led by the African National Congress (ANC), the ripples of ungovernability are still to be seen. Local governments were not elected until October 1995. Provisional arrangements remain ad hoc—the product of ongoing negotiations between civic organizations and the adjacent white municipalities that often provided a caretaker role in the absence of effective township councils.

Preliminary research into the hazard vulnerability of one such South African township in the Greater Johannesburg region suggests that health, safety, and sustainable livelihoods have been blocked—hence environmental rights violated—through the complex spatial and social consequences of struggle over urban occupancy. However, this paper attempts to go beyond describing the hazardous situation thus caused and laying blame to the question of reconstruction and healing. A review of efforts by citizens and their evolving organizations (the civics and other nongovernmental organizations) and a consideration of the policies of the new government provides some room for hope. However, the challenge to both government and citizen-based organizations is not to minimize the extent of the problem. A dual strategy of immediate increase in services and mitigation of the worst hazards must be coupled with two longer-term processes: (1) de-densification through land acquisition and provision of affordable housing, or at least building loans and site and service, and (2) investment in people

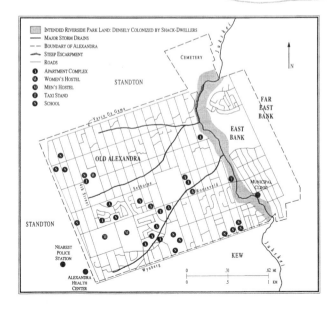

A view of shack dwellings in Alexandra Township, Johannesburg. Photograph by Ben Wisner.

through neighborhood- and community-based capacity building for locally initiated work on what people agree are priority hazards.

Urban and Rural Settlement Ecology under Apartheid

For the majority of people in South Africa, both urban and rural, the system of racial separation distorted relations with nature in a profound way. By allowing residence and land use in only certain places demarcated for "nonwhites," apartheid created overcrowding and made dangerous and environmentally destructive practices necessary for ordinary people trying to satisfy their basic needs for shelter, water, sanitation, and income. In rural areas this took place in two principal ways. As tenants and workers on white-owned farms and ranches, insecurity of tenure for nonwhites and low incomes precluded all but the most modest self-built or self-financed improvements in housing, sanitation, landscaping, and dooryard gardening. In the many small fragments of territory collectively known as the *homelands*, where South Africa maintained the legal fiction that all black citizens belonged, and to which, in principle, they were required to return when not formally employed, sheer population density usually interfered with sustainable land management. Pastures in these former homeland areas are today overgrazed, forests are denuded, stream flow is reduced, soil erosion is extreme.[3]

In urban South Africa, conditions are similar, and for related reasons. Under apartheid only certain so-called townships were designated as residential zones for nonwhites. Even before the campaign of ungovernability and final wave of resistance against "pass laws" (which formally regulated the movement and residence of nonwhites) in the 1980s, houses and home compounds in these townships were subdivided to allow space for relatives coming to the city to work or to rent. Infrastructure and services in the townships was always rudimentary—one of the causes of the "rent and rate" boycotts in the 1980s—but such subdivision made the burden even greater on existing facilities such as water, drainage, sanitation, fire protection, markets, and open space. In addition, attempts by apartheid planners to "rationalize" nonwhite settlement meant that numerous established nonwhite neighborhoods were rezoned and their inhabitants forcefully relocated, usually to sites with only minimal services (water points and pit latrines) at distant locations on the ever-widening periphery of urban areas. Many nonwhite urban dwellers resisted relocation, and their resulting struggle with the authorities resulted in even less access to lifeline infrastructure and even more physical damage to the urban ecology because of arson, erection of road blocks, creation of squatter camps—sometimes overnight—in open space being contested.

Relations between humans and nature in such urban areas were just as distorted as in the homelands and in "white" farm areas. Urban waterways were polluted and often narrowed by the disposal of solid waste. Housing was closely packed, blocking natural drainage lines and precluding the conservation of trees. Open space was rare, and even heroic efforts to maintain vegetation were usually thwarted by sheer weight of usage. Wastewater rutted roads and collected where insects and other disease vectors could breed. The air was often polluted with the smoke of thousands of mineral coal braziers, the principal source of heat for cooking and warmth in the winter. Density of dwellings, narrow and poorly aligned and maintained streets and lanes, both created conditions for frequent injuries of pedestrians—often children—from passing vehicles and increased the danger of fires.

In both urban and rural areas under apartheid, there was, and remains, a gross imbalance between human needs and activities, on the one hand, and, on the other, geographical and ecological conditions such as topography, drainage, surface and ground water, microclimate, soil fertility, and the like. A crisis of environmental health and safety resulted at both the rural and urban end of the settlement continuum. As conditions became progressively worse in rural areas, even more pressure was put on available "nonwhite" space in cities. Then with the lead-up to the elections in April 1994 and the period of the "new South Africa" afterward, a tidal wave of immigrants from the countryside began to reappropriate urban space from which they or their parents had been removed by apartheid. Residential densities soared, and attempts to introduce planned land use and service provision in the new political situation seemed meager, by comparison.

Urban Health and Safety Crisis and Environmental Rights

The editor's introduction to this volume discusses the connections between human rights as conventionally recognized in international law and the notion of environmental rights. The two principal bases for claiming environmental rights are the right to health and the right to a livelihood, or, more broadly, the right to development. By restricting nonwhites in South Africa—some 87 percent of the population—to only 13 percent of the land, the apartheid system clearly violated the right that millions of people had to health and to livelihood. The degradation of rural homelands described earlier has made the population of roughly 10 million living there highly vulnerable to any additional stress, such as the drought in 1992. In keeping with the racial bias governing access to land, employment, housing, and other key material and social resources under apartheid, drought aid during this recent crisis was highly skewed: government allocations of R703 (South African rand) per rural white resident and only R13 per rural African.[4] The unsustainability of rural livelihoods is mirrored in health statistics. Mortality by the fifth year of life, generally thought to be a sensitive indicator of the overall nutritional situation, is around 50 percent in the homelands.[5] Access to improved water supplies in the ten homelands in 1990 was enjoyed by only 46 percent of the people, while only 13 percent had access to adequate sanitation.[6] Violation of the right to livelihood and to health in rural South Africa has steadily increased the numbers migrating to African townships, as described earlier. The result is a housing shortage estimated at between two and three million units.[7] In 1993 estimates of the number of people living in shacks ranged from 5.0 to 7.7 million.[8]

The new South Africa must deal with the human and environmental consequences of its land and housing policies of the past. If, indeed, its citizens are considered to have environmental rights that include healthy and secure shelter, water, sanitation, drainage, clean air, and so forth, then credible and accountable elected authorities should either provide the resources to satisfy claims against these rights, or—in the absence of sufficient resources for direct and immediate delivery—the affected people must be encouraged to become part of a self-help process that will contribute toward satisfying their own needs. As stated earlier, the argument of this paper is that *both* approaches—"top-down" and "bottom-up"—are necessary. Active citizen participation in improving the health and security of urban areas is necessary in the short term, but it is also desirable in the short- and long-term because it empowers participants, builds local nongovernmental institutions, and strengthens democracy.

Urbanization in South Africa

In 1993 the South African population was estimated to be 40 million.[9] Urban growth rates ranged between 3 and 5 percent during the 1980s and 1990s, accelerating rapidly after 1986.[10] African population in cities grew from 8.5 million in 1985 to 14 million in 1993.[11] In 1991 the proportion of people living in urban areas (excluding the former homeland areas) was 57 percent. This is not high by the standards of an industrial country, but the pressures discussed above have resulted in increasing rates of urbanization, especially by poor Africans moving in from rural areas. For example, the African population of Greater Cape Town grew from 200,000 in 1982 to more than 900,000 in 1992.[12] According to one estimate, the urban population is expected to double between 1990 and 2010.[13]

Not only is the rate of urbanization increasing, but also the spatial pattern of growth is highly concentrated. In 1990 some 37 percent of South Africans lived in the country's four largest urban regions:[14]

Greater Cape Town (Cape Peninsula)	2.5 million
Greater Durban	3.4 million
Greater Port Elizabeth	0.9 million
PWV[15]	7.5 million

It is estimated that within a decade three-quarters of the entire urban population could live in the PWV, Greater Durban, and the Cape Peninsula.[16]

Urban Health and Safety: Typical Patterns

Conditions in the townships and more peripheral squatter communities in these major urban regions have much in common, as described above: congestion, poor sanitation and drainage, inadequate access to services such as health care, fire fighting,[17] refuse collection and telecommunications, and high rates of crime. In addition, these communities are often located near heavy industry, because industrial belts were used by apartheid planners as a means to buffer racial groups from one another. Air and water pollution from these industries adds to the insults on environmental health and safety, as does illegal dumping of waste. Particular physical characteristics give rise to special problems in many of the areas within these urban regions.

For example in the Cape Flats to the southeast of Cape Town, the presence of a large aquifer creates rising damp that weakens structures and combines with the cold, wet winter weather brought by the southeastern gales, creating much respiratory disease.

Similarly, some communities in the PWV are built on dolomitic geological formations that are prone to rapid creation of sinkholes, a unique physical hazard. Local topography and regional climate combines in some places such as Soweto and Alexandra in the PWV to create conditions in which smoke produced by burning coal is only very slowly dispersed. The resulting concentration is another cause of respiratory disease in the winter.

Greater Durban's squatter communities are exposed to cyclones and, given the hilly topography in some areas such as Inanda, there is a tendency toward accelerated erosion and mudslides.

Overlying these peculiarities of specific places, African urban inhabitants face a general pattern of combined risk from geophysical, biological, social, and technological hazards.

Megacities and Disaster: The Broader Context

The pattern of exposure to risk and vulnerability to hazards in South African cities should be seen in the context of worldwide experience with the hazardousness of increasingly large, complex urban areas. Within the last few decades we have witnessed the growth worldwide of a number urban regions with many millions of inhabitants in each of them. Despite confusion produced by differing methods for classifying cities and counting people, there is no doubt that the so-called "megacity" is one of the most interesting and troubling phenomena of the late 20th century. These urban regions— whether they be Cairo, São Paulo, Manila, Los Angeles, or Greater Johannesburg (the PWV)—share a number of morphological, socioeconomic, political, and environmental characteristics. They spread and sprawl over very large areas spatially, incorporating smaller preexisting urban places, peri-urban settlements, and newer "edge cities." They are the site of very diverse economic activities and employment patterns ranging from "high-tech" white collar to the semi-proletarian, subterranean, "parallel" economies of large homeless and street populations. There is an ever-increasing income and social distance between the rich and the poor in these urban regions. They are politically fragmented into sometimes hundreds of different administrations and jurisdictions. Environmentally, they import great quantities of energy, food, and water—often from hundreds or even thousands of kilometers away. Their waste stream pollutes the air, soil, and water within the megacity region and sometimes far beyond. Motorized transport—energy inefficient and air polluting—knits these large urban regions together.[18]

Because of the great polarization of wealth in the megacity, its benefits (economic, cultural, environmental) tend to accrue to the rich, while the poor tend to bear the costs of such concentration. In Los Angeles, for example, the predominantly poor Hispanic population lives in the zone of highest air pollution, and it is their housing stock that is least protected against earthquake.[19] To the extent that urban population density is a rough indicator of stress on lifeline services, quality of life, and the potential for disasters, disparities *within* megacities also reveal socioeconomic polarity. Thus, for instance, in predominantly African Alexandra Township, Johannesburg, the density is 688 persons per hectare while in predominantly white areas the density is only 44 per hectare.[20]

Studies of megacities in many parts of the world suggest that they are the sites where people are vulnerable to a wide range of hazards—precisely the range seen in South Africa:[21]

Geophysical/climatic hazards	Floods, drought, wildfires, storms, landslides, earthquakes . . .
Technological hazards	Industrial explosions and fires, air pollution, waste exposure, reservoir failure, nuclear accidents . . .
Biological hazards	HIV infection, drug overdose, childhood cancer, heat exhaustion, water-borne disease . . .
Social hazards	Violent crime, child poverty, homelessness . . .

These hazards interact with each other in complex ways. For example, floods have washed drums of toxic chemicals out of storage yards into residential areas. There are often "cascades" of secondary and tertiary hazards produced by the primary event.

Vulnerability to these hazards in large cities is not evenly distributed. Exposure and the ability to cope and to recover economically are distributed unevenly according to a person's class, gender, age, ethnicity, and whether or not she/he is disabled.

Protecting communities, especially the most vulnerable communities, from such hazards should be one of the major priorities of both environmental and health policies. Disaster prevention, mitigation, and preparedness are activities where the concerns of environmental and health policy overlap greatly. Work on disasters falls squarely into both areas: into the field of urban and peri-urban environmental management and restoration, and into the field of health actions focused on preventing disease, injury, premature death, and loss of livelihood. There are, of course, other areas where environmental policy and health policy interact strongly—for example, in shop-floor occupational health and safety practices as well as in such disease-prevention activities as vector control, water supply, and sanitation.

There is, in short, a crisis with multiple dimensions affecting the South Africans who, for specific historical reasons, are swelling the degraded urban environments discussed. Alexandra Township, the site of recent field work on these issues, provides a case in point.

Alexandra Township: An Extreme Case

Background

Alexandra Township presents an extreme case of the violation of environmental rights. It has historically been one of the chief entry points into the urban system for the environmental refugee from rural areas. It has also suffered in an extreme way the spatial vise grip of apartheid planning. In addition, political struggles over land use and local government have created a culture of ungovernability and violence that now threatens the ability of community-based organizations to engage in reconstruction and development.

Alexandra, the subject of the poem that begins this chapter, is a small area (4 sq km) lying on the northeast edge of central Johannesburg, wedged between affluent white suburbs within a "buffer" zone of light industry. It is an old, well-established African township, officially established in 1905, when it had been possible for Africans to own urban property—an unusual privilege. It has been and remains an important transit point for young people coming to Johannesburg to seek work. Alexandra is thus a mixture of more established households, many of them earning rents from shack dwellers living in tin and wooden shelters built in the "yards" of formerly privately owned homes and the town council's brick houses, and a more transient population. One study in 1990 found that 56 percent of Alexandra adult residents had been living there for more than 21 years, 22 percent between 11 and 20 years, 13 percent between 4 and 10 years, and 9 percent between 1 and 3 years.[22] Alexandra contains great ethnic and national diversity—including a considerable number of Mozambican war refugees.

The people successfully resisted attempts to remove them repeatedly since the National Party came to power in 1948. It was at this time, during the early 1950s, that several African residential areas were destroyed and their inhabitants moved further out into the periphery surrounding Johannesburg. For example, hundreds of thousands of Africans were forcibly removed from Sophiatown to an area some 20 kilometers to the southwest of central Johannesburg, across open land dominated by huge mountains of mine tailings. This settlement subsequently grew into present-day Soweto, with a population of nearly 4 million.[23] Informal settlements grew up in and around many of these new peripheral townships.

From 1960 to 1980 some 3.5 million nonwhite South Africans were removed or relocated as a result of the "logic" of racial separation.[24] In that spirit, the 1960s saw apartheid planners invalidate existing freehold rights held by residents of Alexandra in preparation for reconstructing the entire area as a site for high rise single-sex dormitories (called hostels) for workers. Much housing was destroyed and thousands of people were forced to move to Soweto.[25] However, there was great community resistance and protest, and only a few of the hostels were ever built. Alexandra continued to exist as officially a "temporary" township throughout the 1960s and 1970s.

Beginning in 1979, a series of "upgrading" projects were conceived, though with little community participation.[26] These included work on roads and drainage, provision of water taps and bucket latrines, and expansion of the township house rental stock. Following the mass protests that began in 1986, further "upgrading" has taken place. This has included tarring the roads, provision of some waterborne sewage, storm drains, and some electrification. In addition, approximately 900 homes for middle-income residents were built across the Juskei River in the East Bank area (see photograph).

Unlike Soweto and other townships, Alexandra is very close to the center of Johannesburg and closely borders some of the richest white residential areas, such as Sandton and Kew. Numerous attempts have been made, with the support of township councilors suspected of having personal financial interests, to seize land for lucrative projects such as a convention center.[27] Thus the distance between ordinary residents and their town council widened, eventually leading to a rent and utility fee boycott beginning in the late 1980s.

African townships in the midst of major urban regions did not share a common tax base with the white municipalities that are adjacent neighbors in the urban mosaic.[28] For example, the Johannesburg City Council (serving white municipalities) received 30 percent of its income from the central business district and 70 percent from industry and commerce in the city as a whole.[29] Yet townships such as Soweto and Alexandra received virtually no tax revenue from industry and commerce, because they were (and still are) located outside their borders. Labor power commuted from these townships to work in those industries, creating wealth and making purchases in white businesses whose profits also did not provide tax revenue for the residential home areas of the workers and shoppers.

The late 1980s and 1990s were a period of confrontation and violence. That era also saw the consolidation of popular power through the activities of the Alexandra Civic Organization (ACO), founded in 1986. On the one hand, negotiation with surrounding white municipalities and the Johannesburg City Council continued, as the parties discussed services and the future of local government after the official end of apartheid. Housing, roads, refuse removal, lack of electricity, and street lighting headed the list of residents' concerns.[30] Controversy swirled around a proposed "site and service" scheme offered by the mainstream Independent Development Trust (IDT) that provided 80-meter houseplots, water and electricity connections, and latrines in an area known as the Far East Bank in the former racial buffer zone of vacant land between Alexandra and a major national motorway.[31]

On the other hand, the township was increasingly racked by violent attacks by militant factions, as the date for national elections drew near. For example, in 1991 Zulu migrant workers supporting the Inkatha Freedom Party attacked homes adjacent to their hostel, burning a large area subsequently referred to as "Beirut." In August 1994 refugees from this area were still living in church halls and doubling up with kinspeople, increasing congestion in the township.

Having generated effective forms of grassroots organization over the years (manifesting such institutions as the Ministers' Fraternal and Alexandra Civic Organization), boycotts of rents and utility fees, as well as of the Johannesburg bus system, were effective. The politics of protest culminated in the call by both the ANC and the ACO for a campaign of "ungovernability" in the late 1980s. In addition to the boycotts, the call went out to the rural areas for as many people as possible to come to settle in Alexandra. At that point its population grew rapidly from approximately 75,000 in 1979 to 180,000 in 1986, 360,000 people in 1992, and roughly 400,000 in 1994.[32] Residential density is 160 accommodation units (mostly backyard and freestanding shacks) per hectare. It is this incredibly high, urban density that presents the greatest challenge to the process of "reconstruction and development" launched by the Government of National Unity (GNU) in 1994.

Hazard Profile

Risk, Exposure, Vulnerability, and Response

Alexandra's area is about 1.5 square miles, or roughly four square kilometers.[33] A population of 400,000 (the high estimate) works out to a density of 100,000 per sq km, or a thousand persons on every hectare,[34] for an estimated density of 800 persons per hectare. Alexandra lies on a hillside that slopes from west to east into the valley of the Juskei River. Virtually every square meter of open space has been settled by squatters or otherwise built over. This includes the areas on and near the three major storm drains that run down the hillside into the river. Shacks (*mekhukhu*) fill the backyards of more substantial brick houses. In addition, there are four extensive areas of shack development including one near the cemetery[35] and another along the west bank of the Juskei River. In 1989 approximately 70 percent of Alexandra residents were living in informal housing. Some 14,000 families lived in single rooms attached to houses; 11,000 families lived in freestanding shacks; 6,100 families were in backyard shacks; 400 were in council houses; 1,500 were in apartments in several high-rises built in the 1980s; 1,700 families lived in private houses; and there were 8,400 hostel beds.[36]

Such density exposes the population to a wide variety of hazards. Fires are common. With light shack construction and no firewalls, disastrous fires spread quickly. At present the nearest fire department is in the white community of Randburg several kilometers away, so response time is slow, and given the density of shack development, there are few points of access. Minibus taxis are the main form of transportation to and from work for township residents. Drivers are highly competitive, and traffic is a major hazard to pedestrians, especially children, who have little play space other than the road.

Flood Hazard in Alexandra

Using aerial photographs and household sampling, it has been calculated that a flood of the Juskei River with a recurrence interval of 50 years could destroy nearly 900 shacks, endangering between 4,400 to 10,500 people, depending on one's estimate of family size per shack.[37] Another similar exercise found 1,235 shacks below the 50-year floodline and a total of from 4,940 to 7,410 people exposed to this risk (more conservatively assuming only four to six persons per family, respectively).[38]

The catchment of the Juskei has been rapidly urbanized since 1940 with the consequence that runoff from intense summer rainfall very rapidly finds its way into the main channel. This rapidly peaking storm hydrograph provides little warning to people at risk. In addition, illegal dumping of garbage has narrowed the Juskei, increasing the risk of flood. The people living in shacks in the river flood plain are among the poorest in the township, with few options, little income to facilitate a move, or few resources to help them recover after a flood. They are also some of the most recent arrivals, many of them foreign nationals—including war refugees from Mozambique. They are therefore highly vulnerable to flood, as their poverty, minority status, and lack of social networks lock them into their present exposed locations.

A 20-year flood would presently affect 575 shacks (2,800 to 6,900 persons). Even a relatively common 5-year flood could destroy (and, indeed, has destroyed) as many as 220 shacks (affecting 1,100 to 2,600 persons).[39]

These calculations do not take into account the shack dwellers who inhabit the area adjacent to the three major storm drainage lines. The local runoff associated with a mere 10-year flood could flatten the shacks of possibly 3,000 people who live near these culverts that drain into the river.[40]

Several hundred more families live in shacks on the west bank of the river above the floodline, but precariously near the edge of a steep 15–20 meter escarpment. In flood, the Juskei River undercuts this area, which is highly erodable because it is made up of landfill. The stability of the slope is further compromised by constant seepage of domestic wastewater.

Response to the flood hazard has so far taken the form of an early-warning system based on gauges monitoring river heights and rainfall in the river catchment, together with warning sirens and preestablished assembly points. However, the long history of hostile relations between Alexandra residents and officials has made it difficult to generate public support for this system.

Health Hazards in Alexandra

Many residents burn coal in open braziers for heat in the winter. A pall of smoke settles in the river valley in the evening and in the early morning. Density, poverty, lack of accessible and affordable electricity,[41] and topography combine to create a major risk to the respiratory health of Alexandra's residents, especially those living in the valley (who tend to be the poorest), and especially to the very young, the very old, and those, such as retired miners, who may already suffer from lung disorders or tuberculosis (very common in South Africa).[42] Also related to cold winter weather is the risk of hypothermia on the part of newborn children.[43]

Roughly 25 percent of Alexandra residents use a bucket system for defecation. These bucket latrines are provided by the township council and are, in principle, emptied every week and the buckets cleaned at a facility near the cemetery on the northern edge of the township. The system in itself is unsanitary, and, given the crisis in finance and administration suffered for so long by the township council, maintenance can lapse.[44] In addition, the same washing blocks used to clean buckets serve as an informal site for township laundry. This site is just ten meters from the Juskei River, adding to health risks.

Piles of refuse are a well-known trademark of Alexandra. The extremely high population density and the paucity of government services have created enormous problems of household waste disposal. Vermin abound, providing disease vectors. Stray dogs and rats are a safety as well as health hazard to children.

The response to these and other health problems has been intermittent cleanup campaigns by various citizen-based organizations, political demands by the ACO for the provision of skips (dumpsites) for refuse and a schedule of refuse removal, and small amounts of extension work by health educators and environmental health workers from the Alexandra Health Center.

Composite Urban Risk

In a township like Alexandra, daily life is carried on under the threat of a variety of risks, simultaneously. Violence (including domestic violence), sexually transmitted diseases (including AIDS), hepatitis, and other diseases associated with poor sanitation coexist with the threat of fire, flood, traffic accidents, and chronic or acute illness from a variety of hazardous substances in the air and water. This simultaneity and coincidence in the lives of individuals means that risk perception and self-protective behavior can be quite complicated. Parents may rank risks affecting their children higher than those more generally pervasive in the urban environment. Women suffering domestic violence may not recognize it as a risk they can do anything about until they begin to confide in friends or neighboring women. Disabled people will view risks in terms of the limitations created by their limited mobility, sight, or hearing.

Just as vulnerability is stratified by age, class, gender, ethnicity, or subculture, so are risk perception and behavior modified by these human differences.

So numerous are the risks, and so great the number of people exposed to them in a township like Alexandra, that South Africa has given rise to a new term: the situational *disaster*.[45] Alexandra itself is a disaster. Therefore, the approach to reconstruction has to be holistic. Given that numerous threats exist at any given time and place in the township—plus a shifting kaleidoscope of risk that, changing with small variations in physical topography and political topography, is contingent on the previous night's illegal dumping or a "taxi war" as well as changes in the seasons—one must ask, Who is best placed to prioritize and to coordinate efforts to prevent or limit disasters?

The answer seems to be neighborhood groups that are small and homogeneous enough to experience a similar constellations of risks, yet large enough to have a strong voice in municipal allocation of resources. This leads to a brief discussion of the process of community-based hazard identification and mitigation.

Reclaiming Urban Environmental Rights

Community-Based Hazard Identification and Mitigation

The literature on megacities and disasters, as well as a larger literature on primary health care, self-help housing, community-based environmental management, and so on, is unanimous in finding that community participation is essential in dealing with such complex, changing, and growing hazards. This is because:

- Local knowledge of the environment is often more detailed and accurate, especially in rapidly growing and changing peri-urban situations.

- Participation leads to endorsement and support for action by the community.

- The cost of surveys and mitigating action in so many neighborhoods of so many townships simultaneously would be prohibitive without the assistance of the citizens themselves.

Under apartheid, consultation with communities was rare, and a thoroughgoing participatory planning approach was even rarer. For example, Mashabela reports: "upgrading is not being undertaken in consultation with residents and priorities appear to be determined by military officers in consultation with township officials."[46]

Major partners in the Government of National Unity such as the African National Congress (ANC) are committed to preventive health action, to affordable housing, and to accelerated enhancement of township environments. Community participation is seen as a means to these ends. For example, the ANC's *Policy Guidelines* include the following:[47]

Health and lack of health are rooted in the economic and social fabric of any society. Socio-economic circumstances are more important than medical services in ensuring good health. . . . The primary health care approach is essentially that of community development. It aims to reduce inequalities in access to health services . . . and integrates the many sectors of modern life such as education and housing. Further, it is based on full community participation.

Counter-disaster planners worldwide recognize what might be called a "disaster management cycle" that includes the following phases:[48]

- *Prevention*—when the physical cause of the disaster can be eliminated or the potentially affected populations can move out of its range

- *Mitigation*—when the physical cause or risk cannot be eliminated, but the potential for loss, injury, and death can be reduced

- *Preparedness*—when people can take specific actions in advance in order to increase their personal protection or contribute to mitigation and prevention and to be ready to respond to an emergency or disaster[49]

- *Response*—actions taken by the community and by authorities to save life and property in the event of a disaster

- *Rehabilitation*—actions taken by the community and by authorities to reestablish essential services, as well as social and economic activity;

- *Recovery*—actions taken by the community and authorities to reconstruct housing and facilities and to reestablish livelihoods.

Residents themselves are not only *capable* of contributing considerably to each of these phases, but in many cases *they are the primary actors, by default*. For example, after the major earthquakes of the past decade (Armenia, Mexico City, and others) 90 percent of those rescued were dug out by their neighbors, and not by emergency crews or trained rescue experts.

Preliminary discussions in Alexandra in August 1994 and January 1995 revealed that there is widespread knowledge of the full range of hazards affecting life in the township and that its people are taking initiatives to cope, according to their capacities. For example, parents had built their own speed bumps to slow down the minibus taxis. Groups exist to spread awareness of the hazard of the AIDS virus and to clean up rubbish. Numerous initiatives are taken by church-based groups. In general, the community is active on its own behalf, but efforts are fragmented and not often recognized or supported by official agencies.

As noted above concerning the advantages of community participation, this is not a "second-best" arrangement. Citizens have local knowledge and the intense motivation to improve their lives and environments. In addition, since they are on the ground, they provide vital continuity and the ability to monitor and evaluate actions that have been taken. In this way the vital links between "recovery" and "prevention" and "mitigation" are ensured. That is, ideally, the vulnerability of people in a community is reduced by actions that are taken in the aftermath of an emergency or disaster so that they are *less vulnerable* to the next extreme event or exposure to the next hazard. In many cases, where "top-down" actions have been taken, for example in rehousing disaster victims without their participation in choosing the site, vulnerability has actually *increased*.

Obstacles to Participatory Hazard Reduction

In counter-disaster planning, as in other kinds of field-based, applied research, the attempt is often made to "tap" or utilize something called "local knowledge." Usually this is confined to asking local residents to name or identify hazards, locate them in space and time, and relate their past experiences with, and responses to, these hazards. This has been a fruitful line of applied research,[50] but it is important to recognize the limitations of this kind of knowledge.

All human beings exist within a dense world of meanings. To gain the confidence of a local community and to forge a collaboration between local residents and outside "experts," it is necessary for both sides to become conscious of many more dimensions of their respective world views and life worlds than they do at present.

So-called participatory research has tended to focus too narrowly on "indigenous technical knowledge" (or ITK).

There are, however, many forms of knowledge besides the technical.[51] *Technical knowledge* answers questions such as When?, Where?, and How? For example, discussing the danger of flood along the storm drainage system in Alexandra township in Johannesburg, outside experts and community residents can usefully exchange views on answers to these questions. But there is much more than just these questions. To understand the flood hazard, one must also juxtapose outsider and insider views of *who* it is who lives on or near these storm drains. This involves *social knowledge*. Also included in this category of knowledge are answers to questions concerning agency: Who is it that wants to deal with this "problem"? In whose interest is activity focused around the storm drain problem? In addition, there arise questions about fundamental social and historical causation. This requires *critical knowledge*. Why do people live on and near these drainage lines? Why have "experts" decided to try to help with this situation at this moment in history and not before?

In the cases of both social knowledge and critical knowledge, the outsiders and the insiders may well have divergent views. These divergences must be made explicit and discussed, if mutual respect and confidence between outsider experts and local residents are to be established. Such an exchange can increase the probability of adequate and lasting solutions.

The context of the forms of knowledge just discussed are broader shared understandings. These concern the place of an individual, family, or group in a community, the place of communities in wider society, and the place of people in organic nature. These understandings, more often than not, are unconscious or implicit. This is true of groups of local residents as well as groups of "experts." Here too it can be fruitful for outsiders and insiders to *make explicit* and exchange views on their understandings in these areas.

For example, in Alexandra township the definition of "the community" is very difficult. There are many sets of interests and identities, differing by national origin (e.g., Mozambican war refugees, Nigerians, South African citizens), ethnic origin (e.g., Sotho, Xosa, Zulu), gender, age, socioeconomic class, degree of mobility, acuity of sight, hearing, and so on (e.g., the disabled vs. the able-bodied). Before effective, long-lasting use can be made of even "technical knowledge," it may be necessary to clarify and reach consensus on *minimum common needs and goals* that can provide the basis for common action. Practically speaking, divergent views of the meaning of "community" appear in some people's failing to support flood warning and evacuation plans in their own area—justifiably, because they are afraid that in their absence their meager belongings will be looted by thieves.

In a similar way, Alexandra illustrates numerous possibilities to understand the nature of the society surrounding this little area of five square kilometers. What is "government"? Should it be trusted? Should business interests from the outside be trusted? What, if any, relevance does outside consultants' experience in dealing with flood hazards in Brazil or in greater Durban have for people in *Alexandra*? These are questions that point toward an understanding of the place of Alexandra in a wider social world. The fear of looting that blocks acceptance of a flood evacuation plan proposed by outside experts is partially based on a perception of inability or unwillingness of the greater society surrounding Alexandra to provide police protection for the property of shack dwellers. A difference in the understanding of the place of community in society, of the "resources" of that broader society (such as police protection) that are available, is at issue. During 1996 hundreds of squatters began to build in the area called the Far East Bank (see photograph). Former members of the militant local civic organization who have, since November 1995, been elected to the local government are in the position of trying to evict them. Meanwhile, some consensus needs to be reached concerning options for rehousing those most exposed to flood hazards. Another change in that wider social environment further complicates the "dialogue" between community and outside agents. In May 1996 the administration of the Reconstruction and Development Program (RDP) was moved from its own ministry to the office of the Deputy President. Plans for RDP implementation in urban areas—not unlike trends in many of the world's cities—are placing more and more emphasis on "law and order" in the face of rising crime rates. How will this reorganization of the RDP affect the ability of community members to channel RDP funding into areas of health and safety that are locally defined as priorities?

Finally, there are understandings of the place of humans in the realm of organic nature. Although it doesn't look very "natural" and drains an urban catchment, the Juskei River is still a river. What is the understanding of "river" and the relation of people-to-river that is common among the people who live in Alexandra? What is the *range* of understandings? How do these differ from such understandings held by outside "experts"?

Discussion and clarification of these kinds of understanding and knowledge can facilitate a much richer and more effective collaboration between outside and inside actors in the effort to identify and mitigate hazards.

Disaster and Development: Mainstreaming Prevention

Above, it was argued that hazardous urbanization in South Africa has been driven by the collapse of sustainable livelihoods in rural areas, coupled with constraints on Africans' urban residence and employment in the cities to which they have migrated. The key to unlocking this trap is not to pick in a fragmented, piecemeal way at one or another hazard (flood, or air pollution, or fire). Rather, the way forward is to utilize the opportunities offered by dismantling the apartheid order to draw communities into a systematic process of reconstruction and development.

In South Africa today, that process is said to have a number of elements.[52] It should be integrated, people-driven, focused on promoting peace and security, inclusive of disenfranchised groups, democratic in its methods of decision-making; it also should link reconstruction and development by focusing on critical infrastructure. In early 1995 the national office for this three-year reconstruction and development program (RDP) began to allocate financial resources to the eight new provinces of South Africa. The provinces, in turn, are in the process of creating "local development forums" in the newly formed metropolitan substructures and the remaining transitional metropolitan councils. As accountable and inclusive development forums arise, funds will be passed along for urban infrastructure projects (fire protection, sanitation, water supply, drainage, slope stabilization, electrification, and the like). This is the beginning of urban reconstruction.

Localized identification of priority hazards by development forums in partnership with smaller neighborhood groups could prove to be a way to kick-start the urban RDP process in the most difficult and degraded environments such as Alexandra. The *reverse* is also likely. Linking RDP funding for urban infrastructure to such a participatory process could bring disaster prevention and mitigation into the mainstream of the development process.

Besides investment in urban infrastructure, there is a massive plan to provide loans and grants for affordable housing.[53] The goal is 1 million units over the next five years. Here, too, community-based hazard assessment can help to avoid costly or dangerous mistakes. For example, in principle it is possible to find land on which to house 1 million people within 10 kilometers of the central business district. Much of this land is owned by mining companies, however.[54] *Assuming* for a moment that these companies were willing to provide land for housing, what long-term health and safety hazards may there be on or near old mine sites? In the rush to deliver housing, careful assessment may not be done. However, the existence of community groups sensitized to their rights and ability to call for and participate in hazard assessment makes it more likely that environmental health is considered.

Conclusions

On December 3, 1984, a Union Carbide pesticide factory in Bhopal, India, released a cloud of methyl cyanate into the air, killing (by officially estimates) nearly 7,000 people, and blinding and injuring thousands more. Ten years later nearly half a million people are receiving temporary relief from the Indian government while courts continue to adjudicate claims for compensation. Tens of thousands are being treated for the long-term health effects of toxic exposure. The economic and social cost to a large proportion of Bhopal's population is incalculable.

In another part of the world, South Africa is tentatively feeling its way along in its first year of majority-ruled government. The national elections in April 1994 and local elections in November 1995 finally put an end to apartheid, the system of racial separation. The pent-up demand for higher income and better housing has exploded in a series of wildcat strikes by trade unions and homesteaders' invasions of open land in many cities. As South Africa tries to attract foreign investment to provide more jobs, and as the people spontaneously seek out sites for housing without fear of "pass laws" and other restrictions, the stage is set for dangerous and tragic juxtapositions of industry and human settlement—such as gave rise to the disaster in Bhopal. Other, less dramatic, dangers loom on the horizon. Squatter settlements in many areas of greater Johannesburg, Durban, Cape Town, and elsewhere have taken place far too swiftly in the months following the elections, leaving planners hard pressed to provide basic services—let alone study these sites for hazards such as potential flooding, unstable land fill, buried toxic waste, sink holes, and more. The demand for housing is so great, and has become so powerful a political demand, that even official provincial government plans for new affordable housing may too hastily accept land negotiated with more affluent (usually white) municipalities—even though this land may be hazardous. The potential for situations like that in the neighborhood known as Love Canal, in the United States, is high.

Possibly less well known than Bhopal, Love Canal—near Buffalo, New York—was a site of industrial activity in the past. The site was sold and homes built in ignorance of the fact that the land beneath contained many metal drums of toxic chemicals that had been buried. When children became ill and a group of parents and their advocates campaigned, despite official reassurances, for studies—and, finally, for relocation— there was born the contemporary movement for citizens' active monitoring of neighborhood toxicity. Such citizen groups now number in the thousands in the United States and enjoy the support of such national level nongovernmental institutions as the Citizens' Clearing House on Toxic Waste.

How will such disasters as represented by Bhopal and Love Canal be avoided in contemporary South Africa? How can the precarious environmental health and safety of urban neighborhoods be improved rapidly?

This paper has not answered these important questions, but it has suggested how to approach them. First, consultation with urban residents and respect for their local knowledge must be central to the function of development forums and their relations to new forms of government engaged in implementing the reconstruction and development program. Second, a healthy range of nongovernmental organizations and citizen-based institutions such as the "civics" (ACO in Alexandra, for example) and the Group for Environmental Monitoring (GEM) need to be maintained and strengthened as watchdogs monitoring reconstruction. This is problematic because of a serious decline in funding for NGOs since the elections. Third, new forms of technical assistance need to be devised to aid both these processes—reconstruction and monitoring. Presently there are a number of excellent nongovernmental organizations dedicated to planning and design under a national umbrella called the Urban Sector Network. In addition there are organizations such as the Group for Environmental Monitoring and the Environmental and Development Agency. These need support for innovation in the way they can bring skills and technology to the service of the emerging development forums and other citizen-based organizations.

Notes

1. As a newcomer to South Africa, I was helped in my preliminary research by a very large number of extremely generous people. At Planact there were Graeme Reid, Barbara Schreiner, Wendy Ovens, Mpumi Nxumalo-Nhlapo, Jenny Evans, Chris Benner, Aso Balan, Mzwanele Mayekiso, Patrick Bond, Pat Ramela, Ahmedi Vawda, Cheryl Abrahams, and Penelope Mayson. At University of the Witwatersrand I must thank William Pick, Coleen Vogel, Khosi Xaba, Laetitia Rispel, Alan Mabin, and Chris Rogerson, as well as Prof. W. J. R. Alexander at Pretoria University. I must also thank Toffee Mokonyama and Hans Meeske of the South African Disaster Relief Agency (SADRA), David Fig of the Group for Environmental Monitoring (GEM), Cedric de Beer at the Johannesburg City Council, and Ernest Maganya at the Institute for African Alternatives (IFAA). In Alexandra, I am most grateful to Beyers and Johann Naudé, Kim Goodman, Emanuelle Daviaud, and Queen Cebekulu at the Institute for Urban Primary Health Care. In and around Phambili Books, I was stimulated by discussions with Dale McKinley and Langa Zita. In Durban I learned a great deal from Dhiru Soni, Brij Mahal, Vadi Moodley, Astrid and Ari Sitas, and in Cape Town I benefitted from a conversation with Brett Myrdal. In Pietermaritzburg, Cecil Seethal was my host and guide, and in Ladysmith Indran Naidoo. Finally, I owe Ken Mitchell a great debt for drawing me out of my rural retreat into the world of megacities.

2. A. Vallie, P. Motale, and L. Rispel, "Informal Settlements: Health Priorities and Policy Implications," *Critical Health* 46 (1994) 28–32.

3. F. Wilson and M. Ramphele, eds., *Uprooting Poverty: The South African Challenge* (New York: Norton, 1989); D. Cooper, "From Soil Erosion to Sustainability: Land Use in South Africa," in *Going Green: People, Politics and the Environment in South Africa*, J. Cock and E. Koch, eds. (Cape Town: Oxford University Press, 1991), 176–192; D. Cooper, "Apartheid in South African Agriculture," in *Transforming Southern African Agriculture*, A. Seidman, et al., eds. (Trenton, N.J.: Africa World Press, 1992), 199–216; D. Weiner and R. Levin, "Land and Agrarian Transition in South Africa," *Antipode* 23:1 (1991) 92–120.

4. Love, 1993, cited by C. Cooper et al., *Race Relations Survey 1993/94* (Johannesburg: South African Institute of Race Relations, 1994), 251.

5. B. Wisner, "Commodity Relations and Nutrition Under Apartheid," *Social Science and Medicine* 28:5 (1989) 445.

6. Cooper *et al., op. cit.*, note 6, p. 354.

7. Cooper *et al., op. cit.*, note 6, pp. 319, 322–323.

8. Cooper *et al., op. cit.*, note 6, pp. 319, 328.

9. Cooper *et al., op. cit.*, note 6, p. 82.

10. B. Schreiner, "Urban Planning and Development and the Environment," in *ANC/COSATU/SANCO/SACP Environmental Policy Mission*, Group for Environmental Monitoring and the Environmental and Development Agency (Johannesburg: unpublished report, unpaginated, 1994).

11. Cooper, *et al., op. cit.*, note 6, p. 96.

12. Cooper, *et al., op. cit.*, note 6, p. 101.

13. Schreiner, *op. cit.*, note 12.

14. Cooper *et al., op. cit.*, note 6, p. 95.

15. PWV stands for the urban region encompassing Pretoria, Greater Johannesburg (Witwatersrand), and Vereeniging.

16. Schreiner, *op. cit.*, note 12.

17. For example, during the first two weeks of January 1995, fires destroyed 600 homes in informal settlements in Greater Cape Town alone, including a large fire that razed 500 houses in the community of Marconi Beam. See W. Smook, "50 Fires Each Day," *Peninsula Times*, South Edition, Jan. 18, 1995, p. 1.

18. R. Fuchs, *et al.,* eds., *Mega City Growth and the Future* (Tokyo: United Nations University Press, 1994).

19. B. Wisner, "There Are Worse Things than Earthquakes: Hazard Vulnerability and Mitigation Capacity in the Greater Los Angeles Region," Paper presented at the UN University International Conference on Natural Disasters in Megacities, Tokyo, Jan. 10–11, 1994.

20. Mabin, 1994. In fact 688 persons per hectare turns out to be at the low end of a range of estimates. Others are discussed later in this paper.

21. J. Mitchell, "Natural Disasters in the Context of Megacities," Paper presented at the UN University International Conference on Disasters in Megacities, Tokyo, Jan. 10–11, 1994.

22. M. Mayekiso, *Civic Struggles for a New South Africa* (unpublished manuscript, 1994). This may be an underestimation of the transient component of the population. Another study conducted by the Alexandra Health Centre in 1992 found 43 percent to have arrived within the past five years. See G. Rex and A. Fernandes, "Urbanization and Planning of the Health Services of Alexandra Township," *Critical Health* 46 (1994) 34.

23. Other famous cases of wholesale destruction of vibrant nonwhite communities include District 6 in Cape Town and Cato Manor in Durban. See I. Edwards, "Cato Manor: Cruel Past, Pivotal Future," *Review of African Political Economy* 61 (1994) 415–427.

24. D. Smith, *Geography and Social Justice* (Oxford: Blackwell, 1994), 227.

25. L. Lawson, "The Ghetto and the Green Belt," in *Going Green: People, Politics, and the Environment in South Africa*, J. Cock and E. Koch, eds. (Cape Town: Oxford University Press, 1991), 48.

26. Lawson, *op. cit.*, note 27; Mayekiso, *op. cit.*, note 24.

27. Mayekiso, *op. cit.*, note 24.

28. In January 1995 new "municipal substructures" were created that cut across former racial boundaries, providing a larger tax base for these new, larger urban units and the possibility of cross-subsidies from wealthier to poorer communities. In November 1995, local elections were held to fill executive positions in these new substructures.

29. Schreiner, *op. cit.*, note 12.

30. Mayekiso, *op. cit.*, note 24, cites a survey conducted by the Alexandra Civic Organization in the early 1990s that found that 95 percent of respondents listed housing in their lists of the "five worst problems," 70 percent said bad roads, 66 percent indicated refuse removal, 65 percent lack of electricity, and 55 percent said street lighting.

31. Mayekiso, *op. cit.*, note 24.

32. Mayekiso, *op. cit.*, note 24. No complete census exists. Various surveys, using sampling to give average family size and aerial photography to count shacks, yield different results. There is considerable flux among family members in some parts of the township.

33. Mayekiso, *op. cit.*, note 24.

34. Lawson, *op. cit.*, note 27, p. 48

35. H. Mashabela, *Mekhukhu: Urban African Cities of the Future* (Johannesburg: South African Institute of Race Relations, 1990), 13.

36. Lawson, *op. cit.*, note 27, pp. 49–50.

37. Y. Goosen, "Threat of Future Floods to Life and Property Along the Upper Juskei River," unpublished paper, Dept. of Geography and Environmental Studies, University of Witwatersrand, Johannesburg, 1994, p. 11.

38. W. Alexander, "Flood Risks in Informal Settlements in Soweto and Alexandra," unpublished research note, Dept. of Civil Engineering, University of Pretoria, Pretoria, 1993, p. 1.

39. Goosen, *op. cit.*, note 39, p. 11.

40. J. Naudé, personal communication, Aug. 1994, from the engineer and contractor responsible for recent cleaning out of the storm drains.

41. In 1991 only 25 percent of Alexandra had access to electricity; see Lawson, *op. cit.*, note 27, p. 51. More of a problem is the high connection fee and a system of prepayment that, some argue, works out to a rate higher than that paid in more affluent parts of the urban region. See Mayekiso, *op. cit.*, note 24; *c.f.* E. Kgomo, "Smoke Over Soweto," in *Restoring the Land: Environment and Change in Post-Apartheid South Africa*, M. Ramphele, ed. (London: Panos, 1991), 117–123 on the affordability of coal vs. electricty in Soweto.

42. C. Vogel, "The South African Environment: Horizons for Integrating Physical and Human Geography," in *Geography in a Changing South Africa: Progress and Prospects*, C. Rogerson and J. McCarthy, eds. (Cape Town: Oxford University Press, 1992), 174–175.

43. K. Goodman, personal communication from the director of the Institute of Urban Primary Health Care at the Alexandra Health Centre, 1994.

44. Lawson, *op. cit.*, note 27, p. 50.

45. H. Meeske, personal communicaton from the coordinator of the South African Disaster Relief Agency, Jan. 1995.

46. H. Mashabela, *Townships of the PWV* (Braamfontein: South African Institute of Race Relations, 1988), 10.

47. J. MacDonald, "South Africa's Future Health Care Policy: Selective or Comprehensive Primary Health Care?," in *Sustainable Development for a Democratic South Africa*, K. Cole, ed. (London: Earthscan, 1994), 140, citing ANC, *Ready to Govern*, ANC Policy Guidelines, 1992.

48. Panafrican Centre for Emergency Preparedness and Response (PCEPR), *The Challenge of African Disasters* (Geneva and New York: World Health Organization and UN Institute for Training and Research, 1991); Office of the UN Disaster Relief Co-ordinator (UNDRO), *Mitigating Natural Disasters* (New York: United Nations, 1991); W. Carter, *Disaster Management: A Disaster Manager's Handbook* (Manila: Asian Development Bank, 1992); A. Kreimer and M. Munasignhe, eds., *Managing Natural Disasters and the Environment* (Washington, D.C.: World Bank, 1991); A. Kreimer and M. Munasignhe, eds., *Environmental Management and Urban Vulnerability* (Washington, D.C.: World Bank, 1992).

49. The term "emergency" is generally used to describe a situation or hazard that threatens lives, lifelines such as power and water supply and the like, or livelihoods, and demands that actions be taken immediately to avoid a disaster. "Disaster" refers to the situation in which lifelines and livelihoods have been damaged (without loss of life and injury).

50. G. White, ed., *Natural Hazards: Local, National, Global* (New York: Oxford University Press, 1974); I. Burton *et al.*, *The Environment as Hazard*, 2d ed. (New York: Guilford, 1993); A. von Kotze and A. Holloway, *Reducing Risk: Participatory Learning Activities for Disaster Mitigation in Southern Africa* (Durban: International Federation of Red Cross and Red Crescent Societies and Dept. of Adult

and Community Education at the University of Natal, distributed by Oxfam UK and Humanities Press in the U.S., 1996).

51. I am grateful to Peter Park, Emeritus Professor of Education at University of Massachusetts, for the threefold typology of knowledge. Also see B. Wisner *et al.,* "Participatory and Action Research Methods," in E. Zube and G. Moore, eds., *Advances in Environment, Behavior and Design* (New York: Plenum,1991), 271–296; and B. Wisner, "Teaching African Science," in P. Allen *et al.,* eds., *African Studies and the Undergraduate Curriculum* (Boulder, Colo.: Lynne Reinner Publishers, 1994), 173–208.

52. African National Congress (ANC), *The Reconstruction and Development Programme* (Johannesburg: African National Congress, 1994), 4–7.

53. R. Hartley, "White Paper on Housing," *Sunday Times*, Johannesburg, Dec. 11, 1994.

54. Smith, *op. cit.,* note 26, p. 240.

PART SEVEN

Problems that Push the Parameters of Time and Space

Up to this point, chapters have explored human environmental crises and responses that are lodged in time and space. Crisis genesis, experience, response, and the implications of response are mapped out over a time scale that represents, for the most part, a few generations in time. Some environmental crises, however, defy our conception of time. The nuclear hot spots of the world—places where nuclear power containment mechanisms failed, and places where nuclear weapons were developed, tested, and their waste stored—will continue to contaminate life processes for thousands of years. Our ability to contain, reduce, or even remove their threat is seriously inhibited by the changing, and relatively short-lived, nature of our sociopolitical systems.

The following two chapters explore a few of the dimensions of this complex problem, examining radiation victimization from the community perspective with the aim of understanding how people manage to carry on with life in the midst of death. Holly Barker (who reports on an ethnographic survey of exposed Marshall Islanders) and Paula Garb (who describes problems and response from multiple vantage points in the Chelyabinsk region of Russia) provide some answers, and, in doing so, raise a host of troubling and perhaps unanswerable questions.

In the case of the Marshall Islands, Barker describes a situation of radiation exposure, possibly intentional, for the purposes of furthering scientific understanding of the long-term effects of radiation on human populations. Radiation exposure of the Marshall Islands was carried out in the name of United States national security. For years, institutional response on the part of the U.S. government was to deny culpability and withhold scientific information that would allow Marshall Islanders to understand the full extent of human and environmental exposure. Response on the part of a concerned scientific community included conducting independent research efforts to document the extent of human environmental exposure and the range of related health problems, and using this information in confrontational settings with the goal of getting the U.S. government to acknowledge culpability, an effort that was eventually successful. Response on the part of the newly independent Marshall Islands government was, first and foremost, to regain control over their region. Control required first obtaining a full understanding of the human and environmental problems related to nuclear testing, and then using this information to renegotiate compensatory mechanisms (including medical care and environmental remediation). The act of surveying its citizens, documenting their stories, and using this information in international forums to lobby for change has had far-reaching effects. From the point of view of the victims, the new government's interest in and attention to their stories served to validate and transform their experience. Marshall Islanders are educating each other, taking a proactive look at true dimensions of their world, and channeling this energy in ways that builds communities, and builds nations as well. At a psychosocial level, the knowledge that a wealthy foreign government formally announced culpability allows the affected people to carry on with the day-to-day aspects of life fueled by hopes and dreams that seem obtainable: by documenting their problems they may gain redress, and someday life will be better for them.

In the radioactive regions of Russia, life is very different. Garb describes a situation of radiation victimization where denial is so firmly entrenched in people's responses—at all levels of society—that actions and information that challenge constructed realities are almost impossible to sustain over long periods of time. Victims, scientific and medical personnel, military and other government officials all use denial as a means to carry on. Information that documents the full extent of radioactive contamination, and the full extent of related human and environmental problems, represents threats to the status quo. In the Soviet past, such information was a form of treason, suggesting that the government had made mistakes, and that government action was not in the best interests of the nation. In today's Russia, such information also threatens power structures, by illustrating the inherent weaknesses and inabilities of new governments to understand and adequately cope with the radioactive legacy of the USSR, but also drawing attention to the fact that this is just one in many of what seem to be insurmountable problems. Recent efforts to document, educate about, and formulate responses to the problems of radiation contamination serve in the short term to encourage and empower people as they transform their status from passive victim to proactive agent of change. The opening of such windows is often met with forceful response, as government institutions and officials deny funds, restrict research, and shut down programs, many of which they may have helped start in the first place. The contradictory actions of government on this issue reflect the incredible insecurity and vulnerability of the political and economic structure. For the Russian living in a radioactive landscape it must be quite difficult to construct and maintain the hopeful dreams that fuel activism. Given the apparent hopelessness of this situation, denial plays an important yet dangerous psychosocial role: protecting people from expending their energy on issues that seem to be unsolvable, and allowing people the illusion of more urgent matters.

Radioactive waste, with its lengthy half-life and mutagenic powers, and its ability to promote cumulative, synergistic, and degenerative effects—will be a continual thorn in the government's side for hundreds and perhaps thousands of years. We have the ability to map out radioactive hot zones across the planet: areas where uranium was/is mined, milled, and processed; areas where weapons were or are manufactured, tested, and used; areas where nuclear power plants were or are in service (on land and sea) and where their waste is disposed; and areas where other forms of radioactive materials were and are used and their waste disposed (as in medical technology). Should we partition off regions of the globe, prohibiting human settlement in or near these hot zones? Can we contain radioactive wastes over long periods of time and prevent their release into the air, water, and soil?

Who is responsible for the affected peoples over time? Should we clean up some areas, help some people, and ignore others? What are meaningful responses? Acknowledgment of culpability? Compensation? Long-term medical care that spans the generations? Environmental remediation? Who pays? At what point does government responsibility end? Who is responsible for managing the radioactive legacy of defunct regimes?

CHAPTER 13

Fighting Back
Justice, the Marshall Islands, and Neglected Radiation Communities

Holly M. Barker

I was watching the evening news on my television which told of a person receiving some two million dollars from McDonald's fast food to compensate for the pain and anguish of being scalded by a cup of coffee. Tell me, can that be compared to the pain of watching your first child die of leukemia or your wife giving birth to some monstrous horror?[1]

—Kaleman Gideon, Likiep Atoll

. . . they failed to warn and inform the people about the nuclear tests, and also how they used us as guinea pigs to learn how our bodies could resist or absorb the poison from the tests. Just like when they are about to send a rocket into space they put many kinds of animals (in the rockets) for their experiments. That's exactly what they did with us.[2]

—Tempo Alfred, Ailuk Atoll

Some of the fish that we used to eat are now poisonous. We cannot eat them anymore. And some fruits of the breadfruit tree that shouldn't bear seeds according to the laws of nature, strangely enough, seeds grow in them. Pigs also have defective bodies. Some have twisted legs. Sometimes the (supply) ships wouldn't come for a long time so we had to kill and eat them. What could we do? We were hungry and we needed something to eat?[3]

—Jalel John, Ailuk Atoll

We never had any of these illnesses, these grotesque deformities, these grape-like things (we give birth to) that do not resemble a human being at all. And you ask me what I think! I think that if it were not for the United States and their all-consuming desire for superiority over the Russians, we, the people of Rongelap, would not have to turn our head in shame for fear of being considered freaks of nature. And to add insult to injury, they have heartlessly coined the term "nuclear nomad" to describe our plight, . . . the deaths of our children and the destruction of the islands our forefathers shed their blood for.[4]

—Aruko Bobo, Rongelap Atoll

Introduction

"You can't go there!"
I first heard about the Marshall Islands when the United States Peace Corps accepted my application to volunteer and assigned me to the infant nation. Like many western-

Holly M. Barker is Senior Policy Advisor for the Embassy of the Republic of the Marshall Islands, 2433 Massachusetts Avenue, NW, Washington, DC 20008.

ers, I envisioned a tropical paradise with idyllic beaches and happy people. My dreams were quickly shattered, however, as I shared my acceptance letter with my parents. Instead of joining me in the celebration of my Pacific Island volunteer site, my mother shrieked: "You can't go there!" On the spot, my parents schooled me about the Marshall Islands and their history as a nuclear test site—explaining that the United States had conducted above-ground nuclear weapons tests on its Bikini and Enewetak atolls.

Despite my parents' and my own concerns about lingering radiation in the Marshall Islands, I received assurances from the U.S. government that the islands to which Peace Corps volunteers are assigned are safe for human habitation.[4] Nonetheless, on arrival in the Marshall Islands, I purposefully asked to be stationed in the southernmost village—a location furthest from the "ground-zero" sites. From 1988 to 1990, I lived and worked in a remote island village as a school teacher. At the end of my Peace Corps assignment I found it difficult to simply walk away from the Marshallese and end my affiliation with them. Fortunately, I returned to the United States at precisely the time the Embassy of the Republic of the Marshall Islands (RMI) in Washington, D.C., was looking for assistance.

As the Senior Political Advisor at the Embassy, I work with the RMI national government in its continued effort to secure assistance from the U.S. government for radiation problems associated with the nuclear weapons testing program. For the past two years, I have gathered historical documents and ethnographic data about Marshallese people in communities that were exposed to radiation yet, due to a series of bureaucratic obstacles, remain ineligible for assistance from the U.S. government. In this chapter I present some of this ethnographic and historical data, and describe how the process of compiling and using this information has been working to empower both victims and the newly formed government. I also describe some of the RMI efforts to seek redress from the U.S. government, and how this process is having profound implications on the RMI-U.S. bilateral relationship.

Nuclear Weapons Testing in the Marshall Islands

So many needless deaths and all for the sake of men clear across the world who are obsessed with their games of war and destruction.[6]

More than 50 years ago, the Marshall Islands—an island group in Micronesia, the west central Pacific—was selected as the testing site for the U.S. atomic and hydrogen weapons program because of their geographic isolation.[7] Between 1946 and 1958, the U.S. government conducted 67 nuclear tests above, on, and in the seas surrounding the islands. Many of these tests, including the infamous 1954 Bravo shot (the equivalent of more than 1,000 "Hiroshima" bombs), produced by design as much local fallout as possible.[8] Given the international outcry at this time over worldwide radiation levels tied to the continued nuclear weapons testing of the United States, increasing local level fallout meant decreasing upper atmospheric fallout, and this helped the U.S. government to deflate international protests over its weapons testing program. At the same time, intensive testing in such an isolated region provided U.S. scientists with the perfect laboratory conditions for studying the effects of radiation on human beings and the environment.

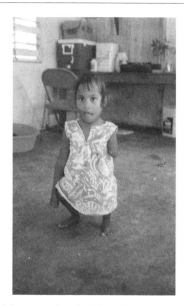

Mimi, an 8-year-old girl from Ailuk. Because her disabilities fall within the "normal" range of abnormalities, she is considered ineligible for U.S. government assistance. Photograph by Holly M. Barker.

From the end of World War II until 1986, the Marshall Islands was a United Nations Trust Territory administered by the United States. Under the terms of the Trusteeship, the United States had direct responsibility for the health and safety of the Marshallese people. Paradoxically, it was this colonial relationship that allowed the United States to justify the detonation of thermonuclear devices deemed too dangerous for testing in the continental United States. The U.S. government thought of the Marshallese as an "expendable population" whose interests were usurped by U.S. national security interests.[9] Even when the Marshallese were legitimately concerned about their safety and welfare, the colonial nature of the Trusteeship arrangement prevented the Marshallese from effectively voicing their concerns. In 1954, the Marshallese people submitted a petition to the UN expressing their concerns about radiation hazards. The Director of the Medical Division of Biology and Medicine in the Marshall Islands, Dr. John C. Bugher, met with the U.S. ambassador to the UN, Henry Lodge, to discuss the political implications of the Marshallese petition. Dr. Bugher convinced both the U.S. ambassador and the Secretary General of the United Nations to delay submission of the petition until the testing series under way in 1954 was complete. As Bugher notes: "This petition has been held by the Secretariat pending the completion of the test series. Ambassador Lodge says he feels that the Secretary General may be embarrassed if there is much further extension of time before release of the petition."[10]

Marshall Island Experiences: U.S. Response

Our question is why didn't they notify us of what they were going to do beforehand so we could seek shelter or take other precautions?[11]

I think (the U.S.) was bound by the purpose of its mission which was the gathering of information to benefit the United States. This, even at the price of the health of a few insignificant "savages."[12]

The Trusteeship arrangement allowed the "selective victimization" of the Marshallese to take place: without their knowledge or approval, the Marshallese relinquished their rights to a healthy life and a clean environment to the U.S. government and its nuclear weapons testing program. The Marshallese people, not the United States, continue to pay the price for the Cold War weapons testing agenda of the U.S. government. The testing program has meant exile, death, illness, and suffering for the Marshallese population. Lingering radiation has caused unquantifiable economic and cultural loss as well. Entire islands were vaporized by the tests, and other islands remain too radioactive for inhabitation or use. In a nation with just 70 square miles of land, land is by no means expendable.

Although radioactive fallout from the tests carried across each of the 29 populated atolls in the country, the problem confronting the Marshall Islands government is that the U.S. government considers only four atolls in the Marshall Islands to have been "exposed." As a result, only four individual atolls receive compensation or participate in a U.S. Department of Energy medical and environmental monitoring program; the two "ground-zero" atolls of Bikini and Enewetak, and two populated atolls that received heavy fallout from the Bravo test, Rongelap and Uterik. Each of these four atolls receive varying amounts of assistance from the U.S. government. The specific nature of the assistance is spelled out in the treaty that governs bilateral relations between the United States and the Marshall Islands, the Compact of Free Association. When the Compact came into force in 1986, the Trusteeship terminated, and the RMI became a sovereign nation for the first time in more than 400 years.

From the beginning of the testing period until termination of the Trusteeship, the Marshall Islands' government was forced to rely on the U.S. government to explain the extent of damage from the U.S. nuclear weapons testing program. As a result of its ability to control access to pertinent information about the testing period, the U.S. determined which atolls were defined as "exposed," and, thus, eligible to receive assistance from the U.S. government in the Compact. Consequently, the U.S. government is able to ignore the needs of entire communities exposed to radiation. A component of the Compact, Section 177, specifically establishes the responsibilities of the U.S. to mitigate the adverse human and environmental effects of the nuclear weapons testing program. If the Marshallese negotiators of the Compact had had access to all withheld information, there is little doubt that Section 177 of the Compact would read quite differently today.

In December 1993, U.S. Secretary of Energy Hazel O'Leary announced an "openness initiative" for her department. In the wake of the Cold War, this initiative made thousands of previously declassified documents available to the public for the first time. For the Marshall Islands, O'Leary's policy meant that approximately 20,000 pages of information pertaining to the nuclear testing program were delivered to the former RMI Minister of Foreign Affairs, Tom D. Kijiner. The RMI government assigned its former ambassador to the United States, Wilfred I. Kendall, responsibility for reviewing the contents of the newly released documents. From the RMI embassy in Washington, D.C., Ambassador Kendall compiled documentary evidence for the RMI national government. This newly released evidence clearly demonstrates that the atoll environment, and surrounding seas, were contaminated to a much greater degree than the RMI government realized. This information has enormous implications for the RMI government, which is struggling to provide for the health care needs of all exposed populations. For the RMI government, these populations include both the Marshallese who were alive during the testing period, as well as those who were born and raised on contaminated atolls where they ate and drank from an irradiated food chain. The truly exposed population in the Marshall Islands cannot be neatly corralled into temporal and physical categories that the U.S. has previously imposed on the definition of "exposed."

The documents also demonstrate that the Marshallese people and the environment were unnecessarily contaminated during the Bravo shot. Although Marshallese populations were evacuated from their home atolls for smaller tests to protect them from fallout, Marshallese living in communities directly downwind from "ground zero" were not evacuated prior to the Bravo shot despite the fact that the Bravo test was designed to produce more radioactive fallout than any previously detonated weapon. Moreover, U.S. government planners knew it was impossible to guarantee that radioactive fallout would not expose inhabited atolls, and that weather patterns in the northern Pacific are unpredictable.[13] A meteorological report was submitted to the Commander of Joint Task Force Seven, Major General P. W. Clarkson, prior to the detonation of Bravo. The report concluded that a high-yield detonation could trigger a cloud of radiation that would expand as it became self-sustained by energy derived from condensation. After considering the recommendations of this report, Clarkson proposed to "treat the report the same as I would a report from any other member of my staff when I do not agree with him. In short, we will kill it and stick it in the file."[14]

Just six hours prior to the detonation of Bravo on March 1, 1954, a briefing was held by the joint task force responsible for detonation of the thermonuclear weapon. During the briefing, the weather forecasters confirmed that the wind was blowing in the direction of inhabited atolls. Despite this dire forecast, a decision was made to detonate Bravo. Precisely as the weather reports predicted, radioactive fallout from Bravo was carried downwind to populated communities in the Marshall Islands.

In the hours and days after Bravo's detonation, the U.S. government instructed airplane pilots to monitor the path of the radioactive cloud. Pilots confirmed that Rongelap Atoll, less than 100 miles away from "ground zero," received near-fatal doses of radiation. Aruko Bobo, a Rongelapese woman, remembers the reaction of her community the morning the U.S. government detonated Bravo:

> I was living with my parents and some other families on an islet across the reef from the main island where we had gone to make copra. On that March morning, my father woke me while it was still pitch dark as I had planned to cross the reef with some of my friends to the main island to purchase some . . . (supplies). There were four of us, three girls and one boy. Well, we were in the middle of the reef between the two islands when the whole of the western skies lit up so brilliantly that it seemed as if it were noon instead of 5:00 o'clock in the morning. The color went from bright white to deep red and then a mixture of both along with hues of yellow. We cowered among the large boulders on the reef, too frightened to decide whether to flee back to the islet or to dash across the reef to the main island. It was the boy who finally galvanized us to make a mad rush towards the main island. Just as we reached the last sand

bank, the air around us was split by a most horrendous noise. I cannot describe what it was like. Perhaps like thunder but the force given off by the sound was so great we could actually feel wave after wave of vibrations. As if the very air had become a living thing. We made the last hundred or so yards to the main island in total pandemonium. There was a man outside the first hut standing beside a fire and gazing blankly at the blazing skies. Some of us ran right into him and draped ourselves all over him. Those who could not find a spot on his body to cling to ran past him and into the hut where they threw themselves onto his wife who was in the process of throwing her clothes on to rush outside to investigate what was going on.[15]

The U.S. military planes also confirmed that atolls where U.S. servicemen and Marshallese resided were exposed to dangerous levels of radiation. Evacuation teams were sent first to Rongerik Atoll where 27 U.S. servicemen were stationed. The U.S. military's final report of radiological safety for the Bravo shot shows that the U.S. government viewed the Marshallese as an expendable population. This perception contributed to the selective victimization of the island inhabitants. The report states that: "In the decision to authorize the Rongerik evacuation, consideration was given to the fact that only the US troops were being removed whereas native populated atolls were also undoubtedly contaminated to the same or higher degree."[16] It was not until 52 hours after Rongelap's exposure that the military evacuated the Rongelapese. Shortly thereafter, another populated atoll to the west, Uterik, was evacuated. Both communities were brought to Kwajalein Atoll where they were unwittingly placed in a biomedical program entitled "Project 4.1: The Study of the Response of Human Beings Exposed to Significant Fallout Radiation."

The 1993 release by the U.S. government of previously classified documents confirmed for the RMI government that those evacuated from the two atolls were not the only communities that were exposed to Bravo's fallout. Records from U.S. military flights over the area after Bravo test confirmed that other communities were also exposed to dangerous amounts of radioactivity. In 1954, the U.S. military considered a 10-roentgen exposure as the dividing line between dangerous and harmless levels of radiation, and 3.9 roentgens was the maximum permissible exposure for U.S. servicemen for an entire year.[17] Rongelap's dose was originally estimated at 175 roentgens although this figure was later adjusted upward of 200 roentgens. Uterik's exposure was estimated at 17 roentgens—substantially less than Rongelap's exposure, yet far in excess of a dangerous dose. The RMI government has evidence from the newly released Department of Energy (DOE) documents confirming that Ailuk Atoll, approximately 20 miles southeast of Uterik, was exposed to 20 roentgens of radiation. When radioactive fallout began to settle on Ailuk and nearby Likiep Atoll, there was no communication system to report the fallout, and no military ships came to evacuate them. Said one native: "Even though we knew and felt that Ailuk was poisoned, we couldn't do anything because we were ignored all along."[18]

Despite the fact that the population of Ailuk was exposed to levels of radiation that doubled a "dangerous" dose, and more than quadrupled the maximum permissible exposure of U.S. servicemen for one year, the U.S. government purposefully decided not to evacuate the Ailukese. This decision was based on the rationale that Ailuk was too difficult to evacuate because of its "sizable" population. In fact, in 1954, there were only 401 residents on Ailuk.[19]

From 1954 until the present, the U.S. government has continued to monitor and study the effects of radiation on the people of Rongelap and Uterik. This medical care contains a research component, though, until quite recently, radiation victims have not been informed as to whether medical interventions were done in the name of personal health or scientific knowledge. Although the subjects have moved to different locations in the nation, the biomedical program that began on Kwajalein after Bravo continues. The U.S. government resettled four communities onto irradiated lands to study the human absorption of radionuclides from an irradiated environment (people from Uterik, Rongelap, Bikini, and Enewetak). Two months after Bravo, the Uterikese were resettled to their home atoll, and more than two years after Bravo, the Rongelapese were told their atoll was safe for resettlement. The Bikinians and the Enewetakese who were removed from their "ground-zero" homes during the actual testing were resettled in subsequent years, and have participated in the biomedical program at different times.

Although researchers monitored the increased body burdens of the four resettled populations, the Marshallese were never told about their increased risk. In the case of the Rongelapese, the U.S. government was aware of high radionuclide concentrations in all of the major foods of the Rongelapese (including coconut crabs, arrowroot, pandanus, bananas, fish, and clams). According to Dr. Esra Riklon, a Marshallese medical officer who accompanied AEC (Atomic Energy Commission) and DOE teams to the resettled atolls:

> . . . the common complaint—because I was the one who translated—was that after they eat arrowroot, they always developed a burning sensation in their throats, and constriction of the throat which caused them to have difficulty in breathing . . . some of them developed rashes, nausea, and vomiting. . . . (The U.S. said) this was an allergic reaction to food. . . . I didn't believe it was allergic. . . . I began to question the integrity of my job. I began to realize that answers given to me to translate regarding important questions were often ambiguous or outright lies.[20]

Incremental increases in the radioactivity of food sources were also monitored by U.S. researchers as radiation from several weapons detonated after Rongelap's resettlement continued to expose the environment and the people.

Coconut crabs on Rongelap were identified by the U.S. government as the most dangerous food source because the crabs primarily eat contaminated coconuts, and concentrate the radionuclides from coconuts in their bodies. Despite the obvious danger associated with coconut crab consumption, the food restrictions that the U.S. government gave to the Rongelapese vacillated: at times they were told coconut crabs were safe to eat, and at other times they were considered off-limits. During each phase of the changing restrictions, the U.S. government monitored the body burdens of the Rongelapese and acknowledged in internal reports that the coconut crabs were increasing the internal radiation exposure of the Rongelapese. These increases were monitored despite an internal policy that the Rongelapese who were already exposed to near lethal levels of external radiation in 1954 should receive no additional radiation exposure for at least 12 years.

How did the U.S. government respond to the increased body burdens of the resettled Marshallese? In 1974, the Atomic Energy Commission (the predecessor to the Department of Energy) relaxed the restrictions for Marshallese radiation ingestion at precisely the time when an increase was needed (because people were returning to their islands, and ingesting contaminated foods). At the same time the maximum exposure levels for the U.S. population were significantly lowered. This loosening up of the exposure levels for Marshall Islanders occurred in spite of an Environmental Protection Agency report that acknowledged that U.S. standards for radiation exposure applied to U.S. activities in the Marshall Islands. As a result of the larger "acceptable" levels of radiation ingestion, the body burden measurements of the monitored populations showed that Cesium-137 was increasing in the populations living on contaminated lands. For example, as noted in a 1982 Department of Energy report, in one year's time alone, U.S. researchers recorded dramatic increases of radionuclides in the Rongelapese as the "body burdens for females less than eleven years of age . . . had increased 82% . . . (and a)dult male burdens were up 56%."[21]

The Bikinians were also ingesting dangerous amounts of radionuclides, having returned to their home in 1972 after the U.S. completed its "cleanup" efforts. Unfortunately, methods used to define exposure dose and risk (and establish "habitability") did not include the cumulative and synergistic effects of drinking water, growing food, eating shellfish, and so forth—of day-to-day life on the island. By 1978 medical researchers found significant increase in exposure levels, and the Bikini islanders were again evacuated.[22] By this time, Bikinians had ingested more radioactive cesium from their environment than any known human population.[23] Even within the DOE, certain individuals recognized that the U.S. failure to provide information on the total radiation exposure of the population constituted a "cover-up." Negotiations are still under way with the U.S. government to engineer a safe resettlement of Bikini. 1996 marks the fiftieth year that the Bikinians have lived in diaspora.

Evidently, Bikini, Enewetak, Rongelap, and Uterik were adequate for the U.S. government's research purposes. Despite the fact that Ailuk received more radiation than Uterik, the U.S. government excluded Ailuk from U.S. medical care or environmental monitoring programs. Unlike the four atolls the U.S. monitors closely, populations from Ailuk Atoll, plus other atolls in the northern and central parts of the country, were not removed when the atolls were at their "hottest." (Many of the most dangerous radionuclides attenuate relatively quickly, as their half-lives are often just a matter of weeks.)

Marshall Islands Government Response

As we are in the same family with America, then America should look after its own people. . . . Help us![24]

Recently, the RMI government has stopped relying on the U.S. government to define the parameters of radiation exposure in the Marshall Islands. The RMI government is conducting its own research of historical documents pertaining to the testing period, and is collecting ethnographic data from Marshallese radiation victims. Those data that the RMI government has begun to amass are a result of its quest for a complete and true understanding of the events that took place within its boundaries. It is clear from the massive amounts of information that the RMI government never knew about that the U.S. government blatantly concealed information about the degree of destruction to the environment and the health of the people caused by such testing.

Furthermore, there is evidence of repeated exposures, increased harm to the Marshallese, and the failure of the U.S. government to provide for peoples it knew were exposed to radiation.

Now that the RMI government is beginning to understand for itself the full impact of the testing program on the environment and its people, it is using this new information in bilateral and multilateral forums to demand that the U.S., as well as the international community that sanctioned the U.S. testing program under the auspices of the UN Trusteeship Council, address the persistent radiological problems in the Marshall Islands. For each statement pertaining to the effects of the weapons testing that the Marshall Islands makes at international and bilateral gatherings, RMI government officials can substantiate their claims with reams of documentary evidence.

Although the RMI government has documentary evidence confirming that additional communities were exposed to radiation, this information alone does not compel the U.S. to change its policies toward the radiation communities. In order to secure assistance for the neglected radiation victims, the RMI government knows it must demonstrate to the U.S. and the international community that the persistent, adverse implications of radiation exposure continue still. To compile this evidence, the RMI government initiated a project to collect ethnographic data from the neglected communities spearheaded by the RMI embassy in Washington, D.C. As an anthropologist employed at the embassy, I was asked to collect ethnographies from Ailuk Atoll and Likiep Atoll. Although scientists now consider both Ailuk and Likiep safe for human habitation, the RMI government believed ethnographic research would illuminate existing environmental and health implications on those atolls resulting from radiation exposure. The purpose of gathering ethnographic data was to help the RMI government identify the aspects of the radiation problem that are actionable,[25] and to provide sufficient justification for the U.S. Congress to broaden its definition of "exposed" in both its spatial and temporal contexts. This present definition is the major obstacle in securing assistance for the neglected communities, because the definition of "exposed" excludes entire populations such as all individuals born after 1954. Although the generation born after 1954 were not exposed to external fallout from the tests, nevertheless they were raised on contaminated atolls and consequently exposed to internal sources of radiation through the food chain.

The neglected communities of Ailuk and Likiep were extremely amenable to the project, since they immediately understood the importance of data ownership. Instead of acting as research subjects for the U.S. government, documentation of their experiences will help their own government—the Republic of the Marshall Islands—request U.S. policy changes aimed at providing tangible assistance to the neglected communities.

Human Environmental Impacts: The People's Point of View

This never happened prior to the nuclear explosions.[26]

As anticipated, there is both observable and ethnographic evidence of acute harm and changes to the environment and health of the populations on Ailuk and Likiep atolls. The people have many stories about the horribly deformed trees, animals, and people in the years following the nuclear testing. In accordance with biological principles of survival, most of these severely deformed plants or people did not survive. The living people, however, can describe these losses clearly. The survivors remember the animals and children born with two heads, or missing limbs. Kajitok and Kiora, an elderly couple from Likiep, distinctly remember one of their children born after the testing period. Kajitok, the husband, recalls that:

> After the testing, . . . (my wife) got pregnant. When the baby was born, it had two heads. . . . Two heads. Two heads. One was on top of the other. . . . (The bottom head was) ripped open here [touches his forehead to show where the second head emerged from]. . . . It looked like the child's head had dents. The baby lived for a moment. . . . It breathed for just a short time when it was born. Maybe not an hour, only some minutes. It was alive, but it wasn't doing well.[27]

In addition to the people, deformed animals were born. Typhoon, a man from Ailuk Atoll, remembers

> . . . sudden changes that we never experienced before the nuclear testings. It happens to trees and even animals and people. . . . A cat for instance. A cat gave birth to a single kitten with what seems like two bodies combined. We might say a "twin" with one body. Eight legs and eight paws.[28]

The trees and food corps on Ailuk and Likiep, like the animals, were also affected by radiation. A woman from Likiep named Alian remembers changes in the food crops:

> One thing which stands out in my mind was the quick and total destruction of all the arrowroot plants on the atoll. Since arrowroot is one of our staple foods, we were astonished to find the arrowroot had been destroyed along with such things as breadfruit, coconut trees, and pandanus. We assumed that whatever caused this was poisonous because it was not only our vegetation at ground level that was destroyed, but also those (crops) growing in the soil.[29]

It is not difficult to ascertain from communities such as Ailuk and Likiep, where people depend on their local environment for their subsistence, that radionuclides deposited from testing fallout worked their way into the environment, through the food crops, and eventually into the people themselves. There are observable effects of health problems induced by environmental contamination. Perhaps the most poignant example is Mimi, an 8-year old girl from Ailuk (see photograph). Mimi is missing half of her left arm. She has no knees, and stunted legs with only three toes on each foot. Mimi's family made a small crutch for her to drag herself from place to place. Mentally, Mimi is normal, but she is embarrassed to leave her family's compound or attend school. She cowers from nonfamily members on the atoll, who are quick to point out that Mimi "ebaam!," which literally means "She is bombed," and connotes that she is irradiated. Mimi is suffering as a direct result of the U.S. nuclear weapons testing program, yet she is ineligible for assistance. Mimi's grandmother recalls how U.S. officials explained Mimi's deformities to her, and the 420 other residents of Ailuk:

> . . . (The U.S. government) told us that approximately 100 newborns will have visible abnormalities on their bodies within the next 30 years. Just this island, 100 newborns. . . . (Mimi is) within the 30 years range predicted by the scientists in 1978 that many babies will be born with abnormalities.

To the casual observer it is obvious that the frequency of disability in Ailuk is not "normal." Yet, compensation for nuclear damage throughout the Marshall Islands is based on the erroneous assumption that Ailuk represents a normal background level of radiation. Because Ailuk was never evacuated after the Bravo travesty, Ailuk was labeled "unexposed" by the U.S. government. Ailuk became representative of a *normal* background level of radiation despite earlier reports confirming radiation doses in excess of 20 roentgens. The U.S. government was able to define "exposed" as simply those four atolls that were evacuated because it had absolute control of the information about the exposure of all atolls. This information was never shared with the RMI government. For Mimi's family on Ailuk, the U.S. manipulation of definitions allowed DOE to justify Mimi's disabilities, and to deny medical care or assistance to Mimi and other neglected radiation victims.

Gender Dimensions

> Four (of my) children were born prematurely. . . . One of them died after his first birthday. Another one was still-born. . . . I have yet to see any doctors.[30]

Marshallese women have a particular need for medical care to address the severe reproductive problems that are ignored by the U.S. government and that were never fully understood by the RMI government. Anthropologists helped disclose the nature of women's birthing problems to the RMI government. Medical anthropologist Glenn Alcalay found a direct correlation between the distance from "ground zero" where women reside, and their incidence of miscarriages, still-births, and birth anomalies.[31] Data I gathered on Ailuk and Likiep for the RMI government confirms Alcalay's findings. Marshallese women who were exposed to radiation are suffering silently and differently from their male counterparts because of cultural taboos, as well as the refusal of the U.S. government to acknowledge the multigenerational implications of radiation. Marshallese women are extremely concerned about their children who were born after the testing:

> You know my children—they say we adults are the only ones who are exposed today—but they are exposed too. If everyone here is exposed, how can they not be? . . . I am one of the poisoned ones. . . . Aren't they contaminated since their mothers and fathers were exposed?[32]

Female radiation victims often do not discuss their birth anomalies with even their husbands because the missionaries had taught the Marshallese that birthing problems are an indication that women are unfaithful to their husbands. There is, however, little doubt that the reproductive problems women are experiencing are connected to their exposure to radiation in their environment. Catherine, for example, moved to Rongelap in 1957 when the U.S. government resettled the Rongelapese who were evacuated after the Bravo incident. Because she did not live on Rongelap in 1954, she was not exposed to Bravo's radioactive fallout. Yet, Catherine lived on Rongelap for several years, and ate from a contaminated environment:

> I returned to Rongelap . . . in 1957, and I saw friends and relatives who were afflicted with illnesses unknown to us. Their eyesight deteriorated, their bodies were covered with burn-like blisters, and their hair fell out by the handful. It was around this time that I had my first pregnancy. My baby had a very high fever when he was delivered, and the attending health assistant conveyed his doubts as to whether my son would survive the night. He was so dehydrated from the fever that his skin actually peeled as I clasped him to me to nurse. The only thing we knew to do was to wrap him in wet towels. And so it was that I held him to my

body throughout the night, changing the towels and willing him to fight for his life. He lost the fight just as dawn broke.

My second son, born in 1960, was delivered live but missing the whole back of his skull—as if it had been sawed off. So the back part of the brain and the spinal cord were fully exposed. After a week, the spinal cord became detached and he, too, developed a high fever and died the following day. Aside from the cranial deformity, my son was also missing both testicles and a penis. He passed water through a stump-like apparatus measuring less than an inch. The doctors who examined him told me that he would not survive. And sure enough, he was dead within a week. You know, it was heart wrenching having to nurse my son, all the while taking care his brain didn't fall into my lap. For in spite of his severe handicaps, he was healthy in every respect. It was good he died because I do not think he would have wanted to live a life as something less than a human.

The health assistant who delivered the child sent a message to Kwajalein, and I am certain those (U.S.) doctors came for the express purpose of seeing first-hand a live "nuclear baby." In fact, they flew in the very same day the message was sent. . . . They were very impersonal, almost casual, when telling me that my baby was not unique and that they had seen other babies like mine in other countries. . . . They did a complete physical (of the baby), took blood samples, and lots and lots of photographs.[33]

Dr. Esra Riklon, the Marshallese doctor working with AEC/DOE, verified that he and an American doctor were immediately dispatched to Rongelap to examine the "monster baby."

The vocabulary of Marshallese women also indicates that their birth anomalies are recent, and therefore could not have existed prior to the weapons testing program. When women describe the deformed, unsuccessful pregnancies they experience, they refer to the children as "monsters," "jellyfish," "grapes," "apples," "octopuses," "clams," and other words taken from objects of familiarity or from their local environment. If these reproductive problems existed before the nuclear weapons tests, the Marshallese would have more precise names for these conditions. Nonradiation induced illnesses have their own labels in the Marshallese language, not names based on comparison to other living objects.

Implications

Exposure will never again be defined in terms of fallout from BRAVO alone, but will now incorporate the cumulative effects of all tests, and the effects of residual contamination in the environment.[34]

In addition to complementing the historical research conducted by the embassy, the ethnographies served several other important functions. For example, Marshallese at the local and national levels are better informed about the extent of radiation problems in the undocumented communities, and, more specifically, among women. Understanding the nature of the problem is essential if the affected communities or the national government are going to increase their ability to solve their own health care and environmental restoration needs.[35]

The neglected communities are putting pressure on their national government to take action, and the national government is responding. This is a clear indication of how the project is empowering both the local and national governments. The historical and ethnographic data justifies the RMI government's demands for the U.S. government to remedy the human environmental abuses immediately, and the ethnographic data demonstrates that the need for action is immediate. Although the RMI government inherited persistent and acute radiation problems from the United States, it is not realistic to expect the RMI to finance mitigation measures.

Because the U.S. government is failing to assume its full responsibility for the lingering radiation problems at the bilateral level, the RMI government is seeking assistance from the international community. The RMI is speaking out about its new information at numerous multilateral forums, such as the UN General Assembly, and the UN Conference on Women in Beijing (September 4–15, 1995). The RMI delegation successfully convinced the international community to refer to the continued need for environmental restoration and health care for the radiation communities in the former UN Trust Territory in the report accompanying the extension of the Nuclear Non-Proliferation Treaty, and the Platform for Action from the Women's Conference. The RMI government also appeared before the International Court of Justice on November 14, 1995, to explain to the Court why nuclear weapons are a crime against humanity that deny basic human rights to a safe and clean environment.

The RMI government is also actively pursuing bilateral remedies for its radiation problems. On January 15, 1994, in the midst of the RMI government's document review, the Clinton administration formerly acknowledged that the U.S. government supported radiation experiments on human beings during the Cold War. Then it established an Advisory Committee on Human Radiation Experiments to investigate the extent of U.S. involvement in human experiments and to make recommendations to the White House about how to respond to biomedical violations. On four separate occasions the RMI government presented its research to the Advisory Committee on Human Radiation Experiments, and, as a direct result of this lobbying effort, the Advisory Committee acknowledged in its final report that more than four communities in the RMI were exposed to radiation, and that it was not merely the Bravo shot that contaminated the environment and exposed the people.[36] It was crucial than an independent, nonbiased committee drew these conclusions, since the Marshallese lack the political and economic clout to have their viewpoints seriously considered by the U.S. government. The Marshallese are not constituents, and it is difficult for the RMI to secure funds from U.S. government policy makers who do not want to appropriate funds or change policies if it is avoidable.[37] For a marginalized, expendable population like the Marshallese, this is particularly true since "existing social policies often serve to perpetuate institutional . . . interest groups . . . (rather than) the interests of those who lack political skills and power."[38]

After reviewing the case of the Marshall Islands, the Advisory Committee concluded that significant efforts need to be made to address the shortcomings of the U.S. government's care for the exposed population. Specifically, the Advisory Committee recommended that the U.S. government:

1. Review the present U.S. medical monitoring program "to determine if it is appropriate to add to the program the populations of other atolls to the south and east of the blast whose inhabitants may have received exposures sufficient to cause excess thyroid abnormalities."

2. Involve Marshallese "in the design of any further medical research to be conducted upon them."

3. Establish a panel to "review the status and adequacy of the current program of medical monitoring and medical care provided by the United States to the exposed population of the Marshall Islands."[39]

While the recommendations of the Advisory Committee represent an important step forward in forcing the U.S. government to acknowledge that it failed to care for all exposed populations in the Marshall Islands, extensive lobbying and political pressure are still necessary to secure policy changes that will provide tangible assistance to all radiation victims. Although the Advisory Committee failed to address the comprehensive needs of the radiation victims in the RMI, the RMI government endorses these recommendations and is working with the Congress and agencies in the U.S. government to implement them.

Changes in U.S. public policy must occur to make the neglected communities eligible to participate in U.S. health care and environmental monitoring programs. An adequate response to the persistent radiation problems in the Marshall Islands requires:

1. A new definition of "exposed" that is not restricted temporally or geographically.

2. Medical care for *all* victims of external and internal radiation exposure.

3. Environmental restoration of all contaminated islands to a level that is safe for human habitation in the United States.

4. Safe storage of all radioactive materials.

5. Increased capacity for the Marshallese to determine what does and doesn't constitute a radiation threat. This includes the training of Marshallese doctors, scientists, and radiation technicians and proper diagnostic facilities for professionals.

6. A nationwide epidemiological study that will identify all types of illnesses associated with radiation, such as women's reproductive health problems.

7. An independent review of all past and present U.S. medical and environmental programs resulting from the nuclear weapons testing.

8. Increased transparency and communication of results to the Marshallese recipients of U.S. programs.

Conclusion

Why didn't they do their experiments in their own country? In America there are deserts, and there is so much unused public land. Instead they chose some small islands to poison and kill the people![40]

The Marshall Islands case provides a grave example of the way in which U.S. colonialist policy and national security interests culminated in basic human environmental rights violations. The U.S. exploited the Trusteeship arrangement in order to establish the world's most superior nuclear arsenal. In its quest to obtain this goal, the U.S. government established the massive weapons testing program thousands of miles from the continental United States, suggesting a government premium on preserving a high quality of life for some American citizens and a complete disregard for other Americans (for the Marshallese were ostensibly U.S. citizens under the Trusteeship). For the U.S. government, the Marshallese were an expendable population: their health and land were of secondary importance to U.S. national security interests. Illness and death for marginalized people, and environmental contamination of their land were justifiable in order to better understand the destructive capacity of nuclear weapons.

It is painful to come to terms with the U.S. government's view of the Marshallese during the Cold War, and to ponder what these attitudes reflect about the values of American society. The Marshallese were powerless victims to the whims of a superpower that controlled what information the people had access to, when citizens could petition the United Nations, what populations of people would receive (or be denied) compensation or care, and what the international community and American citizens knew about the events that took place in the Marshall Islands.

Now that the truth is out, American and Marshallese leaders are compelled to act. The U.S. government has incredible resources that can be used to address many of these problems. Needs include revising the definition of "exposed"—it can no longer continue to be limited either geographically or through time (radiation knows no boundaries). Broadening the notion of "exposed" to reflect radiation realities requires coming to terms with the multigenerational implications of radiation exposure as evident in Ailuk and Likiep atolls, as well as among U.S. servicemen, uranium miners, downwinders, and other populations exposed to radiation as a result of U.S. military objectives.

As a sovereign nation, the Republic of the Marshall Islands will no longer tolerate the subordination imposed on it for decades. RMI government–initiated research into past events legitimizes its request for remedies from the United States and the international community, requests that require the parties to come to terms with the hegemonies allowing these injustices to occur. The simple act of asking questions, listening, and recording the experiences of its citizens has been an empowering experience, both for the island residents and the government that serves them. Compiling a comprehensive understanding of what has been validates and acknowledges the painful past, as well as provides the tools to fight for a better future.

Notes

1. Kaleman Gideon, Sept. 2, 1994. Interview conducted by Holly M. Barker, trans. by Newton Lajuan, Majuro Atoll, Republic of the Marshall Islands.

2. Tempo Alfred, Sept. 8, 1994. Interview conducted by Holly M. Barker, trans. by Newton Lajuan, Ailuk Atoll, Marshall Islands.

3. Jalel John, Sept. 5, 1994. Interview conducted by Holly M. Barker, trans. by Newton Lajuan, Ailuk Atoll, Marshall Islands.

4. Aruko Bobo, Aug. 27, 1994. Interview conducted by Holly M. Barker, trans. by Newton Lajuan, Kwajalein Atoll, Marshall Islands.

5. In Dec. 1995, the Peace Corps informed the government of the Republic of the Marshall Islands that it is suspending the Peace Corps program in the Marshall Islands indefinitely due to budget constraints.

6. Sheiko Shoniber, Sept. 1, 1994. Interview conducted and trans. by Holly M. Barker, Majuro Atoll, Marshall Islands.

7. Barbara Johnston, *Who Pays the Price?: The Sociocultural Context of Crisis* (Washington, D.C.: Island Press, 1994).

8. Atomic Energy Commission, Nov. 11, 1954. Memo from Brigadier General Alfred D. Starbird to Major General A. R. Luedecke, Chief of the Armed Forces Special Weapons Project.

9. Johnston, *op. cit.*, note 7, p. 10.

10. Dr. John C. Bugher, May 11, 1954, Report of meeting with Ambassador Lodge, UN, May 10, 1954.

11. Alfred, *op. cit.*, note 2.

12. Gideon, *op. cit.*, note 1.

13. Joint Task Force Seven, *Operation Castle: Radiological Safety, Final Report,* vol. 1 (Washington, D.C.: spring 1954), F-11.

14. P. W. Clarkson, Dec. 21, 1953. Letter to Dr. Alvin C. Graves regarding the Pate-Palmer Weather Report.

15. Bobo, *op. cit.*, note 4.

16. Joint Task Force Seven, *op. cit.*, note 13, p. K-8.

17. *Ibid.*, p. D-11.

18. Koju Alfred, Sept. 2, 1994. Interview conducted by Holly M. Barker, trans. by Newton Lajuan, Ailuk Atoll, Marshall Islands.

19. Joint Task Force Seven, *op. cit.*, note 13, p. K-64.

20. Esra Riklon, Aug. 18, 1994. Interview conducted and trans. by Holly M. Barker, Majuro Atoll, Marshall Islands.

21. Dept. of Energy, Dec. 16, 1982. Internal memorandum concerning presentation of DOE survey results from the northern Marshall Islands to the government of the Republic of the Marshall Islands.

22. See International Physcians for the Prevention of Nuclear War, *Radioactive Heaven and Earth: The Health and Environmental Effects of Nuclear Weapons Testing in, on, and above the Earth* (New York: Apex Press, 1991), 80.

23. Henchi Balos, Feb. 15, 1995. Statement to the White House Advisory Committee on Human Radiation Experiments on behalf of the Bikini Local Government, Washington, D.C.

24. Typhoon Rellong, interview.

25. William Leap, "Tribally Controlled Culture Change: The Northern Ute Language Renewal Project," in *Anthropological Praxis: Translating Knowledge into Action*, Robert M. Wulff, Shirley J. Fiske, eds. (Boulder, Colo.: Westview Press, 1987).

26. Dikjen Jilo, Sept. 2, 1994. Interview conducted by Holly M. Barker, trans. by Newton Lajuan, Ailuk Atoll, Marshall Islands.

27. Kajitok Lokeijak, Aug. 14, 1994. Interview conducted and trans. by Holly M. Barker, Likiep Atoll, Marshall Islands.

28. Rellong, *op. cit.*, note 24.

29. Alian Alik, Aug. 14, 1995. Interview conducted by Holly M. Barker, trans. by Newton Lajuan, Likiep Atoll, Marshall Islands.

30. Rose River, Sept. 8, 1994. Interview conducted by Holly M. Barker, trans. by Newton Lajuan, Ailuk Atoll, Marshall Islands.

31. Glenn Alcalay, March 15, 1995. Statement to the White House Advisory Committee on Human Radiation Experiments, Washington, D.C.

32. Ellyn Boaz, Aug. 26, 1994. Interview conducted by Holly M. Barker, trans. by Holly M. Barker and Elizabeth Cruz, Kwajalein Atoll, Marshall Islands.

33. Catherine Jibas, Aug. 23, 1994. Interview conducted by Holly M. Barker, trans. by Newton Lajuan, Majuro Atoll, Marshall Islands.

34. Banny de Brum, "Reaction of the Government of the Republic of the Marshall Islands to the Final Report of the White House Advisory Committee on Human Radiation Experiments" (Washington, D.C., Oct. 3, 1995).

35. Edward C. Green, "The Integration of Modern and Traditional Health Sectors in Swaziland," *Anthropological Praxis: Translating Knowledge into Action* (Boulder, Colo.: Westview Press, 1987).

36. Advisory Committee on Human Radiation Experiments, *Final Report* (Washington, D.C.: Government Printing Office, Oct. 1995).

37. Lesley Gill, "Examining Power, Serving the State: Anthropology, Congress and the Invasion of Panama," *Human Organizations* 54:3 (fall 1995).

38. William L. Partridge and Elizabeth M. Eddy, "The Development of Applied Anthropology in America," *Applied Anthropology in America* (New York: Columbia University Press, 1987).

39. Advisory Committee, *op. cit.*, note 36.

40. Alfred, *op. cit., note 2.*

CHAPTER 14

Complex Problems and No Clear Solutions
Radiation Victimization in Russia

Paula Garb

Introduction

The development of nuclear technologies has been accompanied by the potential to cause catastrophic and long-lasting damage to the earth and to the life forms that inhabit it. We have received warnings about these hazards from nuclear accidents that have occurred in different countries, the most notable in recent history being at Chernobyl. However, there have been other serious incidents as well, including radiation releases from nuclear weapons complexes in both the United States and Russia. Sociocultural studies of populations that have been exposed to radiation from such accidents can suggest ways to assist people coping with nuclear age hazards.

With this aim I have studied communities in Russia that have been exposed to radiation from nuclear weapons facilities, working with colleagues at University of California–Irvine (UCI) and Washington State University as part of a larger, multidisciplinary project entitled "Citizen Responses to the Environmental Consequences of Nuclear Weapons Production in the United States and Russia." My focus has been on the divergent perceptions in Chelyabinsk of how the people's health and lifestyles were affected by the radiation, whom they blame, and what strategies they have devised both to ameliorate the problems and to preserve their cultures in these contaminated environments. In this context, I grapple with issues of environmental human rights and environmental racism. I also analyze the responses and discourse on the part of scientists and officials in the nuclear community.

Material presented in this chapter is derived primarily from survey data and in-depth interviews[1] conducted by colleagues and me, mostly in the fall and winter of 1992, in towns and villages in close proximity (from 3 to 30 miles) to a weapons facility known as Mayak Chemical Combine, located in the Chelyabinsk region in the Urals. This facility is situated in Chelyabinsk-65, a closed city that was not on the map until 1989. Mayak was the Soviet Union's first weapons-grade plutonium production center. Throughout the Cold War, Mayak produced nuclear materials for the country's nuclear weapons, and in doing so caused severe environmental contamination to the Chelyabinsk region, which has a current population of 3.6 million. As a result of the

Paula Garb is an anthropologist, Adjunct Professor of Social Ecology, and Associate Director of the Global Peace and Conflict Studies Program at the University of California–Irvine, Social Science Plaza 3151, Irvine, CA 92692. She can be reached via email (pgarb@uci.edu).

accidents, more than 146 million curies of radiation were released over time. By comparison, Three Mile Island, in the United States, released only 14–20 curies. Chernobyl, in the former Soviet Union, released from 50 million to 80 million curies. Most of the radioactive elements released from Chelyabinsk were strontium-90 and cesium-137, but small amounts of plutonium were also lost. About 120 million curies are trapped in Lake Karachay inside the facility; some 120 million were released in a storage tank explosion in 1957; 3 million are trapped in Lake Staroe Boloto; 2.75 million were dumped in the Techa River from the late 1940s until 1956; 600 were disbursed by a 1967 dust storm; and 6,000 curies are in groundwater creeping from the complex toward the city of Chelyabinsk, the region's administrative center with a population of over 1 million.[2]

I also include relevant information from Russia's two other plutonium production sites at Krasnoyarsk and Tomsk, which have released radioactive elements in the environment, causing concern among the population about environmental damage and health effects. This information I acquired during a trip to this Siberian area in September 1994, when I interviewed environmental activists and officials attending a conference on post–Cold War disarmament, conversion, and security issues.

For comparative purposes I cite experiences around U.S. nuclear weapons sites. My sources of information are conversations with officials at a former plutonium production site in the United States at Hanford, Washington, and with U.S. representatives (environmental activists, medical researchers, social scientists) at international conferences that I attended in Chelyabinsk (1992), Krasnoyarsk (1994), and Kaluga (1994).[3] These informants were familiar not only with Hanford, but also with several other nuclear weapons sites in the United States, such as Rocky Flats and Savannah River.

The People of Chelyabinsk

The people living in the Chelyabinsk region include Russians, Tatars, Bashkirs, Chuvash, Mari, Ukrainians, Byelorussians, Kazakhs, Jews, and Germans. Russians form the majority, followed by the Tatars and Bashkirs. Of these groups the earliest settlers were the Turkic-speaking Bashkirs whose history in the area dates back to the 14th century. Traditionally, they were nomads and many aspects of this heritage are still evident today, even though they have been sedentary agriculturalists since the early 18th century. Most Bashkirs in the Chelyabinsk region live in the Argayash and Kunashak districts, both of which are heavily populated with Bashkirs and Tatars and experienced severe radiation exposure from Mayak. Tatars, who speak a related Turkic-language, appeared in the region in the late 17th century. They have a centuries-long history of farming and urban development. Tatars did not settle in compact communities, but were dispersed throughout Chelyabinsk. Despite the cultural differences between Tatars and Bashkirs, due mainly to the differences in their traditional nomadic and farming backgrounds, they share more in common with each other than with the non-Turkic and non-Muslim ethnic groups who are their neighbors. Intermarriage between the two groups is much more common than it is with other nationalities.

Of the towns and villages in the sample, Muslyumovo (population 4,022) has the largest percentage of Tatars and Bashkirs (Tatars number 3,302, Bashkirs 379, Russians

A child and her mother in the leukemia ward of Chelyabinsk Children's Hospital where the survival rate is barely over 50 percent due to a lack of chemotherapy. Studies there show a higher than average rate of leukemia in closed cities, and in the region where Muslyumovo is located. Photograph by Paula Garb.

341). The main occupations in Muslyumovo are related to the operation of the local state farm, which focuses on stock breeding and grain growing, and servicing the local railway station. The village is situated along the Techa River approximately 30 miles from Mayak, and is contaminated both from the dumping of plutonium waste from Mayak in the early 1950s and from the 1957 explosion.

Kyshtym, another town in our sample, is about seven miles from Mayak. It has a total population of 42,283 (of which 38,432 are Russians, 1,365 Tatars, and 931 Bashkirs). Other minorities include small numbers of Byelorussians, Ukrainians, Kazakhs, Germans, Chuvash, Jews, Mordvinians, and Mari. Most of the population work in the city's three major industries—radio, copper, and machine-tool building. Other important sources of employment in Kyshtym are the local railway station, the truck and bus depot, and services industry. Over the decades, employment in the closed cities of Chelyabinsk-65 and Chelyabinsk-70 (focused mainly on weapons research) has been an especially coveted opportunity for people in Kyshtym.

The third town in our study, Dal'naya Dacha, is a community on the outskirts of Kyshtym, and it is closest to the Mayak complex. It was established in the early 1950s to service a health resort built there for the employees of Chelyabinsk-65. Most of the population is Russian, but there are also some Tatars and Bashkirs. The majority of the residents work for the health resort as service personnel. Through their work they enjoy, more than residents in the rest of Kyshtym, better access to the relatively abundant food and consumer goods available to Chelyabinsk-65. Like the people of Kyshtym, many families in Dal'naya Dacha also have relatives who work and live inside the city of Chelyabinsk-65, and through them they have an additional dependence on the facilities.

A History of the Contamination and the Evolution of Perceptions about Mayak

Throughout the construction of the Mayak nuclear weapons facility (1945 to 1949), the people in and around Kyshtym were not told what the facility would be used for—only that it was an important postwar construction site. The facility was a welcomed project, since it provided many unskilled jobs to local residents, especially in the nearest town of Kyshtym.

In 1949, after Mayak's initial construction was completed and the plant began operation, abundant unskilled labor from the local communities was no longer needed and the site was closed to all outsiders. The large numbers of soldiers coming in and out of the gates and the general secrecy that shrouded the plant's activities led local people to conclude that the facility had something to do with the military, although this was never confirmed officially.

By 1952–53, signs began appearing along the Techa River in the plant's vicinity, warning residents that it was dangerous to use the water. People periodically noticed what they described as "pink pieces of fluff" floating in the water, and anglers brought home three-feet long fish that were blind.[4] Officials did not explain why it was dangerous to swim in or use the water in the Techa River. Rumors began to circulate about radiation contamination, but if people knew the term they understood it simplistically, equating its effects with those of an X-ray. Inhabitants claim that officials never explained to them either the scope of the radiation contamination or the health and environmental consequences. About 28,000 people along the Techa depended on the river for drinking and irrigation water.

In the early 1950s, 22 villages along the river in its most contaminated areas were evacuated after a marked increase in disease and deaths were observed among the inhabitants.[5] Whole populations were evacuated, leaving ghost villages. People were moved to other villages in noncontaminated areas. The vast majority were settled in what were to be temporary houses that became substandard in time. These evacuations did not seem to stir any local public protest. No doubt this absence of any public expression of anger by the evacuees was due to the fact that heads of households had to sign papers swearing themselves to secrecy. Another reason is that even though the plant had not hired as many locals as it did during its early construction, it was still regarded as a potential source of privileged employment and was therefore generally looked on favorably as a facility that was economically beneficial to the neighboring area. If a son or daughter was hired by Mayak and moved to the closed city, he or she could share the benefits of their high standard of living with relatives who remained on the outside.

In the late afternoon of September 29, 1957, one of the facility's 80,000-gallon storage tanks exploded, after its cooling system failed. About 20 million curies of radioactive debris were released over a territory about the size of New Jersey, and approximately 10,700 people were permanently evacuated. Over half of these people were not evacuated until eight months after the accident. They consumed contaminated food for three to six months without restriction and continued to eat some contaminated food until their evacuation. The entire population of the region ate the 1957 harvest, which was heavily contaminated with radionuclides.[6]

This is how the events were recalled by Mikhail Gladyshev, formerly director of Mayak's plutonium facility:

> The day after the explosion it was clear that northeast winds were spreading radioactive materials over population centers and waterways, so we began evacuating the population from their native villages. We had to arrange for the issuing of new clothes and other necessities for the evacuees, their decontamination in showers, and resettlement. It took major organizational efforts and expenditures. The overwhelming majority of the evacuees were Bashkirs. It's amazing that the whole evacuation was completed in a relatively short period and without any resistance from the population. The job was finished so rapidly that very soon the people adapted to their new conditions and new life.[7]

Evacuees interviewed for this study confirm that the population did not put up any resistance. The people were conditioned by the strong Soviet government to obey orders and to believe that their leaders knew what was best for them. For the Bashkirs, the tradition of military discipline had an even longer history, going back to the period between 1798 and 1865 when the Bashkirs served en masse as rank and file soldiers in the czarist army guarding Russia's eastern borders. The harsh military discipline imposed on the Bashkirs by their Russian commanders apparently helped to mold an obedient population.

Even though the evacuation met with no resistance and went more smoothly than officials expected, the evacuees suffered deep emotional and cultural trauma from their sudden uprooting from ancestral villages. I talked to people in Dal'naya Dacha who worked at one of the health resorts where evacuees were housed from October of 1957 to May of 1958. They recall caring solely for evacuees from neighboring villages, and doing this job without the assistance of Mayak officials or physicians. Aleftina Fisko, who worked in the cafeteria of the Chelyabinsk-65 resort, told me that throughout the period evacuees were at her resort, no doctors or managers from Mayak even visited the site, "as if," she said, "they were afraid of being contaminated."[8]

Fisko recalled that in early October 1957, several hundred Bashkirs and Tatars, whole families with children and elders, were brought to the resort:

> Most of them did not speak any Russian; they chattered to each other in their own language. They lived in buildings that were only used in summer so they weren't heated, and were given free food for only two months. Afterwards they had to find their own food until they left in May, I have no idea where to. All the belongings they brought with them from home were confiscated and burned. The Bashkir women tried to sneak into the building where they had been forced to leave all their clothing, including their ethnic attire. As soon as they were seen in these clothes they were made to give them up for burning. Some of them were so desperate they even managed to go back to their villages before they were burned down in order to retrieve food and clothing. The women did all the housekeeping and hunting for food, while the men roamed around town and drank vodka.[9]

One of the evacuees from the 1957 disaster told me that when the soldiers came from Mayak to inform his fellow villagers that they had to leave their homes forever the very next morning, they advised the men to drink up whatever vodka they had in stock to protect themselves from the exposure: "The male villagers did as told. We took all the alcohol out of storage in the village store and homes and drank as much as we could. We had a great time." Some men were apparently delighted by this officially sanctioned drinking spree, which may have led to increased alcoholism among this population.

Men and women informants recalled their resettlement with tears in their eyes as they described how they had to slaughter their own animals the night before they left, prepared their homes for burning, parted with family heirlooms, were loaded onto army trucks that took them to barracks or unheated resort facilities, were herded into showers, issued military clothing, and left to gradually rebuild their lives without any government assistance. Some were eventually offered other housing, but many were forced to find shelter and jobs on their own. One major obstacle was that when they were forced to leave their homes they also had to sign a paper promising not to tell anyone why they had moved. When they came to a new place looking for work, they were not able to give a previous reference because they could not say where they were from.

The people who wept in front of me said that for years they had pushed all thoughts about their past from memory, and refrained from talking to anyone about what happened. Some said that I was the first to hear their stories. I felt as though the experiences of the people I interviewed, who were finally opening up about the past, bordered on the cathartic.

Despite the 1957 accident, Chelyabinsk-65, with its Mayak production facility, remained the ideal city of the future to the local people, especially in Kyshtym. Those who worked there boasted to their friends and relatives about the high wages, their interesting and prestigious work, the excellent infrastructure and consumer goods supplies. For young people it was a desirable job. Those who could not get jobs at the closed facilities were envious and, perhaps, somewhat hostile to those who had such jobs. It's as though the people of Kyshtym had a love-hate relationship with the facilities. A man who was in his late fifties said that when he was in his twenties (in the 1960s) the people of Kyshtym started calling the residents of Chelyabinsk-65 "chocolate people," for the chocolate bars (symbols of the good life) available in abundance inside the gates and absent outside. He remembers that teenagers in Kyshtym would get into fist fights over these issues with visiting boys from Chelyabinsk-65.[10]

The people gradually began to understand the effects of radiation on the environment and health as information was released after the 1986 disaster at Chernobyl. However, it was not until 1989, when the government officially acknowledged the Mayak disasters, that the Chelyabinsk population became fully aware of the implications of their proximity to the nuclear weapons facility.

They of course knew of their own health problems, but did not relate them to Mayak until these relatively recent revelations. In Muslyumovo, for instance, the people were told by officials since 1953 that the river was "dirty," but not that the source of the "dirt" was Mayak. The local Bashkirs and Tatars called their "strange" illnesses the "river disease," whose symptoms were periodic, and in some cases constant, numbness in their extremities, aching joints, frequent and severe headaches, bleeding of the nose and gums, and fatigue. People even died of the "river disease."

In Muslyumovo they did not know the name of the river until 1953 when they were told by local officials that it was "dirty" and that they must not use the water for anything. After 1989, when they learned that the "dirt" in the river was radiation and how dangerous it was, the young people of the village renamed the Techa the "atomka," which is a slang derivative from the Russian word "atomic."

The people did not draw a connection between the river and Mayak. Mayak was not allowed to be part of their consciousness because it was a defense plant, and completely hidden from view and from any public discussion. Another factor was that the very inadequate infrastructure (that is, bad roads, no phone lines) in Russian rural areas keeps population centers fairly isolated from one another. Therefore, people did not and do not really know much about what is going on even in their own region. However, secrecy of such a defense facility was the main reason. People did not discuss such matters, pretending that such places did not exist for fear of thinking or saying something that would get them in trouble. It was as if the Mayak and the secret cities were invisible.

The first published information about the health effects caused by Mayak was released in December 1991. The results had the impact of a bombshell on the entire population. The article summed up a study done by a government commission that revealed that since 1950 the incidence of leukemia among the population exposed to radiation along the Techa River had increased by 41 percent (see photograph). From 1980 to 1990 all cancers among this population had risen by 21 percent, and all diseases of the circulatory system by 31 percent.[11] This report is not considered the final word on the tragedy of Chelyabinsk, mainly because the raw data are not available to confirm the results. This work is yet to be done.

Local doctors say it is impossible to obtain completely dependable health data because physicians were supposed to limit the number of death certificates they issued with diagnoses of cancer or other radiation-related illnesses. This was part of the general Soviet practice to control health statistics so that rates of certain illnesses would not be embarrassingly high. My Russian colleague was told by a rural physician in Chelyabinsk that once a certain number of illnesses had been reached, no more were to be reported.

Another problem is that the Muslim Bashkirs and Tatars, due to religious considerations, would not always permit an autopsy to establish cause of death. When they did allow an autopsy they were angered to see that a whole team of physicians were at the side of the deceased within hours after death, whereas during the illness the doctors did not appear once to offer the patient aid.

Perceptions of Health Risks

According to the results of a fall 1992 public opinion survey of residents in the Chelyabinsk Region, among the combined populations of Muslyumovo and Kyshtym, 86 percent feel that their family's health has been affected by Mayak.[12] Approximately half the residents of Chelyabinsk City and Chelyabinsk-70 also say their families have been affected.[13]

In the village of Muslyumovo, Dr. Gulfarida Galimova has been keeping records in lieu of reliable official statistics, although hers may also be flawed. I present her results here because they reflect the depth of the fear so palpable in Muslyumovo. Dr. Galimova claims that every family has someone with the "river disease." She has determined from her own numbers that the average lifespan of the women of Muslyumovo is 47 (72 is the average for the nation), and the average lifespan of the men is 45 (69 for the nation). The death rate in Muslyumovo is 24 percent greater than it is for the noncontaminated villages in the same Kunashak region. The mortality rate at birth is ten times higher. Galimova maintains that sterility and infertility have become commonplace among her patients, especially those who went through puberty in the late 1940s and early 1950s, when Mayak was dumping its radioactive waste into the river. Since 1950 the cases of leukemia have increased by 41 percent and are double those in the noncontaminated areas of the region. The number of asthma cases is four times greater.[14]

Another independent health researcher who worked in the area in the early 1990s was geneticist Nina Solovyova from the Institute of Cytology and Genetics in the Siberian Branch of the Russian Academy of Sciences. She also identified the "river disease" among the subjects of her study and named it the Muslyumovo Syndrome. In addition to the symptoms of the Muslyumovo Syndrome, increasing numbers of children, according to the village schoolteachers, are lethargic and slow learners. Solovyova revealed through DNA and chromosome analyses conducted in 1993–1994 that 30 percent of Muslyumovo residents show genetic deformation.

When Nina Solovyova proposed her DNA and chromosome study to the local government, she was promised funding from FIB-4 (an acronym for the fourth branch of the Institute of Biophysics managed by a classified division of the Ministry of Public Health). FIB-4 is a government institution that has monitored the health of the Chelyabinsk victims throughout the decades. Doctors working there signed sworn statements that they would not tell patients what they were being examined for nor their diagnosis. The data collected is still unavailable to outside researchers. The U.S. Department of Energy is trying to pry loose the information in a major joint project to analyze the data together, but the Russians have made that task very difficult. As Solovyova's preliminary data began to show higher-than-average aberrations, FIB-4 canceled its contract with her because it doubted the validity of her data, since it did not correspond to FIB's data.

When a team of UCI researchers tried to replicate Solovyova's study independently, the project was called to the attention of the local counterintelligence agency (successor of the KGB), which halted the collection of blood samples. In a conversation with the Muslyumovo physician who had asked the Americans to do this study, a counterintelligence officer told her that Muslyumovo blood was worth millions of dollars and therefore she had no right to give it away to anyone. Apparently some local authorities would like to profit from giving foreigners access to such data. This incident and Dr. Galimova's related advocacy for her patients' rights to independent medical opinions have cost the doctor her job. This is perhaps one reason why I was only able to find a few physicians in the region who are active in the antinuclear movement and align themselves politically with their activist patients.

Living with Radiation Contamination: Effects on Lifestyle

It is difficult scientifically to draw a direct link between the above-mentioned health problems and exposure to radiation. To do so requires long-term research by diverse independent scholars who test and retest the data. It will be many years before it is possible to say with certainty that there is or is not a link, and to what extent other types of environmental damage, or perhaps other factors, are involved. However, it is already evident that local people are modifying their everyday behavior in an attempt to avoid or mitigate what they perceive to be the health risks involved in living near or on contaminated territory. This section is devoted to an analysis of these lifestyle changes.

The Bashkirs and Tatars, with their Muslim cultural heritage, who live right next to the contaminated Techa River believe they are at greater risk than non-Muslims from radiation exposure because of their special relationship to water. Practicing Muslims must wash their hands before they say their prayers several times a day. Women, whether they are worshipers or not, must bathe and wash carefully their genitals many times a day. I commonly heard from people a belief that due to these practices they subjected themselves to excessive health risks. They believe that because of these strict rules of hygiene, both for women (frequent washing of genitals) and men (circumcision), in noncontaminated areas Bashkir and Tatar women have lower than average incidences of gynecological cancer, but that the reverse is true in contaminated regions because of the abundant use of water in personal hygiene. For instance, a woman in Muslyumovo attributed the Muslyumovo Syndrome that she suffers to her traditional habits of hygiene. She said that living in her husband's home as a young newlywed in the late 1950s and 1960s, she wanted her mother-in-law to be sure of her concerns for cleanliness in the Muslim Tatar tradition, so she bathed and washed clothes daily in the Techa River right by their home. Had she known about the river's radiation contamination and the health risks, she would have been more cautious, as are today's young village women. In keeping with these views, some individuals said they are trying to reduce the amounts of water they use, particularly from the river.

Adults rarely swim in the river now because of their awareness of the "river disease," but it is still hard to control the children, especially on hot summer days. And even during the winter, it is not uncommon to see teenage boys ice fishing on the frozen waters. Many adults and children alike cross the river daily at its narrowest site to get from one part of the village to another. Large numbers of children could not get to school every day unless they took this convenient crossing.

The food chain is, of course, another important means by which the population is exposed to radioactive elements. Most of the food families consume is grown on their homesteads. Some families who live in close proximity to the river try to sell their garden produce (mainly potatoes), meat, and milk at farmers' markets in the city of Chelyabinsk or the nearby town of Kunashak, and purchase for their own consumption produce from what they hope are noncontaminated areas. But most families in Muslyumovo consume their own homegrown food, including the beef and milk from their livestock that is central to the diet of the relatively recently nomadic Bashkirs and even their traditionally sedentary Tatar neighbors. Since the livestock grazes and drinks at the river, the people perceive these products to be the most damaging to their health.

Milk that is fermented, however, is regarded by the population as an antidote to the "radiation" illnesses. Bashkirs and Tatars have traditionally believed that fermented mare's milk, "koumiss," cures all illnesses. According to medical research in Russia, *koumiss* contains vitamins, especially vitamin C, and antibiotic elements, all of which researchers there say have strong healing qualities.[15] Therefore, koumiss and other fermented dairy products in the traditional Tatar and Bashkir diet are seeing a comeback in the past couple of years in connection with the population's heightened awareness of radiation exposure and the possible consequences.

Also seeing a comeback are herbal and other folk medicines. Traditionally these people have used the skin or mold from fermented products (cheese, buttermilk, farmers' cheese) to heal wounds. Contemporary homemakers maintain that products that have grown mold lose their radioactivity, as though the mold somehow devours the radioactive elements in the milk. They think that the healing qualities of pressed geese and horse dung are also useful in treating cancers. Local people are reviving the use of many herbs to prevent and cure all illnesses, and particularly those they associate with the radiation contamination. Some of the more common ones thought to remove radionuclides and intoxicants from the body are Gledidomium majus, Acorus calamus, Aloe arborescent, honey, pumpkin, and Allium cepa. Gynecological illnesses are treated with Allium sepa, Arctium lappu, Pinus sp., Linum mitatissimuni, Origanum vulgares, and Aloe arborescent. At least two women claimed to have cured themselves of cancer by drinking herbal teas made from hempseed and burdock root.

Folk medicine is the approach women tend to put their faith in to prevent and cure illnesses that they regard to be related to radiation. Alcohol is what the men rely on, particularly vodka. Many informants noted that alcoholism has increased in recent years among the male population. They cannot say what the main cause of this alarming phenomenon is, but indicate that the alcoholics believe they are protected from the consequences of radiation exposure.

In an effort to lessen the effects from what they believe to be contaminated food, the people have introduced some changes to their diet. For instance, even practicing Muslims who won't eat pork themselves do not prevent other members of their families from eating pork because it is regarded as less contaminated than beef. They believe that pork absorbs less radiation because of its greater ratio of fat and meat to bones compared to beef, and also because the pigs stay in their yards and do not drink from the river. However, devout practicing Muslims will insist that a separate set of dishes be kept for serving the pork.

Local residents are taking other measures recommended throughout the country as a way to lessen the general risk of cancer, since they believe they are at high risk already because of the nearby radiation contamination. Thus they are growing more vegetables and eating them more regularly, "like the Russians," as they say, as a means of cutting down beef consumption and adding vitamins to the diet. Finally, they are giving up some of their traditional ethnic delicacies that require extensive frying in large quantities of grease, and smoked meat, the dishes that doctors say are carcinogenic.

The Russian population has also looked to the Bashkirs and Tatars for ways to cut their risks of cancer. They now tend to brew their tea in Bashkir and Tatar traditions, which means they try not to drink tea that has been steeped for more than 5–7 minutes and don't use old brew. This is because they have heard from medical researchers that tea can be carcinogenic if it is not freshly brewed.

Cultural attitudes toward pathology have influenced the way locals express concerns for their families' health, and impact their decision-making about seeking medical care. Muslims in this area, especially the elders, feel it is wrong to call attention to personal misfortune. They are particular about their privacy when it comes to a deformity, pathology, or illness in the family. For instance, a child born with a deformity is regarded as punishment from Allah, and therefore any abnormality should be hidden from others and suffered alone. By contrast, Russian families *demand* public attention to their ailing children and demand special considerations and benefits. Muslim women condemn such behavior, maintaining that a sick or deformed child should not be used as a means to improve a family's living conditions or income.

Another problem is that Muslim women are much more reluctant than other ethnic groups to have gynecological examinations, so such illnesses are often not diagnosed early. Muslim men are more likely not to see a doctor for any ailment. If they are religious they claim that their recovery is in the hands of Allah, and if they are not they say either that they don't have time to see a doctor or that it won't do any good. Men tend to want to be kept in the dark about the risks of radiation more than women. "Better not to know anything. What will be, will be," was a typical male response. And women were more likely than men in Muslyumovo to favor moving out of the contaminated area.

As this whole section has shown, people may not know the exact risks they face living in Chelyabinsk, though they are certain that their health and lives are in danger and they are creatively finding self-help ways to minimize the threat by making dietary and other lifestyle changes. Another solution seen in particular by the people of Muslyumovo is to leave the area by any means possible. Since it does not seem likely that the government will finance their relocation, individuals are seeking the "evacuation" of their own families. One of the local schoolteachers who has three of her own children, and is looking for a way to move out, constantly gives her students these three pieces of advice:

1. Don't have anything to do with the river,
2. Get away from Muslyumovo as soon as possible, and
3. Don't marry each other.

Assigning Culpability

When people are asked who is to blame for their predicament, they most commonly point to Moscow, to the national government that dictated the production policies in civilian and military industry. They recognize that local plant officials did not make their decisions independently of Moscow, particularly in the Stalin period when Beria, head of the NKVD (predecessor of the KGB) until 1953, was personally in control of all the military facilities.

However, they are particularly bitter about what they feel was the betrayal of local officials and doctors who knew about the contamination and the health effects and yet did not inform the public so that they could take effective measures to protect themselves. Special anger is focused on FIB-4, which, as mentioned earlier, for decades conducted elaborate tests on thousands of Chelyabinsk residents to study but not treat the health effects of radiation after the accidents. "If they had only told me how much radiation I had accumulated I never would have had children," was a common refrain I heard from patients who were periodically summoned for testing by FIB-4. It was only in April 1990 that the public was told about the real focus of the institute's research work, although little of the data has been released either to the patients or to outside researchers. Another common complaint about Chelyabinsk doctors was that while a loved one was dying of an illness suspected of being related to radiation exposure, family members sat by the bedside alone. As soon as the patient died, it was common for a whole team of doctors to come at once to do tests. One woman told me, "When these teams come out they are so cold, they do not seem to even notice our anguish. Where were they when we needed them?"

There are also bitter words for Mayak. A speaker at a public rally in Muslyumovo on September 26, 1993, poignantly sums up the sentiment of her neighbors: "We curse Mayak, which robbed us of our parents and our health." I often heard people say that Mayak produced weapons for a cold war during which time no bomb was ever dropped—except on the people of Chelyabinsk!

These expressions of anger do not seem to reflect sentiments against strong defense capabilities. On the contrary, often the same people who were most critical of the facilities also voiced concerns about maintaining Russia's national security. For instance, Gosman Kabirov, a local environmental activist and a Tatar who blames Mayak for his inability to have children and for the illnesses of his parents, brothers, and sisters, has wondered aloud whether western organizations are funding the Russian environmental movement with the goal of using the antinuclear movement to undermine Russia's security. In March 1993, at a conference of antinuclear organizations in the Socio-Ecological Union, he indicated his high evaluation of Mayak's accomplishments both in defense and civilian industry:

> Mayak is a unique complex, not only in our country, but in the world. Indeed, it has brought our country enormous benefit, and made it among the best in the world. The isotope plant that opened in 1962 produces fiber optics, devices for radiation control, batteries for artificial hearts, new materials and reinforced plastics, and new technology for storing nuclear waste (vitrification). All this brings the state hundreds of millions of dollars in profits. And we should not underestimate the fact that Mayak had Americans worried about the Russian bomb. It's no wonder that Chelyabinsk was one of the main targets for a nuclear weapons attack on our country. But at what price? That's what we have to talk about.[16]

While some are concerned with national security, other portions of the population express sentiments tied to the growing nationalist movements of Tatars and Bashkirs throughout Russia—movements that raise claims of genocide and promise to help the people get the justice that so far has not been forthcoming from the national or local governments. The following statement is representative of those used to incite ethnic indignation: "What is the reason for the selective policies in evacuating people from the villages contaminated in 1957 in the Chelyabinsk region after the sudden nuclear explosion of radioactive materials in the storage tank? . . . Tatar and Bashkir villagers were left without help, they were not evacuated to safe places. Meanwhile the population of Russian villages were taken away immediately from the explosion site and their villages were bulldozed."[17]

Without doing a focused study, these charges cannot be confirmed. There are no studies in Russia equivalent to the works of Bullard, Wenz, Johnston, and others who have identified and analyzed environmental injustices against U.S. minority communities and Third World populations.[18] There are local Tatars and Bashkirs who claim that their population was singled out to be the guinea pigs of Russian scientists researching the effects of radiation on humans. They cite doctors who were asked by secret research facilities to identify patients for studies according to their ethnic background.[19] Activists from Bashkiria and Tataria try to incite anger over such accusations of "genocidal" politics. So far, the population resists, telling these outside activists not to put a wedge between the different nationalities of Chelyabinsk.[20] Local environmental activists in Chelyabinsk tend to either deny or play down the possibility that the health and lives of Bashkirs and Tatars were undervalued when decisions were made about evacuations. They fear that raising such issues will generate ethnic tensions that could erupt in violence, which has been (and continues to be) so destructive in other parts of the former Soviet Union.

Activists in Muslyumovo's antinuclear organization known as the White Mice (Russian equivalent for "guinea pigs") hesitate to charge officials with environmental racism, though they are not hesitant to charge them with human rights violations, because the government has not been responsive to their demands that the village be moved to a site farther away from the river. They have written to the UN Human Rights Commission stating their grievances of environmental injustice, but have not framed their complaints as a case of environmental racism.

How do plant officials respond to accusations against them? Yevgeny Ryzhkov, director of public relations for Chelyabinsk-65, focuses all the blame on past production procedures and past policies of not informing the public. "Now," he says, "my policy is to be available to answer any questions from the public so that rumors won't abound."[21] He claims that mistakes were made in the past, but now they are much less likely because of the knowledge and experience accumulated over the years. The population outside the plant, however, continues to mistrust him and other officials, but he says he can't blame them because they were lied to before. That's why his goal is to regain the people's trust by, he claims, always being forthright in responding to their concerns about the facility's activities and concerns about safety today.

Another common remark I heard from officials, scientists, and members of their families who have lived inside Chelyabinsk-65 and Chelyabinsk-70 since before the 1957 explosion is that they as individuals are very healthy and therefore are living proof that even the accidents of the 1950s and 1960s were not as damaging to the people's health as claimed. Some of these informants appear to genuinely believe what they say. However, a couple of them, speaking to me off the record and away from their fellow residents, have said just the opposite. This view was also reflected in the results of a UCI public opinion survey conducted inside Chelyabinsk-70 where roughly half the population claims that their families' health has been affected by operations at the facilities in nearby Chelyabinsk-65.[22] Reliable health data are next to impossible to obtain, so none of these claims can be proven right or wrong.

Officials in local government at the region and district levels seem to talk out of both sides of their mouths. On the one hand, they have fought hard to have the Chernobyl law, which ensures generous government allocations to areas affected by the Chernobyl accident, be applied to the Chelyabinsk region. In doing so they have cited the tremendous health and related social problems caused by the 1957 accident, which released far more curies than Chernobyl. On the other hand, when they are talking to their own constituents and to inquiring guests like myself, they tend to maintain that the environmentalists should be focused on industrial pollutants and low living standards as the main culprits in the region's health problems, not the military complex. At one meeting of several region leaders (September 1992) I heard one of them maintain that the "greens" had done more damage to the country than Chernobyl because they generated "radiophobia," the term used in Russia to denote excessive fear of radiation among the population. They claimed "radiophobia" was far more debilitating than the actual objective problems they faced. Furthermore, the situation was worsened by visiting foreigners (such as myself) asking people questions about how they were affected by radiation. Another official at the same meeting, a physician, claimed that he had gone door-to-door in communities like Muslyumovo where people were convinced that all their ailments were due to radiation, and that he concluded that their illnesses were caused by their low standard of living, not by radiation. None of the officials at this "roundtable" meeting argued against these statements.

Galina Plokhikh, a member of Optima, which is a group of environmentalists in Chelyabinsk secondary schools, is familiar with these attitudes. Speaking at a conference in Krasnoyarsk in September 1994, she said, "We are told that the main source of illnesses and short life is not Mayak but low living standards and general environmental damage. Our officials say, Do not bother protesting because they will help us."

Proposing Solutions

Most of the people I talked to in the vicinity of Mayak, particularly in Muslyumovo, do not see assistance on the horizon or immediate solutions forthcoming—either from their national leaders or from the local government. The most common opinion expressed in Muslyumovo about Mayak is that it is an eternal reality, an inescapable evil that no one knows how to fight. The feeling of doom expressed by all informants was overwhelming. It has been reinforced by a series of disappointments. Just before Russian President Boris Yeltsin visited Muslyumovo in September 1991, the residents unanimously voted for resettlement and hoped that their problems would be solved by the money allocated by the Russian government to compensate for the damage done by Mayak. Instead, the 1 million rubles they received was used in part to pave a road in the center of town where Yeltsin's car would drive, and to build a small hospital that has not significantly improved their health care. People are convinced that the rest of the money, also intended for general improvements to the community (not compensation to individuals), was pocketed by their local officials (Bashkirs and Tatars). In the summer and fall of 1994 they were told that financial compensation would be allotted to anyone who could show that they were victims of excessive radiation exposure. So people began bringing doctors' certificates to a special commission set up to review the applications for benefits, only to find that the fine print of the ruling excluded almost everyone who made a claim. Criteria for the health certificates were so stringent that few qualified. Anyone who no longer resided in Muslyumovo, even if the person had moved away the day before but lived their whole life in Muslyumovo up to that point, was not eligible. And anyone born after 1958—that is, a child or grandchild of victims who may show genetic aberrations—was also ineligible.

The remaining handful of activists in and around Muslyumovo who refuse to be discouraged by these setbacks maintain that they will continue to work toward these two goals:

1. An end to the bureaucratic obstacles to individual compensation to radiation victims and their offspring based on health certificates showing high whole

body counts of strontium-90 and cesium-137, related health problems, and DNA or chromosome changes in offspring

2. An end to government obstacles to independent scientists from Russia and other countries who want to collect and analyze health data

Residents in Kyshtym differ in their approach, in that some still harbor hope that Mayak will come through with some general assistance by sharing its economic benefits with the surrounding community outside the closed cities. The people of Kyshtym think there is a chance that Chelyabinsk-65 will incorporate Kyshtym, especially since the town of Novogorny (right next to Chelyabinsk-65) was incorporated in February 1993. The advantage to the people of Kyshtym is that they hope they will then also enjoy the better city funding and consumer goods supply system. Igor Gul', deputy of a district council in Kyshtym told us in March 1993 that "Our whole struggle for the environment in Kyshtym has been reduced to a fight with Mayak for land and benefits."[23]

Officials at the national and local levels, and especially at Mayak, argue for economic revitalization based on reprocessing spent fuel from Soviet-type reactors in the former republics, Finland, and Germany, and storage at Soviet sites (not in vitrified form). Their argument is that the hard currency earned by handling hazardous waste can be used for environmental cleanup programs. Decree No. 472 signed by President Yeltsin on April 21, 1993, enables the region to keep 25 percent of the profits gained from reprocessing operations to be used by the local governments for "implementation of radiation monitoring, improvement of environmental conditions, and socioeconomic development programs in the above-mentioned regions, and also to carry out scientific research and practical work on enhancing safety in the management of spent nuclear fuel and its waste from reprocessing." This prospect of increased revenues for the ailing region budget is held out to the public as a means by which Mayak can justify its existence to its antinuclear neighbors who are told that they are suffering not from radiation exposure but from a very low standard of living. No guarantees, however, are made about how the extra money will be spent by the local government. Thus, other than government officials, few people support the idea of more money in the budget in exchange for more nuclear wastes in the region.

Some Russian and U.S. Comparisons

Perceptions of serious health problems, whether real or imagined, are common to all communities studied. As noted earlier, according to the results of our public opinion survey of residents in the Chelyabinsk region, among the combined populations of Muslyumovo and Kyshtym, 86 percent feel that their family's health has been affected by Mayak. Moreover, approximately half the residents of Chelyabinsk City and Chelyabinsk-70 also say their families have been affected. Contrasting this information with data from a parallel survey of Washington State residents living in contaminated regions near the Hanford weapons facility in late 1993, only 5 percent of the surveyed Americans fear that Hanford has affected their health or safety, although a third worry about future damage from the facility (these concerns are much greater among residents of Spokane and the towns on the Yakima Indian reservation).[24]

Krasnoyarsk and Tomsk, where plutonium is still being produced, also have their own "Muslyumovos." Lyudmila Fatianova is a high school physics teacher from the village of Atamanovo, which is located about half a mile away from the Krasnoyarsk-26 facility and populated largely by ethnic Russians, but also by Ukrainians and Byelorussians. She claims that out of her village's population of 2,500, the number of patients with cancer is abnormally high: 35 diagnosed as of January 1994, 9 of whom had passed away by September 1994. She is also alarmed that many of her friends are sterile or infertile, and increasingly more of her students show marked learning disabilities. As a physicist she admires the work of her colleagues at Krasnoyarsk-26, but as a mother, woman, and teacher she is totally against it.[25]

A study conducted by Dr. Vladimir Mazharev and fellow research physicians at a nongovernmental research center in Krasnoyarsk shows that the number of adults with psychological disturbances in the contaminated areas of Krasnoyarsk is higher than in noncontaminated areas and higher than among children. Even more persuasive are his data showing that population centers farthest away from the contaminated areas have fewer incidences of leukemia in men and women; lower morbidity among adults due to malignant tumors and leukemia; dramatically fewer incidences of illnesses among children of the respiratory, nervous, or cardiovascular systems; and less infant mortality due to life-threatening birth defects.[26]

Research physician Tamara Matkovskaya reports alarming symptoms among children exposed to radiation releases from the Tomsk accident at its plutonium facility on April 6, 1993. She found that within a couple of hours after the accident most of the children in her sample experienced nausea, vomiting, diarrhea, headaches, and drowsiness. Diarrhea in many of them continued for several months. She maintains that the more long-lasting effects are chronic lethargy, a marked decrease in memorization abilities, less positive emotions than usual, an absence of imagination, and poor motor development.[27]

The United States also has sites with similar health concerns. For instance, for Hanford downwinders, their Muslyumovo is known as Death Mile. It is 11 miles from Hanford's Purex plant, which formerly manufactured weapons grade plutonium. The downwinders claim abnormally high rates of cancer, deformed lambs, hairless cattle, and cancer in their pets.[28] Residents in the vicinity of the Livermore National Laboratories, in California, maintain excessive numbers of people with melanomas, while around the Los Alamos National Laboratories in New Mexico there are claims of high numbers of brain tumors. These are but a couple of the several sites in the United States where citizens voice serious concerns about their health because of the environmental consequences of nuclear weapons development.

In all these cases, the populations that have only relatively recently learned bits and pieces about the activities of the secret operations of these facilities feel that the authorities were not concerned about public health and in some cases deliberately used these civilians as guinea pigs to better understand the long-term effects of low-dose radiation on humans. In Chelyabinsk the ethnic groups most affected were the minority Tatars and Bashkirs because of the large numbers of their populations in the vicinity. At the notorious test sites of Semipalatinsk in Kazakhstan and Novaya Zemlya in Russia, most of the victims were minority indigenous peoples. However, in Krasnoyarsk and Tomsk the vast majority of the population is Russian. It appears as though there has been a general disregard for *all* humans that crosses every ethnic and socioeconomic boundary. Even the elites who were perpetrators of these accidents and experiments and who worked in the closed facilities were also victims, because they were not free to leave their jobs or their own contaminated communities. This was not the case with the employees at nuclear weapons facilities who were free to leave their jobs. However, few of them, especially in the early years of the industry, were aware of the health risks.

In both the United States and Russia, the victim populations are angry because officials did not inform the people of the hazards. Farmers at Hanford's "Death Mile" were not warned of the possible dangers of the routine releases of nuclear materials and accidents of the 1950s and 1960s. Fatianova in Krasnoyarsk said that it was not until 1988–1989 that they heard anything about a contaminated zone that they should avoid. She feels that her infertile friends were the ones who spent the most time swimming in the Yenisei River in that very zone they now know is contaminated.

The common response of plant officials to these claims is that the people should put this in the past. Leonard Lazarev, a prominent nuclear physicist from St. Petersburg, and Russia's main ideologue for reprocessing spent fuel, speaking at a plenary session of the Krasnoyarsk conference, said: "We shouldn't be so emotional about the former accidents. During the Cold War we made mistakes in our haste, but we won't do that anymore." I have heard these arguments from U.S. nuclear weapons physicists as well. I find that the approach does not pacify people like Fatianova, Galimova, Matkovskaya, and others, who believe that their fellow citizens are suffering from present-day problems at these facilities.

It seems as though the nuclear physicists who are convinced that their work does not put populations at risk are not always patient with the accusations leveled against them. At the conferences I have attended on these subjects in Moscow, Chelyabinsk, and Krasnoyarsk, I could see on numerous occasions that representatives from the Russian nuclear establishment smirked and even laughed while testimony of health problems were presented from grassroots activists. I am told by a colleague, Hugh Gusterson, who has studied the culture at the Livermore labs in California,[29] that public relations officers there usually respond to public claims of health problems with sympathy, but at the same time explain that the facility is not responsible. Clearly, there must be Russian public relations officers who would also follow this path, but I have been struck by the frequency with which I observe an openly unsympathetic manner on the part of public representatives of the Russian defense complexes.

Even some sympathetic observers of radiation victimization believe the people would be better off if they did not know about their exposure to radiation or the consequences. They encourage denial. For instance, V. N. Abramova, a psychologist at the Prognosis Research Center in Obninsk, Russia, the home of a nuclear weapons research facility, speaking at the Kaluga International Seminar "Ecological Consciousness—Ecological Security," argued that the less said, the better, since the government cannot provide adequate compensation to people living in high-risk areas, and cannot afford to relocate them. She has observed that it is easier for people to cope when they are doomed to live with radiation if they are not constantly reminded by interviewers and the media, or by discussions of compensation (which she believes are unrealistic because of the state of the economy).

In the discourse surrounding actually trying to tackle the problems of environmental damage, economics is a common theme. In Russia today, while a fierce struggle for power is being waged at all levels of government, while the economy is on the verge of collapse, unemployment is rising, and living standards are plummeting, the people around the weapons sites are truly bewildered as they seek solutions to their plight. They all feel desperate and powerless in the face of the formidable problems posed by their secretive neighbors. Apparently many officials across Russia feel the same way. As nuclear physicist Lazarev said at the Krasnoyarsk conference: "Russia's bank is empty. If Americans don't have enough money to meet their technological challenges, what can we expect from our government? What we need money for is to build roads, homes, make a better life for the population. This is what the people are lacking. The problem is not radiation exposure."

The debate over the real causes of health problems in these areas will not be resolved until data collected by government agencies in secrecy and new data produced by independent investigators are carefully analyzed. Meanwhile, it is necessary to facilitate the process of releasing secret data and allowing new data to be accessed and analyzed. V. G. Khizhnyak, an inspector from the Krasnoyarsk Gosatomnadzor (the equivalent of the U.S. Nuclear Regulatory Commission), maintains that obstacles to this process are still a big problem in Russia, where he charges that research outside the facilities is either discounted or impeded. Just a few examples are Solovyova and Galimova, who have tripped over many obstacles in Chelyabinsk to collect independent data; also interesting, the original data for the study by Tamara Matkovskaya (cited earlier) was stolen from her Tomsk office, while the kind of valuables one would expect a common burglar to covet, such as her computer, were left untouched. Matkovskaya has also had to live with the fear caused by threatening phone calls to her home.

Russia, however, does not have a monopoly on secrecy. Much comparable U.S. data still remains to be revealed. The secrecy often borders on the absurd. For instance, when a photographer tried to take a picture of anthropologist Hugh Gusterson to accompany a magazine article, he posed Gusterson standing against the background of the Livermore labs. A public relations officer was on the spot in a minute to stop the effort. He explained that the blackened windows in the background might give some information to the KGB about what goes on inside. Tongue in cheek, Gusterson suggested that "Maybe guards of both countries could be trained together to save money."[30]

Not only did the Soviets wait until 1989 to publicly admit the explosion at Mayak in 1957, but the United States kept its knowledge of the explosion a secret as well. The CIA and U.S. weapons researchers knew about the explosion not long after it occurred. Presumably the United States chose not to point a finger at the Soviet weapons manufacturers in order not to raise questions among the U.S. public about safety matters at home. A special commission of International Physicians for the Prevention of Nuclear War and the Institute for Energy and Environmental Research, writing in *Plutonium: Deadly Gold of the Nuclear Age*, made the following assessment of this secrecy:

> As mentioned, the government of the United States discovered soon after the accident that there had been some kind of large radiation disaster in the Urals. However, it chose not to publicize this issue, despite the intense hostilities of the Cold War, presumably because questions would have been raised about the prospect of similar explosions in the U.S. nuclear weapons complex. Eventually such questions, among others, were instrumental in stopping

plutonium production at Hanford at the end of the 1980s, just as the Chernobyl accident was instrumental in stopping the operation of the N-reactor of similar design at Hanford.

A complete disclosure of the Chelyabinsk-65 explosion data, along with site-specific data from other centers where high-level waste tanks exist, would allow assessments for other locations regarding the force of possible explosions, the quantities of radionuclides which might be spread in fallout, the potential cancers in surrounding communities, and the health dangers to workers during such an accident and in on- and off-site cleanup. Lack of adequate data from the former Soviet Union about the explosion and from most countries about the exact nature of the contents of their tanks, has prevented us from engaging in such assessments here.[31]

Valery Menshikov, a senior aide for Alexei Yablokov, who is a prominent government critic of the Russian nuclear establishment, is also aware of secrecy problems among the U.S. nuclear establishment. He pointed out at the Krasnoyarsk conference that the U.S. Department of Energy never gave up any data without constant public pressure and that this will also be necessary for the Russian environmental movement to accomplish. "This is the way it works," he said, "in a democratic society."[32]

The solution that the Russian Ministry of Atomic Power has devised to help Chelyabinsk overcome its environmental legacy is a plan to reprocess and resume construction of a new reactor as a way to bring in revenues, especially hard currency. There is an equivalent approach for Krasnoyarsk and Tomsk, where similar projects are the object of public controversy. Valery Lebedev, General Director of the Chemical-Mining Plant at Krasnoyarsk-26, speaking at the Krasnoyarsk conference, made this explanation for their production operations: "We are continuing to produce plutonium not because we are hawks but because our region needs energy and the money." So building more reactors is presented by industry officials as a way to improve the situation. As Yury Fedotov, of the Chemical-Mining Plant, said at the Krasnoyarsk conference, "RT-2 has to be seen as a nature protection plant which will help solve the problem of spent fuel and will be economically beneficial. The economy and ecology are inseparable. No ecological measure is possible without money. We have to make our own money which will also help us solve our environmental problems. All our previous problems were from not having purification installations and from the big rush. Now our work will be safe."

As Russia grapples to resolve these problems, it must contend with a phenomenon unknown in the U.S.: its unique, closed cities. These cities are unique both in terms of the way in which they are not accountable to the local public, only to Moscow (not even to the local KGB and local government), and in terms of the problems they pose for conversion, for reemploying these huge populations and reintegrating them in the larger society (if that's the decision to be made). As Menshikov pointed out at the Krasnoyarsk conference, a special conceptual framework is needed for Russia to conduct conversion, to find alternative ways for these cities to continue developing.

Conclusions

It is clear from this study that environmental disasters around Russia's three weapons grade plutonium facilities have affected populations both inside and outside the closed nuclear weapons cities, prompting citizen organizations to make charges of environmental human rights violations. Even if it were to be proven someday that the health effects from the actual releases of nuclear materials have been insignificant or nil, we can already assert that these populations have certainly been traumatized by their fears of radiation exposure. In the case of Muslyumovo, people are adapting to the predicament in ways that are threatening to long-standing cultural traditions. Further anthropological studies of other population centers at these sites and the areas near similar facilities in the United States could show equivalent modification of culture related specifically to a perception of nuclear victimization.

Bashkirs and Tatars make accusations that their minority populations in Chelyabinsk were targets for selective human rights violations. They make this claim because they believe that Muslyumovo and a few other predominantly Bashkir-Tatar villages were not evacuated from the Techa River deliberately so that the people could be used as guinea pigs to study the long-term effects of low dose radiation. However, no such minority populations exist at Krasnoyarsk and Tomsk, where Russian and other Slavic villagers have also been subjected to nuclear victimization. Thus it is difficult to make unequivocal claims of environmental racism, since it appears as though the leaders of the Soviet defense industry showed a general disregard for the health of *all* civilians. Further studies of this and other environmental disaster areas in Russia may or may not show a more clear pattern of environmental racism.

Representatives of Russia's nuclear establishment argue that all these problems should be put in the past, that the most damaging health risks are from other forms of industrial pollution, or from a low standard of living or from "radiophobia." The solutions they offer involve seeking money from the national government for cleanup and economic development and urging the reprocessing of imported spent fuel for hard currency. Citizen groups oppose these approaches and maintain that the victims never see the money from national and local budgets, and that reprocessing fuel or plans for more reactors will only further the environmental damage. What complicates the resolution of these problems is that whether we look at sites in Russia or the United States, a common pattern is that of withholding information from the public. Both the Russian (formerly Soviet) and American weapons facilities have been allowed to work in secrecy in the name of national defense.

In view of all this, populations around these sites have been traumatized. Their lives have been significantly altered by the predicament they have found themselves in; not by the knowledge they have about radiation exposure, but rather by the absence of information that can help them make rational choices about the care of their health and the health of future generations, information that can empower them to control their own environments.

Several policy recommendations for both countries can be made based on what we know about the environmental situation around such weapons facilities:

1. Ensure access to all related environmental and health information, historical and contemporary, so that it can be processed and comprehended by government and independent researchers, as well as nongovernmental organizations and individual citizens. No longer can national security considerations serve as an excuse for continued secrecy in analyzing existing data and collecting new data.

2. Remove all obstacles to independent research so that carefully reasoned decisions can be made by all interested parties. Experience in both countries shows that it requires strong public and international pressure to pry loose such data.

3. Guarantee complete freedom of citizen action and joint problem-solving between citizen groups and representatives of the nuclear community. While more studies are under way to confirm or disprove linkage between radiation exposure and illness, it is necessary for communication between citizens and officials in the nuclear community to remain open. These officials must acknowledge and accept that residents in these controversial areas deserve respect as human beings and sympathy as possible victims of the Cold War, and should take seriously the concerns of these populations. Populations that believe their human environmental rights have been violated should not be impeded in their efforts to appeal to the United Nations and other international organizations concerned with human rights.

4. Devise a fair and meaningful system of compensation to the victims of environmental disasters.

5. Finally, guarantee full participation of citizens in decisions about new reactors and nuclear production processes. Until greater understanding has been reached on the effects of past releases of nuclear materials, great caution should be taken in proceeding with new projects.

From my own perspective as an anthropologist, I see a real need for research that focuses on the sociocultural experience of radiation victimization—studying changes brought about by environmental damage and deterioration of health, changes including lifestyle change, environmental consciousness, environmental justice, and environmental racism. All too often the national and international agencies assigned the difficult task of assessing the damage of the nuclear weapons industry compile reports replete with numbers that measure curies and proffer involved explanations of technological problems, while descriptions of the predicament of the humans, animals, and plants that live in these environments are virtually absent. These reports provide the basis for policy formation, and their gaps produce significant shortcomings in responding to the needs of nuclear-age disasters. The human environmental dimension needs to be strongly inserted into this debate, and this dimension includes both real and perceived predicaments, response to disastrous conditions, and the biocultural implications of such response.

Notes

1. The survey was of 1,500 people from five sites—Chelyabinsk, Kyshtym, Muslyumovo, the closed city of Chelyabinsk-65, and Chebarkul, a noncontaminated city that was intended as a control site. A random sample was drawn from local electoral lists, which are essentially complete lists of residents in Russian population centers. Interviews were done face-to-face and conducted by local people specially trained for the project. Interviewers had no restricted access to informants. In Muslyumovo, a local official confiscated a few of the completed questionnaires when the survey was finished. I did follow-up in-depth interviews with about 20 people in each site.

2. See Thomas B. Cochran *et al.*, "Radioactive Contamination at Chelyabinsk-65, Russia," *Annual Review of Energy Environment* 18 (1993) 507–28, 513; Alina Tugend, "Victims of Silence," *Orange County Register*, Close-up, June 6, 1993, pp. 1–8.

3. First International Radiological Conference "The Environmental Consequences of Nuclear Weapons Development in the Southern Urals," Chelyabinsk, Russia, May 20–22, 1992; Second International Radiological Conference "After the Cold War: Disarmament, Conversion and Security," Krasnoyarsk-Tomsk, Russia, Sept, 12–18, 1994; International Seminar "Ecological Consciousness— Ecological Security," Kaluga, Russia, Sept. 23–25, 1994.

4. Gosman Kabirov, March 1993, conversation with Paula Garb, Muslyumovo.

5. Cochran, *et al., op. cit.*, note 2, p. 513.

6. Cochran, *et al., op. cit.*, note 2, pp. 521–22.

7. Mikhail Gladyshev, *Memoirs* (recorded by Pyotr Tryakin, 1990), unpublished manuscript.

8. Aleftina Fisko, April 1993, conversation with author, Dal'naya Dacha.

9. Aleftina Fisko, April 1993, conversation with author, Dal'naya Dacha.

10. Sergei Lolovich, March 1993, conversation with Galina Komarova, Kyshtym.

11. Government Report on the Health of the Population of Russia in 1991. *Zelyony mir,* no. 48, Dec. 1992.

12. I participated in this as part of the UCI–Washington State University project mentioned in the introduction.

13. Russell Dalton, Paula Garb, Nicholas Lovrich, John Pierce, John Whiteley, "Chelyabinsk-Hanford Environmental Survey: Survey Highlights," press release, May 5, 1994.

14. Gulfarida Galimova, March 1993, conversation with Galina Komarova, Muslyumovo.

15. *Zelyony mir*, Dec. 1992.

16. Gosman Kabirov, presentation made to a conference of the antinuclear groups in the Socio-Ecological Union, Moscow, March 12–14, 1993.

17. A. Kabirov. "Tyomnye zakoulki rossiiskoi istorii: prestupleniya imperii" ("Dark alleys of Russian history: Crimes of the empire") (Kamaz: Naberezhnyi Chelny, 1993), 60.

18. See Peter S. Wenz, *Environmental Justice* (Albany: State University of New York Press, 1988); Robert D. Bullard, ed., *Confronting Environmental Racism: Voices from the Grassroots* (Boston: South End Press, 1993); Barbara R. Johnston, *Human Rights and the Environment: Examining the Sociocultural Context of Environmental Crisis* (Society for Applied Anthropology, 1993.)

19. Anonymous physician in Chelyabinsk, Sept. 1994, conversation with Galina Komarova.

20. Gulfarida Galimova, Aug. 1994, conversation with author.

21. Yevgeny Ryzhkov, Dec. 1992, conversation with author, Chelyabinsk-65.

22. Chelyabinsk-Hanford Environmental Survey, University of California–Irvine/Washington State University, May 5, 1994.

23. Igor Gul', March 1993, conversation with Galina Komarova, Kyshtym.

24. Survey Highlights, *op. cit.*, note 1.

25. Lyudmila Fatianova, presentation at the Second International Radiological Conference, Krasnoyarsk-Tomsk, Sept. 14, 1994.

26. V. F. Mazharov *et al.,* "Some Indicators of Health among the Rural Population on Territories with Possible Critical Radiation Exposure," *Abstracts,* Second International Radiological Conference, Krasnoyarsk-Tomsk, Sept. 12–18, 1994, p. 107.

27. T. M. Matkovskaya, "Children's Health in a Radiation Zone," *Abstracts*, Second International Radiological Conference, Krasnoyarsk-Tomsk, Sept. 12–18, 1994, p. 109.

28. Karen Dorn Steele, "Downwinders—Living with Fear," *Spokesman-Review*, Spokane, Wash., July 28, 1985.

29. Hugh Gusterson, *Testing Times: A Nuclear Weapons Laboratory at the End of the Cold War* (Berkeley: University of California Press, 1995).

30. Hugh Gusterson, Sept. 13, 1994, conversation with author, Krasnoyarsk.

31. *Plutonium: Deadly Gold of the Nuclear Age* (Cambridge, Mass.: International Physicians Press, 1992), 92–94.

32. Valery Menshikov, presentation at the Second International Radiological Conference, Krasnoyarsk-Tomsk, Sept. 14, 1994.

Crisis, Chaos, Conflict, and Change

Barbara Rose Johnston

Introduction

The stories explored in *Life and Death Matters* cover a broad range of issues with vastly different social, cultural, political, and economic contexts. In each situation there are distinctly different patterns of vulnerability, mechanisms available to negotiate change, and barriers that inhibit access to those mechanisms. These chapters map a continuum, with responses to human environmental crisis that include:

- Passive resistance (efforts to renegotiate conditions in subtle ways)

- Organized efforts to adjust conditions and effect change within existing systems

- Confrontational and violent efforts aimed at transforming both conditions and structures of power

- Efforts to rebuild in the aftermath of structural transformations of power

These chapters also demonstrate the dynamic nature of human environmental crisis. Depending on the conditions and options available and the consequences of previous responses, response to human environmental crisis may include any or all categories in the above continuum. A long history of institutional denial or inadequate response to life-threatening conditions may force people toward action on the violent end of the response continuum. And, conversely, creating and employing mechanisms that allow confrontation, negotiation, and change within the existing system may stimulate the development of further rights-protective problem-solving mechanisms, thus minimizing the potential for future conflict.

In this conclusion I draw on chapter material as well as examples from other sources to briefly discuss the sociopolitical consequences of human environmental crisis. First, I take a moment to outline some of the more promising mechanisms being developed and employed at local, national, and international levels. And then I discuss the connections among response, threats to the status quo, and the rise of reactionary and repressive violence.

Mechanisms that Carry Hope

Promising local-level responses include the creation of structures that foster bottom-up, top-down partnerships with planning, monitoring, and regulatory authority. For example, in Ben Wisner's study of reconstruction and development employed by post-apartheid government planners in Alexandra Township, neighborhoods were surveyed and people asked to define their perceptions of critical infrastructure problems, to prioritize needs, to design solutions, and—with the economic assistance of the government—to implement change. While problems were (and are) seemingly insurmountable, asking targeted people to assess and prioritize and then providing them with the means to make the changes that they feel are important creates an atmosphere where people feel in control, empowered, and connected to their government in direct ways. This is community-based environmental restoration, and this is nation building.

Other examples come to mind of collaborative partnerships where stakeholders are involved in decision-making processes on relatively equal footing. Co-management and other participatory-resource management models represent an example of this,[1] as do the models being developed through community activism in toxic settings. In the past few years a growing number of urban industrial partnerships have been formed where the community (environmental, religious, labor, and other civic organizations) works with local government and industry to monitor and regulate industrial practice.[2] For example, years of activism and protest over the environmental, health, and safety problems created by Chevron Oil at its Richmond, California, refinery resulted in an environmental racism lawsuit, a suit that was eventually settled with a "Memorandum of Understanding Between the Community Groups West County Toxics Coalition, People Do!, and Citizens for a Better Environment, and Chevron Richmond Facility." In this agreement Chevron made a variety of commitments to improving their presence in the community, including environmental remediation and increased access to open space areas; financial support of local nonprofit agencies providing services to nearby residents; training and hiring local residents; establishing a health clinic; and improving a nearby structure to house a Head-Start program. Chevron also agreed to a number of measures designed to improve monitoring capabilities, increase public access to emissions records, and significantly reduce toxics emissions from Richmond Refinery.[3]

There is evidence of change within national political structures as well, especially in the formation and implementation of policies and legal structures that reflect the sociocultural dimensions of environmental crisis. This is illustrated in the chapter by Valerie Wheeler and Peter Esainko, which describes efforts to bring stakeholders together to negotiate national organic standards.[4] Other examples include President Clinton's February 1994 Executive Order 12898, entitled "Federal Actions to Address Environmental Justice in Minority and Low-Income Populations." The main purpose of this order is to require all agencies and departments of the government to take environmental justice issues into consideration as they make their decisions and approve actions. A summary of the strategy reports prepared by the Cabinet departments notes a number of changes that have occurred as a result of this Executive Order, a few of which are mentioned here.[5] At the Department of Defense, environmental justice concerns are being incorporated into the environmental impact statement process to ensure that every major DOD project will include some consideration of potential impacts on the people who live around defense installations. The Department of Housing and Urban Development is funding environmental justice projects in empowerment and enterprise zones that include reducing childhood lead exposure and cleaning up abandoned and hazardous urban industrial sites. And the Department of Health and Human Services has initiated a Superfund Medical Assistance Plan, which provides funds and personnel to work with local residents, as well as with health and environmental institutions, on the public-health dimensions of Superfund hazardous waste sites.

In the United States, national foreign policy increasingly includes recognition of the connections between environmental crisis and social injustice. Speeches and articles by Secretary of State Warren Christopher, Undersecretary of State for Global Affairs Timothy Wirth, and U.S. Agency for International Development Administrator J. Brian Atwood all include references to environmental security—the notion that national security means more than a strong military, but that the security of the nation also rests on our ability to meet basic human needs while ensuring that population growth and consumption do not destroy the lands and waters that sustain our livelihood.[6] In an April 9, 1996, speech at Stanford University, then–Secretary of State Christopher described "policies of engagement" that encompass environmental issues and also announced the formation of new endeavors that improve the flow of human environmental crisis information (including an annual "Global Environmental Challenges" report).

Perhaps the strongest evidence of progressive political change is found in the informal "civic organization" sector, where the ability to organize, communicate, create networks, and form coalitions has meant the emergence of a political force whose power and impact cannot be overstated. With increased access to both information and communication tools, various citizen-action, indigenous peoples groups, and other alliances have organized, formed networks, and created regional, national, and international coalitions. Information flows (publications, videos, fax, cyberspace) and communication forums (conferences, workshops, cyberspace conferences) represent informal political areas where individuals, groups, and communities air their human environmental rights complaints, exchange information and generate support, encourage political action, and apply political pressure.[7] These actions allow otherwise powerless groups a voice and, at times, the power to renegotiate their relationship with the state.

The impact of this point is illustrated by the following example. Beginning October 7, 1995, I received a series of e-mail messages from the Bellona Institute, a joint Russian-Norwegian nonprofit scientific research organization involved in documenting industrial pollution and radioactive waste sites and in developing mitigation and management plans in northwestern Russia. Between October 5 and 16, 1995, Bellona offices in Murmansk and St. Petersburg were entered and occupied by the FSB (the new KGB), which seized data, records, computers, floppy disks, and video cameras. The Institute scientists' homes were entered, and several people detained for questioning. The Bellona Institute was eventually denounced on national television by the FSB for using their environmental organization to conduct an "espionage" campaign (much of the Bellona Institute's current research pertains to radioactive waste stored at Russian North Fleet marine bases). Bellona researchers note that their sources of information were a matter of public record. They worked in collaboration with government officials. No state secrets were disclosed. No laws were broken. Within hours of the first incident, a description of the break-in was sent to 12 different human environmental rights activists and organizations with permission to distribute at will. And within two days of the first incident, formal protests were lodged from the Prime Minister of Norway, among others. In pre–computer network days, the mere rumor of an impending

FSB/KGB arrest was enough to send environmental scientists into hiding or scurrying abroad. Today, people are using the power and scope of cyberspace to communicate with each other and to confront action and authority.

Several chapters in *Life and Death Matters* illustrate the use and power of informal mechanisms. For example, in Al Gedicks's chapter on zinc-copper mining in northern Wisconsin, the struggle became politically effective when Native Americans, environmentalists, sports fishers, and other local groups formed a political coalition across class, race, and cultural lines. Some of the mechanisms used to effect change included placing advertisements and editorials in newspapers to educate and shape local public opinion on the issue, and organizing a five-day conference attended by indigenous activists from throughout the Americas and the Pacific Islands—an event that allowed the exchange of information on the international mining record of the threatening company, Exxon.

Given that many human environmental crises emerge from situations where local people are excluded from the decision-making process, efforts to transform decisions or conditions often hinge on information flows and communication tools. For example, recently the Ukrainian government announced plans to bury radioactive wastes in salt mine shafts. When local activist groups expressed concern over the health risks, the government stated that it was safe because this practice was done in Germany. Local members of the International Environmental Law Alliance contacted advocates in Germany, obtained a report explaining the harmful effects of burying radioactive waste in Germany, and used this report to convince the Ukrainian government to change its plan.[8]

A few formal mechanisms are also beginning to emerge at the international level, many tied to United Nations agencies and entities, some to other international law structures, and others representing bilateral relationships (for example, leverage applied in trade agreements; or requirements, like those used in Australia, to conduct social and environmental impact analyses before funding international development aid packages). International laws, treaties, and conventions are beginning to address the synergistic needs of environmental quality and social justice, and, as evidenced by the United Nations Commission on Human Rights' Draft Declaration on Human Rights and the Environment (see the appendix to this volume), there is some political support to develop a legal mechanism recognizing the right to a healthy environment as a fundamental human right. There are, however, few formal mechanisms that exist that allow peoples to air their grievances against the state in a rights-protective forum.

Ideally, international structures provide the opportunity for affected peoples to lodge complaints against the state, with the goal of negotiating some form of change. As noted by Holly Barker, the efforts by Marshall Islanders to seek redress from the United States for their radiation exposure have taken them to a number of international forums over the years, including the UN General Assembly, the UN Human Rights Commission, and the International Court of Justice. In this case, the independent nation-status acquired in the mid-1970s has enhanced the ability of Marshall Islanders to negotiate with the United States, as complaints can be lodged in existing forums built to mediate state-to-state disputes. Other than the UN Human Rights Commission (UNHCR), few formal mechanisms exist that allow affected peoples—communities, groups, even cultural nations—the opportunity to confront the state in a rights-protective forum.

And even when problems are heard or investigated by the UNHCR, action is often limited to formal expressions of concern.

In most nation-state confrontations, speaking up often proves quite dangerous; it is very difficult for peoples to lodge complaints against the state without experiencing repressive and retaliatory responses, as James Phillips's case of land tenure disputes in Honduras illustrates. Advocacy mechanisms employed in the informal international arena have taken on an increasingly important role in recent years, allowing the airing of complaints in ways that, to some degree, protect affected peoples. In the case of Chiapas, David Stea, Silvia Elguea, and Camilo Perez Bustillo note that informal international attention (communiqués posted on the Internet, media coverage, visits by foreign dignitaries) has at times protected the Zapatistas from heavy military engagement.

Implications of Response

The responses briefly mentioned above seek fundamental transformations in local, national, and international decision-making systems that, first, allow people living with the problem to gain greater control in defining the nature of the crisis, devising equitable responses, and prohibiting the reoccurrence; and, second, allow institutions and organizations that played a significant role in creating the problem to acknowledge their culpability and (through their efforts to respond) to shoulder a greater share of the burden for resolving the consequence. The struggle to achieve these transformations in decision-making systems requires confronting, challenging, and changing the status quo. Backlash is inevitable.[9]

In many cases, governments and industry—the political economy—respond to popular movements by providing services or meeting demands in ways that serve, intentionally or unintentionally, to co-opt the goals of the movement and deflate the power of movement leadership. Disinformation campaigns, publicly acknowledging culpability but responding to problems and victims in relatively minor ways,[10] and creating regulatory and decision-making frameworks that give the image of addressing the concern but are implemented in limited and restrictive fashion—all are actions that neutralize a potential threat to the status quo. For example, government recognition of indigenous land rights in Brazil has been inconsistently enforced, as noted in the chapter by Leslie Sponsel, with greater protection provided during times of global interest on the issue (during and after the 1992 UNCED Conference in Rio de Janerio, for example). In January 1996, the government revised rules for indigenous land demarcation, giving greater voice to those who illegally occupy indigenous lands.[11] Violent conflicts have increased, as has the number of people killed in land conflicts.

In other cases, backlash is of a more overtly violent nature, with actions that terrorize communities and result in the loss of liberty or life. Movement leadership receive threats, find their offices ransacked and records confiscated, are thrown under arrest and imprisoned, or are even killed. Community supporters are threatened, beaten, banished, or "disappeared." Government may be directly responsible, or, through its approval or gazing on the scene with its "blind eye," indirectly responsible.

There is growing evidence that government and industry see environmental justice activism as a form of community empowerment that represents potential future threat.

For example, according to e-mail received from the Bellona Institute in October 1996, researcher Alexander Nikitin remains in custody and faces a death sentence. He is accused of acts of high treason associated with his work on the "The Russian Northern Fleet—Radioactive Contamination" report (despite a finding by the expert committee of MinAtom that the Bellona Report contained no state secrets). Russian constitutional law states that the withholding of information relevant to ecological safety is illegal, but the FSB, on the basis of findings by an ecological committee established by the FSB, has determined that nuclear submarine accidents and safety aspects of such reactors bear no relevance to ecology.[12]

A more widely known example of government-industry backlash to the threat posed by environmental social justice activism is the conviction and execution of Ken Saro-Wiwa, a Nigerian author and activist noted for his efforts to publicize the plight of his tribe—the Ogoni—whose lands and livelihoods have been severely impacted by oil industry production. Saro-Wiwa and 15 other Ogonis were arrested in May 1994, following the deaths of four Ogoni electoral opponents who were killed earlier during a riot at a political rally. Saro-Wiwa was not directly involved in the killings (according to most accounts, the deaths were caused by government troops). Still, according to the government, he was held responsible, because he helped organize the rally. As stated in a recent World Watch report, 25 percent of all oil spills in the world have occurred in Nigeria, most of them on Ogoni land. Saro-Wiwa's activist efforts were successful to the point of earning him the 1995 Goldman Environmental Prize for Africa. Following his execution, Nigeria was suspended from the British Commonwealth, and Nelson Mandela organized a campaign to boycott Nigerian oil imports worldwide. The United States did not join in; it imports roughly 50 percent of Nigeria's oil. Two days after Saro-Wiwa's execution, Shell Oil signed a $2.5 billion gas deal with the Nigerian military government. In May 1996, Shell Oil offered a plan for cleaning up Ogoni land if an agreement can be reached with all Ogoni communities that company staff can return safely to the area. Some 2,000 Ogoni people have been killed since the environmental justice campaign began; no Shell workers have died.[13]

The economic staying power of government and industry opponents contributes over the long run to the relative ineffectiveness of many social movements. Movements lose their mission and purpose when inertia sets in, when successes are followed by even bigger setbacks, when the power of money corrupts the ideals of activism, and when the agenda and strategies to achieve it are co-opted by opponents.

An example of this latter point is the emergence of the wise-use antienvironmentalism movement in the rural western United States (corporate-funded "backlash" aimed at disempowering the environmental plutocracy).[14] People for the West, the Abundant Wildlife Society, Save Our Lands, and the Environmental Conservation Organization are all groups organized at the community level, with agendas that include deregulation, privatization, and unlimited rights for property owners. Supporters see themselves as victims who have become disenfranchised and alienated from resource access and use, by federal regulations that are influenced by the ethics and beliefs of environmentalism. They view "the United States government as the main enemy of personal freedom" and "environmental regulation as one of its most threatening manifestations." Their beliefs and actions are based on moral authority as reflected in the U.S. Constitution and the Christian Bible. Political tactics include media campaigns, lobbying, and sensational incidents of civil disobedience (bulldozing roads across federal lands without permits; vandalizing and attacking federal government offices; publicly confronting and threatening federal employees). These groups are popular and successful (as evidenced by the many county-level property rights laws passed in recent years, as well as the growing number of property rights and antienvironmental bills presented to the U.S. Congress in the last three years).[15]

Crisis, Chaos, Conflict, and the Process of Social Change

The tension that exists between communities of people and larger political economic forces is one of constant struggle for control over the parameters of existence. As exploitation of the world's resources and degradation of the biosphere intensify, movements to reshape priorities and peoples' ways of life will play an increasingly significant role. The fact that many communities around the world are confronting life-threatening situations, finding no help from their government, or thinking of their leaders as being responsible for their plight—this fact certainly suggests a future of increasing chaos. As recent unrest demonstrates, there is a growing use of violence to forcibly transform the loci of power over resource access and use. This is especially true in cases where human environmental crisis is historically ignored and where recent events—framed in a language of positive change—exacerbate existing inequities. The post-NAFTA Mayan uprising in Chiapas is perhaps a good example of this.[16]

However, the rules and tools of the game have changed. Human environmental crises are no longer experienced in singular, silent fashion. Again as the Chiapas case illustrates, global access to computers, fax machines, modems, satellite communications, and solar-powered battery packs has provided the powerless with a voice. Information and communications technology is transforming the human experience of disaster in a myriad of ways. Abuses can be instantaneously reported and responses voiced from around the world. Individual communities and civic organizations form networks and issue-based coalitions that cross race, class, culture, and national lines. They use this broader base of power to renegotiate relationships with government and industry. Absolute control over information is one of the keys to controlling thought and behavior, as information influences and shapes cultural belief systems and legitimizes political authority. Thanks to cyberspace, *absolute* control over information access is no longer possible.[17]

Much of the world's resources are finite. The environmental byproducts of our military/industrial lifestyle are deadly. People, generations, cultures, civilizations—all struggle to survive and thrive in an increasingly toxic world. This is our reality. Struggle means conflict and chaos, with some people winning while others lose.

There are, however, patterns to be seen in the crises, chaos, and emerging responses. Environmental crises are inextricably linked to the abuse of human rights. They emerge from contexts of dysfunctional governance. Inadequate response to human environmental crises contributes to the formation of social movements.[18] And continued threats to livelihood and threats to the status quo both play a significant role in generating violent conflict.

In this study of response to human environmental crises, we found confrontation, conflict, and chaos to be an inevitable part of the process of change.[19] Whether that change is shortsighted or sustaining depends in large part on the structural arrangement of power. Some see a future of crisis, anarchy, and violent conflict; some see anarchy and chaos kept in rein by a future of strong, centralized governance and an efficient management of global resources by multinational corporations and institutions.[20] We suggest that strong governance relies on strong communities. Essential for both are strategies, mechanisms, and institutional structures that close the gap between decision and consequence—allowing people at the bottom *and* at the top to confront and share the misery of crisis and chaos of survival.

Notes

1. As described by Evelyn Pinkerton, *Cooperative Management of Local Fisheries: New Directions for Improved Management and Community Development* (Vancouver: University of British Columbia Press, 1989); Bonnie J. McCay and James M. Acheson, *The Question of the Commons: The Culture and Ecology of Communal Resources* (Tucson: University of Arizona Press, 1990); and Christopher Dyer and James McGoodwin, *Folk Management in the World's Fisheries: Lessons for Modern Fisheries Management* (Niwot, Colo.: The University Press of Colorado, 1994).

2. See, for example, Andrew Szasz, *Ecopopulism: Toxic Waste and the Movement for Environmental Justice* (Minneapolis: University of Minnesota Press, 1994). Promising community-industry-government partnerships have been described in various issues of *New Solutions*, c.f., R. Ginsberg, ed., *Special Section: Risk Assessment* 3:2 (1993); Sanford Lewis, "Corporate Disclosure: Moving Forward toward Environmental Excellence: Corporate Environmental Audits and the Right to Know," *New Solutions* 5:3 (1995) 39–50; and an article on environmental/labor coalitions by Ed Cohen-Rosenthal, "Environmental Action and Social Partnership in North America," *New Solutions* 6:1 (1995) 41–48.

3. The Chevron Memorandum of Understanding was signed May 31, 1994. It is published on EcoNet's ecojustice Internet conference. See (http://www.econet.apc.org) or (http://www.igc.org/envjustice).

4. In that case, though, the outcome is unclear, because the power dynamics among organic farmers, scientists, and other segments of the agricultural sector continually shift, with organic farmers apparently shut out of the negotiation process.

5. Global Action and Information Network, "GAIN REPORT: Environmental Justice—Executive Order 12898 Strategy Reports" (published on the EcoNet Environmental Justice Desk [ejdesk@igc.apc.org], August 30, 1996).

6. The definition of environmental security is a paraphrased statement by Timothy E. Wirth, "The Human Factor," *Sierra* Sept./Oct. 1995: 76–79. Speeches by Warren Christopher and J. Brian Atwood appear in *Environmental Change and Security Project Report*, P. J. Simmons, ed., Issue 2 (Washington, D.C.: The Woodrow Wilson Center, spring 1996), 77–88.

7. See, for example, the Arctic Circle web site, created by anthropologist Norman Chance in 1995, providing a means for people in the Arctic to communicate, a forum to publish environmental quality/social justice information, and "virtual classroom" sites for high schools and universities across the Arctic to tap into. Two years into its cyber-life, close to 60,000 people have logged on (http://www.lib.uconn.edu/ArcticCircle).

8. International Environmental Law Alliance Worldwide newsletter, published on (http://www.igc.apc.org/elaw/) and reported on (gain@igc.apc.org) (Global Action and Information Network), July 12, 1996.

9. The following discussion on backlash and strategies for disempowerment was influenced by Szasz, *op. cit.*, note 2; and Human Rights Watch and Natural Resources Defense Council, *Defending*

the Earth: Abuses of Human Rights and the Environment (Washington, D.C.: Human Rights Watch and the NRDC, 1992). See also Bron Taylor et al., "Grass-Roots Resistance: The Emergence of Popular Environmental Movements in Less Affluent Countries" in *Environmental Politics in the International Arena: Movements, Parties, Organizations and Policy* (Albany, N.Y.: SUNY Press, 1993), 69–89.

10. For example, in July 1995 Unocal acknowledged culpability in a refinery accident that resulted in the release of the chemical catacarb over the town of Crockett, California. Emmissions occurred during a 16-day period, sent 267 people to the hospital, and left the town with a contaminated school near the refinery. A $2.05 million settlement was paid by Unocal, with most of the money going to the county's general fund and used to buy a fire engine and install a warning siren and education system in case of future accidents. No funds were allotted to replace the school or fund a community watchdog group to monitor Unocal practices—requests made by the victims themselves. (Reported in *Earth Island News* fall 1995:4).

11. It is a complicated picture. In the first six months of 1996, 33 people were killed in conflicts between military policy and "landless rural workers," and since the new government came into power in January 1995, 76 people have been killed in land conflicts. With millions of landless poor in Brazil, the politics surrounding indigenous reserves intensify. Families move on their own into the reserves, prompting violent conflicts with indigenous peoples. Landed interests push for reducing reserve size, especially when faced with the possibility of seeing current holdings acquired by the government for use in agrarian reform. See "News from Brazil" supplied by Servico Brasileiro de Justice e Paz, no. 236, July 18, 1996 (printed on the Human Rights Info Network: hrnet.americas). For an excellent review of these issues, see Stephan Schwartzman *et al.,* "Brazil: The Battle over Indigenous Land Rights," *NACLA Report on the Americas*, March/April 1996.

12. This report was released by the Bellona Institute in August 1996 on the Internet (seven months after Nikitin's arrest), and is printed in English, Russian, and Norwegian versions. It is available at (http://www.grida.no/ngo/bellona/ehome/russia/nfl/).

13. Ken Saro-Wiwa's sentence and subsequent execution were widely reported in the news media and on the Internet. See *Earth Island Journal*, fall 1995 and winter 1996, for coverage of this incident. In a paper discussing the growing incidence of violent conflict between Ogoni communities, and between the petro-business–backed Nigerian government and the Ogoni, Okechukwu Ibeanu argues that resolution of conflict and reestablishing order in Nigeria's oil belt cannot be achieved through state violence and forced pacification (which is suggested in the May 1996 Shell Oil agreement), and calls instead for democratization and the scaling down of overdependence on the part of the Nigerian economy and ruling groups on crude-oil rents and exports. The first step, he argues, is letting local peoples have their own democratic organizations. Okechukwu Ibeanu, "Ogoni: Oil Pollution, Resource Flow and Conflict in Rural Nigeria," paper presented at the IUAES/IGU Intercongress meeting, Linkoping, Sweden, Aug. 1996.

14. Brian Tokar, "The Wise-Use Backlash: Responding to Militant Anti-Environmentalism," *The Ecologist* 25:4 (July-Aug. 1995) 150–156. Also see Tokar's forthcoming *Renewing the Environmental Revolution* (Boston: South End Press).

15. Tokar, *op. cit.,* note 14, p. 154.

16. Some suggest that this is the case with regard to Arab-Israeli conflict as well, especially when one considers the role of water and the plight of the Palestinian population. See Rosina Hassoun, "Water Between Arabs and Israelis: Researching Twice-Promised Resources," in *Water, Culture and Power,* John Donahue and Barbara Johnston, eds. (Washington, D.C.: Island Press, forthcoming).

17. This point has clearly been recognized by various governments, as evidenced in the 1996 U.S. Telecommunications Bill, and by recent Internet censorship action by the Chinese government. In 1993 the Chinese government banned private ownership of satellite dishes. In January 1996 it imposed rules that required all foreign-owned economic news services to be distributed through the official Chinese News Agency, and in September 1996 previously independent Internet servers were required to register with the government and sign pledges to limit politically and sexually sensitive materials. China's Internet communications systems flows through a few "choke points," making

censorship relatively easy—by filtering through material for preapproved addresses, and filtering out material with key words in their headings. "China Steps Up on 'Spiritual Pollution,' Limits Web Site Access," *San Jose Mercury News*, Sept. 6, 1996, p. 16A.

18. These points are, of course, made elsewhere, and quite eloquently argued in a paper by William Loker, "'Campesinos' and the crisis of Modernization in Latin America," presented at the Society for Applied Anthropology Annual Meeting, Baltimore, Md., April 1996. See also M. Painter and W. Durham, eds., *The Social Causes of Environmental Destruction in Latin America* (Ann Arbor: University of Michigan Press, 1995); Arturo Escobar and S. E. Alvarez, *The Making of Social Movements in Latin America and the Caribbean* (Boulder, Colo.: Westview Press, 1992); and Susan Stonich, *I Am Destroying the Land!: The Political Ecology of Poverty and Environmental Destruction in Honduras* (Boulder, Colo.: West View Press, 1993).

19. After Allan Schnaiberg and Kenneth Allan Gould, *The Enduring Conflict* (New York: St. Martin's, 1994), 233–234.

20. *C.f.*, Report of the National Commission on the Environment, *Choosing a Sustainable Future* (Washington, D.C.: Island Press, 1993). For a critique of sustainable development that reinforces existing power relations, see Neil Middleton, Phil O'Keefe, and Sam Moyo, *Tears of the Crocodile: from Rio to Reality in the Developing World* (Boulder, Colo.: West View Press, 1994).

Draft Principles on Human Rights and the Environment

United Nations Human Rights Commission

Preamble

Guided by the United Nations Charter, the Universal Declaration of Human Rights, the International Covenant on Economic, Social and Cultural Rights, the International Covenant on Civil and Political Rights, the Vienna Declaration and Programme of Action of the World Conference of Human Rights, and other relevant human rights instruments,

Guided also by the Stockholm Declaration of the United Nations Conference on the Human Environment, the World Charter for Nature, the Rio Declaration on Environment and Development, Agenda 21: Programme of Action for Sustainable Development, and other relevant instruments of international environmental law,

Guided also by the Declaration on the Right to Development, which recognizes that the right to development is an essential human right and that the human person is the central subject of development,

Guided further by fundamental principles of international humanitarian law,

Reaffirming the universality, indivisibility and interdependence of all human rights,

Recognizing that sustainable development links the right to development and the right to a secure, healthy and ecologically sound environment,

Recalling the right of peoples to self-determination by virtue of which they have the right freely to determine their political status and to pursue their economic, social and cultural development,

Deeply concerned by the severe human rights consequences of environmental harm caused by poverty, structural adjustment and debt programmes and by international trade and intellectual property regimes,

Convinced that the potential irreversibility of environmental harm gives rise to special responsibility to prevent such harm,

Concerned that human rights violations lead to environmental degradation and that environmental degradation leads to human rights violations,

Declare the following principles:

Part I

1. Human rights, an ecologically sound environment, sustainable development and peace are interdependent and indivisible.

2. All persons have the right to a secure, healthy and ecologically sound environment. This right and other human rights, including civil, cultural, economic, political and social rights, are universal, interdependent and indivisible.

3. All persons shall be free from any form of discrimination in regard to actions and decisions that affect the environment.

4. All persons have the right to an environment adequate to meet equitably the needs of present generations and that does not impair the rights of future generations to meet equitably their needs.

Part II

5. All persons have the right to freedom from pollution, environmental degradation and activities that adversely affect the environment, threaten life, health, livelihood, well-being or sustainable development within, across or outside national boundaries.

6. All persons have the right to protection and preservation of the air, soil, water, sea-ice, flora and fauna, and the essential processes and areas necessary to maintain biological diversity and ecosystems.

7. All persons have the right to the highest attainable standard of health free from environmental harm.

8. All persons have the right to safe and healthy food and water adequate to their well-being.

9. All persons have the right to a safe and healthy working environment.

10. All persons have the right to adequate housing, land tenure and living conditions in a secure, healthy and ecologically sound environment.

11. (a) All persons have the right not to be evicted from their homes or land for the purposes of, or as a consequence of, decisions or actions affecting the environment, except in emergencies or due to a compelling purpose benefiting society as a whole and not attainable by other means.

    (b) All persons have the right to participate effectively in decisions and to negotiate concerning their eviction and the right, if evicted, to timely and adequate restitution, compensation and/or appropriate and sufficient accommodation or land.

12. All persons have the right to timely assistance in the event of natural or technological or other human-caused catastrophes.

13. Everyone has the right to benefit equitably from the conservation and sustainable use of nature and natural resources for cultural, ecological, educational, health, livelihood, recreational, spiritual and other purposes. This includes ecologically sound access to nature.

Everyone has the right to preservation of unique sites consistent with the fundamental rights of persons or groups living in the area.

14. Indigenous peoples have the right to control their lands, territories and natural resources and to maintain their traditional way of life. This includes the right to security in the enjoyment of their means of subsistence.

    Indigenous peoples have the right to protection against any action or course of conduct that may result in the destruction of degradation of their territories, including land, air, water, sea-ice, wildlife or other resources.

Part III

15. All persons have the right to information concerning the environment. This includes information, however compiled, on actions or courses of conduct that may affect the environment and information necessary to enable effective public participation in environmental decision-making. The information shall be timely, clear, understandable and available without undue financial burden to the applicant.

16. All persons have the right to hold and express opinions and to disseminate ideas and information regarding the environment.

17. All persons have the right to environmental and human rights education.

18. All persons have the right to active, free and meaningful participation in planning and decision-making activities and processes that may have an impact on the environment and development. This includes the right to a prior assessment of the environmental, developmental and human rights consequences of proposed actions.

19. All persons have the right to associate freely and peacefully with others for purposes of protecting the environment or the rights of persons affected by environmental harm.

20. All persons have the right to effective remedies and redress in administrative or judicial proceedings for environmental harm or the threat of such harm.

Part IV

21. All persons, individually and in association with others, have the duty to protect and preserve the environment.

22. All States shall respect and ensure the right to a secure, healthy and ecologically sound environment. Accordingly, they shall adopt administrative, legislative and other measures necessary to effectively implement the rights in this Declaration.

    These measures shall aim at the prevention of environmental harm, at the provision of adequate remedies, and at the sustainable use of natural resources and shall include, *inter alia,*

- Collection and dissemination of information concerning the environment;
- Prior assessment and control, licensing, regulation or prohibition of activities and substances potentially harmful to the environment;
- Public participation in environmental decision-making;
- Effective administrative and judicial remedies and redress for environmental harm or the threat of such harm;
- Monitoring, management and equitable sharing of natural resources;
- Measures to reduce wasteful processes of production and patterns of consumption;
- Measures aimed at ensuring that transnational corporations, wherever they operate, carry out their duties of environmental protection, sustainable development and respect for human rights; and
- Measures aimed at ensuring that the international organizations and agencies to which they belong observe the rights and duties in this Declaration.

23. States and all other parties shall avoid using the environment as a means of war or inflicting significant, long-term or widespread harm on the environment, and shall respect international law providing protection for the environment in times of armed conflict and cooperate in its further development.

24. All international organizations and agencies shall observe the rights and duties in this Declaration.

Part V

25. In implementing the rights and duties in this Declaration, special attention shall be given to vulnerable persons and groups.

26. The rights in this Declaration may be subject only to restrictions provided by law and which are necessary to protect public order, health and the fundamental rights and freedoms of others.

27. All persons are entitled to a social and international order in which the rights in this Declaration can be fully realized.

Index

About the Editor

Barbara Rose Johnston is Senior Research Fellow at the Center for Political Ecology (P.O. Box 8467, Santa Cruz, California 95061) where she coordinates an international and interdisciplinary study on Human Rights and the Environment. She has worked in environmental planning, archaeology, and natural resource management, coached gymnastics, and lectured in environmental studies, anthropology, and sociology at universities in California, Canada, and the United States Virgin Islands. She holds a Ph.D. in Anthropology from the University of Massachusetts–Amherst, an independent studies M.A. in Cultural Ecology from San Jose State University, and a B.A. in Anthropology from U.C. Berkeley. Other books include *Water, Culture and Power* (edited by John Donahue and Barbara Johnston) forthcoming from Island Press, Washington, D.C.; and *Who Pays the Price? The Sociocultural Context of Environmental Crisis* (editor and principal author) 1994, Island Press, Washington, D.C. Comments can be sent to (bjohnston@igc.apc.org).